The Chicago River
A Natural and Unnatural History

Libby Hill

First Edition
Lake Claremont Press
Chicago

4650 North Rockwell Street • Chicago, Illinois 60625 • www.lakeclaremont.com

The Chicago River: A Natural and Unnatural History
by Libby Hill

Published August, 2000 by:

4650 N. Rockwell St.
Chicago, IL 60625
773/583-7800; lcp@lakeclaremont.com
www.lakeclaremont.com

ISBN: 1-893121-02-X: $16.95 Softcover
Library of Congress Catalog Card Number: 00-104566

Publisher's Cataloging-in-Publication
(Provided by Quality Books, Inc.)

Hill, Libby.
   The Chicago River : a natural and unnatural history / Libby Hill. — 1st ed.
      p. cm.
   Includes bibliographic references and index.
   LCCN: 00-104566
   ISBN: 1-893121-02-X

   1. Chicago River (Ill.)—History. 2. Natural history—Illinois—Chicago. 3. Chicago (Ill.)—History. 4. Canals—Illinois—Chicago—History. I. Title.

F548.3.H55 2000   977.411
                         QBI00-534

Printed in the United States of America by United Graphics, an employee-owned company based in Mattoon, Illinois.

04 03   10 9 8 7 6 5 4 3

Author's Note

This book was written for the general reader. It examines the history of the Chicago River and its watershed during several periods: its geological history, the tribal cultures that occupied the land after glacial retreat, the arrival of the Europeans, the changes to the river and watershed that ensued after Chicago was incorporated as a town in 1833, and today's efforts to restore the ecological health of the river. It is the premise of this book that only by understanding what happened to the river, and why, can we create a solid foundation for its continued recovery. Those of us who researched and wrote for the book hope that it will enrich the experience of residents and visitors alike and encourage more people to appreciate the ribbon of water that unites us.

The contributions of my co-authors Steve Apfelbaum, John Elliott, Joel Greenberg, Ed Lace, and Richard Lanyon are gratefully acknowledged as essential portions of the book. Their generous participation and expert knowledge have given greater detail and depth to the story.

Publisher's Credits

Cover Design by Timothy Kocher. Cover photos courtesy of David Ramsay, Friends of the Chicago River (*upper right*) and the Chicago Historical Society [Stereograph; ICHi-0074; View of the River and State Street bridge; Chicago (Ill.); 1873; Photographer—Lovejoy & Foster] *(lower left)*. Interior Design and Layout by Sharon Woodhouse. Editing by Bruce Clorfene. Proofreading by Sharon Woodhouse, Jason Fargo, Amy Formanski, Karen Formanski, Susan McNulty, and Kenneth M. Woodhouse. Photos by Libby Hill and Robert M. Kaplan. Maps by Libby Hill and Robert M. Kaplan. Index by Sharon Woodhouse. The text of *The Chicago River* was set in PenzanceLight with heads and subheads in Poem.

Note

Contents

Preface

If there is magic on this planet, it is contained in water.

—Loren Eiseley, *The Immense Journey,* 1959

A sense of place has always been important for me, and the strongest sense of place has come from rivers. When we moved to Chicago in 1957, my husband, who had lived here earlier, introduced me to Lake Michigan in the hope that I would share his pleasure at living near this inland sea. But the lake seemed flat and featureless to me except on those days when a nor'easter kicked up dramatic waves, and the wild lake resembled an ocean. I craved the excitement and the vitality of a river, of water running in a groove in the earth, an ever-changing drama of ripples and calm, a stream where aquatic creatures hide under stones or skate on the surface, and where low-hanging branches draw reflections in the water. When I found the Chicago River, I felt at home.

The idea for this book came after we had lived in Evanston for 35 years, but I suppose it had been growing and awaiting a precipitating event. That event occurred in 1994 in the form of a comment from Peggy Bradley, public relations director at the Metropolitan Water Reclamation District of Greater Chicago, who lamented that there was no book on the Chicago River and insisted one was sorely needed. Skeptical that no one had written about this river, I searched the libraries, but my searches proved Peggy right. I did find one book, *The Chicago,* written by Harry Hansen and published in 1942 as part of The Rivers of America series. It is a charming book, and I recommend it highly. Hansen uses the river as a starting point for wonderful sketches of Chicago characters, the river being just one of them. Hansen's book wasn't the volume full of the practical information Peggy had in mind, however, the factual kind of history that teachers, students, journalists, and the general public continuously request from her office. So why not write one?

When I set out on my personal journey of exploration, I did not appreciate the degree to which Chicago created the river just as surely as the river itself was the genesis for Chicago. I had learned in fourth grade geography that great cities grew near rivers, but beyond the need for transportation, at that young age I could not have explained why. Later, I learned from traveling in Europe that rivers flow grandly through great cities: Rome, Paris, London, for example, and that they flow between walls of human design, not natural muddy or sandy banks. But as I began to focus on the Chicago, I learned that encasing this river between walls had not been enough.

I began to look at the river through a completely fresh lens. I knew that other cities, London and Athens among them, had poured rivers into culverts and otherwise kept them from offending the residents, but I could not recall any story that rivaled the story I began to piece together: the river's natural history before humans toyed with it, and then the story of the why and how Chicago created today's Chicago River System. This river had played a major role in a drama that was uniquely Chicago. I realized that by telling the river's story, I was telling the city's story, or at least one version of many stories of the Chicago metropolitan area.

For purposes of this book, my husband and I, often with my photographer brother, climbed through brambles, waded through garlic mustard and buckthorn, squealed the car to a halt and backed up to find the shrunken stream sneaking out of a culvert, and took its measure and its picture. We cornered North Branch neighbors to talk about the stream, or as some call it, the ditch. We talked to residents at the trailer park next to the pond in Park City, near Waukegan in Lake County, and to Navy men and golfers at the Great Lakes Naval Base. We watched fishermen at the dam, or "waterfall," at the junction of the North Shore Channel and the North Branch. We explored the Illinois & Michigan Canal and the Sanitary and Ship Canal and stumbled upon the Damen Avenue cross erected to honor Father Marquette. We wandered the banks of Bubbly Creek and hiked through Portage Woods near Summit. I wouldn't have traded these intimate encounters with the Chicago River for explorations of any other river, anywhere.

On the days when I work in the Loop, I observe the river's changing downtown moods. I was working at 120 South Riverside Plaza one October day. South Riverside Plaza is not the name of a street but of a spacious promenade along the Chicago River. According to the weather forecast, this was to be the last fine fall day before rain and cold set in. It seemed as if everyone were eating lunch outside: pasta, salads, gyros bought from one of the many restaurants bordering the river, or sandwiches carried from home in a brown bag, as mine had been. Reclining by the railing at the river's edge, I noticed a fellow river-watcher on the opposite bank doing the same thing. He sat with one leg dangling over the rail as if he were in a boat and trailing one foot lazily in the water.

The river's color was a sort of deep, dark khaki. There was almost as much life in the river as on it. Sea gulls were flying overhead, occasionally dipping down to the river to snatch an unseen snack. Mallards were collecting under the Monroe Street Bridge. Why? I was curious. Two geese joined them. I watched as a homeless man I recognized tossed them bread, making his connection to life.

I finished my sandwich and strolled to the bridge. A cruise ship motored by, the *Ft. Dearborn*, Chicago, Illinois, its upper deck filled to capacity by sun-and river-loving passengers smiling and listening to cruise-talk. A two-man kayak cut sleekly through the water, its paddlers in perfect unison. Now came a working boat, an enormously long barge pushed by the tugboat "Margaret." Presumably tug and barge were making their way west to the Sanitary and Ship Canal, maybe even to the Mississippi River. To my right, separated from the river's edge by a concrete retaining wall, a string of sparkling silver railroad cars stood at rest in Union Station. Only the tops were visible. The riverbank along this reach of the South Branch is low, almost at water level, and I remembered being told that the tracks there have been known to flood. The promenade and buildings are built on air rights over the railroad land. Further downstream, parked along the banks, were a fireboat, a tug, and other small working boats with whose purposes I was unfamiliar.

The river looked amazingly clean, the detritus mostly slim yellow willow leaves, with a few red maple leaves for color, sometimes caught up in a web with a floating can or bottle or a McDonald's bag. For the most part, the scene was one of people stepping up to the river, crossing their arms, leaning on the railing for support, relaxing their shoulders, and quietly gazing at the gently moving current.

It was October 16, 1998, a typical day on the river.

The words "Chicago River" evoke a medley of images to me. They probably evoke different images for each of us. Your image might be the annual flotilla of boats emerging from winter hibernation, locking their way through the controlling works that separate the river from their summer moorings on Lake Michigan. Or the magnificent skyline of architectural history-in-the-making along the river. You might recall strolling along the promenade on a beautiful summer day, waving at the people on the cruise ships as if, for the moment, they were your absolutely best friends, and at that moment, neither of you would ever want to be any place else. Or it might be the ceremony of dyeing the river bright green on St. Patrick's Day.

How about a bike ride over the bridge at the confluence of the Skokie River and the Middle Fork in Winnetka? Or birding or catching blue-gill at the Skokie Lagoons? You might have admired the dignified waterscapes at the Chicago Botanic Garden in Glencoe. Perhaps you have jogged through Lake County's Greenbelt Forest Preserve up in Waukegan, stopping to watch wading blue herons patiently scanning the water for a meal. You might have lost a golf ball in the stream where it runs through the Great Lakes Naval Training Center or any of the other numerous riverside golf courses.

If you live by the water, perhaps you have watched nocturnal animals parading over the footbridges or swimming to the other side. As a volunteer in a restoration project, you might have gotten your feet and hands wet planting seedlings along a wetland restoration at Prairie Wolf Slough on the Middle Fork at Half Day Road, or at Gompers Park at Pulaski Road and Foster Avenue in Chicago.

You might have enjoyed dinner and a play in Chicago's Halsted Street theater district and wondered why the older houses have entrances sometimes into the second floor and sometimes into the basement, or why the yards are below street level. You might have seen the same curious phenomenon in Bridgeport, Pilsen, or other old Chicago neighborhoods. Chances are you didn't associate this phenomenon with the river, but it is a part of the river's story.

A jumble of memories might make up your personal Chicago River, as it does mine. But ours join with others to truly make a stream of consciousness, of connections. The pages of this volume are filled with recollections like these, many from days long ago, before Chicago was a city of skyscrapers. During the nineteenth century, people changed the river almost beyond recognition, beyond being hospitable to aquatic life and far from being a welcome neighbor to humans. During the twentieth century, with the help of another generation with a different vision of the environment, the river began its path to recovery. The memories from each century are very different, and yet, in a way, they are very familiar. The river entered the lives of the people who preceded us, as it does our own.

Chronology

Prehistory through the Eighteenth Century

440 million years-395 million years before the present
Chicago and the entire Great Lakes region lie under quiet tropical seas; vast formation of limestone dolomite bedrock occurs.

20,000-14,000 years before the present (approximately)
Wisconsin Glacier covers the Great Lakes, including the Chicago area.

14,000-13,000 years before the present
Glenwood stage of Glacial Lake Chicago; Lake Border Moraines deposited and outline of Chicago River begins to emerge; formation of Wilmette spit.

13,000-11,000 years before the present
Calumet stage of Glacial Lake Chicago; formation of Rose Hill spit.

11,000 years before the present
Permanent withdrawal of the Wisconsin Glacier to the east and formation of post-glacial Lake Algonquin

13,000-10,000 years before the present
Big game hunters arrive as glacier begins to recede.

Approximately 10,000-3,000 years before the present
Archaic culture succeeds big game hunters.

6,000-4,000 years before the present
Graceland spit formed by Lake Nipissing.

Approximately 3,000 years before the present
Woodland and Mississippian cultures succeed Archaic culture and settle along rivers until official removal in 1833.

1783
Revolutionary War ends; title to Chicago area passes from Great Britain to the United States.

About 1784
Jean Baptiste Pointe du Sable establishes farm at what is to become Chicago.

1794-1795
Treaty of Greenville concludes Battle of Fallen Timbers under General Mad Anthony Wayne; tribes agree to cede a six-square-mile parcel at mouth of Chicago River to the United States.

The Nineteenth Century

August, 1812
Fort Dearborn Massacre.

August 14, 1816
Tribes cede to the U.S. government a tract of land 20 miles wide, ten miles on either side of a potential canal, between Ottawa, Illinois, and Chicago. The outer limits of this tract became known as Indian boundary lines.

1818
Illinois admitted to the Union; northern boundary extended to 42 degrees 30 minutes north latitude to include the southwestern tip of Lake Michigan, so that the entire proposed canal would be within the state.

1828
Officers at Fort Dearborn dig a ditch through sandbar at mouth of Chicago River, but it immediately fills up.

1833
Chicago incorporated as a town; first anti-pollution ordinance for the river; ceremony of Indian removal after defeat in Black Hawk War.

1830s
Settlement begins along North Branch up to Lake County.

July 4, 1836
Illinois and Michigan Canal construction begins.

1837
Chicago incorporated as a city.

April 16, 1848
Official opening of Illinois and Michigan Canal; flow of the South Branch is intermittently reversed.

1849
First big flood in Chicago history causes extensive damage to boats and bridges.

1853
Chicago Land Company under William Ogden buys title to land on North Branch; within the decade the excavation of clay creates the North Branch Canal and Goose Island.

1856
Chicago begins to raise the level of its streets to accommodate E.S. Chesbrough's plan for a sewer system; the sewer system increases the waste load discharged into the Chicago River.

December 25, 1865
    Union Stock Yards opens.

1871
    Deep-cut on I&M Canal completed and rate of reversal of flow in the Main
    and South Branches increased.

1885
    Five and one-half inches of rain falls on Chicago in 19 hours; wind from
    northeast keeps polluted water from reaching the water intakes in the lake,
    preventing an epidemic of water-borne disease.

1889
    General Assembly passes Sanitary District of Chicago Enabling Act;
    referendum approving formation of SDC passes by overwhelming margin;
    first SDC Board of Trustees elected.

September 3, 1892
    SDC begins construction of diversion channel for Des Plaines River between
    Summit and Lockport and construction of Sanitary and Ship Canal between
    Bridgeport and Lockport.

The Twentieth Century

1900
    Sanitary and Ship Canal opens; flow in Main Stem and South Branch
    completely reversed.

1904-1907
    North Branch of the Chicago River between Lawrence and Belmont
    Avenues straightened to receive future discharge of sewage and lake water
    from North Shore Channel.

1905-1908
    Lakefront intercepting sewers built to stop sewage discharge to lake.

1907-1910
    North Shore Channel constructed from Wilmette to Lawrence Avenue in
    Chicago; dam at the confluence of the channel and the North Branch built
    in 1910.

1908
    Union Drainage District No. One in Lake County established on the West
    Fork of the North Branch.

1909
    Burnham Plan for Chicago published.

1914
SDC builds first sewage treatment plant in Morton Grove on North Branch; North Shore Sanitary District formed in Lake County.

1915
Forest Preserve District of Cook County incorporated.

1919
Sanitary District inaugurates 25-year program to build sewage treatment plants based on activated sludge process.

1920
Michigan Avenue bridge completed, setting the stage for the modern downtown Chicago riverscape.

1922
Cal-Sag Channel and controlling works at Blue Island completed, partially reversing flow of the Little Calumet River.

1921-1938
Remainder of historic West Fork of South Branch filled, portion by portion.

1928
SDC opens North Side Sewage Treatment Works in Skokie, discharging to the North Shore Channel all treated sewage originating from the Lake-Cook boundary to Fullerton Avenue in Chicago.

1928-1929
South Branch of Chicago River straightened between Polk and 18th Streets.

1933
Civilian Conservation Corps (CCC) begins work to transform Skokie Marsh into Skokie Lagoons.

1933
I&M Canal officially closed.

January 1, 1939
Controlling works and lock at the mouth of the Chicago River at Lake Michigan begin operation to prevent reversals of flow of Chicago River to the lake and still allow passage of navigation.

1940-1942
North Branch between the dam and North Ridgeway Avenue lined with concrete by WPA.

1955
American Society of Civil Engineers declares the Chicago Sewage Disposal System one of seven wonders of the modern engineering world.

1960-1965

O'Brien Lock and Dam built, completely reversing the Calumet and Little Calumet Rivers, which would now empty into the Sanitary and Ship Canal instead of Lake Michigan.

1965

Groundbreaking for Chicago Botanic Garden begins transformation of last remaining large piece of Skokie Marsh.

1971

Union Stock Yards closes.

1972

Federal Clean Water Act passed.

1979

Friends of the Chicago River formed.

1980-1985

O'Hare, Calumet, and Main Stream TARP tunnels go on-line; fish population in Chicago River begins to rebound.

1987

Lake County begins to create Stormwater Management Commission (LCSMC).

April 13, 1992

Chicago River floods basements in Loop buildings as a result of a construction accident at the Kinzie Street bridge over the North Branch.

The Chicago River
A Natural and Unnatural History

Introduction

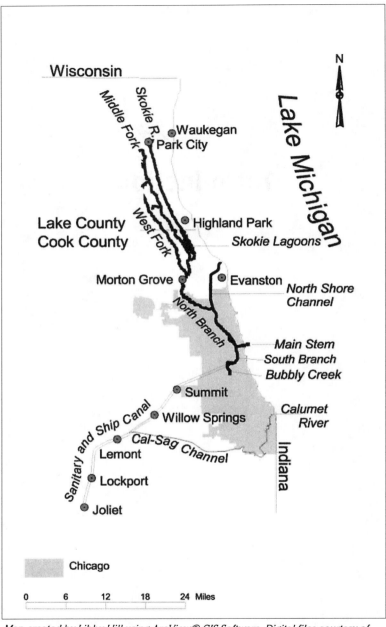

Map created by Libby Hill using ArcView® GIS Software. Digital files courtesy of Northeastern Illinois Planning Commission and Illinois Department of Natural Resources.

The Chicago River: Getting Your Bearings

Introduction

Not content with gathering wild onions or beaver skins, but restless to create something ever bigger, we struggle to put human impact on nature. We shape and reshape nature to our vision. Nature provides a complex situation and challenges. We have our own natures, which include ambition, commercial interests, and, because we are animals, bodily wastes. And so ensues a mighty struggle.

—Robert M. Kaplan

Chicago owes its existence to the Chicago River, and the river owes its present form to Chicago. Had the convenient but capricious portage between Lake Michigan and the Des Plaines River not been such a short way up the river, so attractively, provocatively close, Chicago never would have developed into the nation's central transshipment point. Once the burgeoning city began to stamp its pattern on the low and marshy plain, the river's fate was sealed.

A river is a work in progress, the force of running water sculpting its history on the land. Here in the Chicago area, natural forces took thousands of years to shape and reshape a glacial landscape drained by a river flowing on an almost flat plain. There were no natural waterfalls, no merrily tumbling brooks, no bubbling spring that could be identified as the single source.

"You could not step twice into the same river," Heraclitus reminded us in the fourth century B.C.E., "for other waters are ever flowing on to you." As if in conversation, the Japanese writer Kamo no Chōmei replied in the year 1212, "The flow of the river is ceaseless and its water is never the same. The bubbles that float in the pools, now vanishing, now forming, are not of long duration; so in the world are man and his dwellings." Throughout the written history of the world, rivers have been the metaphor of time, of both change and immutability, of spiritual ritual and connection. Rivers are magical. People are drawn to them as steel to a magnet.

Perhaps that is because rivers are always doing something, even though they often look as if they are doing nothing. They are carrying sediment from here to there, carving and re-carving their banks. They are covering tracks here, uncovering a sandbar there, receiving seepage from beneath their banks, dissolving the life-sustaining minerals for the animal and plant life that rely upon them. Depending upon conditions, the character of a river varies by the climate, by the weather, by the day, even by the hour. Sometimes natural change comes very quickly. In a cataclysmic storm, the river might alter its course, leaving a trace of water in an oxbow lake. Even without a cataclysmic event, the river will change its course due to its tendency to erode and deposit sediments on its banks. It is following natural laws and processes. But when man alters those processes during a few short years, the effects may be devastating.

Imagine a raindrop falling on the land. Every raindrop that falls on a land area is subject to the force of gravity. Gravity pulls it down either into the ground or along a slope, toward sea level. Eventually that raindrop is funneled into a small rivulet that becomes part of a larger series of rivulets that eventually funnel into a particular stream. The entire land area that feeds a stream makes up that stream's watershed.

In the Chicago region, raindrops and snowflakes find their way into many embryonic rivulets of water that weave together into tributaries of the Chicago River's two slow-moving branches. The branches merge to form the main stem that originally emptied into Lake Michigan.

The river's landscape has a long ancestry of gradual evolution from the formation of ages-old bedrock to the glacial and post-glacial events that formed both the river and Lake Michigan. Tribes of people native to the continent settled here first and lived here for 13,000 years before Europeans arrived and immediately contemplated change.

Depending upon an early voyager's experience of rivers, the Chicago looked like a creek, a brook, perhaps even a river. But everyone agreed it was slow-moving. It was "placid," "modest," "a stream with a gentle current," "a sluggish, slimy stream, too lazy to clean itself," and had "the appearance of a canal, narrow and deep." It was "limpid," "clear, transparent." It was given various names, among them "Chikagou Creek," "Garlic Creek," and "River of the Wild Onion," presumably in recognition of the powerful aroma of the plant, which also had various names—wild onion, wild leek, wild garlic—that grew in the vicinity.

When Maj. Stephen H. Long described the river on March 4, 1817, he said of it:

> The Chicago River is but an arm of the lake [Lake Michigan], dividing itself into two branches, at the distance of one mile inland from its communication with the lake. The north branch extends along the western side of the lake about thirty miles, and receives some few tributaries. The south branch has an extent of only 5 or 6 miles, and receives no supplies, except from the small lake of the prairie [Mud Lake, at the portage connection with the Des Plaines]. . . . The river and each of its branches are of variable widths, from 15 to 50 yards and, for 2 or 3 miles inland, have a sufficient depth of water to admit of almost any burden.[1]

R. Graham and Joseph Philips, who were in Chicago in 1819, said the river varied in depth from between ten to 40 feet.[2]

Many early observers commented on the obstructing sandbar at the river's mouth at Lake Michigan. According to Long, the section of river that curved between the mainland and the sandbar was about 30 yards wide. The sandbar itself was about 70 yards broad, covered by water usually no more than two feet deep.[3] Depending upon circumstances, observers said one could even wade across it. They were describing the low, sandy hill along the shore that gradually sloped until it dipped underwater just at the entrance to the river. Its size and shape were probably always in flux.

In 1803 the young United States built Fort Dearborn on a rise of sand across the stream from the sandbar. The new country had to protect its new territory.

Historian J. Seymour Currey contends that the first choice for a fort was at the St. Joseph River, another entrance to a portage route from Lake Michigan to the Mississippi, but the inhabitants were too hostile, and so Chicago was chosen.[4] (Was Chicago already destined for the epithet "Second City"?)

There is a story that when the Potawatomi threatened to attack the fort just before the massacre of 1812, the fleeing Americans, anxious to keep their supply of alcohol from the natives, hastily dumped it into the garrison's drainage ditch that led to the river. This is perhaps the first instance of Chicago River pollution. Following the massacre and the fort's destruction, the soldiers rebuilt the fort and dug a shortcut through the long, narrow sandbar that diverted and lengthened the river's path, and thus their own, to the lake. Although the channel quickly closed up, this is the first recorded attempt to alter the river's course. It foreshadowed the many modifications that human settlement would impose on the river. Even before that cut through the sandbar, the original Fort Dearborn's short drainage ditch into a tributary had begun in a small way to alter the watershed's drainage pattern.

Eventually, the demands of growing commerce led to changes in the river, from the complete removal of the sandbar at its mouth to the replacement of the portage route with the Illinois and Michigan Canal, the fulfillment of a centuries-old dream. As the city grew, the river became polluted by the waste-disposal needs of both people and industry, requiring further changes to the river. The river became a sewer.

Edwin Gale, who arrived in Chicago on May 25, 1835, as a young boy, reflected in 1902 on the fate of the river he loved:

> Nature designed that our creek should flow placidly along from source to mouth midst matted grasses and graceful ferns. Man deemed otherwise. He demanded it should hide the garbage of a large city deeply beneath its transparent surface . . . and that, in spite of all, it should remain as clear as when the paddles of Indian canoes alone lifted its glittering diamonds to the sunshine.[5]

Humans turned the river into a sewer, but the river rebelled and began to threaten the life force of the growing metropolis. It stank. It violently overflowed its banks, carrying the seeds of devastating illnesses out into Lake Michigan and polluting the city's drinking water supply. People just wanted it to go away. Several attempts, very early in the young city's history, did make the water go away from Lake Michigan, at least some of the time, and run unnaturally in the direction of St. Louis on the Mississippi.

The demands for change culminated in the construction of a public-works project of unprecedented scope, the Sanitary and Ship Canal. It permanently changed the river to flow from its former mouth in Lake Michigan upstream through its South Branch and eventually into the Mississippi River. As the city and suburbs expanded, residential and agricultural needs led to major drainage projects and other artificial canals. All branches of the river became increasingly channelized. The river began to seem more a system of urban ditches than a natural, free-flowing stream. With few exceptions, civilization all but obliterated the river's original bed.

The removal of the sandbar and the construction of the I&M and Sanitary and Ship Canals were monumental nineteenth century public works serving both commerce and sanitation. They are illustrative of the proverbial spirit of Sandburg's "City of the Big Shoulders." Chicago met its successive problems by changing the river, sometimes in the process creating new problems, but facing them, too, with its undaunted "I will" motto.

In the earliest years of the twentieth century, though draining and ditching on the upper reaches of the North Branch accelerated, and two new artificial tributaries, the Cal-Sag and the North Shore Channels, were built, human values were in the process of change. The years encircling the turn of the century ushered in a new attitude toward the river and a new aesthetic towards civic projects in general. The evolving science of ecology, the growing sophistication concerning public health and cleanliness, and the emerging ideal of civic beauty impacted the idea of river improvements. As the century matured, an enormous challenge confronted Chicago: how to undo much of what it had done to the river, but within the confines of the metropolitan setting that the river had done so much to make possible.

After the Sanitary and Ship Canal was opened in 1900, the water from Lake Michigan mixed with the river water in the Main Stem, making it clean enough to accommodate an annual swimming race. The event, called the Chicago River Marathon, was held from 1908 through 1930 and extended from the life-saving station at the east end of the Main Stem to the Jackson Boulevard bridge on the South Branch. Johnny Weissmuller of Olympic and Tarzan fame, representing the Illinois Athletic Club, won the three-mile race in 1926 with a time of 56 minutes and 48 seconds and bettered his time when he won again in 1927.

Cruise ships began to ply the waters alongside freighters and other industrial vessels. On the rainy morning of July 24, 1915, the steamer Eastland was docked along a wharf in the river, boarding 2,500 passengers for a cruise to a Western Electric Company picnic in Michigan City, Indiana. In one of the worst maritime disasters yet recorded in the United States, the overloaded ship broke from its moorings and rolled over just a few feet from shore, killing more than 800 people.

By the early 1920s, with the river dredged and widened, the docks neatened, and a gleaming new Michigan Avenue bridge spanning the water, dignified businessmen began to commission solid, dignified buildings facing the river. The South Branch was straightened, and little by little its offensive forks filled in, leaving only "Bubbly Creek," the South Fork of the South Branch, to remind us of the Union Stock Yards and that Chicago was once Carl Sandburg's "Hog Butcher to the World."

Today, the downtown Chicago River is approaching Daniel Burnham's ideal in his 1909 *Plan of Chicago*: a sedate European-like stream flanked by walkways, flowing through a glistening city. Instead of industrial traffic plying a foul-smelling gutter, pleasure boats predominate. Instead of the hodge-podge of docks and wooden swing bridges, handsome drawbridges cross the river, and the seawalls are orderly, if a bit shabby in places. Skyscraper hotels, office towers, and riverwalks line the banks. On late summer afternoons, the sounds of jazz mingle with the conversation of office workers at riverside restaurants. Upscale residential developments, often with public river frontage, are in place or in the planning stages along several reaches of the river.

* * * * *

There were other land and water routes to the Mississippi from Lake Michigan. Why was the Chicago River chosen as the gateway to the interior? The early entrepreneur-explorer René Robert Cavelier sieur de La Salle favored the route of the St. Joseph and Kankakee Rivers instead of the unreliable portage route between the Chicago and the Des Plaines Rivers. How did the sleepy little stream, flowing over land so flat that it could hardly ever carve its own valley, end up in an artificial canyon approximately 12 feet below a major city, or cramped into skinny ditches secreted behind thick lanes of shrubby growth in Chicago's northern suburbs? When and how was the "engineering wonder" of reversing the river achieved? The many changes to the river were influenced by the needs of transportation and commerce, public health and soil drainage, unencumbered by ecological concerns that were not yet part of the civic consciousness.

The good news is that nature is resilient, at least up to a point, and the Chicago River seems to be a good candidate for rehabilitation. We see throughout its story the importance of our respect for natural processes. This respect is the vital key to addressing the problems human beings created by having ignored or misunderstood those processes in the first place. If we learn to respect the natural processes of a river, it can begin to recover its ecological health.

Often reflecting and often leading the national movement to restore a river, the present-day Chicago River pioneers explore new approaches, some high-tech, some low-tech, to improve the quality of the river habitat so that aquatic creatures will return. Ironically, however, our communities continue to build in the Chicago River watershed and even in its floodplain. We pave over the watershed's surfaces, causing increased and faster runoff, enhancing downstream conditions for what are called 100-year floods to strike more frequently than once a century. In our most successful attempts, we work to mimic natural processes. The challenge will take time, money, and experimentation. The river will never completely recover its original processes, but we humans can attempt to undo some of the damage we have done and have a river that can be a safe, healthy, and enjoyable part of our lives.

This book tells the story of the synergy between the river and the people of greater Chicago. In relating the story of the major changes in the river, the book places those changes in the context of their times: contemporary visions of need and possibility and the contemporary state of technological development. The book does not chronicle minor widening or narrowing projects along the river. As for today's vast number and variety of river restoration projects, there is space for only a few examples. The story does not address either the architecture along the river or the history of the bridges that cross it. Many fine books already address these topics, and a list of references will lead readers to such sources.

The Chicago's story is one of degradation and redemption, of scorn and embrace. It is an inspiring story of confident spirit and impressive accomplishments, but also an ironic story of unintended consequences and unforeseen twists of fate. It is the story of people of vision working together. And, for all its local particularity, it is also a microcosm of the uneasy relation between nature and civilization, especially when the welfare of a great city is at stake. The river's story is a good story, and this book undertakes to tell it.

Location, Location, Location

As a place of business, its situation at the central head of the Mississippi Valley will make it the New Orleans of the North; and its easy and close intercourse with the most flourishing eastern cities will give it the advantage, as its capital increases, of all their improvements in the mode of living.

—Charles Fenno Hoffman
Early settler, January 10, 1834

If you were an early visitor, standing on a raised dune on the shore of what is now downtown Chicago, it would have been easy to describe the river scene: one stem, two tributaries, trees scattered in groves along the South Branch, denser forest to the north, marshland everywhere, and to the west, vast endless prairie until the eye spotted the distant line of trees on the east bank of the Des Plaines River.

Anyone delving into the real estate market learns that there are three major characteristics to consider about property: location, location, and location. Combining the advantages of transportation and rich natural history, Chicago's location at the head of the Great Lakes was, and is, unsurpassed. That the marshy land might be a problematic site for a great city with a population in excess of three million was far from the minds of the natives and early settlers who plied its waters with their primitive trade and vessels.

The Riddle of the Divide

If you were a westbound traveler or trader in any typical dry season, you boated five or six miles upstream from Lake Michigan along the South Branch of the river until you could boat no further. At this place, you would be at a sub-continental divide. This divide separates the Mississippi River/Gulf of Mexico drainage to the west and the Great Lakes/St. Lawrence River/Atlantic Ocean drainage to the east.

Geologically speaking, a divide is usually thought of as high land that separates two watersheds. For example, the major North American continental divide, which separates the Atlantic and the Pacific drainages, runs along the Rocky Mountains. But here, at what was to become Chicago, the divide was low, very low. During times of high water levels in the rivers, it was barely visible, and at other times, non-existent. Even so, it is still among the most important drainage divides in North America.

For a traveler in a boat, the importance of a divide is that there is usually dry land between watersheds. To get from one to the other, you have to portage. If you were an early native or fur trader on your way west to the vast, rich interior of the continent along Lake Michigan, you would boat your goods

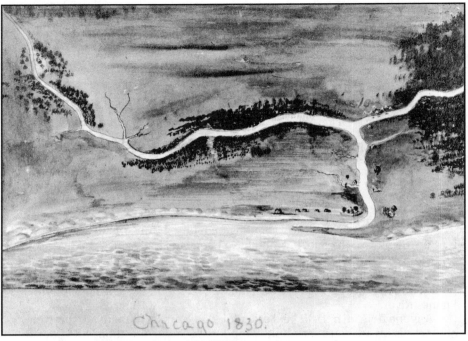

Bird's eye view of yesterday's Chicago, looking to the west. Low sand dunes line the lakeshore. A sandbar diverts the route of the Main Branch of the Chicago River to the south before it empties into Lake Michigan. Sloughs drain the lowland into the river. The slough coming from the north is under today's Merchandise Mart. The North and South Branches meet at Wolf Point and flow into the Main Branch. The South Branch flows from the west from the direction of the Des Plaines River. The South and West Forks of the South Branch are not pictured but are just beyond the illustration's northwest border.

as far as you could, following the Main Stem of the Chicago River, the South Branch, then called the Portage River, and continue up what was later named the West Fork. If you were lucky and the season was wet, the low divide would be completely covered by water and you could sail right along and soon find yourself in the Des Plaines River, on your way to the Illinois River and then the Mississippi.

But if it were a dry season, usually in summer, you could only go so far up-river before your boat would run aground, probably around present-day Leavitt Street. There, you would be forced to lift your craft and cargo out of the water and carry, or portage, them over a slight rise of land in order to reach the Des Plaines watershed where you could again float your boat. Usually you would follow the Portage Road for some distance around a marsh known as Mud Lake.

Alternatively, a traveler could get his boat back in the water sooner by dragging it through Mud Lake, a large, leech-infested puddle filled with dense grasses. Gurdon Hubbard, a young fur trader making his first trip through

Chicago in 1818, described this "shortcut" in graphic detail:

> Our empty boats were pulled up the channel, and in many places, where
> there was no water and a hard clay bottom, they were placed on short rollers,
> and in this way moved along until the [Mud] lake was reached, where we
> found mud thick and deep, but only at rare intervals was there water. Forked
> tree branches were tied upon the ends of the boat poles, and these afforded
> a bearing on the tussocks of grass and roots, which enabled the men in the
> boat to push to some purpose. Four men only remained in a boat and pushed
> with these poles, while six or eight others waded in the mud alongside, and
> by united efforts constantly jerking it along, so that from dawn to dark we
> succeeded only in passing a part of our boats through to the Aux Plaines
> [Des Plaines] outlet. . . . While a part of our crew were thus employed, others
> busied themselves in transporting our goods on their backs to the river; it
> was a laborious day for all.
>
> Those who waded through the mud frequently sank to their waist, and
> at times were forced to cling to the side of the boat to prevent going over
> their heads; after reaching the end and camping for the night came the task
> of ridding themselves from the blood suckers.
>
> The lake was full of these abominable black plagues, and they stuck so
> tight to the skin that they broke in pieces if force was used to remove them;
> experience had taught the use of a decoction of tobacco to remove them,
> and this was resorted to with good success.
>
> Having rid ourselves of the blood suckers, we were assailed by myriads
> of mosquitoes, that rendered sleep hopeless. . . . Those who had waded the
> lake suffered great agony, their limbs becoming swollen and inflamed, and
> their sufferings were not ended for two or three days.
>
> It took us three consecutive days of toil to pass all our boats through this
> miserable lake. . . .[1]

The Chicago portage route of the natives, at the short, low divide between
the Great Lakes and the Mississippi River system, has been called one of the
"five keys to the continent."[2] Chicago is located where it is today because
native tribesmen introduced the French explorers Marquette and Jolliet to this
portage route. They took the path around, not through, the marsh. Jolliet, a
Frenchman born in New France but knowledgeable about hydrology,
immediately envisioned a little canal to breach this portage, eliminating the
need to get out of your canoe even in dry times. He reported that, with just a
little work, a canal would end the need for a portage and open up an easy
route to the Mississippi. To Jolliet, the watersheds of the Des Plaines and
Chicago Rivers were tantalizingly close, separated by but "half a league" (one
and one-half miles).

Jolliet estimated his distance in September, 1673, the only time he crossed
the portage. It must have been a very wet summer, judging by what two
travelers, R. Graham and Joseph Phillips, subsequently wrote:

> The route by Chicago as followed by the French since their discovery
> of the Illinois presents at one season of the year an uninterrupted water
> communication for boats of six to eight tons burthen [*sic*] between the
> Mississippi and the Michigan lake; at another season a portage of two miles;
> at another, a portage of seven miles, from the bend of the Plein [Des Plaines]
> to the arm of the lake; at another a portage of fifty miles, from the mouth of

the Plein to the lake; over which there is a well beaten wagon road, and boats and their loads are hauled by oxen and vehicles kept for that purpose by French settlers at the Chicago.[3]

Fifty miles! Fifty miles of carrying your boat and supplies to the west, or 50 miles of dragging your boat and your precious cargo of furs east. Even though this longest of detours was probably the exception, the more usual seven-plus miles is a great deal of carrying. If, in 1673, crossing the portage had required that much walking, Jolliet might not have imagined that digging a canal would be so simple. Hubbard, whose experience in Mud Lake was so disagreeable, was employed by the American Fur Company, which moved large heavy boats and trade goods across the portage. It should not come as a surprise to learn that he became a leading proponent of a canal.

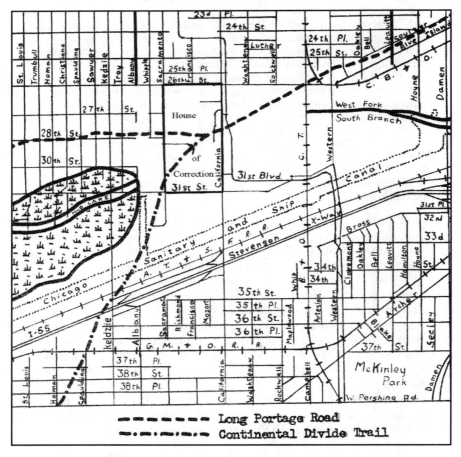

Courtesy of Philip E. Vierling.

"The Old Continental Divide and the Modern City." Albany Avenue and Leavitt Street have been darkened to show the location of Knight and Zeuch's mysterious rise of land that created the divide. Vierling based his map on Knight and Zeuch's "Map of the Old Chicago Portage," which did not show the "original" West Fork. Vierling has added it, showing it rising at the railroad tracks on the eastern slope of the "divide."

Where the Des Plaines arced to the east, a little stream, known as Portage Creek, connected the Des Plaines and Mud Lake. During storms and the breakup of the winter ice, the water in the Des Plaines would rise high enough to break out of its valley and flow east, through Portage Creek, Mud Lake, the South Branch, and the Main Stem, into Lake Michigan. At these flood times, the discrete normal-weather channels of Portage Creek, Mud Lake, and the western end of the West Fork would meld together. There was no need to portage.

But under those conditions, just where was the divide? Robert Knight and Lucius Zeuch, in their exhaustive 1928 study of the Chicago portage, were looking for a definitive location for the divide, and they believed they had found it. They reasoned that,

> . . . there is every indication that the Des Plaines River flowed east . . .
> through the Mud Lake depression and into Lake Michigan by way of the
> Chicago River during a considerable period of time. Then *in some unknown*
> *way* [author's italics] a barrier was raised across the channel near the present
> line of Kedzie Avenue and prevented further flow in this direction. The Des
> Plaines then backed up, turned and flowed southwesterly . . . leaving a slough
> or small lake about five miles long in the depression that had been its former
> outlet to Lake Michigan. This was called Mud or Portage Lake.[4]

Jolliet's half a league sounds very much like Knight and Zeuch's "barrier," which was located between present-day Leavitt Street on the east and present-day Albany Avenue on the west, passing through today's Cook County House of Correction at about 28th Street. The distance between these two streets is just shy of one and one-quarter miles.

Many observed that Mud Lake was the divide in times of wet weather. Maj. Stephen H. Long and William H. Keating, in their earlier visit to the Chicago area during 1817, noted this intriguing peculiarity at Mud Lake. They wrote,

> We were delighted at beholding, for the first time, a feature so interesting
> in itself, but which we had afterwards an opportunity of observing frequently
> . . . viz.: the division of waters starting from the same source and running in
> two different directions, so as to become the feeders of streams that discharge
> themselves into the ocean at immense distances apart.[5]

In 1819, R. Graham and Joseph Philips, the latter having accompanied the Long expedition, attempted to explain the phenomenon. They contended traders who had dragged their goods over the portage had worn down a "gutter." The direction of the current in it depended not on a dividing ridge but literally on which way the wind blew. The increase in traffic was creating many gutters that compromised the divide. They observed:

> This gutter [the original], judging from the appearance of others now
> forming, was, at first, a path worn out by the feet of those who carried things
> across the portage, and afterwards deepened by the attrition of the waters,
> until formed a little canal. The wind, alone, gives the water a current in this
> little canal, and its direction depends upon the source of the wind. Objects
> have been seen to float out of it, from the same point, to the river and to the
> lake.[6]

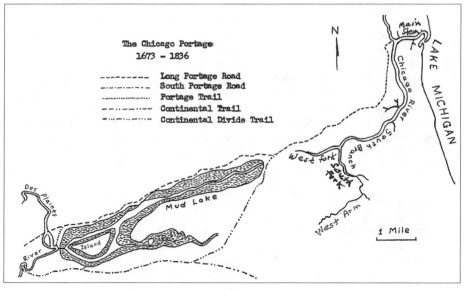

Courtesy of Philip E. Vierling.

Portage Choices.

Due to the expanding fur trade, boats and cargo were becoming large enough that loading and unloading cargo for a portage around Mud Lake on the Portage Road was becoming increasingly time-consuming. "The gutters were probably being dug by heavy boats being dragged or polled [*sic*] through liquid mud in preference to making a land carry [by people like Hubbard]. In this manner the channel through Mud Lake was improved and a connection was established between Mud Lake and the Chicago River."[7]

The gutters observed in the early 1800s were precursors to the I&M Canal, one of the earliest artificial changes to the Chicago River for the purposes of U.S. commerce. To be sure, the two-way gutters, the cuts through the divide, were the unintended result of determined individuals to coax a year-round convenience out of a seasonal occurrence. They created, however, the conditions for the reversal of the river. The gutters were hardly grand public works, but they reinforced the need for a canal.

But where was the divide in dry weather? Knight and Zeuch's thoughts beg the question: since the West Fork had water in it even in dry seasons, where would the source of that water have been? Could there have been an underground stream leading from Mud Lake?

People have so altered the landscape in the vicinity of the divide and the portage route that all geological evidence has been erased.

You cannot see the divide there, much less the West Fork. You may find clues to the existence of the fork, but you will not find a stream. You cannot find it on today's maps. Of all the topographic features in the Chicago area, this divide would seem to be the most significant for understanding Chicago's geographic location and its historical development. You will search in vain, however, on a topographic map for a contour line. A current U.S. Geological Survey bench mark of 594 feet at Albany Avenue is only two feet higher than other benchmarks in the immediate vicinity of Kedzie Avenue.

One can perhaps say that the original divide was physically too insignificant a feature to attract any geological interest, and that its very physical insignificance was partly responsible for its great historical significance. It gave Chicago the crucial edge over other portage routes in use at that time. Did the waters of the West Fork originate in a swamp or on the east side of a low ridge? The answer is probably both, depending upon the wind and the weather.

Part I

Prehistory through the Eighteenth Century

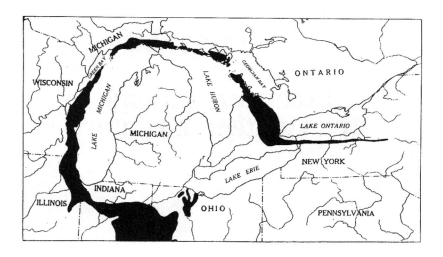

From J. Harlen Bretz, "Geology of the Chicago Region Part I—General," Illinois Geological Survey Bulletin 65 (1939).

Outcrop belt of the Niagaran formation in the Great Lakes region.

Geological Foundations
Bedrock

'You're walking on a history book', said the Professor. . . .

—May T. Watts
Reading the Landscape of America, 1957

To appreciate Chicago's monumental, even startling public works on the river, you must be familiar with the region's geology. You must begin from the bottom up: bedrock.

Legacy of Quiet Seas

The story of today's Chicago River begins hundreds of millions of years ago in Paleozoic time when the bedrock of Chicago was forming under a quiet salt sea. The territory that was to become Chicago was very near the equator. No dramatic episodes of mountain building, spewing volcanoes, or devastating earthquakes created our landscape. Chicago's temperate climate, topography, and natural resources are the result of the slow movement of the North American continental plate away from the equator to colder, more northerly latitudes.

Picture a large, shallow, quiet sea with clear warm water. The sun penetrates the blue water as it does in today's tropics. There are sandy beaches, but it is too early in earth's history for the shade of palm trees. The weather is consistently warm. This shallow sea covers the location of Chicago long ago, approximately 440 through 395 million years before the present, during what geologists have named the Silurian Period. During this time, before there were any Rocky Mountains attached to North America, much of the continent west of the Appalachians lay under this idyllic-sounding sea.

The ocean teemed with sea creatures. Many individual animals had shells of calcium carbonate, like the seashells we admire today. As those cast-off shells accumulated at the bottom of the sea and intermingled with the sand and silt, they eventually formed thick layers of limestone rock. Over the ages, magnesium replaced some of the calcium, forming a very hard rock called dolomite. Also in these warm seas, tiny coral animals assembled into huge coral reefs.

The sea eventually retreated, leaving a flat, featureless lowland. Then, at some time in the far distant past, forces deep within the earth began to elevate and tilt the land. Rainwater and snowmelt drained the higher areas and developed into streams. The streams wore away the weakest rocks, the sedimentary sands, shales, and softer limestone where magnesium had not intruded. The tougher dolomite resisted erosion. Then the glaciers came and finished off the job, leaving only the very toughest layer of dolomite as a cap on the highest cliffs. The cliff-edge of this unyielding dolomite forms a great serpentine shape, called the "Niagaran Escarpment," which stretches across the Great Lakes region. Typically, the escarpment is underground or under water, but it is visible at the Bruce Peninsula in Ontario, Canada and in Door County, Wisconsin, and, of course, in the dramatic exposure at Niagara Falls, where "our" bedrock got its name, "Niagaran dolomite."

Although the deep beds of Niagaran dolomite come near the surface in only a few places in Cook County, such as Stearns Quarry near the Bridgeport neighborhood on Chicago's south side, Thornton Quarry in the south suburban town of Thornton, the Eisenhower Expressway east of Mannheim Road in the western suburbs, the Kennedy Expressway at Chicago's Fullerton Avenue and in the lower Des Plaines River and the Calumet-Sag Valleys, they underlie the entire region and have important implications for our story. The water in streams such as the Chicago River was full of dissolved limestone. Early settlers had to contend with this "hard water" drawn from their shallow wells and streams. Cooking pots would become encrusted with minerals that had to be removed by scraping or soaking in acid. For cleanliness and cooking, settlers turned to rainwater collected in cisterns.

Near the south suburban cities of Lemont in Cook County and Lockport in Will County, where the dolomite lies near the surface, it has been tapped extensively for building stone because of its exemplary quality of breaking easily into neat blocks when quarried. Workers dug the Illinois & Michigan Canal at least partially through this dolomite; blocks fashioned from dolomite line its sides. In 1855, a visitor to Chicago nicknamed this stone "Athens Marble." Local architects refer to it as "Lemont Stone."

Stone from quarries in Athens, Illinois, now part of Lemont, was easily transported by river to Chicago and furnished the building blocks for the Chicago Water Tower and its neighboring Water Works. When you visit Lemont and Lockport, you will see many modest buildings and even sidewalks built from this warm, blond rock.

Where the fossil coral reefs approach the surface in the present-day Chicago area, you will find deep quarries. Where the combined Tri-State Tollway, I-294, and I-80 cross south suburban Thornton, a giant quarry reveals thick layers of coral to the passing traveler. The reef in Thornton Quarry is mined by dynamiting. With each explosion, new layers of ancient fossil creatures are released from their rock tombs. The quarry is a magnet to eager amateur and professional geologists who sift through mountains of rock for ancient fossil treasures. This limestone is ideal for crushed foundations for roadbeds and for bike paths. When you are biking on a crushed limestone path, try considering this: you may be riding on 400-million-year-old stone.

On the larger scale of canal-building, cutting through this resistant dolomite created monumental headaches and budgets which, in turn, led to conflict, compromises, and the development of a new generation of heavy machinery. As Chicago's population grew and sanitation problems caused high rates of waterborne disease, the Chicago Sanitary District built the Sanitary and

Ship Canal, partly blasted through this bedrock, to carry Chicago's sewage to the Mississippi. By mid-20th century, the Chicago area had outgrown the canal. When new federal and state water quality standards were unveiled, the Metropolitan Water Reclamation District responded with a bold, expensive new initiative, one of the major public works of the century, to avert the problems of flooding and lake contamination. The Tunnel and Reservoir Project, or TARP, is literally grounded in the bedrock of the region. The deep tunnels form an underground river system blasted through the dolomite beneath our surface rivers. The storage reservoir will be in limestone quarries.

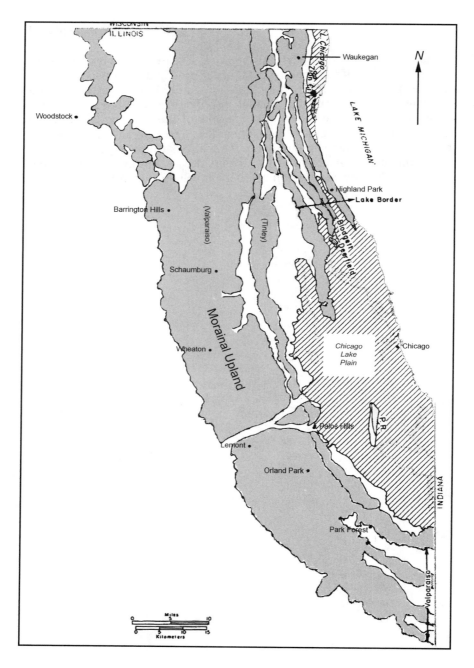

Modified from Willman, 1971.

The high land of the Valparaiso, Tinley, and Lake Border Moraines surrounds the lower, flat Chicago Lake Plain, the bed of Glacial Lake Chicago. White areas are either low, gently rolling ground moraine, glacial outwash, or bedrock. The floor of Glacial Lake Chicago covers about 450 square miles.

The Ice Age and the Legacies of the Wisconsin Glacier
Toward the Chicago River

Shallow seas may have quietly arrived and departed, and coal beds formed in the ground, but in all that time there has been no occurrence that can begin to rival in scope or total change the advent from the north of walls of marching ice.

—Anita Harris, 1983

In Chicago, we would still be enjoying the balmy weather of the tropics had the continental plate on which we sit stayed put. But by 200 million years ago, during the slow movement of the plate to the north, a temperate climate had gradually replaced the equatorial climate. Two million years ago, climatic dynamics we do not completely understand prevented the warm summer temperatures from melting the winter snows. The snow compacted, and glaciers formed. During the next two million years, several great continental glaciers came and went, covering our region and shaping the Great Lakes basin. The most recent one, the Wisconsin, was the glacier that shaped today's Chicago.

Few of us would be likely to consider our landscape "new," but in geologic time it was formed quite recently. A scant 20,000 years ago, hardly a second on the clock of Earth's 4.5-billion-year-old history, much of the northern United States and Canada was locked in this most recent deep freeze of the Ice Age. Our area lay buried beneath a massive glacier. Ice may have been nearly two miles thick at the center of accumulation, north of the present Great Lakes, and perhaps 1,200 feet thick over Chicago. Look up to the top of the John Hancock building on Michigan Avenue and imagine a mass of ice covering the building and extending out for miles, and you will have the general idea of its size. The glacier, called the Wisconsin because its features are best visible in that state, flowed south/southwest from Hudson Bay and reached into central Illinois. It chiseled away the soft shale lying atop the Niagaran dolomite.

In 1837, Louis Agassiz published the first scientific essay on glaciers. He called a glacier "God's Great Plough." When ice sheets advance, they pluck up the rocks and stones in their path and carry them along, usually grinding them down into gravel and scraping the rock underneath. When the ice sheets melt back, they drop this rock debris in unsorted deposits of sand, gravel, and silt along their ice margins, or edges. This unsorted debris is called "glacial till." Where glaciers pause long enough during their recession, they deposit their till in "end moraines." Where glaciers melt back fairly steadily, their till forms low, gently rolling "ground moraines." The Wisconsin Glacier deposited several hundred feet of glacial till over the ancient dolomite bedrock and formed Chicago's current landscape.

The Valparaiso and Tinley Moraines

At its many fairly stationary fronts during its withdrawal from the region, the Wisconsin left a complex system of moraines. The most prominent local legacy is the Valparaiso Moraine. On average, the Valparaiso is eight miles wide. It forms an arc of attractive undulating hills from Valparaiso, Indiana, through the suburban communities of Park Forest, Tinley Park, Orland Park, the Palos area, Wheaton, Palatine, and Barrington and then continues north to the Wisconsin border. One final advance of the Wisconsin in the Chicago area formed the Tinley Moraine, which overlapped the Lake Michigan side of the Valparaiso. As the ice margin finally receded from the vicinity of the Valparaiso, the glacier dropped its till in the slightly rolling Tinley ground moraine, part of which is under today's O'Hare International Airport. The Chicago River does not drain either of these moraines, but its history is related to theirs.

The Lake Border Moraines

As the Wisconsin Glacier continued its recession to the northeast, it formed a series of successively younger end moraines called the Lake Border Moraines. At first, the moraines were most likely partly under water, but as the ice front withdrew, the moraines emerged. The Lake Border system is more than six miles wide, and in our region it lies under Chicago's north suburbs. From east to west, the moraines consist of four north-south trending ridges: the Highland Park, the Blodgett, the Deerfield, and the Park Ridge. At the time geologists named them, they represented major towns on their crests. Since that time, Blodgett has been incorporated into Highland Park.

The Great Lakes

The Niagara escarpment we mentioned earlier fringes part of a low-lying, saucer-shaped depression in the earth's crust called the Great Lakes basin. It was the action of the Wisconsin and earlier glaciers of the Ice Age that formed the Great Lakes by scooping out or enlarging the stream basins that had previously criss-crossed the bowl.

In total, the Great Lakes cover approximately 95,000 square miles and contain the largest expanse of fresh water on earth. They empty into the Atlantic Ocean through the St. Lawrence Seaway.

Glacial Lake Chicago

Anyone who has flown over, sailed on, or tried to look across Lake

Michigan knows that it deserves its appellation as a "Great Lake." Yet, 14,000 years ago, when the Wisconsin Glacier melted back from Chicago toward the northeast, the lake was even greater.

When the glacier finished building the Valparaiso and Tinley Moraines and began to recede to the northeast, it left a giant pool of meltwater trapped in a huge bowl between the Valparaiso and the Tinley on the south and west and an ice dam on the north and east. Scientists have dubbed this giant ancestor of Lake Michigan "Glacial Lake Chicago." At its highest, the water in this enormous glacial lake was 640 feet above sea level, 60 feet higher than our present-day Lake Michigan, which stands at a mere 580 feet above sea level.

Lake Chicago found two low gaps in the Valparaiso, and its water surged through them to the southwest. Meltwater carved two deep, wide spillways known collectively today as the "Chicago Outlet," and known separately as the Cal-Sag and the Des Plaines outlets. As the water spilled out, sometimes catastrophically, it eroded not only the glacial till but also some of the Niagaran dolomite, the stone that would later prove to be a canal-builder's trial.

In geological time, Glacial Lake Chicago lasted barely a moment, but scientists distinguish different stages by name. The oldest and highest, the "Glenwood," stood at 640 feet above sea level between about 14,000 and 13,000 years ago, when water from the Lake Erie and Huron basins flooded west into the Lake Michigan basin. When water in the Huron and Erie basins reversed course around 13,000 years ago and drained to the east, Glacial Lake Chicago no longer had this input and dropped to only 620 feet above sea level. Geologists called this stage the "Calumet."

About 11,000 years ago, the Wisconsin Glacier permanently receded to the northeast, opening the Straits of Mackinac and connecting the water in the Lake Michigan and Lake Huron basins. Geologists consider the creation of this combined lake, known as Lake Algonquin, to be the end of Glacial Lake Chicago. Lake Algonquin lasted for about 500 years, and geologists are still studying it. A current theory holds that at first, Lake Algonquin drained west through the Chicago outlet. When the glacier receded far enough to the northeast to thaw the St. Lawrence Valley and create an outlet for water to empty into the Atlantic, Lake Algonquin switched course and drained to the east. By 10,500 years ago, the water level in the Lake Michigan basin plummeted from 600 to only 230 feet above sea level.

Several additional named lake levels occupied the Michigan basin during the time between Lake Algonquin and our Lake Michigan. The most important for our story is Lake Nipissing, which stood at about 605 feet above sea level between 6,000 and 4,000 years ago. It drained west through the Chicago outlet. About 1,700 years ago, only a geological yesterday, Lake Michigan settled into the basin we know, at 580 feet above sea level, and it has continued ever since to empty through the St. Lawrence.[1] The Glenwood and Calumet stages of Glacial Lake Chicago and post-glacial Lake Nipissing are important in the natural history of the Chicago River because they produced landforms that influence its route today. (See chart on p. 46.)

The Chicago Lake Plain

Geologically speaking, the Chicago Lake Plain, which is the exposed floor of old Glacial Lake Chicago, and post-glacial Lake Nipissing are the youngest features on our young landscape. The Lake Plain comprises most of the flat land between the Valparaiso/Tinley Moraine complex and Lake Michigan. The Chicago River flows between the Lake Border Moraines and across the Chicago Lake Plain.

The plain is a crescent-shaped lowland surrounded by a ring of hills, except where it extends in narrow, fjordlike fingers northward, between the Lake Border Moraines. The gradient of the plain is low, and the base level, Lake Michigan, is only a few feet below the level of the Lake Plain. The river had only to cut a few feet to be at the level of Lake Michigan. It drained the land only grudgingly. Where the plain is not underlaid by sand, it sits on nearly impenetrable blue clay called "hardpan." The combination of the low gradient, poor drainage, and the clay hardpan causes the rain and snowmelt to collect in low-lying areas. This marshy land was home to embryonic Chicago. Carl Sandburg's "City of the Big Shoulders" has feet of clay.

The Spits from the Highland Park Moraine

Chicago is not as flat as reputation has it. The level Chicago Lake Plain is relieved by the hills of "spits." Spits are slim fingers of land originally formed at or above the water line by wave action. The spits on the Lake Plain were created by the waves of each stage of Glacial Lake Chicago pounding mercilessly against the Highland Park Moraine. The Highland Park was originally the broadest of the Lake Border Moraines, but the lake levels undercut and eroded its eastern slope, as Lake Michigan does to its banks today. After any nor'easter, dramatic pictures of homes perched atop eroding bluffs make newspaper headlines. In 1897, old settlers living along the lakefront between Chicago and Waukegan estimated that during the 30 years from 1860 to 1890, a 150-foot-wide strip, representing about 500 acres, disappeared into the lake.[2] Geologist J. Harlen Bretz writes that around 1845 the small village of St. Johns hugged the cliffs on the grounds in the vicinity of today's new north suburb of Fort Sheridan. By 1907, nothing was left but some foundations and a couple of trees, and by the time of his writing in 1937, even these trees were gone.[3]

Where did the glacial till of the Highland Park Moraine go? The waves of the Glenwood and Calumet stages of Glacial Lake Chicago and post-glacial Lake Nipissing eroded the moraine, and the longshore currents, in a process known as littoral drift, dragged the material southward, creating spits.

During the Glenwood stage, the waves formed the "many-fingered" Wilmette spit, which runs from Wilmette to Oakton Street in Skokie. Gross Point Road and High Ridge Road in Wilmette run on its crest. During the Calumet stage, the lake currents formed the slim Rose Hill spit, which stretches from the North Shore village of Wilmette south to Lawrence Avenue in Chicago and is topped by Ridge Avenue. Lake Nipissing's currents formed the Graceland spit.

This low spit begins as a narrow finger in Evanston, runs south near the shoreline, and fans out into the shape of a fat sweet potato from Devon Avenue on Chicago's far north side almost to the Chicago Harbor. The northern stretch of Clark Street runs on this spit. The sandy and gravelly materials in the three spits are easy to dig, and, not surprisingly, a cemetery tops each. Memorial Park Cemetery sits atop the Wilmette spit, and Rosehill and Graceland Cemeteries gave their names to their respective spits.

We are apt, here in Chicago, to think that we have to go to faraway places like Alaska, Norway, or New Zealand in order to see glaciers. Glaciers in action, yes. School children, however, see dramatic glacial features during their field trips to Wisconsin's Kettle Moraine State Forest. We can reinforce the concepts they learn there by appreciating the more subtle traces of glaciers and glacial lakes right beneath our feet, if we know where to look and what to look for.

CHICAGO IN 1832.

Modified from a lithograph created by Rufus Blanchard. Courtesy of Chicago Historical Society ICHi-05947.

View to the north from between today's Randolph and Lake Streets west of Franklin Street, showing the junction of the river's North, South, and Main Branches, all three narrow streams with sedgy borders, and projections into the river on both the east and west. The Main Stem leads off to the right of the picture, the South Branch leads to the left, and the horse and rider are crossing a bridge across the North Branch in front of sand dunes. Wolf Point Tavern is on the left, or west bank, and Miller's store is on the right, or northeast bank, the site of today's Apparel Mart parking lot. The banks would be trimmed 16 years later for a ship-turning basin.

The Chicago River

.... The river is ample and deep for a few miles, but is utterly choked up by the lake sands, through which, behind a masked margin, it oozes its way for a mile or two till it percolates through the sands into the lake. Its banks consist of a black ... fertile soil, which is stated to produce abundantly, in its season, the wild species of cepa, or leek. This circumstance has led the natives to name it the place of the wild leek.

—Henry Schoolcraft, 1820

A shallow, little stream, formed by the junction of two branches half a mile inland, moved in graceful curves to the eastward and added its modest contribution to the great chain of marvelous fresh water seas. ... Along the shore was to be seen a succession of low sand hills, partly covered with a scrubby growth of cedars, junipers and pines. Beyond were detached groves, mostly of small black oaks. A little farther west, reaching to the north branch of the river, were a few noble elms, while further up the stream a fine belt of hickory, maple, beech and a variety of oaks spread gradually wider and wider towards the east until, joining the lake shore timber, they formed the southern outpost of that immense forest stretching to the north, covering the trackless regions. ...

—Edwin O. Gale, 1902

The Chicago River, the main character in our story, is a glacial legacy. It is the only stream that drains the northern two thirds of the Chicago Lake Plain, and under natural conditions, it just barely does the job.

The Main Stem and Wolf Point

For most of today's travelers and visitors, mention of the Chicago River calls to mind the Main Stem in downtown Chicago where the Michigan Avenue bridge crosses the water and magnificent architecture lines the banks. In the early days, the Main Stem was a shallow, sluggish stream fed by the confluence of the North and South Branches at its western end. The earliest settlers called the west bank of the confluence "Wolf Point," or "Wolf's Point," and the confluence was the nucleus of a budding town, with taverns, a school, and a church.[1] Wolf Point and the Main Stem were bordered by rushes, wild rice, and other typical streamside vegetation.

The Main Stem itself had three "tributaries," creeks or sloughs, depending on who was describing them. One slough, 60 feet wide at its mouth, ran north into the river at what is now State Street. (Fort Dearborn fed its ditch into this slough.) A smaller creek ran north between Clark and LaSalle Streets. "The third and most formidable one was on the north side, near Franklin Street, being eighty feet wide at the river and extending north through the Kingsbury and Newberry tracts to Chicago Avenue."[2] It emptied into the Chicago River at the present site of the Merchandise Mart. In addition to the sloughs and branches, the river was fed by water that ponded in low marshy patches on the land surface and slowly soaked through the earth into the stream. One potential buyer recounted:

> I was offered a hull block about where the Auditorium is, as nigh as I can figger it out, for $60. But mud was more'n knee deep on Water and Lake streets [probably today's intersection of Wacker Drive and Lake Street]— the only business streets there wuz then—and the water was so deep and the grass so high when the fellow and I went out to see the land, I couldn't see it when I got there. I couldn't see the pesky town, nuther, the rosinweed and slough grass was so high, and I'd been lost if I hadn't hullered after the chap. He reckoned I wasn't on the buy, so he scooted back for another Sucker. Before I got to the tavern I was that tuckered out wallowing around in the mud I wouldn't er gin ten bits an acre for the whole dod rotted place.[3]

As Chicago grew, the Main Stem became the heartbeat of the ragged, rugged city, and makeshift docks of all sizes and shapes replaced the vegetation. The water that ran from the land into the river now carried an increasing tincture of human occupation. In Chicago's early days, the river flowed to the east, following the dictates of gravity and funneling the united North and South Branches into the Main Stem and then into Lake Michigan, the lowest point on the horizon. Today the water in the Main Branch flows backward to the west, past prized architectural landmarks. It flows through the South Branch into the deep Sanitary and Ship Canal and on to the Mississippi. Since the river's reversal and the construction of other channels leading from the lake, it can be said that its original mouth at Lake Michigan has become just one of its sources.

Around the 1800s, when the river still emptied into the lake, it detoured southward through a narrow channel between the shore and a sandbar. It probably entered the lake somewhere near the location of today's Madison Street, give or take a few feet depending on the day.

The South Branch

The South Branch has only two forks, the South and the West. (Caution: this West Fork should not be confused with the West Fork of the North Branch.) Before the 1930s, the South Branch flowed south toward the Sanitary and Ship Canal in a gentle eastward arc before it turned west; that eastward arc has been eliminated and the river now flows almost straight south from Wolf Point until it bends to the west. During the early days of Chicago's history, the entire South Branch was sometimes called the Portage River. People remember that the Main Stem, the South Branch, and its West Fork provided approximately six miles of navigable river from Lake Michigan to the portage route.

The South Fork of the South Branch became legendary as the site of the

Union Stock Yards. Its history is replete with gruesome tales about the lives of workers and deaths of stock in the yards. The source of the South Fork was south of today's Pershing Road, west of today's Ashland Avenue, in a sort of bayou in the prairies behind the low sand dunes along Lake Michigan's shore. The narrow creek where the water collected was approximately 29 feet wide and flowed to the northeast before turning to the north to connect with the South Branch.[4]

Today, the South Fork is referred to as having had two "arms." The natural little feeder creek running northeast from just below Pershing Road was apparently demoted from "source" to "arm" when the Union Stock Yards dug its twin, a drainage ditch from the east that emptied into the South Fork just below Pershing Road. The South Fork then appeared to have two tentacles below Pershing Road, one coming from the east, and one coming from the west. To lessen confusion, we will use the term "West Arm" when referring to the Fork's original tributary, because that is the way the river has been pictured on all topographical maps since the late 1890s.

The North Branch and the Lake Border Moraines

It was the Main Stem and the West Fork of the South Branch, not the North Branch, which created the conditions for the growth of a metropolis at the junction of Lake Michigan and the Chicago River. But without the contribution of the drainage of the 102-square-mile North Branch watershed, the Main Stem would have been even smaller and slower than it was. The consequences of settlement along the North Branch would be of great significance to downstream Chicago.

The three forks of the North Branch arise in north suburban Lake County and unite in Cook County. In Lake County, it would have been a misnomer to apply the word 'river' to the string of sloughs or marshes that lay in the lowlands between the Lake Border Moraines. These sloughs were only the precursors to today's North Branch forks.

The northernmost point in the North Branch watershed is near a low spot on Grand Avenue at Spaulding Corners in Waukegan, Lake County. This is the marshy vicinity where today's East Fork, or the Skokie River, rises, about two miles west of Waukegan in the valley between the Highland Park and Blodgett Moraines. In the small town of Park City, just to the east of the mobile home village near Betty Limbrunner Park on Knight Avenue, you can see a pond. Its waters drain through a culvert into what becomes the Skokie River. Perhaps the waters of the original northernmost slough, known in the late nineteenth century as "Dady's Slough," have been impounded in this pond.

Between the Blodgett and the Deerfield Moraines, the next hill to the west, lies the valley of the Middle Fork. Today's Middle Fork has its wet weather origin near O'Plaine Road in Waukegan, although historically it probably began some four miles to the south. Its beginning appears to be in a small, very appealing edge of a subdivision, where the original developers sensitively preserved a grove of tall old trees. The land is very wet. The developer probably drained the water off of as much acreage as he could, but one potential lot was too damp for building. The developer appears to have drained the subdivision's very wet land into a narrow channel that may be considered the northernmost reach of the Middle Fork.

A would-be early settler, guided by the Public Land Surveyor's description from July 9 through 12, 1840, would have gained the impression that this land, where the Middle Fork begins today, was dry and supported oak and hickory timber. Surveyor Harrison characterized it as "fit for cultivation," as the surveyors put it. Two miles farther south Harrison found good soil but a little wet for cultivation. Four miles to the south was his first mention of a slough along the route of today's Middle Fork.[5] This vicinity, near the tiny suburban community of Rondout, just north of Rockland Road (Route 176), east of the Tri-State Tollway and at the junction of three rail lines, is where most early writers put the start of the Middle Fork. Perhaps July, 1840, was a dry season.

Searching in southwest Waukegan for today's Middle Fork headwaters in autumn, 1997, a small group of explorers, equipped with a *Hydrologic Atlas of the Libertyville Quadrangle*, arrived at a subdivision located on the map at mile 64. Here, the map indicated the beginning of a small intermittent stream that becomes the Middle Fork. (The *Hydrologic Atlas* is a series of separate maps imposed on the United States Geological Survey (USGS) 1:24,000 Quadrangle contour maps, of the type familiar to hikers. These maps show floods from 1935 through the 1960s.) Our map promised water, but there was none to be seen.[6]

Fortunately, Sandy, a homeowner in the rear of the subdivision, was outside gardening. Intrigued by our quest, she remembered the tiny brook that runs behind the houses near the front of the subdivision. After asking and receiving permission, Sandy, transformed from gardener to guide, led us carefully over the well-groomed lawn to the thick band of shrubs and trees. We were quiet. One at a time, each of the five of us stood in a tiny cleared space and peered through the prickly bushes. There it was. Feeling something like the Lewis and Clark Corps of Discovery, our mounting excitement was all out of proportion to the foot-wide clear ribbon of dark-brown water. We had found it: what the map and we were content to call the headwaters of the Middle Fork. Not the original river, by a long shot, but the beginnings of a stream of water that now connects Chicago to New Orleans. (On July 13, 1999, in the midst of a hot, dry summer, this stream was completely devoid of water. In fact, the Middle Fork was dry until just north of Rondout, supporting the surveyor's conclusions and indicating how vitally important it is to note the month of the early survey.)

Farther west, the valley of the West Fork of the North Branch lies between the Deerfield Moraine and the gentle rise of the Park Ridge Moraine. Today's West Fork of the North Branch (not to be confused with the historic West Fork of the South Branch) rises from marshy land in the southeast corner of the suburban town of Mettawa. Some maps show it emanating from a pond, others just draw a line up onto the area just west of the pond, where water from the soggy land collects in a ditch running parallel to the pond on its west. The pond is indeed one of its origins when it overflows into the channel of the West Fork during springtime. During the dry summer of 1999, however, although there was water in the pond, there was no water in the ditch until nearly a mile south, just above Old Mill Road.

This pond is an artificial creation, appearing on maps for the first time in 1957-1958, simultaneously with the construction of Interstate 94, the Tri-State Tollway. Because of its uniform depth (11 feet as measured by the author in July, 1999), the pond appears to have been excavated as a "borrow-pit," and its soil used for construction of the tollway. Most likely, its soil had a high clay content that could be used to raise the roadbed of adjacent Everett Road over the tollway.[7] According to the *Wheeling Quadrangle Hydrologic Atlas*, the West Fork was relocated in a new channel in conjunction with construction of the highway.[8]

Indicating how close the watersheds of the Des Plaines and Chicago Rivers are in the northern part of the watershed, John Halsey, in his respected 1912 *History of Lake County*, agrees with Harrison in placing the origin of the West Fork at one and one-half miles east of the Des Plaines River and the settlement of Half Day (still an unincorporated area on the fringes of Lincolnshire).[9] Today's changes have moved the origin of the West Fork about two miles to the north. In its natural state, the West Fork was originally less of a slough and more of a channel than the two sloughs to the east, which were known collectively by early settlers as the "two Skokies." Today, the West Fork has been ditched virtually throughout its entire length, with one artificial lake, Lake Eleanor in Deerfield, created in the 1960s and surrounded by housing.

The hills of the moraines diminish to the south, and the forks combine. The Skokie and the Middle Fork join at the terminus of the Blodgett Moraine between Winnetka and Lake Avenues east of Glenview's Wagner Road, in the middle of Cook County's Forest Preserve District holdings. A bicycle bridge crosses the confluence. (The original sprawling sloughs at this junction have been radically altered into distinct channels.) Farther south, this combined stream, known as the North Branch, merges with the West Fork at the end of the Deerfield Moraine on the Forest Preserve District's Chick Evans Golf Course. On Golf Road, east of the village of Golf (tucked between Glenview and Morton Grove), you can ride over the gentle slope of the Deerfield Moraine's tail end. The slight rise between the streams labeled "North Branch, Chicago River" and the "West Fork, Chicago River" on the signs is the moraine. The concrete retaining wall to the north holds the Deerfield Moraine in check. After leaving

Photo by Robert M. Kaplan

Looking east along Golf Road, along the north side of the street in the distance, a retaining wall holds back the Deerfield Moraine.

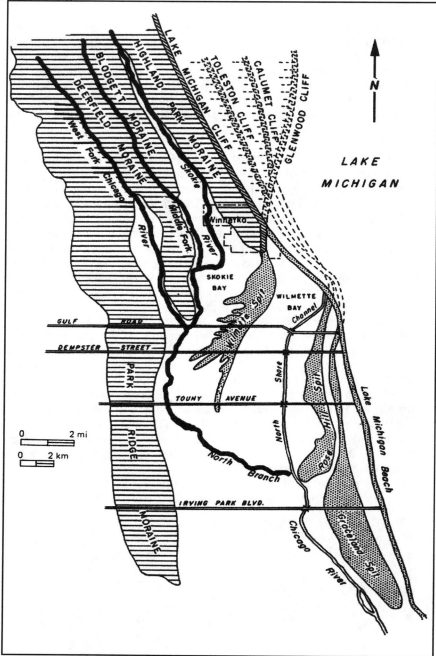

Modified from Bretz, 1952.

The Lake Border Moraines and the spits eroded from the
Highland Park Moraine shape the route of the North Branch.

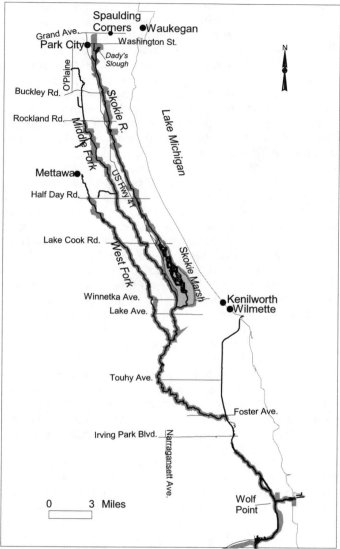

Map created by Libby Hill using ArcView® GIS Software. Digital files courtesy of Northeastern Illinois Planning Commission and Illinois Department of Natural Resources.

A rough approximation of the old course of the Chicago River from Wolf Point north is sketched in black. The present river is in gray. A map of changes made to the South Branch, the South Fork, the West Fork of the South Branch, and Mud Lake can be found on page 212.

the golf course, the combined North Branch flows generally southwest and then southeast on the gently sloping lake plain, its single strand complete.

Here the spits enter the story. The spits formed by the erosion of the Highland Park Moraine shape the route of the North Branch. Geologist Bretz explains that the Skokie River would naturally be seeking an outlet toward Lake Michigan, and its predisposition would have been to flow down into the lake near Kenilworth or Wilmette. However, instead of emptying into the lake in a northern suburb, the Skokie River, and then the combined Skokie and Middle Fork, find themselves landlocked, their route blocked by the Wilmette spit. The North Branch, after joining with the West Fork, has to flow around both the Rose Hill and the Graceland spits. Bretz calculates that the spits cause the water in the Skokie River to flow an extra ten miles out its way before joining the Main Stem of the Chicago River and its final entrance into Lake Michigan.[10]

Originally, the East and Middle Forks, before joining, were just a series of broad, shallow sloughs or marshes, without the energy to carve any sort of a channel. There were no slopes to traverse, no rocky cliffs over which the water could plunge. However, according to Bretz, despite the average low gradient of two feet per mile through which the river runs, the valley of the North Branch is stream-carved from the confluence of the Middle and East Forks between Winnetka and Lake Avenues all the way to Wolf Point. Where the North Branch came to the slope of an old Calumet-level beach of Glacial Lake Chicago, it could descend more rapidly. Because of its greater speed and energy, the water cut down through the slope and eroded a channel. In this short stretch, the river valley is 15 to 20 feet deep, and the river has created a meandering bottomland floodplain. This dramatic and uncharacteristic cut is visible in the Cook County Forest Preserve between Touhy and Foster Avenues (in the Edgebrook area).[11] As the original course of the river continued downstream from the Foster Avenue vicinity, it never again flowed in such a deep natural channel; its route was shallow and meandering, flowing to the southeast close to the spits. It sprawled out over the low, almost flat Glacial Lake Chicago plain, creating a landscape of oxbows, marshes, bottomlands, and summer swimming holes. Today, these meanders are gone.

The Park Ridge Moraine still marks the divide between the Chicago and the Des Plaines River watersheds. At Irving Park Road and Narragansett Avenue, for example, one can detect the low divide of the moraine to the west. Where the moraine subsides, to the south at approximately Chicago Avenue, the Chicago River watershed trends to the southwest on the Lake Plain. South to 83rd Street and west nearly to the Des Plaines River, there were once shallow pockets of marshes drained by either the South Branch or its tributaries, or the Des Plaines River. Mud Lake was one of these. The highest land, if it can be called that, was approximately 594 feet above sea level, 14 feet above the level of Lake Michigan, but barely above its surroundings. In the present-day vicinity of Kedzie Avenue and 31st Street in Chicago's Little Village neighborhood, the situation blurred. Here, in the lowlands, once lay the ambiguous two-foot high divide that created Chicago.

The Natural Chicago River
Animal, Vegetable, and Mineral

. . . Then in winter the Chicago River was our skating rink and our race course. Let me ask John Bates over there if he remembers when we skated together up to Hard Scrabble—where Bridgeport now is—and he explained to me, by pantomime alone, how the Indians caught muskrats under the ice.

—John Dean Caton
Reception to the Settlers of Chicago Prior to 1840 address
Calumet Club of Chicago, May 27, 1879

The sluggish, small stream or lagoon, that by lake-side meandered south, was, in summer, a narrow, green pond when the sand-bars had choked up its mouth; for 'twas only when floods and high water, pushing out with a fortunate tide, bore the creek on to meeting its sweet-heart, and made the lake beauty its bride. In spring time, with thaws and with freshet, the river ran full in its bed, and the natives they cast their bone hooks, catching red-fin and perch and bull-head; here was a clump of green willows, and a few scattering oaks might be seen, but aside from the spots of dry prairie, there were many wet places between. The wild ducks lit down in the slough, foreshadowing a city park lake, where the cygnets now come at the call. . . .

—Knee Buckles
"Chicago in Olden Times"

Not only is the Chicago River positioned at a significant sub-continental divide, it is also in a significant ecological transition zone. The Chicago region is well appreciated as a transition zone between the eastern forest and the tall-grass prairie. Both forest and prairie grew in the watershed along the banks of the river, just waiting, it seemed, for people to come along and capitalize on these riches.

Poised as it is on this ecotone, the greater Chicago region retains vestiges of northern vegetation and also harbors plants and animals of the southern region. In fact, many plants and animals found in the area are at the extreme limits of their ranges. The region's humid continental climate of warm summers and cold winters is moderated by its proximity to Lake Michigan. As this climate altered in response to changing conditions—higher water levels, more or less moisture, for example—even a small change might have given an advantage to forest, savanna, or prairie as they vied to dominate the land.

The lower reaches of the Chicago River flowed sluggishly in a shallow, near-level depression, just barely draining the prairies and the woodlands in its watershed. It was unusual for the river to have anything more than a slight current. In its uppermost reaches in Lake County where the river, particularly the West Fork of the North Branch, ran through land with more slope, there would have been a somewhat stronger current and more riffles and deep pools. The varied characteristics of moving water and streamside vegetation throughout the watershed would have supported habitats for diverse communities of fish, shellfish, and other river and land organisms.

The river reacted not only to slope and climate but also to annual seasonal changes, overflowing its neighboring wetlands in annual spring floods. Rivers like the Chicago, flowing with little slope on sand, silt, and other stream-carried deposits, build up natural levees of sediments as they go through their flood cycle. Before the flood, the river is confined within its banks. As the flood approaches, the water level rises, the current increases, and the river becomes turbid with the increased sediment, either stirred up from the bottom or eroded from the watershed surface by the rainfall and runoff. The river reaches bank-full stage and begins to spread out over the land. The current diminishes, and the suspended sediment settles out. The heavier particles drop out first, causing the land nearer to the river to be slightly higher than the land away from the river. This is the natural levee, perhaps hardly noticeable to the uneducated eye. Away from the river, behind the levee, the lower area remains filled with water, debris, and perhaps fish and other water-dwellers, trapped there and waiting out the flood. Thus, when the water recedes, it leaves a landscape of wet lowland, adjacent levee, and river. The water in the lowland will eventually seep into the ground or evaporate. The entire extent of the belt of low ground likely to be inundated with flood water is the floodplain. The floodplain is an integral and essential part of the river regime. A river channel is dynamic. When the river changes its route, which rivers naturally do, it continuously modifies the profiles of its channel and its floodplain.

In the early Chicago River watershed, life was organized around seeps and mineral-rich deposits, which served as animal licks and wallows. As precipitation gradually percolated through pores in the soil and gravel of the glacial till, it picked up minerals and its temperature cooled. The enriched water re-emerged in springs or seeps, absorbed oxygen, and provided a predictable supply of cool water, high in dissolved oxygen and minerals. Wildlife, including elk, deer, and bison, were drawn to these seeps and used them routinely for primary sources of calcium, sulfur, and iron, as well as for the micronutrients they could obtain here in substantial concentrations. The plants that flourished near these wallows were those specifically adapted to animal disturbance.

In the natural Chicago River, fish came up-river to spawn, and predators (human and animal) caught them. The river provided a life-support system to the animals and plants that used it either as a corridor for travel or as a seasonal or year-round home.

Vegetation in the Watershed

The earliest vegetation in the Chicago River watershed were black spruce, fir trees, low mosses, and low tussock sedges, all plants adapted to the cold post-glacial climate and characteristic of today's northern regions. By the time the Europeans arrived to a temperate climate, the vegetation with which we are familiar—fire-tolerant prairie and oak savanna, as well as oak forests—had long ago migrated in on the south and west winds.

On the west side of the region's flowing rivers were verdant prairies. In summer, they were ablaze with colorful flowers and grasses. In fall, they were typically ablaze with fires set by natives or lightning. The waters in the Chicago River stopped these fierce prairie fires that approached from the west, and the lack of regular fires on the east side of the river favored the growth of trees. The pattern of prairie to the west and woods to the east was typical of all the north-south rivers of northeastern Illinois: the Rock, the Fox, the Des Plaines, and the Chicago.

On high, well-drained land grew fire-tolerant scattered trees, or savannas. The savannas were composed primarily of white oak species, especially the bur oak, with its thick, gnarly bark, but also included white ash and hickory. The open understory of the savannas resembled parks, and early settlers, who found welcome shade there from the blazing prairie sun, called them "oak openings." Oak groves also survived here and there on the prairie, perhaps protected from the fierce fires by barely detectable rises and dips in the landscape, as well as by their own thick layer of protective bark. On the fringes of these upland savannas grew witch hazel, sumac, dwarf huckleberry, two or three viburnums, dogwoods, gooseberry, and currant.[1]

Ravines, low spots, and the east sides of rivers offered cool, moist conditions and protection from the intense fires that seared the prairie. These microsites supported "mesophytic" forest, composed primarily of trees not well-resistant to fire. Swamp white oak, ash, elm, and hickory were dominant and grew alongside butternut, black walnut, and wild black cherry. Maple and basswood, partial to drier feet, grew on slight rises in the low wet land. The fire-tolerant bur oak, with a wide ecological range, was found anywhere in the mix.

Throughout the wetter lands, whether upland or lowland, early settlers reported a wide diversity of understory plants. Among them were quaking and large-toothed aspen, hornbeam, viburnums (maple-leaved, tooth-leaved, nannyberry), dogwoods, prickly ash, and nine-bark. Shadbush (also known as serviceberry or juneberry), wild plum, wild crab, at least ten species of hawthorn, choke-cherry, hazelnut, gooseberry, elderberry, and currant grew along with the others. The hornbeam seedlings, intermixed with hazelnut or other shrubs, often formed extensive thickets.[2] George C. Klehm observed, "Prominent among the shrubbery are large patches of sumac with their splendid crowns in summer and beautiful variegated leaves in the fall season. Hazel nuts, blackberries, red and black raspberries, gooseberries and wild grape are found in profusion; also strawberries."[3] To animals, indigenous tribal members, and early settlers, the broad variety of fruit-bearing trees must have been a treasure trove of dining. In spring and fall, the herbaceous plants and grasses, short and lacking woody stems, decorated the understory of savanna and woodland.

Early settlers called the lowland forests "Big Woods." One Big Woods lay to the west of the small village of Ridgeville, Evanston's predecessor, and east of the North Branch. Settlers built homes on Evanston's oak-lined, well-drained ridges and drained the marshy land between the ridges. The oaks, which seem particularly sensitive to soil compaction and to changing water tables, began to die. Evanstonians, who valued a tree-studded streetscape, reached into their Big Woods nursery and transplanted hundreds of elms to line their city avenues.

Where it was too low and wet even for trees, one could find wet prairie, marshes, and vernal (springtime) ponds. Early settlers in Lake County called these marshes "sloughs." These wetlands and the river edges supported stiff, low, non-woody vegetation including wild rice, blue flag, sedges, and cattails. Trees, such as willow, cottonwood, silver or soft maple, ash, hackberry, and bur oak grew in the floodplain. The streamside vegetation, adapted to a changing flood regime, supported diverse communities of animal life. It stabilized the soil, filtered out silt and other contaminants, and contributed organic resources, or detritus, composed mainly of leaves, fallen tree branches, dead plant growth, and insects. It cooled the water, maintaining a high degree of dissolved oxygen. All of these processes created a healthy habitat for aquatic organisms.

Along the lakefront, low sand dunes supported prairie plants, black oak, some cedar, white pine, cottonwood, and low-spreading juniper. Today, Illinois Beach State Park, near Zion and the Wisconsin border, preserves a landscape similar to that of the original Chicago lakefront, with alternating dunes and swales and the Dead River, which runs through the park. The Dead River, with its sandbar, probably resembles the Chicago River's original mouth at the lake.

Wildlife of the Watershed

When Europeans arrived, the whole Chicagoland region was a wildlife haven. A soldier stationed at Fort Dearborn and known to us only as J.G.F. in historian Henry Higgins Hurlbut's 1886, *Chicago Antiquities*, described the marshland wildfowl in Mud Lake:

> The prairie between these streams [the South Fork of the Chicago River and the Des Plaines] is at all times swampy; but during the spring floods, a considerable lake is formed. . . . Here, after the waters have subsided, vast quantities of aquatic fowl congregate to feed upon the wild-rice, insects, etc. that abound in it. Swan, geese and brant, passing to and fro in clouds, keep an incessant cackling; ducks of every kind, from the mallard and canvass-back, down to the tiny water-witch [possibly a horned grebe] and blue-winged teal, add their mite to the 'discord dire,' while hundreds of gulls hover gracefully over, ever and anon plunging their snowy bosoms into the circling waters. In April, myriads of plover and snipe take the place of the aforementioned; still later, great quantities of woodcock, grouse, and ortolans [probably bobolink] make their appearance in the neighborhood.[4]

Scores of animals abounded in each community: the woodlands, the wetlands, the river, the floodplain, and the prairie. Some of the animals used several different habitats. In the deep woods of the North Branch were large populations of woodchuck, gray squirrel, fox, skunk, wolf, deer, elk, bobcat, and even mountain lion and black bear, as well as bald eagle, crow, and wild turkey. Nearer the river were fisher, beaver, otter, and marten. In springtime, the heart-pounding sounds of the ruffed grouse resonated from the aspen groves. And, in early morning, the booms of prairie chickens rose from nearby prairies. In some years of heavy migration, so many passenger pigeons perched in the trees that the branches bent low to the ground. Hunters on the prairie found some "woodland" mammals, as well as the now long-gone bison and the now-returning coyote. The marshlands were alive with birds: herons, egrets, swallowtailed kites, long billed curlews, whooping cranes, sandhill cranes, American bitterns, trumpeter swans, and ducks of nearly every variety. LeConte's sparrow, upland sandpipers, and ravens (outnumbering the crows) ranged throughout the drier habitats.

To the north of the river, in a broad basin roughly defined by the 600-foot contour line and stretching from Foster Avenue in Chicago to Wilmette, lay a basin of wet land that drained into the Chicago River through intermittent streams. The basin contained rich loamy soils with a high water content. Where the basin was too low to support trees, wet prairie prevailed. Close to the river at Foster was a game preserve known as Budlong's Woods. Lyman A. Budlong, famous for Budlong's pickles, owned a large wooded patch in the midst of truck farms. The woods extended from the North Branch near Bowmanville, now a residential enclave on Chicago's north side, nearly to Lincoln Avenue. A 1902 newspaper article described it:

> Extending eastward for half a mile from the bank of the North Branch of the Chicago River, in the 27th Ward, is a great belt of native timber unscarified as yet by the ax of civilization. This big patch of woods, with its huge trees, is on the property of Lyman A. Budlong, who has lived near the timber and has jealously preserved it for nearly half a century. The woods constitute the only game preserve in northern Illinois, and the birds and animals which live within the shadow of the trees are descendants of those who made their home there time out of mind. . . .[5]

The article claims that the huge trees were between 20 and 25 feet in circumference. It describes the great quantities of woodcocks, "jacksnipe," and wood ducks that could be found there in spring, as well as quail, ruffed grouse, and songbirds. The large raccoons of the timber were hunted occasionally in the fall. Budlong's preserve was private, and invitees had to show passes or paid admission receipts in order to enter. At the time the preserve was the subject of this newspaper article, it was already doomed by the inevitable encroachment of town lots, although it took until the 1940s to obliterate it completely.[6]

In the river itself, life teemed with fresh-water mussels as well as fish, frogs, insects, and turtles. Near the old river mouth at Lake Michigan, in today's downtown Chicago, was expansive marshland fed by the detritus delivered by the river. Because of its connection to the Great Lakes system, the Chicago River supported many species of Lake Michigan fish that came upriver to spawn. Floodwaters from typical 'freshets,' as the early settlers called the heavy rains, triggered biological movements of fish and other organisms. In the spring, lake sturgeon migrated upstream to spawn. Walleye and suckers and even some trout species gathered in the pools by day, moving into the riffles to spawn at night. Northern pike spawned in the marshes. Brook trout spawned in the fall. Fish species in the rivers of northeastern Illinois differed in different watersheds. Those of the Chicago River differed from those of the Des Plaines and the Mississippi. Since the waters met on occasion at Mud Lake, however, there was surely some crossover at this point between the Great Lakes and Mississippi watersheds.

This was the land of vast natural richness that greeted successive tribes, European explorers, French fur traders, and the first American settlers. What it lacked in the grandeur associated with mountains and rushing streams, it made up for in the sheer diversity and abundance of plant and animal life that complemented the clear, clean waters of the river and lake.

As long as the Chicago River watershed was dominated by its original vegetative cover, and no artificial ditches drained the water from the sloughs or marshes, the river would have been in tune with the cycle of nature. But the enormous settlement rate of Chicago and its outlying areas led to plowing the prairie, cutting the trees, and draining the moist land. By the last quarter of the nineteenth century, the raindrop that had been able to take its time percolating through the soil to emerge in a seep or dribble down to one watershed or another to join a rivulet, found itself in a hurry, dashing off plowed farm fields, roofs, compacted soil, paved streets, and sidewalks. By the 1930s, it joined not a lazy, winding rivulet or a wetland but a straight and narrow artificially carved ditch that hurried it even faster to the river. Water was increasingly extracted from the lake for drinking purposes, and it drained as waste into the river, adding to the river's burden. No river, neither the Des Plaines nor the Chicago, was ecologically equipped for this amount of stress, and its pulsing energy simply collected and delivered the goods—water, sediment, detritus from the entire watershed—so quickly that it inundated the built-up landscape downstream. Humans had so reworked the landscape that the natural ecological processes of the river and its watershed could not function in the face of the seasonal weather cycles.

Tríbal Lands

Ye say they all have passed away
That noble race and brave.
That their light canoes have vanished
From off the crested wave.
That midst the forests where they roved
There rings no hunter's shout,
But their name is on your waters,
And ye may not wash it out.

—Mrs. Hemans
Edwin O. Gale's *Reminiscences of Early Chicago and Vicinity*

Humans ventured into the Chicagoland area approximately 12,000 years ago as the glacier receded and the climate became more inviting to plants and animals. Their successive cultures adapted to the changes in the landscape as the lakes ancestral to Lake Michigan varied in size.

If man or animal lived here before the Wisconsin glacial episode, all evidence was removed by the action of the ice. Huge animals came in as soon after the glaciers as the area was habitable for them. It is hard to imagine the immense woolly mammoth, a beast with long shaggy hair and huge curved tusks, grazing here in the meadow, while its smaller but still enormous reddish cousin, the mastodon, browsed on the trees and in the grasslands, perhaps in the neighborhood of your own backyard. Both animals, relatives of the elephant, were probably common, and both were ideally suited to the cold climates that followed in the wake of the glaciers.

The earliest human culture following the glaciers were the nomadic Paleo-Indians. They lived in a land of spruce forests, tundra, grasslands, sloughs, and bogs on the high land, where there were also wetlands full of rich aquatic resources. Current research suggests that their game diet may have consisted more of smaller mammals, such as caribou (if caribou can be thought of as small), rather than of huge mastodons.

Around 10,000 years ago, the Archaic culture followed that of the Paleo-Indians, on the cusp of a warming climate. The lake level fluctuated to much greater extremes than it does today. As the temperature warmed, deciduous trees replaced the cold-loving spruce and fir, and prairie grasses extended into the region from the west. By 9,000 years ago, the lake had diminished dramatically from 620 feet above sea level to only 230 feet above sea level. Geologists call this phase Lake Chippewa. (It is helpful to remember that today's Lake Michigan is more than twice that height, 580 feet above sea level.) Forests covered gently sloping hills. People could probably have walked in a direct line from present-day Chicago to Michigan City, Indiana. This lowest lake level coincides with the early years of the Hypsithermal period, which lasted

| YEARS BP | 15,000 | 14,000 | 13,000 | 12,000 | 11,000 | 10,000 | 9,000 | 8,000 | 7,000 | 6,000 | 5,000 | 4,000 | 3,000 | 2,000 | 1,000 |

LAKES: Milwaukee · Chicago · Algonquin · "Post-Algonquin" · Chippewa · Nipissing · Algoma · Michigan

LAKE PHASES: Glenwood I · Intra-Glenwood low · Glenwood II · Two Creeks low · Calumet · Kirkfield · Post-Algonquin · Chippewa low · Nipissing I · Nipissing II · Algoma · modern

LAKE LEVELS: Present lake level — Michigan (177m) low · Algoma (179m) · Toleston (184m) · Calumet (189m) · Glenwood (195m) high

CULTURAL CHRONOLOGY: PALEO-INDIAN · EARLY ARCHAIC · MIDDLE ARCHAIC · LATE ARCHAIC · E M L WOODLAND · MISSISSIPPIAN

| YEARS BP | 15,000 | 14,000 | 13,000 | 12,000 | 11,000 | 10,000 | 9,000 | 8,000 | 7,000 | 6,000 | 5,000 | 4,000 | 3,000 | 2,000 | 1,000 |

Courtesy Illinois Historic Preservation Agency. Chart modified from Charles W. Markman, in Ardith K. Hansel, David M. Mickelson, Allan F. Schneider, and Curtis E. Larsen, "Late Wisconsinan and Holocene History of the Lake Michigan Basin," in P.F. Karrow and P.E. Calkin, eds. Quarternary Evolution of the Great Lakes, Geological Association of Canada Special Paper 30, 1985, 39-53.

Chart showing the water levels in the Lake Michigan Basin
overlaid with North American tribal cultures.

from 8,700 to 5,000 years before the present. The Hypsithermal was not only hot but it was also dry, and prairie grasses extended even further at the expense of forest. Marshlands and bogs, hitherto sources of valuable resources for the inhabitants, began to shrink.

Between 6,000 and 4,000 years ago, the waters rose again to around 600 feet above sea level and post-glacial Lake Nipissing took shape. Succeeding generations of the Archaic culture would have been forced to retreat to dry land. At these high lake levels, the volume of water carried by rivers would have increased. Permanent streams most likely began to play a greater part in the lives of the people, who probably settled in and around the river floodplains. Large shell mounds provide evidence that they exploited the river environment. Deer were probably their greatest source of protein in the Chicago area, supplemented with an occasional elk, bear, or bison along with small mammals, fish, and migrating waterfowl. Nuts from forest trees became a particularly important part of their diet. At this time, we have evidence of early agriculture and growing trade within the region.

Around 3,000 years ago the Archaic evolved into the Woodland culture, although this evolution did not take place uniformly everywhere. Population was on the increase. Woodland people built permanent villages high above the rivers. They practiced extensive horticulture. Trading for exotic materials from afar was particularly important to this group, and thus rivers took on even more importance.

In much of Illinois, the Woodland culture was replaced about 1100 years ago by the Mississippian, a way of life marked by large urban or semi-urban centers on major rivers, hence the name. In our area, from Minnesota to Ohio, the culture has been named "Upper Mississippian," to differentiate it from the more complex cultures farther south along the Mississippi River. The Upper Mississippians were still mostly hunter/farmers who depended less than their southern neighbors on agriculture, but they continued to rely upon the river. They still followed the seasons for wild food and productive wetlands, especially the Chicago Lake Plain marshes, provided important resources.

The Miami were most likely Mississippian, and the Potawatomi perhaps late Woodland or Mississippian. A village site on the North Branch of the Chicago River in LaBagh woods near Sauganash Prairie attracted all cultures and has yielded artifacts from the Archaic, Woodland, and Mississippian cultures, indicating the importance of the river in providing the necessities of life.

A Woodland/Upper Mississippian culture site had four necessary ingredients: water, a source of food other than from agriculture, tillable soils for farming, and a source of fuel. The Chicago River provided all four: the river, springs, and backwaters provided water and attracted prey animals; tillable soil was in the floodplain; and trees grew along the banks.

These peoples lived within the seasonal cycles of the river. They burned the prairie, reinforcing the fire-dependent ecosystem that provided open views for hunting, protection from enemies, and open space on which to practice agriculture. They may well have built stone or wood fishing weirs in the river itself, changing the riffles in the water, but we have no evidence that they purposefully changed its course or its natural processes.

A spring near the river provided running water even in winter. Animals and birds were attracted to the water, and the river supplied them with fish and freshwater mussels. Backwater lakes or vernal ponds would flood in the spring and then, as the water receded, fish would be trapped and the villagers would help themselves. Around the pond edges grew wild rice and other edible vegetation. Evidence from archeological digs in and near Chicago shows that fish and other river life such as beaver, otter, muskrat, and turtles were important resources for food or fur.

The floodplain would have been an ideal area for planting. Floodplain soil was soft and loamy and could be easily worked with simple tools. Planting after the spring flood receded usually yielded a good harvest by August or September. Villagers could have planted corn in late May and the corn would have been available for picking 90 days later. Downstream, on a slight rise, perhaps along a ravine, a maple grove would have afforded maple sugar.

The trees of the forests and savanna provided one necessary ingredient for survival: energy. Aspen and other poplars were common near the river. Because it was women and children who broke off the dead lower branches of these fast-growing trees to use for cooking fires, such fuel became known as "squaw wood." Burning hot and fast with little or no smoke, this soft wood was an important energy source. After several years of cutting and gathering firewood, an energy supply would be depleted. When collecting wood required a two- or three-mile walk, it was only logical to move to a new stock; relocation became a way of life for the Woodland peoples. Wood was a renewable resource, however, and in a generation or so a former home would be re-populated with trees, and the village would return and rebuild in the same spot or nearby.

The Mississippian culture flourished at the time of the cold and wet "Little Ice Age," from 1450 to 1850 A.D., encompassing the year 1673 when the Indians introduced Father Jacques Marquette and Louis Jolliet to the Chicago portage. High water levels during the Little Ice Age may lend credibility to claims by Jolliet that only a short canal would have been necessary to bridge the distance between the Chicago and the Des Plaines Rivers.[1]

By approximately 1600-1700 years ago, the waters in the basin had reached 580 feet above sea level and taken form as Lake Michigan, although the water level varied, as it continues to do. Maps of the recent tribal settlements show villages located on high land overlooking a river, although occasionally the villagers may have moved downhill in the dry summer months to set up small, temporary tent encampments along the stream. One village was located at Bowmanville, near today's Foster Avenue bridge on the North Branch of the Chicago River. Another village, located in the general vicinity of present-day Golf Road and the North Branch, extended north into Harms Woods and south onto the Chick Evans Golf Course parking lot. Its center was on the site of today's Glen View Club at the southern terminus of the Deerfield Moraine near Golf Road. The ground there was full of chert, a rock similar to flint, composed of fine quartz and often found in crumbly limestone. Here was a rich quarry for this raw material for arrowheads. Albert Scharf, who studied the native sites intensively at the beginning of the 20th century, called it "the most romantic and homelike spot in the whole Chicago region—the gem of the Green Bay Trail."[2]

Whether Woodland or Mississippian, villages were located along the rivers. The Chicago River, its tributaries, and other area rivers were a lifeline for the tribes. Without beasts of burden or carts to carry their possessions or their items for trade, they relied on their canoes.

But canoes presented their own challenges. Raging floods could be treacherous to small craft, and drought could leave a boat moored as if in dry dock. Rocky rapids were obstacles even in the flat northeastern country. Getting around these problems and traveling from stream to stream required carrying, or portaging, canoe and possessions. Portaging was a way of life.

Thus, portage routes were of critical importance in trade, migration, and exploration. Though easier than walking and carrying, canoeing presented its own difficulties and hazards that could be ameliorated by a portage. In flood, small streams could be treacherous, and larger rivers could become raging torrents. In dry spells, there might be long stretches without enough water to float a canoe. Even in the relatively flat Illinois country, there were rocky rapids to portage around, and there was always the problem of getting from one stream to another. Under these various conditions, portaging became an

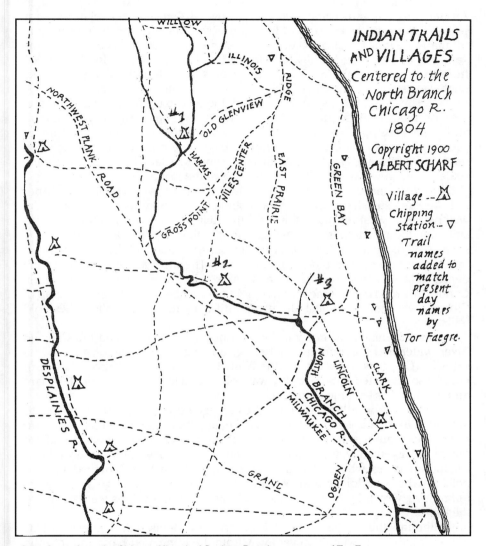

Scharf map from the Chicago Historical Society. Drawing courtesy of Tor Fagre.

Indian trails and villages near the North Branch of the Chicago River. Three village sites have been added by the author: Village No. 1 is at the junction of the North Branch and the West Fork just north of Golf Road on the site of today's Glen View Club, Village No. 2 is in Chicago's Forest Glen neighborhood, and Village No. 3 is in Chicago's Bowmanville neighborhood on the Rose Hill spit.

essential part of travel by water.

The most important of the portages were those linking major routes. Around the southern Great Lakes were several that allowed relatively easy passage from the lakes to the Mississippi River system: from Lake Erie into tributaries of the Ohio, from Green Bay into the Wisconsin River, and two at the southern end of Lake Michigan, both leading into the Illinois River. One led from the mouth of the St. Joseph River on the southeastern shore of Lake Michigan, starting in today's Michigan, down to an approximately five-mile portage (by current maps) at South Bend, Indiana to the Kankakee River, and then on the Kankakee into the Des Plaines River, and finally into the Illinois and the Mississippi. The other was at Chicago. There were also many minor portages between the Des Plaines and Chicago Rivers, including one between the Des Plaines and the Chicago near present-day Glenview, which the early settlers used in wet weather for traveling down the North Branch into Chicago.

Besides canoes, the only other method of early travel was on foot. Tribes followed an extensive network of trails, some for wet weather and some for dry weather. Wet weather paths followed the high ground of the moraines and spits, and today's various roads named "Ridge" follow these trails, as do others, such as Waukegan Road, and Elston, Milwaukee, Ogden, and Archer Avenues. In dry weather, trails could follow the rivers. The trails radiated out from the center of the Chicago area in a form mimicked by Chicago's railroad network. Connecting roadways formed a sort of grid pattern. Looking at a current map of Chicago, we see that almost all curved and diagonal streets follow these old trails.

Over the millennia, many different tribes lived in and used the Chicago River watershed for hunting, gathering, and agriculture, among them the Ojibway (Chippewa), the Ottawa, the Winnebago, and the Kickapoo. European contact so disrupted these peoples' ways of life and locations that tribal warfare and dislocations became common.

Marquette and Jolliet learned of the Chicago portage when they were far to the south, in Arkansas. When they arrived near the Chicago area on their return route, they were met by the Miami. Shortly thereafter, the Iroquois forced the Miami out. Eventually, the Chippewa, Ottawa, and Potawatomi, closely related Algonquin tribes who called themselves the "Three Fires," moved in. The natives who led Jolliet and Marquette to Chicago's portage route were unknowingly sealing their own fate; their last territorial claims were ceded to the United States in 1833.

Although the central area of Chicago now yields little evidence of its former inhabitants, when you get away from the populated parts and into the parks, farms, and forest preserves, there is plenty of evidence of thousands of years of tribal occupation. Archaeologists know where to look for the prehistoric and historic sites based on the site requirements of the different cultures. Because even small hunting camps needed a water source, most such sites can be found close to the rivers and wetlands.

Passages and Treaties
On the Path to a Canal

Few of us North Americans, whether of Canada or the United States, realize what a nuisance our continent was to Europe before the days of colonization. . . . [W]hen American rivers flowing from the west into the Atlantic were explored, it was less with a purpose to find in them, or in their surroundings, any values related to climate and soil, or even to gold, than to discover if one of them headed near enough to a west-flowing river, or to the Western Ocean, to serve as a route through the continent to the Pacific.

—Vilhjalmur Stefannson
Northwest to Fortune, 1958

While the North American Woodland tribes were shifting to the Mississippian cultures in the thirteenth century, the Venetian Marco Polo was making his historic journey to China. He wrote of the fabulous riches of the Far East. He wrote before the time of the printing press, yet his book was so popular it was copied by hand and distributed to a fascinated public. The idea of finding a northwest route to the riches of the east by sea rather than by land, on the uncomfortable humps of stubborn camels, took hold of restless European imaginations. During his voyages, Christopher Columbus often referred to Marco Polo's book of travels. Columbus's discoveries increased the passion for finding a route to China by promoting the possibility that it could be reached through North American continental waters.

Thus it was that, in the 1600s, nationals of three European countries were poised on the edges of North America, seeking to lay claim to the continent's treasures or looking for that fabled Northwest Passage. The French were to the north in New France (Canada). They were primarily traders, explorers, and missionaries who, unable to penetrate the land of the antagonistic Iroquois just to their south, found riches in the fur-bearing animals of the Middle West. The souls of natives were also acceptable quarry; the French built a chain of forts and missions along their route between New France and Louisiana. The English settled along the mid-Atlantic coast, while the Spanish dominated what is now Mexico, California, and the southern part of the United States. Only the Spaniards were not a part of the territorial disputes over the Chicago portage or land surrounding the future Illinois and Michigan Canal.

The French, and Jolliet's Idea of a Canal

In 1534, Jacques Cartier "discovered" the St. Lawrence River and claimed its valley for France, but it was Samuel de Champlain, known as the "father of

New France," whose imagination was fired by the potential of the inland wilderness and especially the Mississippi River. In 1611, he established a trading post at Montreal and began to trade with the natives for skins and copper ore. In 1661, when Louis XIV ascended the throne of France, he had a bulging royal treasury and ambitions to expand France's power in the New World. He supported the explorations into the interior in principle, if not always financially.

Louis Jolliet, Father Jacques Marquette, and Rene Robert Cavelier sieur de La Salle were the major Frenchmen whose names are connected with early French interest in our vicinity. Louis Jolliet, born in 1645, was a Jesuit-educated native of New France. He was reported to have a gift for languages. He had studied hydrography in France, and having lived there for a time, he was aware of the implications of the great canal system being planned for the French interior. He was an experienced trader by the age of 27 when he led an expedition to the Mississippi, accompanied by Marquette. Jolliet's personal interest in the expedition was finding the way west to China.

Marquette was born in France in 1637, eight years before Jolliet. He did not seek the riches of the east but for many years yearned to be a missionary to the natives in New France. He was serving in that capacity at the Jesuit outpost of St. Ignace on the Straits of Mackinac that separate Lakes Michigan and Huron when Jolliet stopped for him on his way to the Mississippi. Marquette was assigned to this expedition because during their early years in New France the Jesuits had provided invaluable experience in dealing with the natives. Today's general wisdom is that, as a reward for their contribution, a missionary was included in the expedition. Marquette had been the natural choice. He was fluent in tribal languages and much beloved by the natives to whom he ministered.

In 1673 Marquette and Jolliet went searching for the Northwest Passage. They reached the Mississippi by following the Green Bay/Fox River/Wisconsin River route, portaging at present-day Portage, Wisconsin. The Mississippi took them south, however, not northwest, and they turned back as the season grew late. They were befriended by the Miami, who told them of the Chicago portage route. Marquette and Jolliet inadvertently wrote the first lines of modern Chicago history when they crossed that Chicago portage on September 1, 1673. Our only records of the journey are Marquette's journal of their travels and Jolliet's dictations to Father Claude Dablon, a Jesuit priest and the Superior of the western missions until he was recalled to Quebec. These reveal Jolliet's immediate grasp that a canal could substitute for the portage and secure strategic influence for France. He told Father Dablon of

> . . . a very great and considerable advantage and one which it will perhaps be difficult to believe; it is that we should be able to go easily by ship to Florida, by means of a very good waterway. There would be only one canal to make and that by cutting through only one-half a league of prairie to enter from the lower part of the Lake of Illinois [Lake Michigan] into the river St. Louis [the Mississippi].[1]

It may not have been the fabled northwest passage, but Jolliet's creative idea spawned a dream of untold riches for the country that would control the

Photo courtesy of Edward A. Ayer Collection, The Newberry Library, Chicago.

This portion of Vincenzo Coronelli's Italian map of 1697 illustrates the two portages at the southern end of Lake Michigan. La Salle's favored portage is clearly marked at the southeast end of Lago Illinois, d Michigami [Lake Michigan]. It begins with Miamis Forte, goes up the Miamis R. [the St. Joseph], and after the portage, goes west on the Keatiki [Kankakee] River. The Kankakee joins with the Chikagou R. [the Des Plaines] to form the Illinois River, which flows to the Mississippi. Coronelli also clearly marks the Chicago Portage at the southwest end of Lago Illinois. Lake "Frontenac" is now Lake Ontario. The R. des Iroquois flowing out of Frontenac to the Atlantic Ocean is today's St. Lawrence River.

portage route.

For the 25 years after Marquette and Jolliet first crossed the portage, it was busy, principally with commerce involving the fur trade. One of the traders was René Robert Cavelier sieur de La Salle, a farmer attracted to developing a business in the fur trade and establishing a monopoly on that trade for France. He was born on November 22, 1643, in Rouen, France, and, like Jolliet, was educated by the Jesuits. Unlike Jolliet, who was the son of a wagon-maker, La Salle was born into wealth. When he emigrated to New France in 1666, at the age of 23, he received a grant of land just west of Montreal on the St. Lawrence River. While there, he dreamed of finding that water route to China. According to historian Francis Parkman, after an exploring misadventure during which some of his crew returned home, his land was christened LaChine, "in derision of the young adventurer's dream of a westward passage to China."[2]

La Salle crossed the Chicago portage only once, in the winter of 1682. He much preferred the route along the St. Joseph River. He vigorously disagreed with Jolliet about the ease of building a canal along the Chicago portage route and wrote a full account of its difficulties (modern names are substituted for archaic names in the quotation):

> There is an isthmus which is 41 degrees 50 minutes elevation from the pole [the equator] on the west of Lake Michigan where one goes [west] by a channel [the Chicago River] formed by the junction of several small streams or gullies of the prairie. It is navigable about two leagues to the edge of this prairie. Beyond this at a quarter of a league distant toward the west there is a little lake [Mud Lake] a league and a half in length which is divided in two by a beaver dam. From this lake issues a little stream [Portage Creek] which after twining in and out among the rushes for half a league falls into the Des Plaines and from there into the river of the Illinois. When this lake is full either from the great rains in summer or from the floods of the spring, it is discharged also into this channel which leads to Lake Michigan whose surface is seven feet lower than the prairie where it is situated. . . . The Des Plaines does the same in the springtime when its channel is full. . . . At this time should one make a little canal *of a quarter of a league,* [author's italics] says Jolliet, from the lake to the basin which leads to the Illinois river, ships could in the summer enter into the river and descend into the sea. That might perhaps happen in the springtime but not in the summer because there is not enough water in the [Des Plaines] river as far down as Fort St. Louis where the navigation of the Mississippi River begins at this season and extends as far as the sea. . . Also I would not have made mention of this way of communication if Jolliet had not proposed it without sufficiently examining the difficulties.[3]

La Salle understated Jolliet's estimate by half; was this purposeful? Ironically, Jolliet's notes, along with the lives of his crew, were lost in their entirety as he attempted to run the LaChine rapids of the St. Lawrence—the same rapids purportedly named for La Salle's folly—when he was nearly home in Montreal. Jolliet should have portaged.

According to Clarence W. Alvord, an early authority on Chicago history, Jolliet's failure to convince La Salle of the efficacy of a canal might be attributed to factors other than physical barriers. He speculates that because Jolliet was allied with other Jesuits searching for a water route from New France to the continent's interior through the St. Lawrence, the dominance of the Chicago portage would have been a triumph for Jolliet. La Salle's dream was to establish a trade route down the Ohio and the Mississippi to the Gulf, headquartered in Louisiana, not in New France. La Salle had rebelled against the Jesuits early in his life and did not like them any better now. He would have had no interest in promoting a canal which would favor the competition.[4]

By the early eighteenth century, La Salle's interests were winning. It was a time of conflict between the French, the British, and the Fox tribe, and Illinois became a sort of "no man's land," not safe for European travel. As early as 1701, the French had shifted their attention to the middle Mississippi Valley and Louisiana, and in 1717 Illinois came under the jurisdiction of Louisiana rather than Quebec. The Ohio, Maumee, and Wabash Rivers substituted for the Chicago portage as water routes between Lake Erie and the Mississippi River. The Chicago portage was not in use by Europeans during the majority of the eighteenth century. Although the French never reestablished a foothold there, the dream of a canal over the portage route stayed alive, if dormant.

Making the Land Safe for a Canal

After the British defeated the French and their allied tribes in the Seven Years War (French and Indian War) in 1763, nominal title to the entire Chicago area passed to the British. They never established real control west of Detroit or south of Mackinac, however. Even after the Revolutionary War, the Potawatomi continued to control the Illinois Territory and the portage.

Then, on August 20, 1794, General "Mad Anthony" Wayne led the Americans to a major victory over the Northwest Indian Confederacy at Fallen Timbers, in northwest Ohio. The defeat of the Confederacy, comprised of the Miami, Potawatomi, Shawnee, Delaware, Ottawa, Chippewa, Iroquois, and others, forced the British, who had been their allies, to turn over their posts to the United States. The dream of the canal, which had been dormant throughout the century, began to re-emerge. The Miami, who had introduced Marquette and Jolliet to the portage, were now considered an impediment to progress. They and other tribes were about to pay a very high price.

The 1795 Treaty of Greenville, which settled the battle of Fallen Timbers, showed that Americans meant business about a potential canal over the portage route. This treaty secured from the tribes a six-mile-square parcel at the mouth of the Chicago River and another parcel of land at the mouth of the Illinois River where it empties into the Mississippi, giving the United States control over both ends of the potential canal. It also required the tribes to allow United States citizens free passage and free use of harbors and mouths of rivers that adjoined tribal lands.

In 1803, Thomas Jefferson negotiated the Louisiana Purchase with the French. This purchase approximately doubled the entire existing area of the United States, adding in excess of 800,000 square miles to the country. The purchase only enhanced the potential canal's strategic position for commerce and the probability that the dream would become reality. In that same year, the U.S. government built Fort Dearborn, named after the then Secretary of War, Gen. Henry Dearborn, at the mouth of the Chicago River. The fort's purpose was to establish a U.S. presence in the area as a signal to both the British and the tribes that this was U.S. territory, and the U.S. intended to protect it. But the natives continued to present problems for the American settlers at Chicago. In 1812, soldiers and civilians, fearing violence, fled the garrison. The Potawatomi killed many of the soldiers and civilians who took flight and then burned the fort.

In 1816, an impatient United States signed another treaty with the native tribes, extending control over not just the two ends of the canal but the land in between, a ten-mile-wide strip of land on either side of the supposed route of the canal. The boundaries that enclose this cession of territory are known today as the Indian boundary lines. The northern line starts in Chicago's far north neighborhood of Rogers Park along Rogers Avenue and runs diagonally through Cook County, becoming Forest Preserve Drive, and continuing to near Lockport and Plainfield in Will County. The southern line runs diagonally from the vicinity of Calumet Harbor to the Kankakee River.

The Ceremony of Tribal Removal

Chief Black Hawk of the Sauks in Wisconsin led a band of Sauk and Fox who refused to recognize prior treaties that ceded their ancestral lands to the young United States. A series of skirmishes, beginning in 1831, bedeviled the U.S. military and its volunteers and became known as the Black Hawk War. It reached a crescendo in 1832, and finally, on August 2, Black Hawk and his followers were defeated at the Battle of the Bad Axe River in Wisconsin. The Treaty of Prairie du Chien officially ended not only the war but also the tribal presence east of the Mississippi, at least in this region. The treaty required all natives to leave Illinois, but there were exceptions. Many "friendlies" and persons of mixed race were allowed to remain and received land grants, several of which were on or near the Chicago River. Billy Caldwell, the son of an Irish-American army officer and a Potawatomi woman, was one of these biracial individuals who smoothed the tribal-versus-American diplomacy of the time. Known to the natives by the Potawatomi name "Sauganash," meaning "white man," Caldwell was rewarded by the U.S. government for his efforts with a grant of land along the river near today's far northwest side. The Sauganash neighborhood in Chicago bears his name, as does the area known as Caldwell Reserve in the Forest Preserve District of Cook County.

Ceremonies finalizing tribal removal took place in Chicago in September, 1833. An enormous council of natives assembled to sign the treaty that would end the war and displace them forever. Popular historian Eleanor Atkinson described the scene:

> Five thousand Indians of the allied tribes were camped all over the prairie to the north. . . . A council house had been built of poles and bark. . . . There were four hotels . . . all full of transient guests drawn here by the treaty. Hundreds of migrants were living in prairie schooners waiting for the conclusion of the treaty before seeking homesteads in the Indian lands. Horse dealers and stealers, peddlers, sharpers, whisky sellers, contractors for feeding the Indians, speculators, and adventurers—enough rogues to keep the new log jail on the public square filled—were in town. Every man had a claim, genuine or spurious, against the Indians, and schemed to get some of the cash which the government was sure to distribute with a liberal hand.
>
> The village was a chaos of mud, rubbish and confusion. The Indians kept up the wildest uproar day and night, singing, howling, weeping, yelling.[5]

The natives did not all leave immediately, of course; that took time, and some stragglers remained in the territory. But the great majority of the Potawatomi crossed the Mississippi to Iowa, and today their descendants may be found on a reservation near Independence, Kansas. Caldwell divided his grant and sold it off before 1842. This was the bitter ending of the tribal chapter on this land, a chapter that had lasted for nearly 13,000 years. The first tribal-European contact must have come soon after the French landed in New France after 1534. Three hundred years later, the natives were gone, and the land was available for United States settlement and a canal.

On the Verge of a Canal

The Americans did not wait for removal of the natives to begin their planning. As the tribal threats receded at the end of the eighteenth century, trade opened up. Travelers and permanent settlers came into the area. By 1800 at least one resident, Antoine Ouilmette, after whom the village of Wilmette is named, was regularly engaged to transport goods across the portage, and the trader John Kinzie, Sr. also offered his services. In 1830, even as the Black Hawk War was brewing, and three years before the ceremony of tribal removal, James Thompson was platting the towns of Chicago and Ottawa, at the eastern and western ends of the imminent canal, for the state canal commissioners. Many Americans who had fought in the skirmishes of the Black Hawk War had come from the east, and seeing the riches of the Chicago area, had resolved to return with their families and make it their home.

Part II

The Nineteenth Century

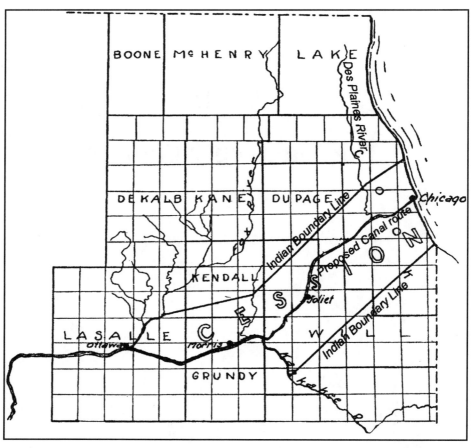

Modified from Milo M. Quaife, Chicago's Highways Old and New *(Chicago: D.F. Keller & Co., 1925), 17.*

The Indian Boundary Lines and the proposed Illinois and Michigan Canal route. The U.S. secured this strip of land in 1816 through a treaty negotiated with the allied Chippewa, Ottawa, and Potawatomi tribes, only four years after the Fort Dearborn Massacre and two years before Illinois became a state.

The Illinois and Michigan Canal

But as the country had never been carefully examined by men of science and observation, it was difficult to ascertain what were the facilities of forming an artificial communication. All talked of the project as practicable, but none knew the manner in which it was to be accomplished . . .

—Lewis C. Beck
Gazetteer of the States Illinois and Missouri, 1823

In the early nineteenth century, the westward movement of the nation demanded transportation. As the center of population moved away from the East Coast, products needed to be moved cheaply and dependably between city and country, coast and interior. Wagon freight was expensive and slow, roads were poor or nonexistent, and railroads were a thing of the future. Boats were the preferred mode of travel. This was the era of canals. The Erie Canal, which opened in 1825 and connected the Hudson River to Buffalo, New York, was a huge success, pouring commerce and people toward Chicago as soon as it was considered "safe" from tribal threats.

In 1833 alone, after native removal, enormous numbers of people arrived in Chicago by boat—20,000—according to the authors of the Federal Writers' Project in their 1939 *Descriptive and Historical Guide to Illinois*. These pioneers were the first travelers in a wave that swept easterners toward the west, but few stayed in Chicago. For most, the vast western plains beckoned, and they traveled on.[1]

The Erie Canal shifted trade toward the Great Lakes, away from New Orleans and St. Louis. Writing in *The Tale of Chicago* in 1933, Edgar Lee Masters, the famous poet and author who practiced law in Chicago beginning in 1891, says:

> . . . But the Erie Canal did more than pour the wealth of the West into New York; it brought to Chicago the blood of that State and of New England. It changed the character of Illinois, making it over from a State dominated by men from the South, to one ruled by men of New England and New York.[2]

The type of men about whom Masters is speaking became tireless advocates for the proposed Illinois and Michigan Canal. They had connections to money. They arranged for the canal's funding, turned it into a Chicago enterprise, and changed the face of the city and the fate of the Chicago River. It is impossible to overestimate their importance.

Hurdles

Despite the moves by the young United States toward treaties that brought

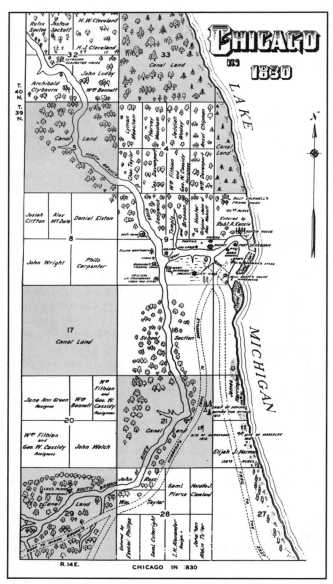

Map based on an original drawn by J.L. Dobson and published by J.C. Elder & Co., Surveyors and Map Publishers. It was retraced on February 14, 1934, by C. A. Erickson and printed by the U.S. Engineer Office, Chicago, Illinois. Courtesy of the Army Corps of Engineers Chicago office.

The shaded sections, in a checkerboard pattern, were designated as canal land that Illinois could sell to finance the project. Sections are one mile square. The canal commissioners controlled the odd-numbered sections.

the portage route under its control, it was by no means certain that there would be a canal. Uniting the country's commerce was not always seen as federal business, and at first Congress voted down proposals for the I&M Canal. In 1808, Albert Gallatin, who was Secretary of the Treasury first during the presidency of Thomas Jefferson and then under President James Madison, recommended to Congress that the government build an I&M Canal. The country was still young, however, and opinions about the role of the federal government in public works differed sharply; Jefferson himself was opposed to a strong central government role in such projects. Congress rejected the canal. In 1814, Madison asked Congress to permit construction of a canal at the Chicago Portage for the passage of warships to compete with the British. This proposal also failed, but the idea persisted. The 1816 treaty relegating the tribes to territory outside the Indian boundary lines allowed engineers safely to explore routes for the artificial waterway. Maj. Stephen H. Long was sent out to prepare a topographic survey for the War Department. Long's work convinced him that the waterway, if used by small boats, would need "but little more excavation to render it sufficiently capacious for all the purposes of a canal." The only other necessities he perceived would be a dam across the Des Plaines and locks at either end.[3] Major Long, like Jolliet, was an optimist.

Thanks to the proposed I&M Canal, greater Chicago is today a part of Illinois rather than Wisconsin. Prior to its admission as a state in 1818, almost all of Illinois's population was in the south, and the northern boundary of Illinois was to extend only to the southern tip of Lake Michigan. Upon statehood, and under the assumption that Congress would eventually authorize a canal, the border was extended about 50 miles north from its original designation, so that the canal route would be entirely within the state.[4]

In January, 1819, Secretary of War John C. Calhoun gave a report to the House of Representatives recommending a network of canals and roads to defend the country. He included the I&M Canal. Almost ten years later, in 1827, after the state had surmounted many roadblocks, Congress granted Illinois every other section of land in a five-mile-wide strip on each side of the proposed canal. This "splendid gift of Congress," as historian Alfred T. Andreas characterized it, amounted to 284,000 acres of marketable land, which could be sold by the canal commissioners to raise construction money for its venture.[5] The state appointed a Board of Canal Commissioners with general responsibility for realizing the canal. Thus, Chicago became a company town: a canal town, not in the sense that the company organized the lives of those who lived there, but in the sense that it was laid out by the commissioners for a single purpose.

A River Ran through It

Because of the land grant, Chicago did not begin life as a jumbled arrangement of shops of would-be capitalist dreamers who built helter-skelter on crooked streets, as did many cities that chose rivers as their lifeline for goods and services. The framework of Chicago's streets, backdrop for the brash, cluttered, often tumultuous frontier atmosphere, was dictated by the methodical federal government land office policies, carried out in the survey conducted by surveyor John Walls in 1821. The land office surveys carved up the land into one-square-mile areas, known as sections, and ignored any natural geographic features such as rivers or marshes. These were the sections every other one of which the federal government granted to Illinois for the canal.

A section needed to be further subdivided into lots before the land could be sold. In 1829, the canal commissioners hired James Thompson, a canal surveyor, to plat the land, and he produced a town map of Chicago in August, 1830. As his base map, he used the rigid section lines of the 1821 government land survey. Therefore, future subdivisions were platted as if the river did not divide them in two.

The Growth of Chicago

Here was a plum ripe for the picking by land speculators. You bought your property from the canal commissioners according to township, section, range, and lot number on the grid. You put up your business, or, more likely, you put up your land for sale. The more you bought and the better you advertised it, the quicker you sold it and the richer you became. Stories abound of people who got rich overnight, and of inflating land prices, such as those for the lot sold by the canal commission in 1832 for $100; on March 11, 1834, for $3,500; in June, 1836, for $15,000.[6]

There were plenty of eager buyers. The potential for making money from land speculation obsessed the minds of most of those willing to suffer the crudities of the frontier atmosphere. Canal workers and land speculators combined to create a breathtaking growth in Chicago's population. In 1829, only about 30 people lived in the little settlement along the Chicago River. By 1831 the population had doubled. Chicago was on the brink of transformation from a bucolic encampment to a village of near-frantic activity and explosive growth. In 1832, Cook County was incorporated, with Chicago as its county seat. In August, 1833, Chicago was declared a town, and its population was estimated at 350. After the departure of the natives, bewitched immigrants swarmed into the town as if propelled to a gold rush. In 1837, with a population of 4,170, Chicago received its city charter.

Money Problems

The state had to take responsibility for building the canal because the federal government continued to resist participation in local projects. There were legislative hurdles to surmount, commissioners to appoint, surveys to conduct, and the route and design to determine. Most important of all, there was money to be found; the state did not have it. The lack of steady financial backing would continually plague canal authorities, and, in the end, would determine that a cheaper, less efficient canal would be built.

Chicago might have lost its position at the head of the canal, according to

Henry W. Blodgett, were it not for Gurdon Hubbard. Hubbard had been part of the Chicago commercial landscape since moving to Illinois in 1818. In his travels as superintendent for the American Fur Company's posts on the Iroquois and Kankakee Rivers, he frequently used the Chicago portage on his way to its headquarters in Mackinaw, on northern Lake Michigan. In addition, he supplied Fort Dearborn and the Chicago settlement with livestock. Although he lived downstate, he had set his sights on Chicago and moved there permanently in 1834. Chicago's position at the head of the canal (or a railroad) would have been crucial to his interests. Blodgett asserts that Gurdon S. Hubbard deserves the credit for influencing the canal's final route:

"As representative of Vermillion County in the Illinois General Assembly of 1832-33, Gurdon Hubbard introduced a bill for the construction of the Illinois and Michigan canal. It was passed by the House, but defeated in the Senate. He immediately substituted a bill for a railroad, defeated by only the casting vote of the presiding officer. Every session of the legislature thereafter found Mr. Hubbard present to urge the passage of a canal bill, until it was effected in the session of 1835-36. It is Hon. Henry W. Blodgett who states that Illinois owes a debt to Mr. Hubbard which has never been duly accredited to him; namely, the settlement of the question of the location of the terminus of the canal. It had been strongly urged that it would be cheaper to follow up the Calumet, to what is known as the Sag, and thence down the valley of the Des-plaines River, than to cut through the hard ground between the south branch of the Chicago River and the Desplaines. After hearing the arguments upon this point, Mr. Hubbard took a map and called the attention of the members to the fact that the mouth of the Calumet River is within a few hundred yards of the Indiana state line, and suggested that it was expected that wherever the canal terminated, a great city would grow up, and pertinently asked, whether it was desirable that the coming city should be as much of it in the state of Indiana as in Illinois, when the entire expense of construction would devolve upon our state. This practical view of the question settled it, and the mouth of the Chicago River was made the terminus instead of the mouth of the Calumet." Thus had the faith and courage of Chicago's champion saved her from a fate of possible mediocrity or extinction as a city.[7]

The original 1823-24 construction estimate by the first surveyors, engineers Col. Reno Paul and Col. Justus Post, fell between $640,000 and a little over $700,000 for a canal that would accommodate boats 13.5 feet wide drawing three feet of water. But in 1833, just as the Illinois legislature was deciding on the route, a shocking new estimate put the construction figure at approximately $4 million.[8]

The problem was the design, called the "deep cut." Under the deep-cut plan, a 30-mile-long trough through glacial till and hardpan (very tough clay) would carry the water of Lake Michigan directly to that point on the Des Plaines where the levels of Lake Michigan and the Des Plaines were the same. This point was called the "summit" level. From that point, the Des Plaines gradually descended west to the Illinois River. The canal was to enter the Illinois River at LaSalle. Estimates suggested that only a moderate flow over and above the normal level in the Chicago River would be necessary to satisfy the need to fill up the low-water stretches of the Illinois. (Note that this plan, although not advertised as remarkable at the time, would have reversed the flow of the

Chicago River.)

Every surveyor had noted that limestone bedrock was nearly at the surface at the highest level of the proposed canal near the Des Plaines, and that cutting through it would be an expensive proposition, but by far the most effective one. It was the expense of blasting through the ancient limestone that almost doomed the planned canal; plans were put on hold, and other routes and even a railroad were investigated as substitutes. The state chose to stay with the original canal and resorted to loans to raise the larger amount. On January 9, 1836, the Legislature passed a bill authorizing the state to issue bonds. The original design was replaced with a more commodious plan: 60 feet wide at the surface, 36 feet wide at the base, and six feet deep. Cost estimates doubled to approximately $8.6 million. But with the backing of public and private purses, the work was ready to begin.[9]

Construction at Last!

Construction began on July 4, 1836. There was great fanfare as the commissioners, financiers, politicians, and just plain folks left Chicago for the long-anticipated "shovel-day" at Canal-Port, near Bridgeport. Canal Commissioner Col. William B. Archer turned over the first shovelful of dirt, and Gurdon Hubbard was on hand to wield the spade "with his strong hands and long arms and to deliver the closing address, complete with memories of the 'luckless trader' . . . wading 'waist-deep' in the morass of Mud Lake."[10]

From Deep Cut to Shallow Cut

In March 1843, work on the canal ceased for lack of money. In a flurry of revenue-raising activity, Chicago promoters persuaded capitalists from the east and Europe to come to the rescue. The condition for the loans, however, was that a cheaper, or "shallow cut" plan be followed. This plan relied on the surface waters of the Des Plaines and the Calumet as feeders for the upper reaches of the Canal, leaving the Chicago River out entirely. (It is remarkable that the canal planners were willing to depend upon the inconsistent Des Plaines River. As noted by La Salle years before, the water level in the Des Plaines was notoriously erratic and particularly low in summers. The Calumet was a much more dependable feeder.) One man, Russel E. Heacock, owned land at both the northern and southern outlets of the canal and saw his future livelihood linked to the canal business. He was determined to see the canal built, even if cheaply and less effectively. He lobbied so incessantly that he received the nickname "Shallow-cut."[11]

Andreas observes: "But although the Legislature had 'authorized' the finishing of the canal on the 'shallow-cut' plan, it could not decree that water should run up hill."[12] More water than would be available from the Des Plaines and the Calumet would be needed to fill the canal. More experts, more money, and a trio of trustees were assembled to solve the problem and approve a revised plan, which included pumping water from the South Branch of the

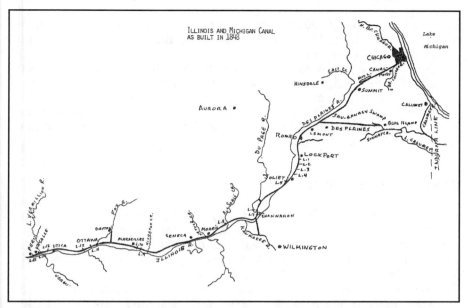

Drawing courtesy of Mary Yeater Rathbun. The map appeared in the draft version of "The Illinois and Michigan Canal," written for the Illinois Department of Conservation, Division of Historic Sites, Office of Research and Publications, 35a.

The I&M Canal began at Canal-Port on the South Branch of the Chicago River and ran to Peru on the Illinois River. The drawing shows the location of the locks.

Chicago River into the canal near the summit.

As finally built, the canal was much greater in scope than ever envisioned by Jolliet. It did not just breach the divide; it ran 97.24 miles from Bridgeport near Chicago to LaSalle, which was then the head of navigation above Lake Peoria, a wide spot on the Illinois River. The canal was designed to bypass the Chicago portage, low water in the rivers, and the rapids between Chicago and the Peru/LaSalle region. Locks were an integral part of the canal. Instead of the two locks envisioned by Post and Paul, 15 lift locks—each 110 feet long and 18 feet wide—raised or lowered boats to the next level between Lockport and LaSalle. Two lift locks of a different design helped boats across the summit. Four "guard locks" were designed for traffic control rather than for lifting. One was located at Joliet where the Des Plaines and the canal intersected, and another was in Ottawa where there was an entrance to a lateral canal leading to businesses. A 16.8-mile feeder canal from the Calumet River supplied water to the summit. Aqueducts, tow-paths, mules, and other typical canal accessories completed the picture.

Two guard locks were placed at Bridgeport on the South Branch. Here, the I&M began the fulfillment of the longed-for westward connection over the portage route between the Chicago River and the Des Plaines. Two approach channels were dug just east of Ashland Avenue. A pumping plant at Bridgeport contained two pumps, each with a steam engine of about 160 horsepower.

Each engine pumped 7,000 cubic feet of water per minute. The purpose of the Bridgeport plant was to lift water out of the South Branch and force it into the artificially dug supply channels.[13]

Even though there was no purposeful diversion of water from Lake Michigan for the canal, residents observed that sometimes when the Bridgeport pumps were in operation, the river current ran from east to west. In fact, the pumps were diverting approximately 250 cubic feet per second (cfs) from the lake. Still, under the shallow-cut design, the Chicago River continued to flow into Lake Michigan.

Opening Day and Success

The canal was completed in 1848, 12 years after construction began. The official opening took place on April 16 at the canal town of Lockport, with a celebration more festive even than the groundbreaking ceremonies. The canal was an immediate success. Grain and lumber were the major cargoes hauled in freight boats pulled by mules plodding along the towpath.

The canal was facing obsolescence almost as soon as it was completed, as railroads began to lure passenger service away from the slow canal packet boats. By 1854 the Rock Island Railroad extended to the Mississippi. Even so, the canal was still viable for bulky cargoes that did not require speed. Competition between the two systems helped keep shipping charges low, another boon to the incredible growth of the region. Chicago grew from a town of a few thousand in 1836 to a city of 30,000 in 1850, and ten times that 20 years later. Lockport, Joliet, Ottawa, LaSalle, and other towns, buoyed by shipping and industry along the canal, prospered too.

Ironically, the I&M bypassed the shallow crooked channel of the West Fork of the Chicago River, which had conducted many a boat over the portage route through Mud Lake.

But the sandbar still blocked the harbor, excluding ships of the size anticipated in the canal. Removal of the sandbar was crucial to the canal's success.

Redesigning the Harbor
Fighting Nature and Politics, 1833-1875

*That ponderous dredge, that mechanical elephant, which feels with
its seeming intelligent trunk far down below the surface of the water,
removes the sandbar and the coveted harbor is obtained. . . .*

—Edwin O. Gale, 1902

La Salle, who had been so prescient about the challenges involved in
building a canal, was no less so in the matter of the harbor. He noted:

> . . . . It is true that there is still another difficulty which this ditch [the
> canal] one would make could not remedy, it is this: The Lake of the Illinois
> [Lake Michigan] always forms a sand bank at the entrance of the channel
> which leads to it. I doubt very much in spite of what anyone says [referring
> of course to his rival Jolliet] whether this could be cleaned out or cleared
> away by the force of the current of the Chicago River when it was made to
> flow therein, since much greater currents in the same lake cannot do it.[1]

The sandbar yielded to the power of the United States War Department and
the federal dredge. The project was played out within the context of one of the
major constitutional questions of the nineteenth century. In the young republic,
what did the Constitution say about who was responsible for internal, local
improvements? We have already seen Congress's response to the earliest
requests for the Illinois and Michigan Canal. Because of their importance in
military defense and foreign trade, harbors were early considered part of the
jurisdiction of the federal government. But interest was limited to those harbors
deemed to affect the broad national interest. When the issue focused on local
river and harbor improvements, the extent of the government mandate was at
issue. In this matter, Chicago took center stage.

The Sandbar Problem

Before emptying out into Lake Michigan, the Chicago River originally
detoured to the south through a passageway between the mainland and a
substantial sandbar, what scientists call a "baymouth bar." Most of the sandbar
appeared as a generous beach to the east of the river, but some of it was
underwater, creating a boating hazard.

The sandbar offered protection for small craft that remained in the river's
mouth, and it protected the shoreline from erosion by breaking the energy of
the waves. Fort Dearborn was built on this protected shore at today's Michigan
Avenue, where the river originally curved to the south.

Although the sandbar provided protection for some purposes, it was a major navigational inconvenience. It was a particular hazard for large ships that would eventually pass through the Chicago River between Lake Michigan and the I&M Canal. First, the sand made the harbor too shallow for large vessels. Second, the sharp turn at the river's mouth made maneuvering in and out of the river difficult. Third, a baymouth bar is by nature an unstable, unpredictable landform. It would have to go.

How to Build a Sandbar

Removing the sandbar was not a simple matter. To understand the problem, one must understand how the sandbar formed in the first place.

The river deposited only a small amount of sand in the bar; most of the sand came from the lake. The water in a river carries sands, silts, and clays in an enclosed channel. When a river reaches its mouth and the channel can't confine the water any more, the river's energy is reduced. It can no longer carry its load of sand, silt, and clay. Sand, being the heaviest material, drops out first. Even though the river had little sand to contribute, it may have influenced the shape and dimensions of the bar in times of high water.

Chicago's prevailing southwesterly winds cause little erosion on the west side of the lake. But if a storm comes from the northeast, Chicago's location on the southwestern shore of the Lake Michigan makes it extremely vulnerable. The northeast waves carry a tremendous amount of energy because they arrive in a long-distance "fetch," uninterrupted for approximately 200 nautical miles by any land between Chicago and the Leelanau Peninsula in Michigan. The strong winds and waves in these storms erode the bluffs adjacent to the lake, and the eroded materials end up tossing about in the churning water. The storm subsides, but the materials remain suspended in the water.

Particularly after a nor'easter in late fall and early spring, the waves will be approaching from the northeast, picking up the eroded debris from underneath the water surface and tossing it back and forth. The closer a wave gets to the shore, the more energy it loses to friction.

When the wave finally rides up on top of the beach it loses even more energy. Some of the water will percolate through the beach sand, and some of the debris will drop out onto the shore. But some will remain in the water and roll back into the lake with the receding wave. The wave does not roll back to the northeast, from whence it came, but returns to the lake in a direction nearly perpendicular to the shoreline, or perhaps a little to the south. As a result, the sand and gravel suspended in the water move a little farther to the south. With the next wave that approaches, the process is repeated. This incessant, repetitive, zigzag motion of waves both eroding and depositing sand along the shoreline is known as littoral drift; the wave action in the breaker zone is called the longshore current. The current and the drift not only assure development of a beach that will extend as a sandbar across the mouth of a river, but also that the sandbar will continually be reshaped.

This was fine for dynamic, ever-changing nature, but when humans opened a channel, they meant it to be permanent. To retain the opening, people built piers. Piers cause their own problems. Any sort of breakwater, even a boat that has run aground on the beach, interrupts the process of littoral drift by trapping the sand carried toward it by the longshore current. Sand builds up on the north side of the pier and then creeps around into the end of the pier, filling in the opening. Meanwhile, the beaches south of the pier are starved of their "just" supply of sand. The north beach gets bigger, and the south beach erodes away.

Removing the Sandbar: The Federal Government in Action

In 1833, Chicago's harbor was deemed important enough for the federal government to authorize improvements. But it was one thing for the government to approve a project and quite another to accomplish it. From beginning to end, it took 42 years, until 1875, before a satisfactory harbor was achieved.

The natives in their light canoes probably had not considered the sandbar a problem. In about 1784, however, Jean Baptiste Pointe Du Sable, a mixed-race, free-born black man who is considered Chicago's first non-native resident, established a farm at the mouth of the river and lived there until about 1800. (De Sable is considered the correct spelling of his name by historian John F. Swenson.[2])Trading with both natives and Europeans, he might well have thought the sandbar an annoyance. In a fictionalized account in *Gateway to Empire*, author Allan Eckert depicts Du Sable in a thoughtful moment on July 4, 1779 (earlier than he actually lived here, according to Swenson):

> He studied the river upstream and down. Just below where he stood, the river turned southward and angled to the lake, deflected in its eastward course by a dense sandbar twenty yards in width. With that bar removed, the man mused, the river would have a straight shoot into the lake and commerce would be improved considerably. Why could not the sand from there be removed and placed across the present river mouth, opening the one and closing the other and, in the process, creating a still-water harbor of great value?[3]

No one knows, of course, if Du Sable thought this, but it is not unreasonable, given his commercial experience and ambitions. After the establishment of Fort Dearborn in 1803, when it was a safe prediction that Chicago would become a major commercial center, others had the same idea. In 1805 an agent at the United States Indian Factory, a newly established trading house in Chicago, recommended that the federal government dig a narrow ditch so that the small, flat-bottomed Mackinaw boats could sail right up to the door of his business. His idea went nowhere.[4]

Major Long, the U.S. Army topographical engineer who had been so optimistic about the ease of constructing the I&M Canal, thought it would be just as easy to remove the sandbar. John Larson, in his account of the Chicago District of the U.S. Army Corps of Engineers, quotes Long in 1813:

> "The entrance into Lake Michigan...which is 80 yards wide, is obstructed by a sandbar about 70 yards broad." [Note how the width changes here from Du Sable's sandbar.] Where the bar was highest [beneath the entrance] the

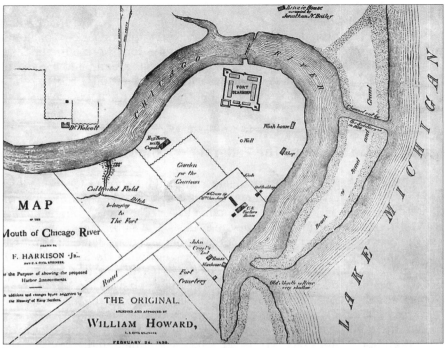

Courtesy of Chicago Historical Society ICHi-21558.

An 1830 map of the sandbar, showing the channel
cut by soldiers and the old mouth of the river.

water rarely exceeded 2 feet in depth. It would be easy to remove the bar.
"Piers might be sunk on both sides of the entrance, and the sand removed
between them." Since the river and each of its branches for 2 or 3 miles
inland have "sufficient depth of water to admit vessels of almost any burden"
removing the sandbar . . . would provide "a safe and commodious harbor for
shipping. . . ."[5]

When the scientist-explorer Henry Schoolcraft visited in 1820, he thought it
might be feasible to build an island in the lake at the mouth of "Chicago
Creek," to accommodate ships and wharfing needs. A bridge would connect
the island to the mainland. He noted that plenty of rock for the foundation was
available at Green Bay (where the Niagaran escarpment was visible in Door
County).[6] He was unaware of the treasure-trove of Niagaran dolomite beneath
the surface in today's Lemont vicinity. Nothing came of his proposal.

The garrison at Fort Dearborn, frustrated by always having to skirt the
sandbar to get in and out of the lake, took matters into their own hands and
tried to cut through the sandbar several times between 1816 and 1828.[7] The
openings never held against the natural force of the wind and waves. In the
spring of 1828, as Gurdon Hubbard remembers it, the river was running high
and strong. The soldiers dug a ditch through the bar down to river level in only
an hour or so, and the powerful current in the river rushed through the

channel, cutting it 15 feet deep. The ditch promptly filled up again with sand.[8]

In 1830, a federal government agent mapped out Chicago's harbor. He proposed to dam the original outlet and cut a channel through the bar 1,000 feet to the north.[9] The channel would run between two piers that would extend southeast. This plan bore fruit, at least politically. It was bundled with the canal recommendations and a map was added to show the platted sections of the town and its contemplated subdivisions. Altogether, these plans made a convincing argument that the canal commissioners had made good on their 1827 government grant. Congress was persuaded Chicago would be expanding at a rapid rate and would need an ample harbor. In March, 1833, it appropriated $25,000 for the project.[10]

Tentative Beginnings

Preliminary work began in the summer of 1833 and progressed slowly. Since this was a federal project formally under the management of the War Department's Board of Engineers, predecessors to the Army Corps of Engineers, the supervisors were officers in that department. They were moved around whenever the army saw fit, which was often.

The project began under the supervision of engineers who had no experience on this type of project. Compounding the problem was that the officer in charge had no money on hand, banking facilities were unavailable in Chicago, and the infrequent mail made it difficult to ask questions and receive either guidance or money. Labor was difficult to come by because many new arrivals found it more profitable to engage in land speculation than in the trades. There was great competition for the materials needed to satisfy the construction demands of the expanding population, and prices for what was available were high. Little equipment and few supplies needed for the harbor project could be obtained in or near Chicago. The only local construction materials were dolomite from what is now the Stearns Quarry at Halsted and 27th Streets, about three miles up the South Branch; some timber from the Calumet area; and some oak, which would be used for pilings, about 12 miles up the North Branch. Most of the big timber would come from Wisconsin and Michigan.

The first superintendent over the harbor work was Maj. George Bender, who had just become the commander at Fort Dearborn in 1833 and was a novice at this sort of engineering. He was frustrated on all accounts—lack of labor, lack of materials, and lack of money. While he was waiting for instructions, his men began some preliminary digging across the bar in July under the supervision of a civilian, Henry Handy, but every time they dug a channel it immediately filled up with quicksand. Somehow, Bender and Handy actually managed to begin work on the south pier. Bender resigned his post at Fort Dearborn in October, 1833 (not surprisingly), and Handy temporarily replaced him as supervisor of harbor work. In January, 1834, 2nd Lieut. James Allen from Fort Dearborn was appointed supervisor. In something of an understatement, he was told, "There is a probability of your meeting with some difficulty in the prosecution of your operations," and he was given a raise.[11]

On the 13th and 14th of February, 1834, nature provided assistance when a 24-hour deluge raised the river level by three feet. The bulging river coursed through the sandbar into the lake, creating a channel 30-40 feet wide and ten feet deep, north of the south pier. About half of the river's volume flowed through this channel, and, that year, 180 vessels used this new route to carry their cargo into Chicago.

Work on the north pier began in August, 1834, but progressed very slowly. By the fall of 1835, the north pier had grown to 1,260 feet long and the south pier to 700 feet. However, the 200-foot wide channel varied in depth between three to seven feet, hardly sufficient for the increasing amount of commerce. On October 14, 1835, Allen, having fully understood the nature of his work, requested a dredging machine. Then, in an augury of things to come, in the fall of 1836, while awaiting arrival of the machine he had ordered in Albany, Allen headed off on a special assignment: a survey of the Calumet harbor as Chicago's alternate to the Chicago River harbor.[12]

Such were the frustrating beginnings of harbor work. There was no fanfare comparable to that which would attend the groundbreaking for the canal three years later. Chicago was still a town with a small population, and there was no single event that one could call "groundbreaking." All was experimental, and the federal government's commitment was unpredictable, appropriations sometimes coming so late in the season as to erase any lead time in finalizing contracts.[13] The undertaking was hardly grand enough to engage the imagination, let alone inspire confidence. Although in hindsight, modern-day historians can point to regular federal funding from 1833 to 1838, the manager on the ground at the time could not be sanguine.

By 1837, only a small tongue of the old sandbar remained and the channel was a minimum of ten feet deep. The work proceeded in fits and starts because of the unreliable appropriations, but it *was* proceeding.

Allen stayed until 1838. At that time a complete reorganization of the bureaucracy of harbor-building took place. The Corps of Topographical Engineers replaced the Engineer Department, and Capt. T. J. Cram became the supervisor of work on all Lake Michigan harbors. Before Allen left he would confidently write that the harbor now provided a secure and easy entrance to lake vessels but he would just as confidently warn that sand was beginning to accumulate on "the weather side of the north pier."[14]

Sand vs. Humans

Allen's warning was apt. As the piers were being extended and the channel dredged, the scourge of the project was emerging. The natural process of littoral drift was quickly piling up sand on the north side of the north pier. The fear that the sand would encroach on the harbor entrance and cut it off was justified.

By the early 1840s, Chicago's population had grown and included many men from the east who were both ambitious and resourceful. Chicago citizens began to take great interest in the harbor project. Even though the canal was not yet in service, commercial vessels were using the harbor and the main channel in increasing numbers. Edwin Gale said, "The work of construction was very interesting to our little community, which turned out every Sunday afternoon in summer to inspect the work, to congratulate itself on the progress made and to enjoy the cool lake breezes." But, Gale commented, "Congress was so dilatory with appropriations that the public became impatient, and in 1842 the merchants and vessel owners contributed $970 for the deepening of the channel."[15]

From 1843 to 1846, Capt. John M. McClellan was the War Department's engineer in charge of harbor work. McClellan was an original thinker and an astute observer. Noting the lack of sand accretion to the south of the south pier, he thought that building a new pier to the north of the north pier might produce the same results; that is, no sand accretion on the north pier's south side, which was the harbor. This innovative idea was rejected as too costly.

Then the wind began to cause problems. Blowing sand was building up north of the north pier adjacent to the shoreline, drifting over the pier, and filling the river. McClellan's solution to this problem was to build a fence in the sand, parallel to the pier but a bit to the north, to catch the blowing sand. His strategy resembled the snow fences we place along our beaches today. To stabilize the sandbank he planted trees. The fence proved so successful that he installed another.

In addition, McClellan replaced the deteriorating piers and used the dredge continually (when it was working), deepening the channel to 12 feet. McClellan's improvements allowed Chicago to claim that by 1846, two years before the opening of the I&M Canal, it was one of the "best and safest harbors on the lake."[16]

The River and Harbor Convention: Reaction to a Presidential Veto

On July 5, 1847, even before the opening of the I&M Canal, Chicago sprang into the national limelight on the subject of harbor improvements. In 1846, President James Knox Polk was preoccupied with the Mexican War and the dispute with Britain over the Oregon Territory, reflecting his interpretation that the mission of the federal government was to annex adjacent lands. Despite his interests in other pressing matters, on August 3 of that year, Polk took time out to write a passionate veto message of Congress's River and Harbor Bill, which contained money for Chicago's harbor. He argued in favor of a limited central government. He regretted that the bill contained too much money for unconstitutional local improvements having nothing to do with foreign trade at the expense of the national treasury. His veto stirred up an enormous, pent-up resentment. Not only Chicago, but other cities to the north and west of Mason and Dixon's line were incensed by this veto, which was inspired, as they saw it, by southern interests.

The idea of a united, conspicuous display of strength against the veto, and what it stood for in the eyes of the bill's supporters, led representatives from 18 states to convene at Chicago for the first River and Harbor Convention in July, 1847. The meeting lasted for three days and drew 20,000 out-of-towners. One of the speakers was a fledgling Representative from Illinois named Abraham Lincoln. The convention reminded Washington, in no uncertain terms, that the federal government had a duty "to improve navigable rivers and harbors for the benefit of all commerce, and that the Atlantic coast had been allotted an unfair portion of the money thus far expended on such improvements." "All" was an important operative word here, because that included commerce in the nation's interior ports, some of which Polk referred to as mere creeks.

Unfortunately, this convention did not free up money for harbor improvements, which continued to proceed only gradually. But an extremely significant consequence of the meeting was to establish the host city, Chicago, as a leader on the crucial subject of inland rivers and harbors. Chicago so impressed its guests by putting on a grand parade and offering such fine hospitality that visitors left with high praises for the city.[17]

The Sand Continues to Creep

Political speeches and parades could not make the sand stay put. In the fall of 1849, when the next topographic engineer, 1st Lieut. Joseph Dana Webster, arrived, he noticed the sand defying McClellan's fences and creeping around the outer end of the north pier, threatening the harbor. By now the I&M Canal had opened and shipping business was lively. Webster, like McClellan before him, speculated on ways to work with rather than against nature. His innovative idea was that of a "jetty pier," a separate breakwater built to the northeast of the north pier to funnel water between the two piers and force it to drop sand at a harmless distance from the harbor. His suggestions were ignored.[18]

While work was progressing on the piers and the sand was accumulating to the north, south of the piers the lake was remorselessly eroding the shoreline because the construction of the piers and their capture of sand were starving the southern beach. In 1852, when the Illinois Central Railroad built a breakwater parallel to the shore, this erosion problem was unwittingly solved.[19] The longshore currents and littoral drift could operate as nature intended. Sand was caught up in the breakwater and began to replenish the eroded beach.

The Federal Dredge

The government provided only one federal steam dredge for all the harbors being developed along the entire western lakeshore. The dredge was a ponderous affair, moving under its own power at barely six miles an hour, unable even to tow the four scows necessary for its dredging operations.[20]

In the spring of 1854, the Chicago harbor was virtually closed by sand; lives and boats were lost. Webster, now a captain, was in Washington trying to straighten out his own affairs, and his successor, Lieut. Col. James D. Graham, had not yet arrived. The Chicago Board of Trade, which naturally took great interest in the harbor, found itself without a friend on the scene. It offered to borrow the federal dredge, pay all costs for opening the harbor, and return it in good condition. The federal government did not reply in a timely manner, and the frustrated Board, in cooperation with the Common Council of Chicago, seized the federal dredge and began to scoop out the harbor. Upon his arrival in spring, 1854, Graham retrieved the dredge and continued the work. By the late summer, 18,000 cubic yards of sand had been dredged, towed far out into the lake, and dumped. The dredging created a new channel 600 feet wide and from $11\frac{1}{2}$ to 13 feet deep and was so successful that Graham recommended that instead of continuing to build ineffective jetties, regular yearly dredging would be a better solution. But for that, Chicago would need its own dredge. During each of the 12 years that he was stationed in Chicago, Graham requested in his annual report to the Topographic Bureau that a first-class steam dredge be assigned specifically to Chicago, but nothing ever came of it.[21]

The Incident of the Hostage Dredge

Unfortunately, in the summer of that same year, another sandbar built up in the Chicago harbor. This time the federal dredge was up in Kenosha. Chicagoans wanted it, but Kenosha refused to relinquish it. On September 27, 1855, officials in Kenosha, faced with the dredge's imminent removal, boarded it and removed various pieces of equipment, among them the critical iron scoop. A member of the Kenosha City Council got into a "scuffle" with the vessel's custodian. The sheriff of Kenosha County, obviously in sympathy with this piracy, seized even more U.S. equipment from across the harbor, with the backing of Kenosha's mayor. Graham was not amused and vigorously admonished the Kenosha officials. The dredge was returned nine days later, but not before the Kenosha City Council restored the town's dignity by voting its consent.[22]

Solving the Sandbar Problem

In 1863, Colonel Graham's annual report summarized the condition of the harbors under his control, listing Chicago typical of those in "more or less delapidated [*sic*]" condition, since no federal appropriations had been made since 1852.[23] Andreas says,

> The Government still seemed loath to recognize Chicago's importance as a commercial emporium, even by so much as making a modest appropriation by which her decaying harbor piers could be kept in repair. The city herself therefore took up the matter, trusting to the future for re-imbursement [*sic*]. In the fall of 1859 a small sum was raised by the Board of Trade to preserve a portion of the North Pier, which was fast rotting and falling into the lake. In 1861 and 1862 the repairs undertaken by the city were just sufficient to prevent the harbor improvements from becoming utterly useless. . . .[24]

By the end of the Civil War, Chicago had emerged as the giant of Great Lakes shipping, both in rail and water. During the war it had become a major supply center for the North. Acknowledging its importance, beginning in 1866, federal harbor appropriations became steady and generous.

Maj. Junius Wheeler became the government's man-in-charge of harbors on Lake Superior and Lake Michigan in 1866 and remained at his post until 1870. He was not content with simply extending piers. He endorsed a proposal by the Chicago Canal and Dock Company for a major ship basin with an entry to the harbor from the north. Major Wheeler further recommended building a 455-acre enclosed outer harbor to the south. A 4,000-foot-long breakwater would be built at a right angle to the south pier, to create a 12-foot-deep protected area that would include piers and slips as well as harbor space. Another pier was to join the new breakwater to the shore. Because the Chicago harbor now ranked as the country's second or third major port, he persuaded the government to commit funds for the outer harbor construction. In 1867, after the Civil War was over, the Chicago Canal and Dock Company built their proposed Ogden Slip (along which today's North Pier is located). Afterwards, the piers were extended once again.

Unfortunately, Major Wheeler left in 1870 before he could oversee his project. His successor, Maj. David Crawford Houston, supervised construction, but because he was uncertain about the eventual need for the pier enclosure to the south, that portion of the project was never built.

Maj. George Gillespie replaced Houston in June, 1874. He completed the superstructure for the breakwater but did not enclose the basin. Major Gillespie was favorably impressed with the effects of the new outer harbor on the sand accumulations, which had ceased.[25] Though the sand must have continued to drop out, it probably accrued (and is still doing so) in deeper portions of the lake.

Of the history of constructing the harbor, Andreas acutely observed: ". . . it would seem . . . that the task of protecting the harbor entrance would be an indefinite contest between the governmental purse and the natural forces of wind, wave and current."[26]

The Sands and Streeterville

Andreas also noted: "The same forces that caused the bar across the mouth of the river in times of yore, have made hundreds of acres of land upon the north side of the pier, and the detritus and deposit that was formerly a formidable obstacle to navigation has become dry land, and a valuable accessory to Chicago's greatness."[27] These hundreds of acres of new sandy land were not, of course, on the original federal government Public Lands Survey Map made in 1821 by John Walls, who had precisely delineated Lake Michigan's shoreline. As the sand accumulated, maps located the shoreline farther to the east. In 1883, one map showed a shoreline almost a third of a mile east of Walls's line. Who owned this land that had been created by improving the mouth of the Chicago River? It had never been platted for the canal commissioners to sell. Did it belong to the landowners who had legally purchased acreage along the lakefront? Squatters did not worry about these legal niceties. They took possession of it and, according to historian Currey, built "rude shanties and obtained a livelihood by fishing and collecting debris which had floated ashore, and which had a salable value."[28] The acreage

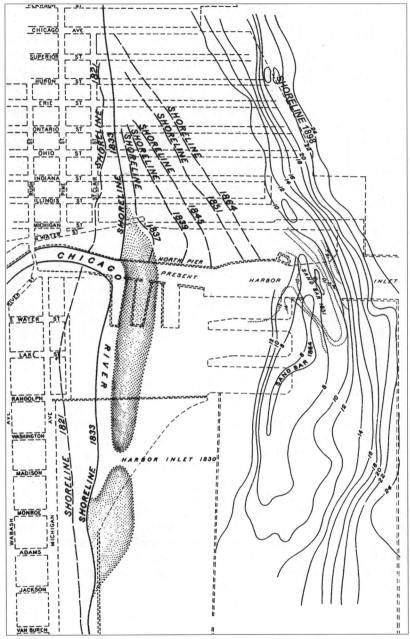

Modified from J. Harlan Bretz, Geology of the Chicago Region, Part I, General, 1939, based on U.S. Geological Survey, Geologic Atlas of the United States, Chicago Folio [No. 18], Fig. 13, 1902, 11.

The incessant accretion of sand at Chicago's Harbor.

became known as the "Sands" and began to add its own rich lore to Chicago.

"The area," according to historian Carl Smith, "had a notorious reputation since the 1850s as a morally as well as geographically marginal neighborhood congenial to the most suspect human impulses and activities, notably gambling and prostitution, which were unofficially tolerated by the authorities. In April of 1857, Mayor 'Long' John Wentworth . . . led thirty policemen in a raid in the area . . . [that] scattered the men and women of ill-repute all over the city." It was to the Sands, adjacent to the lake, that many fled to escape the flames of the great Chicago Fire of 1871, " 'only to find that the fire seemed to revive the old spirit of the Sands.' The fire created an instant democracy, uniting 'extremes of wealth and squalor' so that 'inequalities of societies were now leveled off as smooth as the beach itself.' "[29]

It is probable that Capt. George Wellington Streeter, a circus promoter from the Michigan Woods, ran his boat aground on this same un-platted asset in 1886, at what is today Superior Street. Sand accumulated around his boat just as it had around the piers, and he claimed 168 acres of land as his own, calling it a new district because it had not appeared on the original government survey. He replaced his ship with a shack and proceeded to sell off the land. Regardless of his influential and wealthy neighbors' opinion of him as a low-life, he was not evicted until after World War I, when he was caught violating the law that prohibited the sale of liquor on Sundays.[30] Even though he is gone, his name is memorialized in Chicago's Streeterville section, which encompasses glittering North Michigan Avenue, some of the world's most expensive real estate.

The Aftermath

The mouth of the river had changed. The sand accretions may have stopped and the harbor been made commodious, but the story continues. Wheeler had proposed building a pier to enclose the outer harbor, but because Houston felt the pier was unnecessary, as noted above, it was never built. Ships found the opening a convenient approach to the main harbor. This channel became a focal point for federal and city conflict. In 1875, Gillespie was pleased that ships were using this entrance to the outer harbor. But to his dismay, he soon discovered that the City of Chicago was using it as a dumpsite for dredgings from the Chicago River, thus building up a potentially dangerous shoal. Gillespie suspected that the dumping was taking place at night when his officers were off duty. Eventually the mayor promised to halt the practice, but it seems to have continued.[31]

Early Settlement
on the North Branch

We the surface broad surveying,
We primeval forests felling,
We the virgin soil upheaving,
We the route for travel clearing,
O resistless, restless race!
Pioneers! O Pioneers!

—Walt Whitman
Pioneers! O Pioneers!

As the federal government was improving the harbor and the I&M Canal commissioners were still planning their waterway, pioneers were beginning to move up along the North Branch. European and Yankee immigrants began displacing tribal settlements in the wake of the official native removal in 1833, some even earlier. As the small number of early migrants grew, settlers reworked the hydrology of the watershed in northern Cook County and northeastern Lake County, draining its sloughs and wetlands, ploughing the prairies and felling the woods. By 1860, perhaps even by 1849, Chicago would feel the impact.

The North Branch was early called "Gaurie's River" because a French trader named Gaurie built a house and trading post just above the forks around 1778. He is said to have surrounded both of his buildings with a picket fence in order to protect his "livestock—chickens, ducks, hogs, sheep and cattle—from marauding wolves [probably coyotes], bobcats and occasional bear." He lived there for 14 years.[1] Archibald Clybourn's slaughterhouse came later, but it still preceded the large migration up the North Branch. Clybourn opened his business in 1827, at a bend in the river just south of Armitage Avenue in Chicago, near today's Clybourn station on the northbound Metra commuter train line. It was the first enterprise that probably affected the quality of river water. Although there is no proof that Clybourn dumped any of the offal from his operations into the river, it would have been typical for that category of business. Clybourn was official butcher to the Potawatomi and to the military personnel at Fort Dearborn, and his clientele also include the ordinary citizen. A Clybourn handbill, dated December 3, 1833, shows the extent of his production:

> BUTCHERING—The subscriber intends butchering from 400-500 hogs this present week, all of which have been well fatted on corn. He wished to inform his old customers and the people generally that he intends selling cheap for cash at wholesale at his butcher shop, two miles from Chicago, and at wholesale at his market on the market square in Chicago. He further

wishes to inform the public that he keeps constantly on hand and for sale at his farm two miles from Chicago work oxen and beef cattle. Beef both fresh and salt at wholesale and retail at his market in Chicago.

A. CLYBOURN[2]

Although the infamous Union Stock Yards would eventually be located on the river's South Branch, Clybourn was Carl Sandburg's first "Hog Butcher"—if not for the world, at least for Chicago.

The Earliest Settlers

Before the land was surveyed in 1839 and 1840, anyone who lived north of Bryn Mawr Avenue and the North Branch, or north of the Indian Boundary Line, which ran diagonally along Rogers Avenue in Rogers Park, was a squatter, but that did not seem to hinder settlement. According to Andreas, the first land claimant on the North Branch in Jefferson Township was most likely John Kinzie Clark, also called "Injun John" Clark or "Prairie Wolf" Clark. He claimed land eight miles up from Wolf Point on the North Branch, just barely south of the Indian Boundary Line. In 1830, Clark moved to his claim and built his log house with its shake roof out of the native woodland materials. At that time, the North Branch watershed was so heavily wooded that his house was nearly invisible until one was almost upon it.[3] The forest protected the house from the fierce winter prairie winds, and the forested watershed soaked up the precipitation, slowly releasing its nourishing waters to the river. (The highly respected Clark soon moved north to suburban Northbrook, tried farming, and gave it up for a job as postman. He ran the mail between Chicago and Waukegan through Lake County, sometimes acting as unofficial real estate agent. He knew what was for sale and put sellers in touch with prospective buyers.[4] One of today's major wetland restorations along the Middle Fork bears his name.)

Andreas names several early pioneers who settled along the North Branch shortly after Clark, but he says that 1834 was the year that immigration on the North Branch began in earnest.[5] People moved upstream and built along the river or on the high ground near the river, as well as inland. It was probably in 1834 that John Miller built the first sawmill on the North Branch just south of present-day Dempster Street in what is now Morton Grove. His mill was below the junction of the West Fork with the combined Middle and East Forks, and perhaps the extra current from the fuller river attracted his attention. To run his wheel, he built a dam on the river's gravel bottom, raised the water level a few feet, and diverted the water into a new ditch. The mill produced sawed boards instead of the whole logs that had previously been used for construction. Lincoln Avenue, near the junction of the railroad tracks just south of Dempster, is also known as "Miller's Mill Road." Its name reflects the route cut out of the forest so logs could be hauled to the mill by teams of oxen. The only vestige of the millrace today is a small backwater down a hill, just west of today's Chicago, Milwaukee and St. Paul Railroad tracks and just south of Dempster in Morton Grove.[6]

Mark Noble's steam-powered sawmill, near what was to become the lower end of Goose Island, was another early North Branch enterprise. The mill, later known as Huntoon's Sawmill, processed trees from the surrounding forest, including oak, elm, poplar, and ash. During the summer of 1835, the mill sawed three-inch oak planking for the harbor's north pier.[7]

Lake County and the Chicago River

In about 1835, one Jacob Miller was said to have "rowed and pushed a boat laden with about thirty bushels of potatoes, beside other family supplies, up the north branch of Chicago River to its source in what is known as the Dady Slough, a little west of the city of Waukegan." The source of this story, *The Historical Encyclopedia of Illinois*, continues: "This fact will serve to illustrate the difference between the then and the now as regards surface water. In winter skaters not infrequently made long trips on the ice, following the streams and sloughs for scores of miles. Trips to Chicago were often made in this way. Now, except where lakes or rivers provide the opportunity, the average school boy must learn the art of skating, if he learns at all, upon a pond his father or grandfather would have looked upon as entirely too small for even an amateur to practice on."[8]

The sloughs of Lake County play a starring role in the story of Jim Mooney, who arrived in Lake County with his family at the behest of his fellow Irishman, Mike Meehan. When Meehan greeted Mooney's boat on the shore of Lake Michigan in the vicinity of Highland Park in autumn, 1844, and guided him to his new home, they had to walk

> . . . about two miles from the lake when they came to the brink of a muddy, swollen stream. Mike halted the oxen: "This is the east slough [the Skokie]. It's flooded this time of year, so we'll have to lead the team across." Mike removed his shoes and let the cold mud under the marsh grass close over his feet. Jim Mooney helped his two older sons into the cart. The children clung to the sideboards and cried in panic when the wheels lurched forward into the icy stream. Jim Mooney wanted to rest when they reached the west bank. Mike motioned him on to higher ground: "The land you should claim is just beyond the slough; it's two-thirds timber—if all else fails at least you won't freeze to death. . . ."
>
> Besides furnishing logs for the hearth, the trees served as wind-breakers against November gales which swept around the cabin. Jim Mooney was glad too, that his farm was near the slough. At daybreak he followed light thuds of deer hooves through the swamp grass or he watched for ducks to circle over the water. When blizzards froze the stream and locked fish inside, the only meals he could count on were those he tracked in the forest. He learned to make traps of willow branches and grain, which sometimes yielded game. More often, wolves made off with the catch before he could make his way through snowdrifts.
>
> Spring came; melting snow swelled the slough again and ran in muddy streams over soft, fresh earth. Jim Mooney scooped out soil with his hands and planted seeds. When a summer sun baked the ground, he brought count-less pails of water from the slough. Slowly, precious green sprouts began to

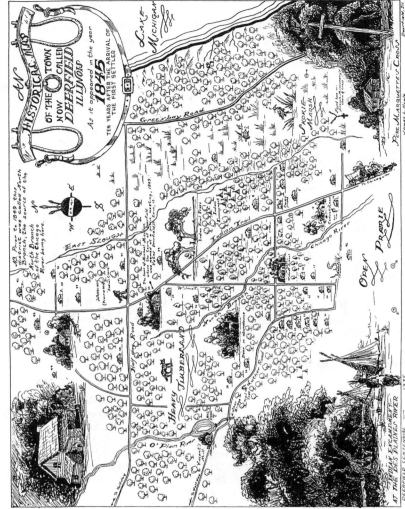

Map drawn by James L. Heale and printed in The Bicentennial Plus Three, A History of Deerfield, *by Paul Pritt, 1979. Courtesy of the Village of Deerfield.*

Romantic map of old Deerfield in 1845. The cartographer has caught the wooded aspect of the land but had omited the Middle Fork, once known as the West Slough. It would have run just east of the Indian Trail. The West Fork is here called the North Branch, Chicago River, as it was often referred to by early historians. The Des Plaines is called by one of its early names, the O'Plain. The cartographer has placed Mike Meehan's house just south of Half Day Road and east of the Indian Trail, atop today's Prairie Wolf Slough restoration site on the Middle Fork. The map is definitely not to scale. Its charming features are best appreciated through a magnifying glass.

push their way out of the earth. The younger boys searched the woods for butternuts and berries. . . .[9]

What the plough was to the prairie, drain-tile was to the wet land. Most early settlers, like Mooney, probably owned a pocket or two under water which they wanted to dry up and cultivate. They had two incentives: to drain the land to farm the fertile bottomland underneath and to get dry, early access to the land so they could work the soils over a long growing season. To accomplish their goals, they removed most of the existing vegetation and installed ditches and an underground network of drain tile. The story of the Chicago River in Lake County is the story of the tiles and ditches that fingered out in a dense network under the land.

What the plough was to the prairie, and drain tile to the wetland, the ax was to the woodlands of the North Branch watershed. All up and down the North Branch, in Lake and Cook Counties, were settlements of farmers. They cleared the woods and sold the wood for charcoal and later for fuel to the railroads. In Lake County, the ground was such heavy clay that it was said the first generation of Irish settlers was worn out from clearing the forest and draining the land.[10]

Farmers of Cook County

Having cleared and drained the land, the primarily English and German truck farmers in Cook County raised oats, corn, barley, wheat, onions, and potatoes, plus other crops. Some specialized in horse radish, celery, pickles, sauerkraut, or greenhouse flowers. Their cattle and hogs grazed freely in the oak woods, the hogs fattening up on acorns. Niles Center, the future north suburban village of Skokie, became the market for all the surrounding territory, where farmers from miles around came to market days on the first Tuesday and third Thursday of each month to sell vegetables, pigs, and poultry.[11] The town of Lake View (now Chicago's northside Lakeview neighborhood) became known as the celery capital of the world.

Early residents' memories of the shallow North Branch, whether slough or river, are replete with swimming holes, skating parties, hunting, and fishing. In what became today's village of Golf, John Dewes once owned 400 acres along the West Fork of the North Branch, where he did some farming from 1840 to 1850. He lived in an old log cabin near what is now the 17th green of the Glen View Club. Dewes found the hunting easy because of the river corridor. "Game in those days was plentiful and it was not necessary to step off the little porch facing the river to bring down a deer of the many who followed the stream."[12]

The Goose Island Story

No story of the river would be complete without Goose Island. Small islands dotted the original North Branch, but Goose Island was not one of them. An early map of the area shows the river making a lazy, bow-shaped bend to the northwest as you look upstream, close to the city between what was to become North Avenue on the north and Chicago Avenue on the south. The astute observer may be struck by the potential of making a shortcut up the river here, the straight "string" of the bow, so to speak. The idea also occurred to entrepreneurs, and in 1853, the new Chicago Land Company purchased canal land at this spot. By 1857, the company was excavating the clay on the eastern side of the island and making bricks. As they progressed in their digging, the workers were creating a channel that became a shortcut up the North Branch. The channel was known as the North Branch Canal, or Ogden's Canal, after William Ogden, Chicago's first mayor, who was a trustee for the Land Company. This channel moved the head of navigation up to North Avenue, the island's northern border. Goose Island is almost one and one-half miles long, and nearly one-half mile at its widest, extending south to Chicago Avenue. There was no bridge to the island until after the Chicago Fire of 1871.

By most popular accounts, before the land became an island, the Irish were the early squatters there, coming as early as the 1830s and 1840s to work on the I&M Canal. Those accounts report that the Irish settlement was regarded by others as a lawless, vermin-infested pit. Some say it was called "Kilgubbin," others say that refers to a place farther west, or to wherever any Irish lived. Squatters kept pigs, geese, and cows, fed with slops from a nearby distillery.[13] To what extent the crowded ragtag squatter settlement with its people and animals would have polluted the river is unknown.

There had always been industry on the island, but after the channel was dug, industry displaced most of the squatters. Many of the industries that moved onto the new island were anything but river-friendly: lumber yards, coal yards, tanneries, tanbark dealers, stone and gravel yards, shipyards, distilleries, a rolling mill that made steel rails, and a city gas works. It has been alleged that the segment just south of Goose Island now contains the most toxic materials in the entire riverbed.[14] Despite several studies, as of this writing the content of the sediment has not been definitively determined, aside from a surprising amount of silver residue from an unknown source, possibly photographic processing. As of 1998, there were proposals to fill in the artificial channel and reconnect Goose Island to the mainland.

From the viewpoint of the river story, the significance of Goose Island is not the colorful tale of who lived on it at what time, but that it redeveloped into an industrial and manufacturing zone with significant degrading consequences for water quality and aquatic life.

Effects of Early Settlement

It cannot be said of the fledgling North Branch communities, as it can of Chicago, that the river made them possible. It was neither the focal point for most settlers nor the central *raison d'être* for the towns that would emerge. But it can certainly be argued that the settlers' draining and deforesting began to transform the watershed and the river by hastening water runoff and soil erosion, increasing the river's sediment load and making it more flood-prone. As the amount of farmland under cultivation or used for animal production increased along with the human population, downstream Chicago felt the repercussions, both in floods and sewage. The little upstream farming settlements along the Chicago River and the giant industrial and commercial center of Chicago were woven together by this mere slip of water.

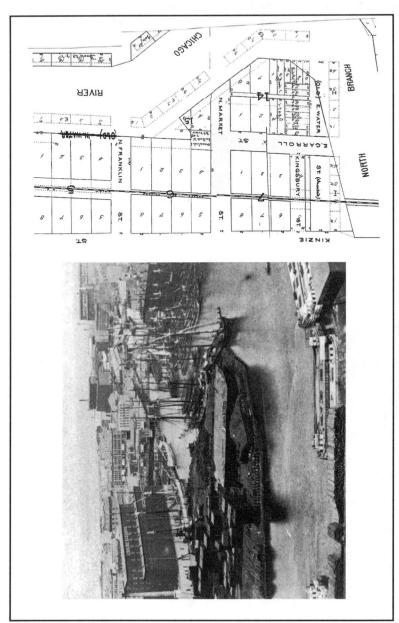

Peltzer map courtesy of Illinois Regional Archives, Northeastern Illinois University. Photo courtesy of Chicago Historical Society.

The Peltzer map on the right shows city block and lot numbers. The dark line represents the shape of the new basin. Note the removed wedges of blocks 14 and 15. The dotted lines represent water lots vacated for widening. The photo on the left, taken in 1875, shows that the scar on Wolf Point's northeast side was still clearly visible 27 years later.

Early Commerce and the River

That little stream, whose crystal waters had never been parted by any-thing heavier than a canoe, now buoyed the massive barks of traffic, and became polluted with the sewage of a growing city. And thus the great transition came, and we were wont to curse the sinless streamlet for it.

—Edwin O. Gale, 1902

Shipping did not wait until the portage was breached by the Illinois and Michigan Canal or the sandbar removed from the harbor. It began immediately after Chicago was recognized as a political entity. Ships sailing on Lake Michigan needed moorings, piers, wharves, and a deeper river. Once the I&M Canal opened, canal barges and boats joined the vessels. Locks and movable bridges became necessities. Commerce increased population, and population increased commerce. The more the river was improved for navigation, the more it needed to be improved. Retaining structures and docks proliferated along the banks. Heavier cargo ships have greater drafts, hence the need for an even deeper and straighter river, stronger docks, and the removal of the center-pier bridges. The need for some sort of plan was obvious, but there was none.

Early Trade

In its earliest years, Chicago had imported almost all of the necessities of life. But very soon the balance of trade switched from a net inflow of goods to a net export of goods. According to Andreas, as early as spring 1833, a bill of lading for a vessel headed for Detroit, read, "287 barrels of beef, 14 barrels tallow, 2 barrels bees-wax, 152 dry hides, weighing 4659 pounds. . . . From this shipment dates the beginning of Chicago commerce."[1]

Much of the trade during the first two decades of the town came from slaughterhouses and associated businesses, all of which used the river for dumping. By 1845, these discharges made the river extremely offensive.[2]

As commerce grew, so did the size of commercial vessels. Iron mills; grain elevators; cement factories; lumber yards; and dealers of sand, stone, and other building products all required larger, heavier ships. In the early days, when boats were very small, the Chicago River was navigable up the North Branch to Chicago Avenue, up the South Branch, and, depending upon the size of the vessel, up the West Fork to the portage. As the amount of shipping traffic grew, the size and number of vessels the river had to accommodate and the accouterments needed to service that commerce made a shambles of the riverbanks. It was said that the river was so thick with boats one could walk across it on the decks of the vessels.

Wharves and Wharfing Privileges: Early Bones of Contention

Because Chicago was to become a quintessential transshipment point, it was inevitable that the crystal waters of Edwin Gale's youth would quickly disappear. And while the surveyor could lay out neat lines, neither the town nor later the City of Chicago could make the behavior of the men who did business along the river conform to any uniform rules. As early as 1833, the town began to define wharfing privileges and sell the land fronting the river for wharves, but the system had disintegrated into a non-system that led to bitter disputes, violence, and complete disarray.

By 1847, "lumber yards, elevators, shipyards, warehouses, and factories lined the docks of the river jammed with sail and steam craft."[3] As completion of the I&M Canal neared, it became clear that some agency was needed to assume control over the navigable reaches of the river so that it could be widened and straightened, turning basins built, and riparian owners identified. The issue of wharfing privileges became contentious.

Mayor James Curtiss, in his inaugural address on March 9, 1847, included an extensive paragraph addressing the problem: "There will be no matters presented to your consideration, of more importance than those connected with the 'Wharfing privileges' so called. The value of the property involved in the question connected with these privileges, has been estimated at a half a million of dollars."[4] In October, 1847, the city's Common Council took charge of examining old titles and vacating streets along the waterfront.[5]

Improving the River: Public Responsibility

Starting in 1848, the first year of operation of the I&M Canal, the Chicago River became the focus of ceaseless improvements by various governmental entities. Activities included dredging, redredging, widening, deepening, making turning basins, repairing deteriorating piers, everything and anything that could improve shipping safety and accommodate the ever-increasing size of vessels using the route.

The year the canal opened, the canal trustees began work on a "commodious" turning basin at Wolf Point, the confluence of the North and South Branches. At that time, "commodious" did not mean what it does today, as ships were still relatively small. But even a modest turning basin required that the original Wolf Point be decreased by dredging back its banks. The city passed vacation ordinances for the new basin and established new lot and dock lines. On the west bank, West Water Street was eventually vacated between Fulton and Kinzie Streets. On the north and south banks of the Main Stem, the affected banks lay between State Street and Wolf Point. Ordinances vacating all streets named Water Street (South, East, and West) were enacted. Some ordinances affecting these streets came as late as 1858.

The *Peltzer Atlas of Chicago* of 1872 shows the basin's final shape as well as the old streets and docklines.[6] The most noticeable changes were on the northeast bank of Wolf Point, under what is today the Apparel Center's (the commercial building west of the Merchandise Mart) parking lot, where the land was sliced away at sharp angles. The photograph of Wolf Point in 1875 illustrates the unnatural look that resulted. Today, this point curves once again, and because it looks so natural and is masked by brush, it can entice people into believing that it is the original river bank.

At the same time, where the river curved around the site of Fort Dearborn, the city decreased the angle of the river, dredging away part of the land originally covered by the fort to make a smoother arc.

The Flood of 1849

With the canal open, the turning basin completed, and commerce and population on the increase, the city was about to experience its first encounter with another unanticipated scourge. Against this scourge the City of Chicago's ordinances were utterly powerless. The first history-making flood of calamitous proportions occurred on the river on March 12, 1849, only 11 months after the opening of the I&M Canal. Three days of heavy spring rains followed a long spell of freezing weather. The ground and the rivers were frozen thick. The Des Plaines River, unable to penetrate its own ice dam to drain into the Illinois, went on an eastward rampage, overflowing its banks into Mud Lake, part of the former portage route. From there the torrent of water and ice flowed into the Chicago River and out to the lake. Estimates say that nearly 100 boats were in the harbor that day, most of which were destroyed; the rest were seriously damaged. Many of the boats were canal boats, along with lumber ships and schooners that had over-wintered at the wharves. Rufus Blanchard described the scene:

> Of course, each owner or person in charge at once sought the safety [from the oncoming tide] of his vessel, added additional moorings to those already in use, while all waited with anxiety and trepidation the result of the totally unexpected catastrophe. It was not long in coming. The river soon began to swell, the waters lifting the ice to within two or three feet of the surface of the wharves; between nine and ten A.M. loud reports as of distant artillery were heard towards the southern extremity of the town, indicating that the ice was breaking up. Soon, to these were added the sounds proceeding from crashing timbers, from hawsers tearing away the piles around which they were vainly fastened, or snapping like so much pack-thread, on account of the strain upon them. To these in turn were succeeded the cries of people calling to the parties in charge of the vessels and canal boats to escape ere it would be too late; while nearly all the males, and hundreds of the female population, hurried from their homes to the banks of the river to witness what was by this time considered to be inevitable, namely, a catastrophe such as the city never before sustained.[7]

The ice and swirling water demolished and swept away every bridge over the South Branch and Main Stem on their way out to the lake.

The rivers had probably gone on a water rampage many times before when few people lived in the vicinity. But now, with Chicago bursting into a major shipping and population center, property and lives were lost. The flood of 1849 was the first—but hardly the last—time that the citizens of Chicago would be

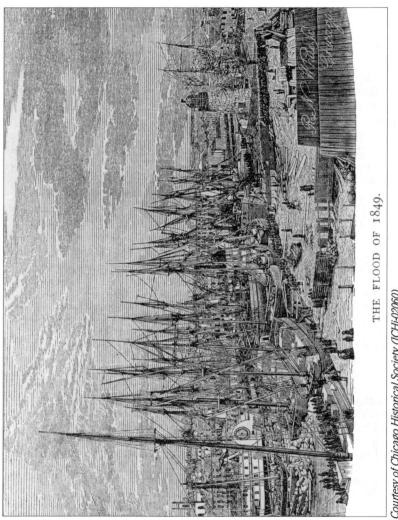

THE FLOOD OF 1849.

Courtesy of Chicago Historical Society (ICHi-02060).

The tangle of boats and debris in the river after the flood of March 12, 1849.

subjected to this particular force of nature. Chicago had already reckoned with disease, particularly cholera epidemics, but untamed rivers were another matter. The definition of "flood" changed from a natural occurrence to a natural disaster. Against this force, the mayor and city council were powerless; humans could declare that the new river boundaries were "here," but nature could not heed them.

Little Goose Island

In the vicinity of Wolf Point during 1865 and 1866, the new Department of Public Works's annual report recorded the removal of a little island of about 20 square yards of yellowish clay. In the spring floods, this little island was covered by water, but when it emerged in dryer weather, it was covered with geese.[8] Whether above or below water, it would have been a hazard to large boats turning or going up the North Branch. To complete the improvements, some planned public dock space was added along the main stem, presumably to the satisfaction of Mayor Curtiss.

Tunnels for Pedestrians

Improvements made to the river for commerce before the 1860s might have helped navigational interests and some pocketbooks, but pedestrians were suffering. All of the boats using the river had to pass under the movable bridges, which were controlled manually by bridgetenders. It turned out that a bridgetender could be an unruly member of the municipal body. When a ship approached one of the swing bridges over the river, the tender would open the bridge promptly, but he would take his sweet time closing it. In January, 1854, according to Andreas, an ordinance designated bridgetenders as special policemen and required them to open and close the bridges "as quickly as possible." This ordinance seemed to make no difference, depending, as it did, upon each tender's definition of "as quickly as possible."[9] As Andreas says, before mid-century,

> . . . all the sectional jealousies (south, north and west) entered into, and raged around the question of locating the early bridges of the city. But by 1857-58, the marine interests of Chicago had increased so prodigiously, that all local feelings in the breasts of landsmen had been thrown aside; and all the pugnacity of the city was divided in the fierce warfare which raged between river navigators and those persons who were obliged to use the thoroughfares. What constituted the respective rights of land travelers and water travelers, and what was their relative importance in the community?— this was the question which vexed the public for many a long and weary month. So far as it related to the question of the conveniences of land travel, the problem was to be partially solved by the construction of the two river tunnels.[10]

The city built two tunnels under the river for foot and horse traffic to relieve

In this 1873 picture, all bridges are open on the Main Channel, severing
the connection between the northern and southern sections of the city.
The State Street bridge is in the foreground.

the long-suffering public from the tyranny of the bridgetenders. Both tunnels
were similar in construction. The Washington Street tunnel opened on January
1, 1869, and the LaSalle Street tunnel on July 4, 1871. One Chicago resident's
1880 opinion of this latter tunnel is quoted in Meyer and Wade:

> It is a marvelous underground highway, containing two passageways for
> vehicles, besides a footway for pedestrians, passing not only under the river
> but also under several squares either side, making it an easy grade, and, with
> its long row of gas-lights, a very "cheerful tunnel." [11]

Interestingly, Andreas's descriptions of the tunnels include their length (1,605
feet for Washington Street and 1,890 feet for LaSalle Street) and, in the case of
the Washington Street tunnel, its depth to the bottom of the river bed (32.4
feet). Andreas never mentions the figure from the low-water level of the river to
the top of the tunnels. The shallow water over the tunnels was to prove a major
sticking point for commerce, as the depth would prove insufficient for the
larger vessels at the turn of the century. [12]

SECTIONAL VIEW OF LA SALLE STREET TUNNEL, SHOWING MASONRY, ETC.

Courtesy of Chicago Historical Society ICHi-05569; from Seven Days in Chicago, *published by J.M. Wing & Co., 1877, Chicago.*

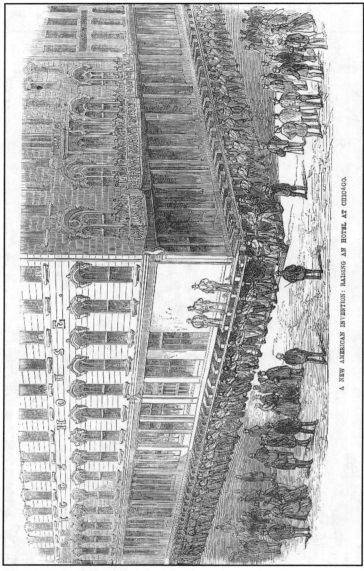

A NEW AMERICAN INVENTION : RAISING AN HOTEL AT CHICAGO.

Entire buildings were moved or lifted to the higher level necessary to accommodate the sewers. At Lake Street, for example, the grade was raised to 8.62 feet higher than low water in the Chicago River, as determined in 1847 by the canal commissioners (Andreas, vol. 2, 59). Here, the Briggs House at the northeast corner of Randolph and Wells Streets, is being lifted in 1857. The men under the building are working in complete harmony to turn jacks and keep the building intact. No wonder the spectacle attracted onlookers.

The Chicago River
From Clean Stream to Open Sewer

> *Oh, Chicago, you make me shiver*
> *With your dirty streets and your stinking river.*
>
> —Sailor's chanty

> *It is said of his converts that no one of them was ever known to be a back-*
> *slider. If you could see the cakes of ice that were raked out to make room for*
> *baptismal purposes, you would make up your mind that no man would join*
> *a church under such circumstances unless he joined to stay.... One cold*
> *day, about the first part of February 1839, there were 17 immersed in the river*
> *at the foot of State Street. A hole about 20 feet square was cut through the ice*
> *and the platform was sunk, with one end resting on the shore.... Recently*
> *our Baptist friends have made up their minds that our lake has enough to do*
> *to carry away all the sewerage of the city without washing off the sins of the*
> *people.*
>
> —Rev. Isaac T. Hinton
> Baptist clergyman, 1839

The days of the Chicago River's crystal clear waters nestled in a bucolic setting had disappeared. A glut of docks and ships replaced the grasses and canoes. The city's growth was exciting, but the expanding population and industry each generated an increasing amount of filth. Where could the city dispose of this very inconvenient by-product? The Chicago River turned out to offer a very convenient, although problematic, answer.

Early in its history, Chicago's leaders worried about the sluggish nature of the river and foresaw that it could pose health and drainage problems. They were well aware they were carving this future metropolis out of poorly drained marsh. On November 7, 1833, the progressive little town tried to protect its drinking water and prevent offensive odors by enacting an anti-pollution ordinance. By the terms of the ordinance, citizens were forbidden to use the river as a receptacle for "dung, dead animal carrion, putrid meat, or fish entrails, or decayed vegetables, or any other offensive substance whatever."[1] In 1834, in the throes of a cholera scare, the town adopted a more stringent ordinance, but when the scare abated, offensive substances penetrated the waterway. By 1845, the Chicago River, the dumping ground of refuse from the slaughterhouses, had become foul.[2]

Primitive Water and Sewage "Systems"

Two major problems beset the young city: obtaining a supply of potable water and safely disposing of wastes. The first priority was getting a safe supply of drinking water. For this Chicago's earliest residents had turned to the river and to shallow wells. In the 1830s, "water peddlers" began to provide drinking water from the lake at prices of five to 25 cents a barrel.[3] Water delivery improved slowly, but outhouses were a continuing problem because of the need to dispose of the wastes. In the early years, businesses arose to perform that chore too: scooping out the refuse and hauling it to someplace where it would be out of sight and, thus, out of mind. As the population increased and industry diversified, it became obvious that individual entrepreneurial services were inadequate. Safe water and safe sewage disposal required a centralized government that assumed responsibility for modernizing both systems.

A great population upsurge in 1846-1847 laid the groundwork for an upsurge in disease. In 1848 both cholera and smallpox broke out in epidemic proportions. In the early 1850s Chicago experienced outbreaks of dysentery and cholera. To assure a uniformly safe water supply throughout the city, in 1851 the city replaced the private Chicago Hydraulic Company with the newly incorporated Chicago City Hydraulic Company. But the new company could not act quickly enough. In 1854, cholera took the lives of nearly six percent of the city's population, leading the Illinois legislature to authorize the creation of the Chicago Board of Sewerage Commissioners.

Meanwhile, the streets had become open sewers on purpose. Beginning in 1849, oak gutters had been laid in street centers to serve as drains, and planking was laid atop the principal streets. The results were far from satisfactory, and the August, 1850, edition of the weekly *Gem of the Prairie* included a long list of complaints and demanded action:

> Many of the populous localities are noisome quagmires, the gutters running with filth at which the very swine turn up their noses in supreme disgust. . . . [T]he gutters at the crossings are clogged up, leaving standing pools of an indescribable liquid, there to salute the noses of passers by. . . .The only condition of health and decency, is a regular, thorough system of drainage. Such a system is feasible, and must be adopted if the "Garden City" is to be habitable.[4]

In 1850, the population was nearly 30,000. It was destined to double within three years.

Draining the City

In 1852, the Illinois legislature appointed a drainage commission that immediately went to work to dry up marshy land to the south and a little to the north and west of the city, making more land habitable and available for farming. The water from the new drains emptied into either the Chicago or the Calumet River. By 1854, the *Democratic Press* boasted that this commission had also removed the surface water from streets and the flooded cellars, which, "otherwise, become a pool or an eelpit." The newspaper was over-optimistic, perhaps a sign of the times, but it also sounded a note of caution:

> There was never, perhaps, a city with features better fitted for drainage than this. The peculiar shape of its river, with its two branches, gives easy and short access to it from every section of the town; while there is, from every square rod of its surface, a gradual and sufficient inclination to the adjacent bank. The sewers only need to be extended as they have been begun to render the town as dry as is desirable. As they are, however, of a temporary and experimental make, if they are also to be made channels of the filth of the town, they will require to be laid in a more permanent manner.[5]

Chesbrough's Sewage System

In February, 1855, the city appointed a Board of Sewerage Commissioners. The commissioners chose Ellis Sylvester Chesbrough, then city engineer for the City of Boston, to be chief engineer in charge of developing an overall sewage plan. *Chicago Public Works: A History* quotes an unnamed source extolling Chesbrough as "the most competent engineer of the times." The board gave Chesbrough two guidelines: "remove sewage and drain surface runoff."[6] His background was in canal and railroad construction, and he had received training in hydrology.

Being American and never having worked abroad, he had no experience in building sewer systems. At the time, no American city had one. Debate and experimentation with sewage systems was more advanced in Europe, especially in Great Britain, where London had built a system of intercepting sewers to prevent pollution of the Thames River.[7] In 1856, Chesbrough toured cities in Europe and, as a result of his investigations, he compiled a manual that became a standard for sewer-building. Even before his trip, he was considering four alternatives for Chicago: turning waste into fertilizer by using sewage farms; dumping undiluted waste into Lake Michigan; directing the waste to the Des Plaines and Illinois Rivers via the Chicago River and canal; and draining sewage into the Chicago River where it would be diluted before being discharged into Lake Michigan.[8]

Chesbrough considered sewage farms too expensive for Chicago and thought draining directly into Lake Michigan would cost more than draining into the river. His optimal long-term choice was to send the sewage down the Des Plaines. He knew a canal for that purpose was too expensive at the time, though he predicted one would eventually be built. He was left with only one option: draining sewage into the river that would then drain into the lake. Even though science had not advanced sufficiently to prove the relationship between disease and imbibing poor-quality water, Chicagoans were already familiar with suspicious-looking water when they saw it running from their taps—sometimes complete with fish. They needed reassurance. Responding to concerns that directing sewage into the river would endanger the city's Lake Michigan reservoir of drinking water, he said,

> It is proposed to remove the first objection by pouring into the river from the

lake a sufficient body of pure water to prevent offensive or injurious exhalations, by means which will hereby be described. . . . For the purpose of keeping the water in the South Branch fresh, it is proposed to construct a canal twenty feet wide and six feet deep at low water between the lake and the south branch through North (Sixteenth Street), and for the purpose of purifying as much of the North Branch as possible it is believed that the necessary canal should be located as far north as Center Street [between North and Fullerton].[9]

Ultimately, all of the channels constructed by the future Sanitary District of Chicago would follow his model of pulling in lake water to dilute the sewage-laden branches of the Chicago River.

Raising the City

Chesbrough designed a "combined" system to handle both stormwater and sewage. His sewers would be three to six feet in diameter and were to be laid under the city streets. This was a problem. Since the sewage would be gravity-fed into the river, there had to be a slope. But Chicago was built on land that was, at the time, only five feet higher on average than either the lake or the river and had no slope to speak of. In addition, the sewers had to be far enough below ground so they would not freeze in the winter and so that surface waters and refuse would drain freely into them. Since neither the lake nor the river could be lowered, the only solution was to raise the city.

It is almost beyond today's imagination to try to recapture the people's reaction to this suggestion. The desperation level, however, must have been great enough to lead the city council to authorize just such a project. Starting in 1856, over the next two decades, Chicago raised the grade level of its streets anywhere from two to eight feet, depending upon the location. Sand and clay dredged from the river to deepen its channel provided fill for the streets and the low ground between them, 1,200 acres in all.[10] "The new streets were huge ramps that ran level with second-story windows until people either jacked up their houses or converted their original ground floors into cellars. For years the sidewalks climbed and dipped like roller coasters. Half the town was in process of elevation above the tadpole level and a considerable part on wheels—a moving house being about the only wheeled vehicle that could get around with any comfort to the passengers. Some buildings were raised and some were not."[11] George Pullman, who went on to design the Pullman railroad car and the Pullman community south of Chicago, ingeniously designed jacks that could raise buildings without disturbing their occupants. Those who visit Bridgeport, the theater district on North Halsted Street, or other old city neighborhoods can still see how homeowners adapted various solutions to the raised streets outside their doors.

Drinking Water from Lake Michigan

Since the sewers were now emptying into the river and the river into the lake, and the lake supplied the city's drinking water, contamination of the drinking water was inevitable, despite Chesbrough's assurances. The water supply was piped from an intake in the lake to the city. By the 1860s, the city was forced to move the water intake cribs farther out in the lake and build a large tunnel to bring the lake water to the city for distribution. Meanwhile, during the Civil War, factories were running at full capacity all day long, seven days a week. This was good for the North and for the economy, but so much refuse did nothing to help Chicago's health problem. The situation was growing out of control.

By 1862, the downtown North Branch had become so putrid that the engineer from the city's Board of Public Works denied the city's new sewer outlets were responsible and claimed "that in 1860 the discharge from piggeries and cow stables high up on the North Branch made that stream exceedingly offensive at its mouth."[12] Perhaps the accumulated excrement from the live-stock foraging on the many upstream farms was the cause, or perhaps Clybourn was still growing and slaughtering livestock on the North Branch; he remained in business until his death in 1872. The engineer, reportedly Chesbrough, did not point to any particular guilty parties releasing fetid byproducts well up the North Branch.

The South Branch and the Union Stock Yards

Adding to the river's problems was the growth of the meatpacking industry. The South Branch and the Healy Slough, which emptied into the South Branch near Bridgeport, were home to many scattered packinghouses, all of which used the South Branch for disposing of unwanted by-products of their operations. Even though local governments wanted control over these industries, they seemed unable to exert their authority over this sector of business. Chicago's anti-pollution ordinance was enforced irregularly, if at all. In order to try to separate the citizens from the disease-producing and generally unpleasant conditions, it was becoming a national urban practice to relegate "nuisance" industries to the outskirts of town.

Louise Carroll Wade, writing of the stockyards, provides some particulars:

> Hoping to cure the so-called Bridgeport nuisance, Chicago extended its southern boundary from Thirty-first Street to Thirty-ninth Street in 1863. Prisoners of war were set to work cleaning up the South Branch debris, burying it in pits, and covering the excavations with lime and clay. All slaughterers, packers, and renderers on the South Branch and the Healy Slough just to the east were warned of the city's intention to enforce its ordinances. Thirty-three companies promptly signed contracts to sell offal to the Wahls, the owners of a fertilizer factory with brand new drying equipment. These actions, it was hoped, would solve the crisis....But one month into the packing season of 1863-64 the South Branch was "thick as mud, black as ink," and "sickening" to smell. All the slaughterhouses were obeying the law, said the Times, yet in some occult way the offal does move, notwithstanding, down the bed of the Chicago River.[13]

As part of this sanitizing movement, the separate stockyards were consolidated into a single entity, the Union Stock Yards, in a marshy location just south of the city limits. But the Union Stock Yards still used the Chicago River as its ultimate sewer. Octave Chanute, the resident engineer of the stockyards, designed 30 miles of channels to drain the land into two sewers, one leading to the South Branch, the other running along 39th Street and emptying into the South Fork. He designed a new ditch at the northern limits along 39th Street to receive the offal of the yards and to channel that filth, too, into the South Fork of the South Branch. The fresh water for the animals, 500,000 gallons per day, came from the clean water upstream from the sewer outlets on the South Fork. Chanute built a stone dam there to create a large reservoir from which water was piped for a mile to a well inside the yards.

Packing the slaughterhouses together did not make them more receptive to regulation. The city tried to require all slaughterhouses and related industries to obtain licenses to operate in the city, but to no avail. When the Chicago Board of Health was re-established in 1867, it was given the power to recommend ordinances to protect the lake and the Chicago River. Shortly afterwards, the city council issued the following ordinance, which bears some similarity to the original 1833 law:

> No person or persons shall throw, place or deposit, or cause to be thrown, placed or deposited any dung, carrion, dead animal, offal of other putrid or unwholesome substance, or the contents of any privy upon the margin or banks, or in the waters of Lake Michigan within the limits of said city of Chicago, or upon the margin, banks, or into the waters of the Chicago River or either of its branches . . . under the penalty of twenty-five dollars for each and every offense, and further penalty of five dollars for each and every day the same shall be allowed to remain after a conviction for the same offense.[14]

The stockyard powerbrokers were influential, united, wealthy, and fiercely independent, and the ordinance was not enforced. They continued to pour into the river the unwholesome substances prohibited above by law.

From Frogs to "Bubbly Creek"

James O'Toole, who lived in the neighborhood that came to be known as "Back of the Yards," remembered "his after school expeditions to the meandering western branch [the West Arm] of the South Fork, at that time a clean little creek with apple trees and hazelnut bushes along its banks."[15] "Old Nathanial Hart still remembers and talks of the laying of the first plank which converted the bog into a teeming mart, and exchanged the croaking of bullfrogs for the grunting of swine and the chirping of reed birds for the voices of men."[16] Soon, the South Fork became so polluted that it acquired the appellation "Bubbly Creek." Ed Lace, who grew up near the yards, tells this story:

> During the era just preceding the Civil War, a commission was formed to find a location for a combined stock yard and slaughterhouse. Too much

butchering was going on inside the city, and the resultant mess, particularly the odor, affected the sensibilities of those not making a living in the industry. A member of the commission, a Mr. Hoxie, owned property in Thornton, Illinois, which already had a railroad and two major roads passing through it, as well as a navigable stream, Thorn Creek, which was available for drainage. His recommended site was sidelined as most of the commissioners thought the location was too far from the city.

They finally agreed on an area just outside the city's southern boundary, which at the time was 39th Street. Construction began on June 1, 1865. On Christmas Day the Union Stock Yards opened, with the slaughterhouses and processing plants occupying most of the land between 35th and 47th streets and from Halsted to Ashland.

The river was the reason for locating the yards there. Blood, guts, and other waste emptied into the lower portion of the South Fork. From there, the offal oozed into the South Branch, but it could not take enough of the odor away from the main part of the city.

Nothing yet devised by the city regarding sewage control could help the South Fork, as most of its flow was not water. As the offal settled to the bottom it began to rot. Grease separated and rose to the surface. Bubbles of methane formed on the bed of the river and rose to the surface, which was coated with grease. Some of these bubbles were quite large and when they burst a stink arose. There were many local names for this part of the river, most unprintable. The one that stuck was Bubbly Creek.

Every once in a while, people who lived in the Back of the Yards, Canaryville or Bridgeport areas would take a ride over to "Bubbly Creek." As a kid in the area whose father drove a truck for Armour's Soap Works, I got to see the creek many, many times. There was a bridge over a branch of the creek, the West Arm, on Iron Street. That part of the creek is filled in. The surface of the creek looked like solid ground and legend has it that chickens could walk on it. A tale is told [by Upton Sinclair, in *The Jungle*] of an unhappy soul who sought to walk upon the water. Enough about that.

The stockyard barons were as famous for getting as much profit as possible from their industry as they were for their most famous by-product: pollution.

> Profits for such tycoons as Gustavus F. Swift and Philip Armour also came from hides, hair, wool, bones, horn, fertilizer, glue, fats and materials for toothbrush handles, chess pieces and strings for musical instruments. It became a commonplace that Chicago packers used every part of a hog but its squeal.[17]

The Union Stock Yards lasted for 105 years, finally closing in 1971. For seven weeks in the fall of 1904, Upton Sinclair roamed unchecked through the stockyards, dressed as a workingman, carrying a lunch pail, and investigating the lurid details of the workingman's Packingtown. In 1905 he published his novel, *The Jungle*, describing in agonizing detail the workers' physical and mental misery, the animals' suffering, and the industry's abominably filthy practices that led to tainted meat. Mark Twain called the book "the *Uncle Tom's Cabin* of wage slavery."[18] The book's primary social effect, however, was on food inspection laws. As Sinclair himself commented, "I aimed at the public's heart and by accident I hit it in the stomach."[19] The public appetite was greater for safe meat than it was for social justice.

In 1877, a new health commissioner, backed by reform organizations, generated enough support to indict the leading polluters, who pleaded guilty. But the court could find no precedent for what amounted to forcing a business to alter its practices, and it thus levied only nominal fines. In 1878, the city council passed an ordinance putting the police department in charge of enforcing the regulations pertaining to slaughterhouses. The industrialists did not give up quietly, but challenged the ordinance in court. It was only after the Illinois Supreme Court upheld the ordinance that businesses hastened to comply.[20] An attitude change was coming, though slowly, to the entrepreneurial frontier.

Today, you can canoe or boat on Bubbly Creek, but you may still see bubbles rising to the surface, especially on hot summer days. The bubbles come from the decomposition of organic matter on the bottom of the creek. These sediments are a combination of old by-products from the stockyards plus the more recent organic matter that is released from the Racine Avenue pumping station in big storms. As recently as March 1997, Mayor Richard M. Daley "talked of sealing off Bubbly Creek to improve water quality in the Chicago River. . . ."[21]

The I&M Canal
From Shipping Channel to Sewer

The flow of "Garlic Creek" (The Chicago River) was reversed in 1871, and some of its foul waters were carried down the Illinois into the Mississippi, but not in sufficient quantity, so that sewage continued to pour into the river and the lake, to be thrown back at Chicago by the winds and waves.

—Federal Writers' Project of the Work Projects Administration, 1939

Even before the Union Stock Yards began to discharge filth into Bubbly Creek, the Chicago River had become exceedingly offensive. The degree of offense depended upon the amount of rainfall during the summer months. There was little or no problem during a wet summer, when enough rain fell to dilute the river water. In dry summers, however, a very unpleasant odor emanated from the river. In addition, when the river water reached the drinking water cribs in the lake, disease rates began to rise.

By July 1860, due to low rainfall, the stench in the river had become strong enough to provoke the Chicago Board of Health to appoint a committee to meet with I&M Canal representatives, to "ascertain what arrangements could be made for pumping water from the river at Bridgeport into the canal, so as to create a current from the lake which should supply the river with fresh water and relieve it of the offensive sewage matter." In 1862, $10,000 was appropriated for pumping at Bridgeport.[1] Presumably the pumps began to work, because effects were felt downstream. The *Joliet True Democrat* complained that the water reeked "enough to make a horse sick."[2] The 1860 inquiry was the first record of investigating the possibility of reversing the river. Although this pumping action did not officially reverse the I&M Canal, since much more work was needed, it was the first step.

In 1863, during the height of the Civil War, 5,000 delegates from the northern states arrived in Chicago to attend the national ship-canal convention. The delegates urged the federal government to enlarge and deepen the I&M Canal so that the new and larger gunboats needed to protect the east-west trade routes from the Confederacy could travel through it.[3] The idea of enlarging the canal for military and commercial purposes fell through, but the idea of enlarging it for civilian sanitary purposes endured. On February 16, 1865, almost ten years after the Chicago River had become the city's official sewer, the state assembly approved construction of the I&M on the original deep-cut plan: cutting through the limestone bedrock at the summit section and pulling in Lake Michigan water by gravity. The idea was to dilute the water in the Chicago River sufficiently to flush it and then send the diluted water downstream. Engineers calculated that pulling 1,000 cubic feet per second (cfs) from the lake would be enough to flush the Main Stem and the South

Branch, even when the rainfall was low. By constructing the deep cut, the city believed its sewage problems would be solved. Thus, the dubious honor of carrying Chicago's diluted waste was awarded to the cherished dream of the earliest Chicago promoters, the I&M; it was to be reincarnated as a sewage channel.

By 1865, however, the river's condition was so offensive that Chicago could not wait for the deep cut. The city and I&M Canal officials agreed to increase the flow rate from the present 250 cfs to 417 cfs through the South Branch and the canal in the interim period, using the canal pumps until the enlarged canal was finished.

Making the Deep Cut

There seems to have been no formal shovel day for the deep cut. The work was begun in the late autumn of 1865 after the canal closed for the season. The work continued for six years during the off-season until it was completed in 1871. During the actual work, the pumps at Bridgeport were set in motion whenever they were needed to pull water from the lake. Fortunately, the pumping capacity at Bridgeport had been enhanced in 1859 by the addition of two steam engines.

While the Main Stem and South Branch benefited from the pumping, conditions on the already noxious North Branch deteriorated further. Experiments showed that during times of low water, the pumping in the South Branch even seemed to result in stagnant conditions on the North Branch, somehow keeping its water from emptying into the lake.[4]

By July 15, 1871, the canal had been enlarged and deepened at the summit, and the old locks in the South Branch removed so that they would not interfere with the increased rate and amount of water flowing west toward the Mississippi. It was time to celebrate. On that day, the mayor, other notables, and ordinary citizens turned out to watch the cutting of a temporary dam that had been built across the canal. They crowded onto banks and bridges to celebrate as the river reversed its course. At least one spectator saw immediate improvement in the color of the river. Other skeptical citizens watched straws floating on the surface of the water hesitate before reluctantly flowing in the direction of the canal. Andreas's personal observations were optimistic: "Quite a current was at once created, and an entire change of the water in the main river and South Branch was effected in about thirty-six hours. The 'new' I&M also had a good benefit on the North Branch, although more benefit was derived by abstaining from throwing garbage, offal and distillery filth into the Branch."[5]

Andreas reports that three days later, by the morning of July 18, 1871, "the Chicago River, with all its filth, had taken the place of the heretofore clear water at Lockport, the people of Chicago rejoicing in the great relief furnished by the deep-cut, which caused the South Branch of the river to run 'upstream.' " Shortly thereafter, the clean water from Lake Michigan reached Lockport, and the water there was "almost as clear and blue as the waters at the Falls of Niagara."[6]

The Failure of the Deep Cut

Reversing the river did not alter the weather. Conditions in the river and the canal continued to vary not only from year to year and from season to season, but also from day to day, depending upon rainfall and lake level. Storms, known locally as "freshets," continued. Freshets from the west usually caused the worst problems. They re-reversed the river and once again forced the polluted water out into the lake, fouling the drinking-water intakes.

Exacerbating the problem, the canal banks had a tendency to cave in, reducing the channel's capacity. The slower the water, the less effective the canal in reversing the flow in the South Branch and the more offensive the odor.[7] In winter, when the canal was frozen, the situation could be oppressive.

Fixing the Deep Cut with Pumps

Conditions in the entire river throughout the city were unpleasant. Conditions on the reversed canal and the river, particularly the North Branch and the South Branch's West Fork, the old portage route, had become so offensive that more action was necessary. But what? Between 1870 and 1874 there was constant discussion about the best method of alleviating the problems. Finally, adapting a previous idea suggested by Chesbrough in 1857, engineers came up with a scheme. They would build a tunnel from the lake to the North Branch at Fullerton Avenue, which is approximately three miles north of the confluence of the North and South Branches at Wolf Point. The tunnel would have reversible pumping works. The pumps could bring clear water in from the lake or deliver it out to the lake, whichever direction was necessary to flush the North Branch.

The other set of pumps would be built at Bridgeport. They would be extremely powerful and would be able to create such a strong southerly current that, when necessary, they could induce the polluted North Branch water to bypass the Main Stem and flow directly into the South Branch and down into the canal. Thus, the North Branch could be cleaned under any set of conditions.

Condition One: Current in the North Branch was slight and an artificial current was required to flush it. At those times, the pumps at Fullerton Avenue would pull lake water *into* the North Branch. Simultaneously, the powerful pumps at Bridgeport would pull the diluted North Branch water into the South Branch and then into the I&M Canal. The Bridgeport pumps would also pull the water in the West Fork, which was by now also polluted, into the South Branch. Therefore, in low water conditions, the West Fork and the North Branch waters would become de facto auxiliary channels to the South Branch and the I&M Canal.[8]

Condition Two: A nor'easter. These heavy storms would force large amounts of water from the lake through the Main and South Branches. To deal with this water, the Bridgeport pumps would be silenced. The lock at the South Branch, which had been installed to prevent backflows, would be thrown open. The force of gravity would pull all of the filth and sewage from the Main

Stem and the South Branch down the canal, chased by diluted lake water. Unfortunately, this rush of water tended to push the polluted water in the North Branch back upstream. To alleviate this situation, the Fullerton pumping works on the North Branch would pull the sewage flowing up the North Branch into the conduit and push it out into the lake. It was an ingenious scheme. As long as the filth pushed into the lake through the Fullerton Avenue tunnel didn't end up near the entrance to the drinking-water supply tunnel, it might have worked.

The construction phase had begun by June 1, 1874. The 12-foot-diameter Fullerton Avenue conduit, or tunnel, was 11,898 feet long. The powerful pumping machinery was located at the river end and consisted of two propellers and three boilers. At Bridgeport, new pumps were also required. After the I&M Canal was rebuilt on the deep-cut plan, the old Bridgeport pumps had been considered superfluous and were sold in 1873.

Problems Downstream

While the dual pumping works were being planned and built, problems continued downstream in the Des Plaines Valley. Joliet residents, who had grumbled before, continued to complain. In early 1878, the Secretary of the State Board of Health asked the locktender at Joliet to monitor daily conditions at his station for 14 months. By accident of nature, these were months of consistently low water. On September 30, 1878, the locktender reported that, following a particularly low stage, all the fish in the river had died. Residents of Joliet became so agitated over the odor that public meetings were convened to "demand relief."[9]

Pumping Fails

The Fullerton assembly was completed on January 9, 1880, and the pumping works at Bridgeport were completed in 1883. Andreas noted that in 1884, the result was "unsatisfactory, the water in the North Branch quickly becoming foul and fermenting, and in the main river, in three or four days during the summer solstice, becoming very offensive, even while pumps in the South Branch were in operation."[10] Andreas noted that the pumps were also ineffectual on the South Branch, which received the offal from the stockyards. The pumps were already discharging "the full volume of water that could be carried away by the canal without its overflowing its bank."[11]

Author Charles S. Winstone reported problems in the lake soon after completion of the pumping scheme:

> Complaints of impure water at the lake crib were investigated, and it was
> found that the pumps at Fullerton were sending the water from the North
> Branch through the conduit into the lake, instead of in the opposite direction.
> The water of the North Branch was indescribably filthy, polluted as it was
> by distilleries, glue factories and tanneries. Pumped into the lake it formed
> a distinct stream of inky blackness. When the winds blew from the northwest,
> as they often did, this stream of pollution flowed straight to the crib.[12]

It was becoming clear that the little I&M, the canal that had fulfilled Louis Jolliet's dream, provided the very stimulus for the town of Chicago, lured immigrants to the area from all over the world, and helped make Chicago the busiest shipping center in the United States, was inadequate for its second task: to be the city's second open sewer. After 1900 and the opening of the Sanitary and Ship Canal, the rate of water passing through the canal was reduced solely to that required for navigation. The I&M Canal was to be eclipsed by a bigger brother. In 1933 it would officially be closed.

Toward the Sanitary and Ship Canal
From 1880 to Shovel Day

A drought set in, in July, 1837, and from the 19th of that month until Novem-
ber, no rain fell. The streams dried up, the springs gave only brackish and
impure water, and from the low lands and partially dried up marshes and
bogs a fever-breeding miasma floated unseen to pollute the air. . . .

—Alfred T. Andreas
History of Chicago, 1885

One hot Chicago day, in the summer of 1879, a man, despite all of his efforts to hurry, was caught at an opening swing-bridge over the Chicago River, which at the time was "a serious matter to the olfactories." The man was impatient. He worried more about his health than getting to an appointment on time. "He hardly dared to draw a full breath for fear of inhaling the poisonous miasma, but he was unable to escape, and began to calculate what his chances were of escaping the terrible disease likely to be engendered by the poisonous vapors which he was obliged to breathe." The following conversation ensued:

"Pretty bad smell from the river to-day."

"Yes," answered the elder of the two [bridge-tenders], Martin Casey, "it is so bad it nearly makes me sick."

"Must be rather unhealthy to breathe such an atmosphere," said our friend, who stood trembling in his boots for fear the odor which <u>nearly</u> made the tender sick would fill his system with the poisonous virus of that odor.

"Yes," replied Casey, "I guess it is not very healthy to breathe till one gets used to it; but I have got used to it."

"Got used to it? What do you mean? How long have you breathed this terrible odor?"

"I have not breathed it all the time, of course, for I am here only half of the time during the day and night; but I have breathed this kind of air ever since I commenced being bridge-tender, which was in 1853."

"You don't say you have breathed this air during the last 26 years and not been sick?"

"Yes sir," said Casey, "I have worked on these bridges for 26 years, and the river has been awful sometimes, but it never made me sick, only to be a little sick at the stomach."

The bridge turned and our friend walked off, and wisely concluded that the odors from the Chicago River were decidedly more disagreeable than dangerous.[1]

The Miasma Theory: Disagreeable Odor Breeds Disease

The above conversation illustrates the state of public knowledge about infectious disease in the late nineteenth century, as well as the state of the river: dismal. The consensus was that disease came from the "miasma," noxious vapors generated from decaying organic matter. But here was evidence to the contrary from a bridgetender. Why? What was "known" about disease and sewage treatment as the world entered the twentieth century? Were there any realistic alternatives to the dilution strategy?

In the last half of the nineteenth century, under the rubric of the "Sanitary Movement," the miasma theory dominated public policy in health matters. While it aimed to alter the way people looked at personal hygiene, it stretched beyond the personal to the public arena. Sanitarians advocated cleansing cities by constructing large public works to provide clean water and to dispose of sewage. "Water carriage technology," or, in the common terminology—sewers—would convey human waste by water to an area far removed from the city.[2]

Germ Theory

If it wasn't the odor, what was it that spread infectious disease? The French chemist Louis Pasteur, born in 1822, unselfishly devoted his entire professional life to investigating industrial, agricultural, and medical problems. He hypothesized that the cause of infectious disease was "germs," tiny bacteria that could be transmitted from person to person through air, water, or food. New theories, however, take time to be accepted. It was not until the 1870s, 20 years after he began his work on bacterial theory, that he, Robert Koch, and Joseph Lister finally convinced the scientific community that bacteria caused typhoid fever, cholera, and dysentery.[3] There was a gap, however, between scientific acceptance and public application of the theory. It was during this very interval between "proof" of theory and development of proven technologies that Chicago found itself in desperate need of a solution.

Chicago's Dubious Distinction: First City of Filth

Public health policy shaped by the miasma theory advocated removal of organic matter before it could putrefy. Emptying sewage into a waterway that both diluted the organic matter and carried it away, far away, was the obvious answer. The I&M Canal, however, the waterway that Chicagoans used, couldn't carry the diluted waste away far enough and fast enough. The river's reversal had been in complete conformity with miasma theory and the sanitary movement, as had Chicago's sewage system that emptied into the Chicago River in 1855, but ideological conformity hardly ensures success.

Chicago's Lyman F. Cooley, soon to be chief engineer in charge of building the Sanitary and Ship Canal, spared no words describing Chicago's dire predicament in 1890. Chicago had become the First City in regard to filth.

Cooley wrote:

> Chicago produces more filth per capita than any other city. She has
> filth-producing industries of enormous proportions; her plumbing is more
> universal than any American city, certainly more than any foreign communi-
> ty, and there are no cesspools, and the soil is, for the more part, impermeable,
> —in fact, it may be said that the organic wastes of no other city, in so large
> proportion, reach the sewer outfalls. The organic wastes received by the
> South Fork alone, with a tributary population of only 150,000 people, exceed
> the produce of one million people in London, or in Massachusetts cities.
> There is very little data to indicate the product of the city as a whole, but it
> certainly exceeds that of two million, and may be as great as that of three
> million people, on the basis of cities above mentioned. About nine hundred
> and fifty thousand people are tributary to the river and its branches and forks
> (some two hundred and fifty thousand being directly tributary to the lake or
> unsewered), the sewage from which nominally reaches the Bridgeport
> pumping station and the Illinois and Michigan Canal.[4]

Chicago's major health problems were not only its stupendous production
of filth but also the typhoid fever epidemics that followed the overflows of
polluted Chicago River water into the drinking supply in Lake Michigan.
Freshets from the west, causing the Des Plaines to spill over into the Chicago
River and pour into the lake, were the most troublesome, and the Des Plaines
was overflowing its banks eastward with increasing frequency and volume. The
cause of the increased flooding was the expanding population on the Des
Plaines's upper reaches. Increasing numbers of farmers were draining the
grassy wetlands adjacent to the river. These wetlands had originally taken days
to absorb and release heavy rains; now the water cascaded off and reached
Chicago in only hours.[5]

The Ogden-Wentworth Ditch: From Bad to Worse

Exacerbating the "mischievous effect" of the Des Plaines was the "Ogden-
Wentworth Ditch." William B. Ogden and "Long John" Wentworth, both former
mayors of Chicago and big Chicago boosters, owned land in the Summit area
near Mud Lake, the fabled marsh around or through which so many had
portaged only 40 or so years earlier. Wentworth's Summit farm was over 4,700
acres.[6] According to Andreas, in 1868 Ogden and Wentworth had drained their
marshy lands in the Des Plaines Valley into a 200-foot-long, 20- to 30-foot-wide
ditch running north through Mud Lake and then turning east, emptying into the
old West Fork.[7] Knight and Zeuch disagree about the direction of flow, stating
that the Ogden-Wentworth Ditch generally followed the course of the original
channel through the north end of Mud Lake, though it was straighter and
emptied west into Portage Creek. They also describe another ditch, Nickerson's
Ditch, which generally followed the old south channel and also drained into
Portage Creek. Knight and Zeuch say that in low water periods, the "Upper Des
Plaines" diverted from its normal channel and flowed through the deep ditches
into the West Fork.[8] What is indisputable is that, during times of flood, the Des
Plaines overflowed into the ditches and on into the West Fork.

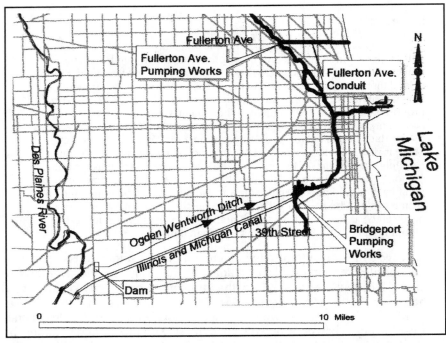

Map created by Libby Hill using ArcView® GIS software. Digital files courtesy of Northeastern Illinois Planning Commission and Illinois Department of Natural Resources.

The Ogden-Wentworth ditch and the pumping station for the deep cut scheme. Under "normal" circumstances, the water from the ditch would have flowed into the West Fork and down the reversed I&M Canal.

To prevent the overflow, in 1874 (or in 1876-1877, according to Knight and Zeuch), the city built a dam across the east arm of the Des Plaines at the same level as the adjoining land. "Its crest was about one foot higher than the old Continental Divide, the effect of this being to move the Divide west to the location of Ogden Dam, to cause the Upper Des Plaines again to flow down the valley and to lengthen the West Fork of the South Branch of the Chicago River more than six miles."[9] While the dam served its purpose on most occasions, according to Andreas it did not sit well with adjacent property owners. Entrepreneurs that they were, they wanted the land flooded in fall and winter so they could harvest crops of ice to sell; in spring and summer they wanted the land dry for agriculture. Andreas describes how, for years, these neighbors destroyed and rebuilt the dam on this cycle. Finally, in 1885, the state foiled these enterprising men and built a dam that could not be broken. The dam was built of concrete and enormous cobbles and topped by a road.[10]

Chicago on the Brink

Confronted by the failure of the deep-cut I&M, the increasing number of times the Des Plaines overflowed into the Chicago River, and the lack of effective germ theory technologies, Chicago needed to do something, but it dragged its feet. As early as 1881, even before the Fullerton Avenue conduit was finished, the city had hired Rudolph Hering, a renowned expert on sewage, to study alternatives available to Chicago for safe sewage disposal. One technique he considered was the use of "irrigation farms." Under that alternative, the city would acquire a large amount of land outside Chicago, and the city's wastes would be delivered there through an intercepting sewer. The soil on the farm would absorb the sewage, separate out the solids, and leave the cleaned effluent to be conducted into nearby waterways. Crops would grow on the fertilized soil. This idea was so radically different from the old system that it generated too much animosity for fear of smell and the cost of acquiring the amount of necessary acreage. And it was still not based on germ theory. Hering's recommendation was to forget the ineffectual I&M Canal and build an entirely new channel through which sewage could be thoroughly diluted by a great deal of lake water and flushed into the Des Plaines.[11] This idea echoed that of Chesbrough nearly 30 years earlier and garnered the support of concerned citizens.

Thus it was that the Sanitary and Ship Canal would be built on the cusp of technological breakthroughs that applied the new germ theory. (Dilution is still considered a necessary tool, just not the only tool.) Ironically, the nearly outmoded, though still useful, sewage-disposal practice of dilution, based on miasma theory, would dictate the construction of one of the most innovative engineering projects the world had ever witnessed.

Citizens Take Action

By 1880, the Chicago water supply and sewage systems were serving over half a million people. Devastating rains during the summer of 1879 had caused 30 consecutive days of discharge from the foul Chicago River into Lake Michigan. Chicago's public works, simply put, were not working for the public. Once more the water supply was polluted, and this time, exasperated citizens were provoked into action. In 1880 they formed a Citizen's Association of Chicago and appointed a Committee on Drainage and Water Supply. This Committee, following the dilute-and-send-it-away theory, suggested the construction of an entirely new channel, to be called the "New River," which would carry diluted sewage downstream. It would run in a corridor sandwiched in between the I&M Canal and the Des Plaines River, starting at the West Fork of the South Branch and ending at Joliet, $31\frac{1}{2}$ miles away. The committee proposed that this channel carry not only sewage but also ocean-going vessels. It also recommended the Ogden-Wentworth ditch be closed. The estimated cost of the New River was $7 million.[12]

The Flood of 1885 and the Epidemic that Never Occurred

Saturday, August 1, 1885, was a typical Chicago summer day. A brutal August heat wave seemed to have abated in the face of a fresh breeze off the lake. The *Evening News* had carried another in its series of editorials excoriating city officials for inaction on the foul condition of the river and the threat to the drinking water:

SLOW SANITARY MEASURES;
Experiences which Have Afflicted the City Through Official
Procrastination and Indifference;
THE RIVER AS A DISEASE-BREEDER.
Nothing Accomplished in the Way of Purifying the Stream
Which Defiles the Water Supply.

The article charged:

Most of the city officials who say the water is pure and good enough are rich enough to keep a supply of mineral water at their homes, or even to drink champagne. The mayor is so careful of his health that he keeps a tank of Waukesha [spring] water in his private office at the city hall. While the present council, which has practically succeeded itself for the past six years, has been fairly liberal in making appropriations for the health department, they have neither conceived nor advised the adoption of any practical plan for permanently purifying the river and protecting our source of water supply [Lake Michigan]. It is the poor people . . . who are the sufferers.[13]

Saturday's *Evening News* also carried the weather forecast for Sunday on the front page: "light local rains, followed by fair weather, variable winds; nearly stationary temperature."[14] The Sunday weather forecast in the *Chicago Tribune* conveyed its hope that "if it [the unexpectedly good weather] does not wear itself out before today, those who attend church may be able to go without their fans."[15]

By Monday morning, August 3, the tone had changed markedly. The *Tribune* headlined:

AND A FLOOD CAME.

Over Five and One-Half Inches of Rainfall in Nineteen Hours
in Chicago. Sewers Too Small to Carry Off This Great Quantity—
Many Basements Submerged.[16]

So much for weather forecasts.

Both newspapers reported that Sunday had been a disaster. At 4 P.M., the storm center was in Chicago but the storm itself stretched from St. Paul on the north, to the Mississippi River on the west, to Philadelphia on the east. This was an enormous tempest. Hailstones as big as hickory nuts were reported. Flood damage was tremendous. Basements all over town were soaked. The Washington and LaSalle Street tunnels filled with six feet of water. The lake piers and Lake Shore Drive were damaged severely by the "furious sea." All except one telegraph wire was out. But the immediate consensus appears to have been that it was a good thing the rain fell on a Sunday, although people in flooded areas were greatly inconvenienced trying to get to work the following day.[17]

Tuesday's *Tribune* explained why the storm did not cause an epidemic of disastrous proportions. The paper reported that:

> At that critical point where the Illinois & Michigan Canal and the south and the west forks of the South Branch converge there might, under ordinary circumstances, have occurred a flood of disastrous consequence. In a word, if the currents of these three streams—two of which are artificial—had been subverted toward their sources, that whole district of the city must inevitably have been drenched, not only with water but with the bulk of the city's filth. Happily, however, the force of the downward current was sufficient to carry the natural sewage toward the lake. This sufficed for the minor branches, while the direction of the wind—only from the northeast—sufficed to keep the stream within its natural boundaries. The ultimate effect of Sunday night's drenching has been much lighter than was to have been anticipated from the severity of the storm.[18]

The August 3 *Chicago Daily News* evening edition had gone even further:

THE SEWERS THOROUGHLY CLEANSED.
In this way the Storm was a Benefit to the Entire City.[19]

By August 17, in an article entitled "Fortunate Chicago," *The Daily News* wrote:

> Had the heavy rainfall of two weeks ago been followed by the usual August temperature and the usual southwest winds the chances are that we would have been in the height of a cholera excitement about this time. With such a mortality as obtained in the latter half of July [of this same year], and the river reeking and festering in the hot sun, it would only have needed a death or two from green apples to furnish some local "Dr. Beale" [an illness chaser] the material for more free advertising. . . . A phenomenal prevalence of easterly winds and an unusual low temperature have combined to reduce sickness and the death rate far below the average of this season of the year. The first fifteen days of August show a reduction of fully one-third in the number of deaths as compared with the last fifteen days of July. Nature has been very kind to us. On the last of July we were about as dirty a city as there was north of the Ohio River, and our death rate was about the highest of any large city in the country. On the 3rd of August we were undoubtedly the cleanest city on the continent externally, and since then our death rate has been the lowest of any large city probably in the world. Chicago may not be a pattern of morality nor an illustration of the highest wisdom in civic administration. But Chicago is very fortunate.[20]

In the end, Chicago's mortality rate for typhoid for the entire year showed only a slight rise. Asiatic cholera, which had not been present in Chicago since the late 1860s, did not reappear. The death rates from disease kept within their usual pattern.

Every Chicago River buff is familiar with the urban legend that the flood led to subsequent outbreaks of cholera, typhoid, and other waterborne diseases estimated to have killed 12 percent of the population of approximately 700,000: one out of every eight people. This would have been an epidemic akin to the

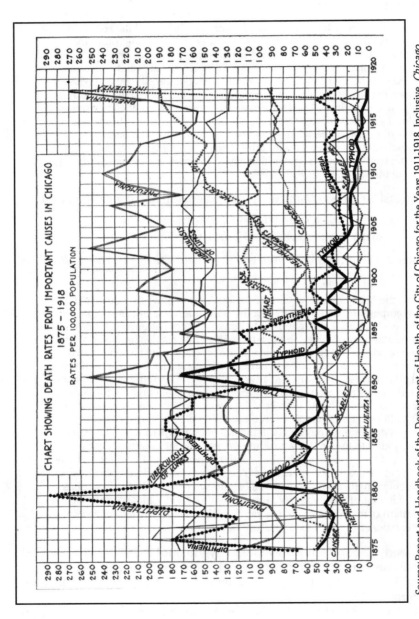

Source: Report and Handbook of the Department of Health of the City of Chicago for the Years 1911-1918, Inclusive, *Chicago, 1919.*

Note that there is no cholera, which had last been seen in the city in the late 1860s.

Black Death in fourteenth century Europe. The statistics do not support this. Finding the origin of this legend would make an interesting challenge.

Proposal for a Sanitary and Ship Canal

On January 27, 1886, the city responded to the actual flood damage and the enormous anxiety regarding water-borne disease by creating a new official body of its own, the Drainage and Water Supply Commission. Its mandate was to recommend a plan to protect the city water supply and ameliorate the condition of the Chicago River. In its early deliberations, members debated various alternatives: continuing to discharge sewage into Lake Michigan, but as far away as possible from the drinking water intakes; disposing the sewage in land reservoirs, from which the sewage could be reclaimed as fertilizer; and expanding the existing system for sending sewage down to the Mississippi.

The Commission finally recommended an incontrovertible reversal of the flow of the Chicago River by cutting a new channel along the lines proposed earlier by the Citizen's Association. While the new channel was Chicago-style bold in sheer magnitude, we can see that the proposal did not represent a significant departure from the collect-dilute-and-deliver-downstream technology in style at the time. In the new plan, the proposed canal entered the Des Plaines at Joliet. Down-river traffic would continue to use the I&M Canal. The Commission estimated the maximum Chicago River flood flow (the volume of water that passes by a particular spot in a particular time interval) at 10,000 cubic feet per second (cfs). Economist/historian Louis Cain, who has written extensively about the canal, says this was "the crucial factor in projecting its necessary size."[21]

Creating the Sanitary District of Chicago

Harvey Hurd, who headed the first drainage district in Illinois in the area centered in Evanston, crafted the legislation to create a Sanitary District for Chicago. Why was it necessary to form yet another governmental body to accomplish the task at hand? Money. Chicago was in debt to the legal limit, and the task at hand—construction of a canal—would require considerable resources. A new entity encompassing a larger area could borrow anew from a larger tax base than the city.

When the legislation was considered on the floor of the House in 1887, it was referred to a committee of five, made up of the mayor of Chicago, two members of the House from different parties, and two members of the Senate. The committee's instructions were to report to the next legislative session, two years hence. Their charge was to determine whether the people downstream would be affected by the diversion of sewage into the Des Plaines.[22] During the legislative hiatus, Chicago lobbied everyone possible to increase the constituency favoring the canal. Some proposed making the canal large enough for steamboats. Now, industrialists from all parts of Illinois, plus many from states downstream on the Mississippi, paid attention. They saw the potential for fulfillment of the dream of a "Great-Lakes-to-the-Gulf Waterway" and came on board. Proposals that the canal be a shipping channel also produced visions of competition between river and railroad that would result in depressed freight charges. This solution would both shunt the waste away from the lake and enhance the opportunity for money-making river traffic between the Mississippi and Lake Michigan.[23] Both of these purposes are reflected in the channel's name: Sanitary *and* Ship Canal.

The "Act to Create Sanitary Districts and to Remove Obstructions in the Des Plaines and Illinois Rivers" was reported out of committee in 1889 and approved on May 29. The act covered all potential sanitary districts within the state but contained particular provisions for Chicago. It is popularly referred to as "The Sanitary District Enabling Act." Sanitary districts were restricted to contiguous incorporated cities, towns, or villages within the same county. The restriction to a single county could encourage county communities to cooperate, but it would have troubling implications for the Chicago River, as it flows through two counties, Lake and Cook, and the proposed canal would run also through Du Page and Will Counties.

The mission of a sanitary district was to protect the public health by draining away wastes. But a canal with the capacity and the dual purpose of the proposed Sanitary and Ship Canal would have to be declared legally navigable. This status was fraught with difficulties.

Backers of the proposed district had to gather 5,000 signatures on a petition containing the proposed name and intended boundaries of the district and present them to the county judge. The judge would select two judges of the Circuit Court to join him in serving as the board of commissioners. After hearing comments, this commission would fix the boundaries of the proposed district. Finally, the legal residents of the proposed district would vote approval or disapproval of the district on the first Tuesday after the first Monday in November.[24]

Enough signatures were collected, and the commission set the boundaries of the proposed Sanitary District of Chicago (SDC) as all of the city of Chicago north of 87th Street, the incorporated towns of Cicero and Lyons, and a part of Lyons Township—in all, 185 square miles. The exclusion of the area south of 87th Street was at least partly because it was in the Calumet River watershed. North and northwest areas were excluded because they were primarily devoted to farming. On November 5, 1889, in a landslide vote, epic even by Chicago proportions, the citizens of the proposed Sanitary District voted 70,958 for and 242 against. The judges lost no time in performing their duties, and the required nine-member Board of Trustees was elected in December. The first meeting of the Board of Trustees was held on January 18, 1890. The SDC was a reality. Although a canal was not actually required by the Enabling Act, several sections attended to specifications "if" a canal should be built for sanitary purposes between Lake Michigan and the Des Plaines River.

Section 17 of the act empowered any sanitary district to " 'enter upon, use, widen, deepen and improve any navigable or other waterway, canal, or lake' when it proved necessary."[25] Sections 23 through 27 were specifically addressed to the proposed Sanitary and Ship Canal. Section 23 specified:

If any channel is constructed . . . by means of which any of the waters of Lake Michigan shall be caused to pass into the Des Plaines or Illinois rivers such channel shall be constructed of sufficient size and capacity to produce and maintain at all times a continuous flow of not less than 300,000 cubic feet of water per minute [cfm, or 5000 cubic feet of water per second (cfs)], and to be of a depth of not less than fourteen feet, and a current not exceeding three miles per hour, and if any portion of such channel shall be cut through a territory with a rocky stratum [which of course it would be, the Silurian dolomite] . . . such portion of said channel shall have double the flowing capacity above provided for. . . . If the population of the district . . . shall at any time exceed 1,500,000, such channel shall be made and kept of such size and in such condition that it will produce and maintain at all times a continuous flow of not less than 20,000 cubic feet of water per minute [333.33 cfs] for each 100,000 of the population of such district, at a current of not more than three miles per hour. . . .[26]

Using these figures, if the population reached 2,500,000, then the channel would need a capacity of 8,333 cfs. If the Drainage and Water Supply Commission were right about how much water per second the system could deliver in total, that is, 10,000 cfs, and if the law were right about how much was needed per 100,000 of the population, then the system could accommodate 3,000,000 people. The law allowed a 10,000 cfs flow *if* the channels of the Des Plaines or Illinois River were appropriately deepened. Note that the formula was based on population; the needs, uses, and effluent of industry were not part of the calculation.

The act established a maximum current in the river (three miles per hour) and the depth of the waterway under various conditions, and created a commission, responsible to the governor, that would attest to the satisfactory completion of a canal before it could be opened. Section 24 specified that, once the channel was completed, if the "general government" improved the Des Plaines and Illinois Rivers, the new canal would be declared a "navigable stream," but the general government would not be able to "interfere with its control for sanitary or drainage purposes."[27] Although the act did not require that a canal be built, it obviously anticipated such a venture. The question was still on the table as to what form the canal would take. Two things were certain: Chicago's big plans for sanitation and shipping meant that the SDC would have to widen, deepen, and improve the Chicago River at considerable expense. Conflict with the federal government, which by the turn of the century considered itself in charge of navigable waterways, was inevitable.

Population Growth of Chicago 1833-1900	
1833:	about 350*
1840:	4,470
1850:	29,963
1860:	112,172
1870:	298,977
1880:	503,185
1890:	1,099,850
1900:	1,698,575
1910:	2,185,283
1920:	2,701,705
1930:	3,376,438

Source: Bureau of the Census, U.S. Census of Population: 1950.

* Andreas, vol. 1, 174.

Planning the Canal

Lyman Cooley, instrumental in forming the SDC and disappointed not to be on the original Board of Trustees, was appointed first chief engineer of the district. Cooley, perhaps by inclination or perhaps in response to the inaccurate estimates for the reversed I&M Canal, left no stone unturned and no reach ungauged in documenting the requirements for a successful channel. Exasperated by his slow pace, the board terminated his services by a vote of five to two without a mention of cause. Then, three trustees resigned during the first year. When time came to replace them, in a nice piece of irony, Cooley was elected to one of the seats.

The SDC Board vs. the I&M Canal Commissioners

Meanwhile, the board was wrestling with the channel route between the South Branch and Summit. Three possibilities were under consideration: enlarging the I&M Canal, building a new channel which connected to the West Fork, and building a channel that followed 39th Street and connected to the West Arm of the South Fork, where the putrid effluent of the stockyards was at its worst. Based on cost, the board decided on an enlarged I&M Canal, with a substantial pumping station at Summit. The I&M Canal property was available to the SDC for free, or so the SDC Board was advised, and the route offered fewer problems with railroad crossings. The plan was short-lived, however, as the I&M Canal Commissioners raised objections, and the SDC attorney rendered an opinion that a limited-capacity channel and pumping station were contrary to the enabling statute.

Perhaps the nail in the coffin was the demand by the I&M Canal Commissioners to maintain control over the new canal and charge for its use. That brought the Illinois Attorney General into the dispute. It appeared that the only way to settle the questions between the SDC and the I&M Canal was to submit to a lawsuit with uncertain outcome and delay. In May, 1893, the SDC Board reconsidered and selected a route that would provide for a new large-capacity channel connecting to the historic West Fork at Robey Street (now Damen Avenue). The I&M Canal was not to be disturbed.

Rerouting the Des Plaines

To enable digging in the Des Plaines riverbed, the SDC had to re-route 13 miles of the Des Plaines River into a diversion channel. For this purpose, it built a 19-mile levee to separate the Des Plaines from the new channel both during and after construction. Work began on August 24, 1892. While the diversion channel and the levee were under construction, it was necessary to limit the flood flows in the Des Plaines. A spillway was built near the present-day western suburb of Riverside so that excess water in the Des Plaines would be diverted through the Ogden-Wentworth Ditch to the Chicago River. This plan was taking an obvious chance on the weather. Fortunately, a major flood did not occur during the period of construction. The spillway was eventually raised to the level of the levee to prevent floodwater from heading toward Chicago.

More than 100 years later, this levee still separates the Des Plaines from its old bed. It is wide and substantial and invites a good hike into history.

Shovel Day

"Shovel Day" for the Sanitary and Ship Canal was September 3, 1892, although groundbreaking had already taken place for the Des Plaines diversion channel. *The Chicago Tribune* championed the event, considering it comparable in importance to driving the Golden Spike, the historic moment that had joined the eastern and western sections of the first transcontinental railroad in 1869. Chicago dignitaries turned out in full force and fancy dress for the festivities, as they had for the commencement of work on the Illinois and Michigan Canal, though this time few common folk were represented.[28] Mayor Patrick Haley of Joliet, one of many speakers, gave an address indicating the relief the long-suffering citizens of Joliet were anticipating when enough water to dilute the sewage would run in the Des Plaines. He said, "Our citizens and committees representing them have co-operated with like committees from Chicago, in framing the present act under which the work which was so auspiciously begun today is expected to be consummated. All the people of the valley and all the people of Joliet are satisfied when the Board of Trustees honestly and in good faith live up to the letter and spirit of the law."[29] The ceremonies inaugurated what president of the board Frank Wenter proclaimed as "a mighty channel which will rank with the most stupendous works of modern times. . . ."[30]

An End to River Fires

One more insult to the Chicago River that was to be abated by the new canal was fire. According to some accounts, its oily surface burned. In 1949, an anonymous writer reminisced about going down to the river as a child to watch the flames. He says that it was not unusual for the river to burn, but says

> . . . it was still something of a show, however commonplace. . . . The fire
> that we watched from a south side bridge on that mellow spring afternoon
> in 1889 may well have been the last of its kind that Chicago was to see, for the
> opening of the sanitary canal in January, 1900, restored the river to a more
> or less liquid consistency. It was a weird exhibition more memorable for the
> attitude of the crowds than for anything startling in the play of bluish flames
> across the surface of the water.
> "Looks better at night" said an experienced river-fire watcher who stood
> next to me at the rail. "You can see it better at night, account of the dark."
> Somebody behind me asked a policeman: "Is there water under there?" And
> the policeman answered wearily, "I wouldn't be sure." Come to think about
> it, I wasn't so sure myself. It lacked smoke, and brilliance, and flying sparks,
> and uproar and fire engines and the other things that might make such shows

memorable. There was some dramatic expectancy about it, thanks to the policemen who wouldn't let anybody loiter on the bridge except those who could find a place at the rail and every now and then shouted instructions about what to do when and if the pier took fire.

But the day was saved, really, by a tug that came along pushing a contrivance of sheet iron that looked something like a snowplow. This device rolled the fire ahead of it and actually mixed it up enough to toss up a lot of sparks and a column of greasy smoke. "Well," said somebody, a little sadly I thought, "that saves the grain elevator." I took another look to see the blaze being herded into the middle of the river. And then my grandfather took me home. So far as I know the river hasn't burned since.[31]

Fire department records for the City of Chicago show no responses to river fires because real property was not burning. The fire department responded to burning tugboats, barges, and various ship paraphernalia, but the total number of records of anything burning on the river is insignificant and far less than the number of prairie fires responded to by the department.

Both wildfires and rivers are almost irresistible elemental forces to people. Witness the fascination recorded in diaries about huge prairie fires lighting the sky. When fire and water combine, it is no wonder that they cause more than a little nostalgia.

Building the Channel that Saved Chicago

I have often wondered if science will not some time provide a better way to utilize our sewage than to spend $33,000,000 in throwing it away.... However, I am delighted to think that I have been permitted to see the day, when the river, partly freed from its pollutions, promises to be restored to its original condition, and that it may again swarm with its former finny occupants.

—Edwin O. Gale

In the 1850s the city council had ordained that the level of the swampy city be raised ten feet, and it had been done. In later decades the municipal authorities had ordered that the flow of the Chicago river be reversed, and so it was reversed. The achievements of government in Chicago at times rivaled the feats of the Old Testament God.

—Jon C. Teaford
The Unheralded Triumph, 1984

The Sanitary and Ship Canal was not designed all at once. Many decisions were made and many different contracts let at various times during construction. In just the four years between 1889 and 1893, there were four different chief engineers. After being hired in 1893, however, Isham Randolph, brought a new era of stability to the project when he retained the position for 14 years. One of the issues he resolved was the conflict over whether a powerhouse at the terminus of the channel would be within the financial ability of the district. He was able to recommend a low-cost approach within their means but without a powerhouse.[1]

The Design

The channel as finally completed ran for 28 miles from Robey Street (Damen) to Lockport. To the "summit" (now the village of Summit), 7.8 miles, the Main Channel was built through soils of various textures on the Chicago Lake Plain. This section of the channel is 162 feet wide at the bottom and 234 feet wide at the water line. From Summit to Willow Springs, 5.3 miles, the soil layer thinned and the channels were cut mostly through glacial till. This section is 202 feet wide at the bottom and 299 feet wide. From Willow Springs to Lockport, 14.95 miles, the bedrock was at or near the surface, and after the mantle of soil was removed, the rock had to be blasted. This section is 160 feet wide at bottom and 162 feet wide at the water line. Throughout its 28-mile length from Robey Street in Chicago to Lockport, the channel bottom has a

Courtesy of the Metropolitan Reclamation District of Greater Chicago.

Men guiding a hopper into place under the cableway on August 31, 1894, near Lemont. At this location the channel is cut out of solid rock for its full depth. The solid rock has been broken up by dynamite and will be manually loaded into the hopper. The men are guiding an empty hopper that was just lowered from the cableway. Next to it lies a full hopper. The chains and yoke will be disconnected from the empty hopper and connected to the full one. The full hopper will be hoisted vertically and to the side where its contents will be dumped onto the spoil piles seen in the background. The cableway spans the entire breadth of the work area from towers on each side. One tower can be seen in the background. The towers are mounted on tracks so that the cableway can move along the length of the excavation. Several cableways were in use so that rock removal could proceed at several locations simultaneously.

slight slope, dropping 5.7 feet.

The discharge from the channel was through the Lockport Controlling Works. These works consisted of seven vertical sluice gates and a horizontal gate called the "Bear Trap Dam." The vertical gates were lifted by chains and hoists, and water could flow under them when they were opened. The Bear Trap Dam was so-named because it resembled the jaws of a bear trap. When the dam was lowered, it would allow water from the channel to pass over it, thus providing a means of flushing debris and ice downstream.

In addition to the Main Channel, the original project involved building 31 bridges, relocating the Des Plaines River in the construction zone, and erecting the terminal controlling works at Lockport. The final construction cost of the channel from Robey Street to Lockport was $31,163,032.

Moving Earth: Ingenious Inventions

The completed canal constituted the largest public works excavation project ever undertaken up to that time. More earth was moved than in any previous effort. It resulted in a gigantic stride forward in the technology of earth moving. New and powerful steam shovels, developed before canal construction began, made up the majority of the machines in use. Each of the conditions required its own unique technology. The Heidenriech Incline, the Mason and Hoover Conveyer, and the Bates Conveyer were among the innovations born of this project. The techniques used became known as the "Chicago School of Earth Moving."[1] Carl Condit observes that, "The machines and techniques of excavation developed for the Chicago project demonstrated the feasibility of digging the Panama Canal from 1906-1914."[2]

Sidewalk Superintendents

During construction of the canal, spectators, including visitors to the 1893 Columbian Exposition, thronged to the site. Seymour J. Currey, an historian and contemporary observer, describes a typical visit:

> Excursion parties from the city and other localities frequently visited the scene. The view in the rock section was especially impressive. Beneath was a level floor of rock, while on either side of the channel rose the perpendicular walls, cut through the stratified layers of limestone, rising to a height of thirty

Courtesy of the Metropolitan Water Reclamation District of Greater Chicago.

Two inclines at the rock section near the Cook-Will county line on May 17, 1895. This part of the excavation is nearly completed. In the background, beneath the tilted inclines, work is proceeding in the removal of rock at a facing. The loose rock will be loaded onto hoppers suspended from the lowest end of the incline. When the hopper is full it will be lifted off the ground and pulled up the slope of the incline to the upper end, where the contents are dumped onto the spoil pile. The incline on the left appears to be in the process of dumping rock. The photo illustrates the river-canyon effect.

feet or more for many miles. Temporary stairs and ladders were in use at various points to permit of entering and leaving the channel. The long vista between these walls, running true and straight as far as the eye could reach, made an impression on the beholder comparable to that of standing at the bottom of a river canyon in the west.[3]

Resorting to the Court

When the members of the SDC Board of Trustees were planning the canal, they were following their legislative mandate. Their priorities were to keep drinking water safe, to dilute and drain away polluted water, and to provide for navigation.

The issue of water quality in the Mississippi at St. Louis was the first major sticking point. St. Louis lies just below the junction of the Illinois and Mississippi Rivers, and the Mississippi was the source of drinking water for that city. The canal was to flow into the Des Plaines, which combines with the Kankakee to become the Illinois River. Conflict with St. Louis furnished much of the drama as the day of completion drew near.

St. Louis had become concerned about the potential polluting effects of the Sanitary and Ship Canal on the Mississippi River as early as 1898, but it

Courtesy of the Metropolitan Water Reclamation District of Greater Chicago. Description from the February 10, 1897 Proceedings of the Board of Trustees of the Sanitary District of Greater Chicago, 3839.

Just downstream of the present confluence of the Calumet-Sag junction with the Main Channel, where a 19-foot-high rock wall was built atop the bedrock, there was a great rock slide on the night of September 23, 1896. "The entire wall . . . went into the Channel and was buried by a mass of muck and soft clay which extended across the Channel for about 130 feet."

wasn't until April, 1899, that their study committee reported a probable threat. St. Louis decided to petition the United States Supreme Court to enjoin the SDC and the State of Illinois from discharging sewage into the new canal. Legal wheels sometimes turn slowly, and unfortunately for St. Louis, the word of its intent was out well before any legal action was taken. It wasn't until mid-January, 1900, that Missouri, on behalf of St. Louis, joined court proceedings. By then, it was too late to be effective.

When the SDC got word of the threatened injunction, they faced a dilemma. The Sanitary District Enabling Act required that all work on the canal, including the enlargement of the Des Plaines River below Lockport to Joliet so the Des Plaines could accommodate the additional flow, had to be completely finished before the governor could approve opening the channel. The governor had appointed a three-person commission to advise him as soon as the work was done. By December, 1899, seven years and four months after it was begun, most of the canal was complete. Only the work on the Des Plaines section remained unfin-

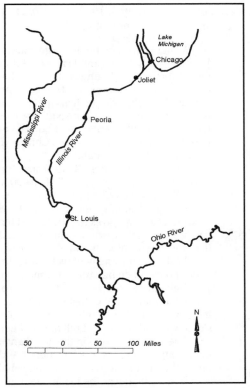

Map created by Libby Hill using ArcView® GIS software.

The geographic relationship of St. Louis and Chicago, with St. Louis on the downstream, or receiving end.

ished, but that was enough to delay the commission's approval. There would have been no hurry to open the canal except for St. Louis's legal threat. After all this work, nothing was going to stop Chicago from opening its pride and glory, especially not this last-minute maneuvering by St. Louis. Afraid that any prior notice of opening would speed up the Court's schedule on the injunction, Sanitary District officials acted in the frigid early morning hours of January 2, 1900.

The setting was near Kedzie Avenue at the Collateral Channel, which the SDC had built on a line with Albany Avenue to connect the West Fork to the Sanitary and Ship Canal. There, about a mile west of the starting point of the canal, the "needle dam," a temporary barrier at the head of a temporary wooden flume at the top of the embankment, was holding back the waters of the Chicago River. The flume led down the slope to the bottom of the canal. When the dam was removed, only a controlled amount of water would enter the new channel, thus preventing a too-rapid filling that would have caused erosion. On January 3, 1900, *The Chicago Tribune* brought alive, in great detail, the previous day's activities:

> Water was let in the drainage canal from the Chicago River yesterday [January 2] morning, and last night a thin coating of the murky fluid covered the bottom of the channel as far as Willow Springs. The opening of the greatest ship canal ever constructed in America and the informal completion of one of the engineering feats in the world's history was accomplished without ceremony. The nine Sanitary Trustees with their engineer, Isham Randolph, simply went to the Kedzie avenue [*sic*] connection of the West Fork of the South Branch of the Chicago River and the canal and saw the thin ridge of earth cut through.
>
> The consummation of the project, on which the people of Chicago have expended upwards of $33,000,000, was free from the formalities which marked "shovel day," when the work was inaugurated on Sept. 3, 1892. But there was no fear of injunctions on "shovel day." The enemies of the project by which Chicago gives to the State a ship canal were not so persistent on that day as they have grown to be as the canal, in spite of all obstacles, has neared the time when water should fill its banks. . . .
>
> While the turning in of water was simple and business-like, it was attended by much nervousness among the trustees for fear of injunctions. Two belated newspaper reporters who came rushing across the earth piles caused a small panic until it was seen they carried no injunctions with them. It was with a feeling of relief that the water finally was seen pouring down the sluiceway without a legal bill having been called.
>
> The trustees started in the gray light of dawn, and their coming was unannounced except to a few friends and two newspapermen; who at midnight had received a tip that the canal was to be opened.
>
> B.A. Eckhart was the first to reach the narrow watershed at Kedzie avenue and Thirty-fifth street. He jumped out of his carriage, dragging with him a set of new shovels for the trustees. The shovels were of the common kind with no silver handles.
>
> "I had an awful time getting these shovels at this time of day," said Mr. Eckhart, as he deposited them on the bank, just above the place where a dredge was already hard at work throwing up the clay from the cut. . . .
>
> Before long trustees Carter, Braden, Jones, Wenter, Kelly, and Mallette arrived. Seizing the shovels, the trustees jumped down the embankment and began throwing the loose earth out of the cut. Loud shouts of approval greeted their efforts, but a few shovelfuls apiece sufficed to cover the honor of opening the canal. It was plain that the Big Dredge No. 7, when it came to throwing earth, was worth several hundred of the most distinguished trustees ever produced. The trustees crawled back and waited. By this time there were fifty or more people gathered around the cut.
>
> After a while the dredge gained a point where its great arm could reach no further. Large chunks of ice and frozen clay blocked the way. Less than eight feet separated the waters of the lakes from the waters of the Mississippi, but the solid nature of the soil made the obstacle almost as great as if the distance had been as many miles. Some one set up a plea for blasting out the ridge. Soon a dozen brawny arms were driving in the bars which were to make the holes for the blasts. It was exceedingly slow work, for the clay was like a rock in its hardness. Four large charges of dynamite were placed in the ridge. The crowd, which by this time had grown to a hundred or more, beat a retreat and hid behind timbers or sought shelter [behind] a stationary dredge

near by. It was expected that the earth would yawn as by magic under the power of the explosive and the drainage canal would be opened amid salvos of dynamite and the rush of flying clay. President Boldenweck, who had arrived sometime previously in company with Trustee Smyth, claimed it as a prerogative of his office that he and he alone should touch the button. Thereby he cut short a controversy between Trustees Carter and Braden as to which one should have the honor.

The button was officially touched and a sullen roar was the answer. A few fugitive pieces of clay did fly into the air, but as a grand opening it was a failure. When the crowd rushed back to the cut it looked about as it did before. Then the ambitious trustees, armed with their shovels, descended into the cut and began to push away the pieces of clay and ice which held back the lakes. President Boldenweck was particularly active in the futile endeavor. Chief Engineer Randolph watched the rivulets of ice water trickle through the breaches the official shovels had made in the ridge and bethought himself of the dam, or sluice gate, which had been made at such expense and foresight to keep back the waters he was now so anxious to see pouring through. A gang of workmen was ordered to remove the dam before it ever had been used. The trustees gave up their feeble endeavors to keep the blocks out of the cut and fell on that dam with vigor.

For an hour previously some of the spectators had maintained a fire with old timbers and the general riff-raff of canal building. The fire in no small degree had kept the crowd from freezing in the bitter wind from the western prairies.

"Put the dam in the fire," commanded Mr. Jones, and into the fire went the structure which for so many days had been pointed out as evidence of good faith in not opening the canal until the State commission had given its consent.

Then the crew of the dredge renewed their efforts to get within range of the cut. If its great arm could not cut a hole through the narrow ridge of clay and ice the day would end in another defeat of the trustees. The crew tugged and pulled to get their unwieldy craft into the breach. At last the "spuds" went down to the bottom of the river again and the long arm was extended towards the Mississippi. It reached. A great shout went up when the dipper brought up as much earth as a team of horses could have hauled away.

"It is but a question of a few more shovelfuls now," exclaimed Mr. Wenter, as the long arm swept to the westward and dropped its load on the spoil bank. With the regularity of a pendulum the arm of the dredge swung back and forth. Each time it carried a load of clay from the fast-disappearing watershed. The ice from the river rolled in and blocked the channel which had been cut through by the dredge.

"Push the ice gorge away with the arm," shouted the foreman to the man who controlled that mechanism. The arm dropped behind the ice gorge, and then with resistless motion swept the whole of it into the Mississippi Valley.

". . . . It is open! It is open!" went up from scores of throats as the water at last, after two hours of constant endeavor, had been made to start down the toboggan slide into the canal. The fall from the surface of the collateral branch, as it is called, of the West Fork of the South Branch of the Chicago River, to the bottom of the drainage canal was $24\frac{1}{2}$ feet. The cut through the bank of the canal was about twelve feet wide and was planked up for some ten feet. The cut ran nearly straight almost to the bottom, and then shot eastward until, where it emptied into the canal, it was nearly at right angles to the channel. This was to avoid washing away the banks on the other side by the rush of water.

"It is the Niagara of Chicago," Mr. Eckhart said, as he stood watching the waters of the West Branch, together with the ice and clay bowlders [sic], sweep down the chute and drive far into the wide canal, whose surface already was beginning to take on a rich mahogany brown as the river water covered the boy's skating pond.

The consummation of the great event was celebrated by the trustees by gathering on the timbers at the end of the chute and having their pictures taken in a group. Engineer Randolph stood at the end of the structure and waved his hat triumphantly. The flooding waters sent heavy spray over the feet of the men on the pier, and threatened to carry the group, the pier, and all the rest into the canal beneath. Like school boys on a vacation, the drainage officials waved their arms and shouted. It was soon over, however, and the crowd returned to the dredge, whose clicklike motion was steadily widening the cut through the watershed. As each dipperful was taken out the flow of water was increased and the spray at the foot of the chute went higher and higher."

Then the trustees went to celebrate over lunch at Trustee Kelley's home.[4]

When writing officially of the occasion, Chairman of the Board Frank Wenter gave a more modest account of events. He recommended the following be printed in the proceedings: "On the morning of January 2nd, 1900, at about 10:35 the barrier which held back the water from the flume . . . was cut and the waters rushed into the Main Channel . . . "[5] The wastes that entered the Chicago River now spilled away from Lake Michigan and began to fill the new channel. But the Bear Trap Dam at Lockport was still high. Lowering the dam would allow water from the canal to pour over it into the Des Plaines. This action also required approval of the three-man commission and a signal from the governor. After 12 days of filling, regardless of the fact that the Joliet section remained unfinished, it was time to lower the dam. Again, subterfuge was the order of the day. In the early hours of January 17, 1900, knowing that the injunction on behalf of St. Louis against the canal was pending that very day, the special commissioners and canal trustees inspected the still unfinished Des Plaines riverbed section near Joliet. The dissembling commissioners then contacted Governor Tanner by phone at dawn, requesting—and receiving—his consent to open the dam. Cain describes how, "By 11 A.M. on January 17, 1900, a 'crowd of men, weary and worn from loss of sleep and looking haggard in the foggy morning light' were assembled to witness the lowering of the bear-trap dam at the Lockport Controlling Works. By mid-afternoon the trustees were celebrating at a big lunch in Chicago as word came that St. Louis had filed for an injunction that morning."[6] It was too late for St. Louis. In Chicago, jubilation filled the air. The *New York Times* hailed the event, exclaiming, "The Water in the Chicago River Now Resembles Liquid."[7]

The Sanitary District Report of the same event was more reserved:

. . . . The Bear Trap Dam was used, and at 11:05, in the presence of Trustees Boldenweck, Braden, Carter, Eckhart, Jones, Kelly, Mallette, Smyth and Wenter, the crest of the dam was lowered until a thin sheet of water flowed over it. In this position it was held until President Boldenweck introduced Col. Isaac Taylor, President of the Special Commission, who in a few appropriate words stated the facts relating to the satisfactory completion of the work and the permission granted by the Governor. As soon as he ceased speaking, President Boldenweck gave the word for action. The valves were opened and the massive steel dam settled beneath the torrent which rushed over the crest, and at 11:16 the official act was accomplished and the flow of the Sanitary Channel was passing into the Des Plaines Valley.[8]

Historian Currey reminisced about the huge project in a 1914 newspaper article:

In the course of construction the total amount of material excavated amounted to some 43,000,000 of cubic yards, the whole volume of which, if it were deposited in Lake Michigan in forty feet of water, would make an island one mile square, with its surface twelve feet above the water line. It is no exaggeration to say that the Chicago Drainage canal is one of the greatest artificial waterways ever constructed. Other canals may have cost more, and they may exceed this in depth, but this canal has a greater cross section than any other in existence. None has presented half the difficulties which were encountered and overcome in this undertaking, but to this work neither the general government nor the State of Illinois has yet contributed a single dollar.[9]

The New Channel: Long, but not Long Enough

The new channel did not go far enough for SDC purposes. Although navigable, it came to a dead end at Lockport. The channel and I&M Canal paralleled each other for 28 miles from Robey Street to Lockport, but did not interconnect. If the navigable channel could extend as far as Joliet, it could replace the I&M Canal. Also, the Des Plaines dropped some 36 feet between Lockport and Joliet. The SDC wished to recover the lost energy in the cascading Des Plaines for the purpose of generating electricity. The original 1889 act did not authorize the SDC to build a powerhouse and sell electricity, but the act had been amended for these purposes in 1903. Prior to that year, the SDC planned the channel extension from Lockport to Joliet.

Building the extension took from late 1903 until 1907. The four-mile extension consists of two miles of channel between parallel levees above the floor of the Des Plaines Valley bottom and another two miles of channel cut in rock. The powerhouse is at the midpoint of the four-mile extension. Here the water level drops 36 feet from the Main Channel on the upstream side of the powerhouse to the Des Plaines on the downstream side. Adjacent to the powerhouse, the SDC built a navigation lock and a discharge control gate. The navigation lock was small, but allowed for expansion for the planned Great-Lakes-to-the-Gulf Waterway. At the time of construction, it was the highest lift lock ever built, allowing boats to overcome the 36 feet difference in the reach between Joliet and Lockport.

From 1907 until 1928, the SDC sold electricity to municipalities for street lighting. Subsequently, it was used by the SDC to operate the West Side Treatment Works. After 1939, the electricity was "sold" to Commonwealth Edison as a credit for electricity purchased elsewhere from the utility company.

To enhance hydroelectric generation, the SDC built the Willow Springs

Spillway in 1908, one mile below Willow Springs Road on the northwest bank of the channel. This spillway allowed excess flood flows from the Des Plaines to discharge into the channel. Extra water meant more electricity and more revenue for the SDC. The entire cost of the Main Channel extension was $7,114,000.

The Aftermath: Water Quality Downstream

Had the fears of St. Louis been on target? In 1902, the SDC released a report of a survey supervised by Arthur R. Reynolds, the commissioner of health for the City of Chicago, and carried out by scientists from the University of Illinois and University of Chicago. The survey claimed that if St. Louis's water was foul, the slaughterhouses and distilleries at Peoria and Pekin were to blame for polluting the Illinois River. The problems could not be traced to the reversal of the Chicago River:

> Of the facts demonstrated in the report, your attention is especially invited to that which shows that running streams, adequately diluted, do purify themselves from sewage pollution. . . . All talk of Chicago sewage injuriously affecting the drinking water at St. Louis is thus completely and effectually disposed of by the work of these investigators. . . . As to the improvement of the river and the South Branch, no one who crosses a bridge from Rush street to Robey, or who lives, works or offices in the vicinity of the main river and South branch, can fail to notice the change in the atmosphere since that date [that the channel was opened in January, 1900].[10]

The State of Missouri v. the State of Illinois and the Sanitary District of Chicago was the first pollution case brought before the U.S. Supreme Court. In over 8,000 pages of testimony for both sides, experts testifying on behalf of Chicago stated that at the confluence of the Illinois and the Mississippi Rivers the water in the Illinois was of superior quality to the water in the Mississippi. In 1906, Justice Oliver Wendell Holmes, Jr. delivered the majority opinion, which supported Chicago and the continued operation of the Sanitary and Ship Canal. Subsequently, St. Louis built filtration works.[11]

The canal had been predicated on the assumption that the SDC service area would grow to a population of three million. If the region's population had grown no larger, the canal (along with its sister canals soon to be built by the Sanitary District) might have been an adequate solution. But the Chicago area continued to grow. By the turn of the century there were already 1.7 million people living in Chicago alone. No city in the history of any civilized people had ever grown so large so fast, in just 70 years. Population in the SDC service area reached three million before 1920.

Were the outfalls of waste turning portions of the Des Plaines River, Illinois River, and maybe even the Mississippi River into an open sewer? Had the population growth already outstripped the Sanitary and Ship Canal capacity? Were other measures necessary to supplement the canal? Did the prior positive research hold up? Two biologists from the Illinois Natural History Survey described what they found in the summer of 1911:

> [We] had . . . what may be called septic conditions for twenty-six miles of
> the course of the Illinois from its origin [at the confluence of the Kankakee
> and the Des Plaines Rivers approximately twelve miles downstream of Joliet]
> to the Marseilles dam. At Morris, which is on the middle part of this section,
> the water . . . was grayish and sloppy, with foul, privy odors distinguishable
> in hot weather. . . . Putrescent masses of soft, grayish, or blackish, slimy
> matter, loosely held together by threads of fungi . . . were floating down the
> stream. . . . [12]

It appears that, in this study at least, Chicago's canal was implicated after all.

The latter part of the nineteenth century had seen years of near astounding technological progress. It seemed that nothing was impossible. David McCullough has written that

> . . . there really seemed no limit to what man might do. . . . While an official
> report . . . might contain the expression "under Providence" (in conjunction
> with certain accomplishments), such terms seemed perfunctory. Man, mod-
> ern man—the scientist, the explorer, the builder of bridges and waterways
> and steam engines, the visionary entrepreneur—had become the central
> creative force. [13]

In this context, it might be argued that the technological marvel of reversing the Chicago River was something not so much to be amazed at as to have been anticipated. It was as much a product of its age as it was of Chicago's "I Will" spirit.

Part III

The Twentieth Century

From The Evanston Small Parks and Playgrounds Association's Plan of Evanston, *1917.*

"The Affluent Boating on the Effluent." The vision of the channel banks by Evanston planners, including Daniel H. Burnham, Jr., in 1917. On the left is a high-speed boulevard and on the right is a bridle path. The North Shore Channel winds to the northeast toward Lake Michigan in the distance. Today the banks are tree-covered to the waterline. Ladd Arboretum lies between the banks and the road, McCormick Boulevard. Although those familiar with the North Shore Channel will think this bridge is Church Street, the drawing's caption in the *Plan of Evanston* says the view is from the bridge at Emerson Street.

Photo by Robert M. Kaplan.

The pumphouse beneath Sheridan Road at Wilmette Harbor, with the Bahá'í House of Worship in the background.

The North Shore Channel and Straightening the North Branch

In three years we will see pleasure boats running up and down on its blue waters.

—George W. Paullin,
Shovel Day, September 26, 1907

In other words, the affluent would go boating on the effluent.

—Anne O. Earle
"Intake and Outflow" Slide Show and Talk
Evanston Historical Society, February 6, 1987

It is nighttime along the North Shore Channel. The foresters are at work taking down the cottonwoods. These foresters do not work for union wages; they are a beaver family, whose bank den has yet to be discovered. Take a walk on a spring morning, making your way down through the scrubby growth to the chain-link fence next to the canal. There you will find fresh woodchips at the base of conical tree stumps, a dead giveaway that beaver are at home here on this eight-mile-long artificial waterway. The channel, built by the Sanitary District of Chicago between 1907 and 1910, is a magnet for waterbirds, warblers, and people seeking solitude. It does not meander like a real stream, there are no rocks and riffles, but there are surprises for the onlooker at every bridge. Deer find this corridor appealing and, with luck, could start along this channel and stroll all the way from Wilmette Harbor close to downtown Chicago.

The channel was not built for the sustenance of wildlife or the regeneration of the human spirit, though it serves these purposes. It was built, plain and simple, to get rid of the decomposing and noxious filth in the Chicago River's North Branch. The North Shore Channel and the associated widening of the North Branch into which it emptied were the Sanitary District of Chicago's first twentieth-century projects after the furtive opening of the Sanitary and Ship Canal. The channel did not signal a new vision as much as, once again, it represented the application of the old dilution approach.

By 1863, Chicago had annexed territory north to Fullerton Avenue. Fullerton, therefore, was the farthest north the city could build a conduit and pumping works to bring Lake Michigan water into the North Branch to overcome the shortcomings of the reversed I&M Canal. But in 1889, the same year the Enabling Act for sanitary districts was passed, the city annexed a large amount of territory. It expanded its boundaries north to Devon Avenue, absorbing the Town of Jefferson and the City of Lake View. These communities had been involved in bitter dispute over the location of sewers; neither wanted sewers located within their boundaries. When both communities were simultaneously annexed to Chicago, the debate was resolved. One sewer serving both communities was built along Montrose Avenue, emptying, of course, right into the river and exacerbating the already noxious conditions.

When the Sanitary and Ship Canal was designed, it was not intended to solve problems on the North Branch, just those on the Main Stem and the South Branch. In its earliest discussions, the Chicago Sanitary District deliberated several options to address the problems of the North Branch within the city. The solution they finally chose was the excavation of an entirely new channel from Wilmette to the North Branch at Foster Avenue, in Chicago, to carry a big flush of Lake Michigan water.

Before the North Shore Channel: The Big Ditch(es)

The general route the SDC chose for the new channel had already been used for a drainage ditch. On February 15, 1855, the state legislature had incorporated a drainage commission that included parts of Niles, New Trier, Jefferson, and Evanston Townships, south to Bowmanville in Chicago. Harvey Hurd of Evanston, later the co-author of the original legislation for the Sanitary District, was secretary and guiding spirit. The commission raised money by assessing people who lived along the route of the planned drainage ditches and had the most to gain from the commission's projects.

Perhaps Hurd's initial interest in drainage was associated with his interest, along with that of his law partner, Andrew J. Brown, from 1850-1854, in purchasing and platting a large tract of real estate in what was to become the western part of Evanston.[1] In this vicinity, water was trapped in a low wet prairie basin between the Rose Hill and Wilmette spits, created by Glacial Lake Chicago's erosion of the Highland Park Moraine. The formation of the Hurd Commission in 1855 and its major undertaking, the "Big Ditch" to the east of the "Big Woods," in the general area of Hurd and Brown's proposed "development," is certainly suggestive.

The Big Woods was a large wooded tract, emerging from the wet prairie at approximately today's Prairie Avenue in Skokie and stretching west toward the North Branch and northeast into Wilmette. Low, wet prairies and marshes were interspersed with the woods.

The Hurd Commission's first project was to dig a ditch to the east of the Big Woods and create a road, so that Benjamin Emerson, said to be Chicago's first milkman, could get his product to market. Emerson's 160-acre claim lay just west of the corner of what is now Golf Road and McCormick Boulevard, on the border of Skokie and Evanston. He had hewn most of his farm from the Big Woods. (The author lives on what was Emerson's sheep pen.) The process of building the road was to dig a ditch and throw the dirt up into a dike. Many of Evanston's first streets were laid out in like manner by this same commission.[2]

The Big Ditch was the commission's second project. The ditch followed the contour of the lowest-lying land from Wilmette at Lake Michigan south to the North Branch at Foster Avenue. It was located about halfway between the Big

Woods on the west and Ridge Avenue on the east and was designed so that there was a divide at what is now Central Street in Evanston. North of Central, the ditch emptied into the lake near today's Wilmette Harbor. South of Central Street, the water traveled about six and one-half miles to empty into the North Branch near Foster Avenue. This ditch, whose depth or width we do not know, was probably dug in the late 1850s and early 1860s.

After the commission completed the Big Ditch to its satisfaction and added a commissioner from Glencoe, its next objective was to drain the Skokie Marsh, the lowland on the western borders of Winnetka, Glencoe, and Highland Park. This new drainage ditch emptied into the East Fork of the North Branch, or the Skokie River. In times of flood, however, the North Branch backed up through this ditch into the Skokie Marsh. The commission took another tack. It excavated a ditch eastward through the Wilmette spit to Lake Michigan at the northern end of Kenilworth. The Skokie, being about 40 feet above lake level, provided ample fall for a watercourse, and this "Kenilworth Ditch" successfully drained the southern end of the marsh, "reclaiming" valuable acres of farmland.

The commission's work was so successful that it considered extending the ditch farther to the north and/or to deepen it, a project that met with fierce resistance and a lawsuit. One George Hessler, a district resident, refused to pay his assessment. The commission sued. It won the suit in a lower court, but in January, 1870, the Illinois Supreme Court declared the commission unconstitutional on the grounds that it was a private corporation whose authority to tax had not been granted by vote of the people.[3]

Since all of the records of the Hurd Commission were burned in the Chicago Fire of 1871, detailed research into the commission's projects is impossible. We do know from reading the minutes from Evanston Board of Trustees meetings that in March, 1868, the commission had collected $371 for digging the Big Ditch and spent $368.99. The minutes also reveal that the Big Ditch was not working as expected. The water at the south side of town was flowing northward toward the village, and the trustees wished the ditch to be dammed.[4]

By mid June, 1872, another drainage commission had been appointed under a new drainage law. This commission also embarked on a project called the Big Ditch, but limited it to Evanston alone. This "new" ditch began one and one-half miles west of "Calvary Station" near Oakton Street and ran straight northeast to empty into Lake Michigan. On June 15, 1872, the *Evanston Index*, never even referring to Hurd's work, reported: "One of the most important works now in progress . . . is commonly known as 'The Big ditch.' . . . There is a long wide stretch lying a mile or two west of the lake which, though gradually growing better, was, only a short time ago, little better than a lake, fit only for the dwelling place of frogs. The improvement named will transform this wilderness into a garden and make it 'blossom as the rose,' while the land so lately worth very little will sell for enough to pay the necessary assessments, and give the owners large profits. We shall watch the progress and completion of this 'Big ditch' with a good deal of interest."[5]

The new commission acquired land and dug a ditch four miles long, an average depth of six or seven feet, 20 feet wide at the top and six feet wide at the bottom.[6] Although some people complained that this drainage was drying up their wells, the commission continued its work. It had completed enough of the ditch by June 10, 1874, for the *Index* to notice that developers were buying land in west Evanston and that property values were on a dramatic rise.[7]

What became of Hurd's Big Ditch? At least a remnant of it was still there by century's end, though "out of commission."[8] Its profile still appeared on a USGS topographic map in 1895. Hurd was a strong advocate of Evanston's annexation to Chicago's Sanitary District. He was skeptical that the SDC's original plans to build a pumping station at Lawrence Avenue, just south of Foster, to draw a large amount of lake water westward to flush the North Branch would not succeed. He argued that the North Branch would have to be deepened considerably in order not to flood Evanston in cases of heavy rain. The problem was his own Big Ditch. In times of flood, the North Branch had backed up through it into the wet prairie as far as the south boundary of Evanston. In order to protect Evanston's sewer system from further flooding, a dike had been built on the south and west city limits to stem the tide.[9] It is unclear how this dike relates to the dam requested by the Evanston Board of Trustees in the late 1860s. Inclusion of the North Shore Channel satisfied Hurd's concerns.

The SDC: Annexing the North Suburban Communities

The proposed North Shore Channel ran through territory originally outside of the jurisdiction of the Sanitary District of Chicago. The district found it necessary to extend its boundaries to the north to flush the North Branch, as well as to the south to accommodate the needs of Chicago's growing Calumet area.

As of 1901, some prominent property owners in Evanston were still wary of joining the SDC. Skeptics feared that the new canal could not work as planned, so that even if they joined the district, they would never gain anything from it. They worried that this proposition was simply a ploy by their southern neighbor, Chicago, to annex their city.[10]

Spring, 1902, was very wet and was followed by a particularly devastating summer rainstorm. Cases of diphtheria escalated, and the weekly *Evanston Index* printed an interview with Dr. Henry Hemenway, a prominent local physician who went on to become a linchpin in the Illinois Department of Public Health. Dr. Hemenway linked the incidents of disease with the poor drainage in the western part of the suburb where poor people inhabited poor dwellings. He stated:

> . . . . Again, within the city of Evanston there are many humble homes unprovided with pure water, without drainage, and often surrounded with water which stagnates under their floors. Disease that attacks the occupants of those homes may easily be communicated to the children who live in palatial dwellings. . . . Probably the Evanston sewers now take as much water as did the old ditches [the Big Ditches] but that is not sufficient. . . . The Niles land [the land to the west] is better ditched today and more water is delivered on our border. It seems to the writer that we cannot afford to risk our water

supply which would result should efficient drainage to the lake be given. There is only one really satisfactory solution to this problem, and that is to become eventually a part of the drainage [SDC] district. . . . [T]here is too great apathy on the part of Evanston to this subject of drainage. Don't wait for an epidemic of diphtheria, for example, but begin to study the subject at once, for purely selfish if no higher reason, for whether we will or no, we are our brother's keeper.[11]

Perhaps this argument had its impact on the skeptical property owners.

In May, 1903, the Illinois General Assembly passed an act to enlarge the boundaries of the Sanitary District. The *Index* supported the proposition specifically because the legislation prevented the SDC from levying special assessments on local territories for local improvements, but required the entire district to pay for all projects. Evanston and Wilmette would not have to bear the financial brunt of the channel. The *Index* regretted that the citizens would not have a vote of ratification, but it felt that a timely solution to the growing problem of polluting Lake Michigan more than compensated for this "coercion." A process of petitioning and voting throughout the entire district had been provided for in the legislation, if there were interest; if there were none, the act would be in force. The *Index* feared that voters in the district as a whole might not vote in favor, and that, in any case, the vote, which could not be held until the November, 1904, election, would delay plans for the new channel. No petition was circulated and no vote held. The 1903 boundaries became law. The SDC now included almost the entire North Branch watershed up to the northern border of Cook County, with the exception of a very small portion of the West Fork, just south of today's Lake-Cook Road.[12]

The Sanitary District set to work immediately on a final design of the North Shore Channel. Since the channel would only run through the communities of Wilmette and Evanston, it was assumed that Evanston and Wilmette would somehow automatically be connected with the new channel, while the northern and western communities would have to make their own arrangements for hook-ups with the Sanitary District.[13]

It turned out that even Wilmette and Evanston had to make individual arrangements with the SDC.

Straightening the North Branch Meander

The intersection of the proposed new channel with the North Branch posed two problems. The first was that the channel would join the North Branch just above a natural meander in the river, and the second was that the bed of the natural North Branch was higher than that of the proposed channel. As Hurd had argued, the North Branch would have to be considerably expanded.

More than enlargement was called for. The river meandered for a two-mile stretch between Lawrence and Belmont Avenues, flowing through an area of cultivated fields and pasture, meadows, clay pits, brick ovens, a mushroom patch, and backing onto subdivisions and Sharpshooters Park, the precursor to the famous amusement park, Riverview, which sat at Belmont and Western

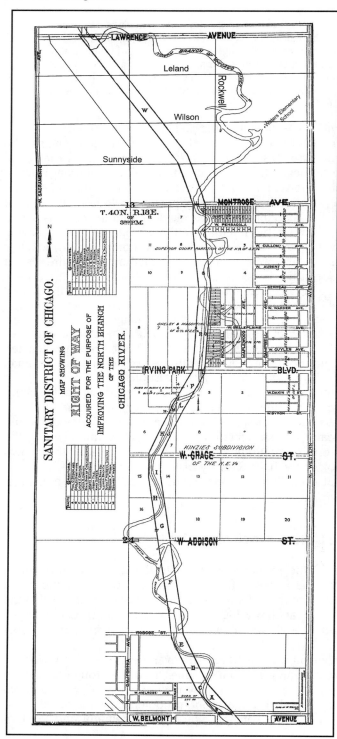

The Sanitary District of Chicago's map showing the old and proposed channels of the North Branch between Belmont and Lawrence Avenues. Streets have been added to the large parcel, W, above Montrose Avenue. The greatest distance between the old and new channels is less than 2,000 feet at Wilson Avenue. The total distance from Western Avenue to Sacramento Avenue, from the right to the left sides of the map, is only three-fourths of a mile.

Avenues. In the vicinity of Chicago's current Wilson Avenue, the "weedy ditch, harboring a few small islands," swung lazily to the southeast. A Mr. Peter Haual remembered that it "overflowed its low banks in spring and extended for about an eighth of a mile in each direction."[14] The perhaps apocryphal tale told of one Miss Sarah Argo, the first school teacher in Albany Park, probably around 1911, sheds light on the fickle nature of the North Branch above Belmont.

> Since Miss Argo's (one room) school was so far from the city, she decided to move into this neighborhood, so, one fine spring morning she came to the suburb of Albany Park to look for a house. It differed from the Albany Park of today. Weeping willows lined Lawrence Avenue instead of telephone wires. Enterprising realtors put up gay lanterns. It was beautiful, in the country, away from the city noises. Houses were few and far between and one could see Western Avenue on the east, the horizon on the west, and on the north the river. When Miss Argo saw that river she was sure Albany Park would be her home, and she picked a site overlooking it. Since she was born in a small Illinois town on the Mississippi, she loved the sound of the current. Now she was to live near the big city and still have her countryside and river. That very day she signed the deed.
>
> But alas, her joy was short lived, for when she returned to her new found paradise, the next week, her beloved river had dwindled to but a trickling stream. Nevertheless, Miss Argo never regretted her moving to this district. Even if the river wasn't roaring, there was running water, electricity, telephones and other modern conveniences that weren't in every day use at that time.[15]

In order to accommodate the increased flow of water from the North Shore Channel, the Chicago River from Lawrence to Belmont would have to be channelized into a relatively straight line. The river route below Belmont flowed in gentle curves and was not an impediment; its route was never changed, only dredged.

The SDC's Subcommittee on the Improvement of the North Branch of the Chicago River was appointed on January 30, 1901, to acquire rights-of-way to the necessary land. The subcommittee took almost as long to assemble the 23 individual parcels as its original optimistic two-year time frame for all activities, letting of contracts, and actual construction.

The project was divided into two sections. Section 1 extended from Belmont Avenue to Montrose Avenue, and the contract was awarded to Great Lakes Dredge and Dock Company. Section 2 extended through the Northwest Land Association's holdings, between Montrose and Lawrence Avenues. Callahan Brothers & Katz, an Omaha, Nebraska firm, won that contract. Each company assumed the responsibility for investigating the nature of the land by inspecting clay pits and the river bank to determine "the character of the material to be encountered."[16]

Callahan Brothers & Katz began construction on May 10, 1904, on Section 2. They began the cut with a machine capable of digging through dry land. But the company had badly miscalculated. By October 5, the "contractors unexpectedly encountered a soft, wet and soggy material commonly called 'swamp muck' " that would not support "steam shovels, cars, horses or scrapers."[17] With the approval of the SDC, they conveyed their contract to Great

Lakes Dredge and Dock, which was working from south to north. Without great additional expense, however, Great Lakes Dredge and Dock could do no work on Section 2 until its machines, excavating from the south in Section 1, reached Montrose. The company finally resumed work on Section 2 in June, 1906; completed the entire channel; and let water into it on August 13, 1907. By December 2, 1907, three years past the original due date, they had leveled the spoil banks and filled in the old riverbed. The final result, 2.2 miles of a sweeping arc of a river, 90 feet wide and 12 feet deep, was straight enough to carry the combined waters of the North Shore Channel and the North Branch.

The contractors' responsibility was to dig the new channel and use the dredgings to fill in the old, plus the adjacent low-lying lands. In some cases, they agreed to cover an area with black dirt sifted from the diggings. Ravenswood and Albany Park farmers were said to be very happy with the project because they were paid to haul dirt from the new channel to fill in the old.[18] The farmers could only have trucked fill between May and October, 1904, for Callahan Brothers & Katz, however, because Great Lakes Dredge and Dock pumped the excavated wet and dry dredgings to the old channel meander through a conveyor.

The delay in construction plus a disagreement about the process of depositing the fill, a method that had created a "landscape" of mud and water, resulted in a rather bizarre lawsuit filed against the SDC by Chicago Title and Trust as trustee for the Northwest Land Association. The association had deeded, at no charge, a right-of-way along Section 2, knowing full well that the SDC would fill in the soggy land for free and create land that the association could then sell for a killing. But a full two years after the channel had been completed, on January 20, 1909, Chicago Title and Trust posted signs along the channel, reading "Private property of trust company, trustee." Two days later it began court action, charging, among other things, that the SDC had not adhered to its promised timetable and had not put all of the dredgings from the channel on its land; it demanded the return of the right-of-way that it had donated. The SDC lost the first round, but in April, 1917, the Illinois Supreme Court reversed the verdict.[19] Charles Yerkes, the rapid transit tycoon, and his Northwest Land Association had gotten all they wanted or needed: dry land suitable for development, to which Yerkes's transit lines could carry the new residents. The Sanitary District retained its right of way on the river channel.

Building the North Shore Channel: Evanston on the Alert

With straightening of the North Branch nearly complete, the way was clear for construction of the North Shore Channel. Shovel Day was September 26, 1907. Evanston Mayor Joseph E. Paden was on hand to praise the project, but he gave the SDC public notice that Evanston would be closely monitoring the character of the workers on the channel. "It is quite probable that many people will be brought temporarily into the city who are not accustomed to the surroundings which exist here. The policing of the district will be a great problem . . . We are also vitally interested in the question of having the work done in such a way that the appearance of the city will be preserved and all unsightliness eliminated."[20] That was a tall order for a construction project, particularly one that was to go the entire length of Evanston, and adhering to these requirements cost the SDC considerable expense.[21] Judge Harvey Hurd, the Evanstonian, the man with the longest history in drainage in Illinois, and the strong advocate of expansion of the Sanitary District, never lived to see Shovel Day; he died in 1906.

It is unclear from sources whether work began immediately after Louise Paullin, the 12-year-old daughter of SDC Trustee George Paullin of Evanston "put her tiny spade into the earth and filled the small bucket that stood at her feet with dirt,"[22] or whether, as historian Seymour Currey says, work did not really commence until the following April.[23] Regardless of the schedule, Currey reported that slides on the slopes occurred during construction because 20-30 feet of very soft clay underneath the banks slumped under the weight of the spoil piles. Slumping would not be a problem once water was turned into the channel. When the 8.14-mile channel was completed, it was 90 feet wide at the surface, 30 feet wide at the bottom, and varied from 11 feet to 13 feet deep. (Today, with sedimentation, it is much shallower.) The Sanitary District itself hired most of the workers, desiring "to inconvenience the residents as little as possible."[24]

Some Evanston and Wilmette residents had high hopes for recreation on the channel. The *Plan of Evanston*, published by the Evanston Small Parks and Playground Association in 1917, contains a drawing that depicts pleasure boats plying the channel. On Shovel Day, Louis G. Pierson, a member of the state legislature from Wilmette, voiced his enthusiasm: "The other day my boy wrote an essay in which he said that some day one could take a pleasure boat at Wilmette and ride in it to New Orleans. He was a prophet. That's what we shall be able to do when the system of which this branch of the drainage canal is a part is completed."[25]

To get the lake water into the channel it was necessary to design pumps because, at the time, the lake level was usually below the level in the channel. The pumping works were housed in an attractive building topped by Sheridan Road just west of today's Wilmette Harbor. They consisted of four screw pumps and a 140-foot-long lock, which was 11 feet deep and 30 feet wide. Bill Wente, executive director of the Wilmette Harbor Association, describes how the lock worked:

> On the east side, a gate slid back and forth, like a pocket door. On the west side there was a gate that opened out into the canal. When the channel got too high they let the water run through to the lake. In the early days, when the locks were in working order, people in little pleasure power-boats would make advance reservations to lock through on Saturday and Sunday afternoons from noon until four. There were no sailboats because of the bridge.[26]

The spoil from the excavation not only piled up on the banks next to the canal, but went for fill for the shallows along Evanston's lake shore and also to make land that was to become Wilmette's Gillson Park along Lake Michigan. Wilmette's problem with turning the land into an attractive park illustrates the nature of the spoil described by Currey: "As this land consisted of nothing but

Photo by Robert M. Kaplan.

The sluice gate that controls the flow of water from
Lake Michigan into the North Shore Channel.

impervious blue clay, nothing would grow on the new land. It took six years of cultivating, plowing with horse teams, and planting with cow peas, until finally about 1917 they were able to get grass and trees to grow."[27]

Lake water was turned into the channel on November 29, 1910. The channel's completion was hailed by the traditional fanfare. Evanston expected that very soon its waste and stormwaters west of the watershed divide along Ridge Avenue would flow through new sewers, away from the lake and into the canal. On September 7, 1912, Paullin promised speedy relief to Evanston and recommended a "proper proportionate contribution of the City of Evanston" for the connecting conduits and where those outlets would be."[28] The SDC not only balked at paying the entire cost of the conduits, but also, it wished the connection to be at Colfax and Noyes Streets, near the northern boundary of Evanston and close to the channel. This location would have created an open sewer running through most of the city, and Evanston did not approve.

The negotiations were complicated by court action brought against the SDC by an Evanston resident who challenged the SDC's right to build a pumping station and intercepting sewers leading to the channel. The Illinois Supreme Court decided for the SDC, supporting the district's right and responsibility to build intercepting sewers to keep pollution out of Lake Michigan. But, as the old cliché goes, the devil is in the details. The SDC and the city eventually reached a compromise agreement calling for the SDC to pay for the connections to be made at Lake Street, just outside the western city limits, with Evanston responsible for maintaining the bridges over the channel. It was not final until 1916, four years after negotiations opened.[29] By 1920, outlet sewers to the North Shore Channel had been built at Emerson and Lake streets and a pumping station was in operation draining the low land along Evanston's lakefront. The SDC was now pumping Evanston's raw sewage away from the lake, into its artificial arm of the Chicago River, the North Shore Channel.

Building the Dam: Problems and Solutions

As noted earlier, the level of the North Branch was higher than the level of the proposed channel. The junction would create an unstable situation in which the natural North Branch would drain from the west into the lower waters of the newly deepened and widened North Branch just below the confluence. To address this problem, the SDC built a dam to restrain the North Branch from eroding its banks and silting up the waterway to the south.

The 82-foot-wide, eight-foot-high-dam was constructed in 1910. It was designed so that, in flood, the water would pass over the entire 82-foot-width. A shallow notch, 12 feet wide and two feet deep, was built into the top to allow lower flows to pass over the dam. At an even lower level, the SDC cut a small circular gated outlet, two feet in diameter, to permit water to pass through even at times of lowest flow in the river. It seemed as if the dam would work under all conditions.

All was not well with the dam, however. One problem was flooding basements. Another was increased river erosion behind the dam, and a third was the dam itself.

In 1938, in the heart of the Depression, the City of Chicago requested Works Progress Administration (WPA) funds to rehabilitate the North Branch reach from the dam north to Devon Avenue, the city line.[30] A few years earlier, from September, 1934, to May, 1935, an Illinois Emergency Relief Project had employed approximately 500 men to clean and grade (dredge) this same section of the river and establish a uniform North Branch profile that would reduce flooding and remove stagnant pools. It is unclear from the Department of Public Works records whether the work proceeded beyond Crawford Avenue (now Pulaski Road) to the city limits at Devon, but it is clear that the entire project did not receive a good report card.[31] And whatever positive results had been accomplished had not been effective near the dam.

In 1939, the Chicago Department of Public Works received approval to proceed with one mile of the new WPA project from the dam to Lawndale Avenue. This time the work would involve more than just grading the river bottom; the natural river bed would be re-surfaced by an 18-foot concrete slab. The slab would be designed in such a way that, after a flood, the receding water simply could find no low recesses in which to form stagnant backwater pools. Banks were to be reinforced at riverbends, offending trees were to be removed, and timber-cored levees were to be placed where areas of high flooding were anticipated.[32]

WPA Project No. 30284, "Cleaning and Grading the North Branch of the Chicago River between the North Shore Channel and North Lawndale Avenue," began on February 23, 1940.[33] High water in the spring and summer of 1942 hampered progress, and the concrete lining was only installed to Ridgeway Avenue, less than one block west of Lawndale. Because it was wartime, materials were in short supply, and the project was terminated in September;

Photo by Libby Hill.

Looking north, the dam is on the left and the North Shore Channel is on the right.

no work was ever performed by the WPA in the reach between Ridgeway and Devon.

Residents living near the newly-lined riverbed were enthusiastic about the project. Water stayed in the bed of the stream even during times of high rainfall instead of invading neighbors' basements. No silt could erode from the concrete bed and even the shored-up banks appeared solid. The upstream and downstream channels seemed safe, at least temporarily.[34]

Unexpectedly, ponding began to appear behind the dam in periods of low water. In 1940, the SDC cut a deeper notch into the dam. This notch, more toward the center of the dam, was nine feet wide at the top, six feet wide at the bottom and six feet deep. But even this notch proved to be too narrow and frequently became clogged with logs. Much later, in 1965, the SDC established a metering system to measure flows passing the dam, but the clogged notch disrupted even the ability to make accurate measurements of the flow. To solve the clogging problem, the SDC widened the notch to 23 feet. The new part of the notch was four feet deep. Now, both debris and water could pass through it.[35]

The 1950s: Surging Population and Surging Water

After World War II, well after sewers had been installed and the North Shore Channel was no longer an open sewer, population swelled in the North Shore suburbs and inland North Branch communities. The more people, the more baths and showers, car washing, dishwashers, washing machines, and all of the other amenities that characterized post-war suburbia. Hence, the more sewage.

On October 10, 1954, and again on July 12, 1957, torrential rainstorms hit the Chicago area. Sewers overflowed into the North Shore Channel and the only recourse was to let the sewage out through the harbor into the lake. At Wilmette, in July, 1957, "They waited too long to open the gate. The water level in the channel rose so high it poured over the locks. The gates wouldn't open so the pumping station was flooded to the brim; the pumps were completely inundated. It was a very costly affair."[36] The pumps, despite their soaking, were operational until 1975 when, in order to prevent excessive leakage through the pump tunnels, the gates on the pumps were sealed.[37] They can be re-opened manually if necessary, to draw water into the channel.

In 1961, the SDC replaced the old lock gates with a vertical sluice gate, the same width as the old lock chamber. The gate, when fully open, could allow a boat to pass, since the bottom of the gate could be raised as high as the bottom of the Sheridan Road bridge. To pass a boat, however, the water levels in the harbor and channel would have to be the same. Obviously, this retrofitted structure was not designed to be used as a navigation lock. There would be no more weekend pleasure-boat outings.

The first time the Sanitary District opened the new sluice gate to let stormwater into the lake was on September 13, 1961. They did so without forewarning the harbormaster. "The surging water played havoc with the boats moored in the harbor. Three Flying Scots were washed out into the lake and were recovered off Evanston, six other boats were sunk, and Dr. Kent's 38' cruiser, 'Lolita' had a large hole punched in the topsides. The harbor crews worked from 12:45 P.M. when the locks were first open until 4:30 A.M. the next morning trying to save boats. The sluice gates have been opened many times since but the Sanitary district now provides a warning so that the harbor can be better prepared."[38]

The Wilmette Harbor's picturesque location is set off by the Bahá'í Temple in the background. The attractive pump house, the sandy beach, the boats in their moorings, and the landscaped hills form an appealing entrance to the North Shore Channel. Bill Koenig, a member of a family with a long history in the area, recalls that as late as the 1960s, "we would drive to the harbor to buy fresh perch from commercial fishing boats docked at the lock."[39]

The policy of the landowner, the Metropolitan Water Reclamation District of Greater Chicago, has been to lease land on either side of the channel for recreational uses. The communities along the banks of the North Shore Channel have nurtured street-level projects that enhance this open space. The city of Evanston, along with the Evanston Environmental Association, for instance, maintains the Ladd Arboretum, anchored by the Ecology Center. Skokie has developed a sculpture park between Dempster Street and Touhy Avenue and a boat launch at Oakton Street. And an uninterrupted bicycle path connects the communities of Evanston, Skokie, and Lincolnwood with Chicago. The steep banks of the channel remain untamed, mostly inaccessible to humans but a corridor for wildlife.

The challenge for the communities living along the North Shore Channel is to develop a common plan for the corridor. The MWRD's challenge is to balance at least four requirements, only one of which is in its mandate. It needs to keep the water flowing by clearing debris and over-vegetation; that is its mission. It must control the sometimes unpleasant odor emanating from the stream, particularly during a string of dry weather during the summer. It must satisfy the residents' desires for peace, beauty, and recreation. And it must continue to provide for wildlife's needs for a green corridor. The MWRD's sensitivity to these diverse needs is crucial to its good government image. This artificial extension of the Chicago River system, with its densely wooded banks, its misty summer evenings, and its animal life, has become a precious amenity, a haven for people seeking tranquillity and wildness.

Reconnecting the City and the River after the Turn of the Century

Make no little plans. They have no magic to stir men's blood and probably themselves will not be realized. Make big plans. . . . Let your watch word be ORDER and your beacon BEAUTY.

—Attributed to Daniel H. Burnham[1]

At the dawn of the twentieth century, after the construction of the Sanitary and Ship Canal and the improved water quality it brought to the Main Stem and South Branch, Chicago's attitude towards the downtown river began to improve. Pivotal to new prospects for the river was the shift of heavy commerce and its bulky accompaniments to the southern part of the city at Calumet Harbor. Another element was a positive national change in attitude toward the environment and toward public participation in public projects, especially city beautification. The consequences would be felt not only downtown but on all of the Chicago River's branches.

The Ascendance of Calumet Harbor

The Chicago Sanitary District's reversal of the Main and South Branches was accompanied by the river's slowly declining importance in the commercial life of the city. Because the harbor at the Chicago River was unavailable to vessels during rough weather, Congress had appropriated $50,000 in 1870 for improvements at Calumet Harbor, also in Chicago. The now-familiar enhancements were undertaken there: deepening and widening the Calumet, removing a sandbar at its mouth, and building parallel piers into the lake. By the late 1880s bulky raw materials for steel went to Calumet, while less bulky products still came through the Chicago River.[2] The city would lose no revenue, but the exodus permitted the downtown river to evolve from a cluttered, unsightly channel jammed with ramshackle wharves, all types of cargo vessels, and sprawling warehouses, into a majestic stream dominated by pleasure boats and bordered by buildings of architectural significance. Capt. William Marshall of the War Department had foreseen this transformation. He favored a commodious Calumet Harbor because he believed the crooked Chicago River had reached its capacity and because he foresaw that Chicago's river banks would be more valuable for uses other than for grain elevators, lumber yards, coal yards, docks, and wharves.[3]

A Proliferation of Voices

By the turn of the century, a host of new voices was demanding to be heard regarding the river. It was no longer possible for one government bureau to make decisions on its own. In 1880, the Citizens Association of Chicago had been a single voice demanding attention be paid to the health of the city. Now, many governmental agencies and jurisdictions, special interest associations, and citizen groups had to review and approve any changes to the river. In his history of the Chicago District Army Corps of Engineers, John W. Larson observes:

> . . . though such a trend was still in its infancy, there began to be a prolifer-
> ation of government and quasi-governmental agencies as well as private
> associations, corporations and firms that had to be consulted. In the course
> of carrying out the 1909 survey [for improvements of rivers and harbors at or
> near Chicago], Corps officers at Chicago consulted with the State of Illinois
> Rivers and Lakes Commission, the Sanitary District of Chicago, the Chicago
> Harbor Commission, the Mayor of Chicago, the Chicago Plan Commission,
> the City Council of Chicago, and officials of adjacent cities. Among the
> associations which became involved in the study were the Citizens' Associa-
> tion of Chicago, the Lumbermen's Association, the Chicago Association of
> Commerce, and the Shipmasters' Association, plus businesses and hundreds
> of smaller organization which were asked to provide information on their use
> of water transportation needs.[4]

The Committee on the Universe: An Informal Voice

In this fresh atmosphere of reform and citizen participation, some influential Chicagoans were defining their personal responsibilities for Chicago's future. During a 1990 interview, Larry Perkins, son of Dwight Perkins, founder of the architecture firm of Perkins and Will, described this thoroughly unstructured group who met for lunch and at each other's homes a century ago as their schedules permitted:

> These people called themselves by the rather self-effacing title of the
> "Committee on the Universe." . . . and the Committee on the Universe was
> where they had the conversation . . . that led to the Chicago Small Parks
> Board. Some put in time on that, but some of the people out of that picked up
> one ball and some picked up another. . . . They were just fun people who felt
> they had some responsibility about what they could do something about.
> The Forest Preserve was one of those sparks thrown off by this group. . . .
> [The group] later evolved . . . into the Cliff Dwellers, [who were] heavy into
> the fine arts and oh, as you very well know I'm sure, Grant Park and that
> whole concept. It was Mr. A. Montgomery Ward's moral force that forced that
> one through.[5]

The Burnham Plan's Prescriptions for the River

The advantage of Daniel Burnham's 1909 *Plan of Chicago* was that it fused earlier recommendations, such as Montgomery Ward's vision of a grand lakefront and the Committee on the Universe's forest preserves, with some original ideas of its own and related them all in context. A cityscape and its river are symbiotic; no one understood this better than Daniel Burnham. The Burnham Plan's first mention of the Chicago River indicates that it was still the case in 1909, that

> the Chicago River, which gave to the city its location and fostered its commerce, has become a dumping spot and a cesspool; bridges of every possible style and condition span it at irregular intervals and at all angles; and year by year riparian owners have been permitted to encroach upon its channel until there are to be found as many as four lines of docks, each newer one having been built further into the stream.[6]

Never one to just wring his hands, Burnham considered this degraded environment an opportunity for comprehensive planning. In losing commerce to Calumet, he saw the potential for enhancing the river banks with service facilities and aesthetic improvements.[7]

Burnham agreed with the Committee on the Universe that a city needed breathing room. He promoted the idea of forest preserves in his plan, though for the most part they were to lie outside of Chicago proper. He thought "the wooded bluffs and ravines at the northern boundary of Cook County in Glencoe mark a natural park entrance from Lake Michigan. . . . At a distance of a mile inland the valley of the North Branch of the Chicago River is reached. In this valley the views are particularly beautiful, especially where the stretches are unbroken by constructions of any kind. . . ." He was taken by the "Skokee" marsh, saying, ". . . in beauty [it] vies with the Lake itself."[8] He fully understood not only the synergy between river and city but among river, city, and suburb.

He also supported the idea of straightening the South Branch of the Chicago River in conjunction with the construction of new passenger stations. He recommended that boulevards, a favorite of City Beautiful enthusiasts who were building parks and boulevards in cities throughout the nation, be built along both the North and South Branches, raised above the normal traffic level.[9]

The Changing Face of the Riverfront: A Crescendo of Construction

Burnham's boulevard idea culminated in Wacker Drive, the double-decked street that mirrors the curve of the river. Wacker Drive's first portion was finished in 1926, the entire street by 1929.

The city's first major improvement preceded Wacker Drive by several years. It was the Michigan Avenue bridge. The new bridge, begun in 1918, opened in May, 1920, to a huge public celebration. Simultaneously the city witnessed the beginning of a private building boom along the river. First came the Wrigley Building at the northwest corner of the bridge, built in two sections. It was begun in 1919, and by 1925 both sections were completed. Across the street, the Chicago Tribune Tower was built between 1922 and 1925, its design

Aerial view looking west at the changing skyline and prominent skykscrapers
along the Chicago River around 1927. The Michigan Avenue bridge is flanked
on the northwest by the white Wrigley Building and on the northeast, set back
from the river, by the tall and slender Tribune Tower. The southwest corner
of the bridge is anchored by the London Guarantee Building, almost out
of the picture on the left side.

the result of a worldwide competition that attracted 264 entries.[10] Soon, the
bridge was flanked on all four sides by impressive skyscrapers. Land values
north of the bridge skyrocketed, as did the tax intake for the city.

Building on railroad air rights also changed the appearance of the
riverbanks. The Chicago Daily News Building at 400 W. Madison Street was
built over the Chicago Union Station tracks and completed in 1929. But it was
the two-block-sized Art Deco Merchandise Mart, conceived in 1923 and ready
for occupancy on May 1, 1930, that historian Ann Durkin Keating says "em-
blemized the transformation of the river from railroad transshipment point to a
post-industrial center of consumerism. . . . The massive building used the river
as its front yard, providing room for Chicagoans to once again see their river
from its banks (and not just from its bridges)."[11]

The Civic Opera Building, erected during 1927-1929, is often used as an
example of the city "turning its back on the river." It fronted on the new Wacker
Drive and backed up to the South Branch. Since it originally drew water from
the river to power changes in stage sets, it is no accident, nor is it an insult to
the river, that the massive and handsome rear of this powerful building seems
to rise out of the river.

The Depression of the 1930s and World War II temporarily broke the cycle of recovery along the downtown river. After the war, architectural redevelopment returned slowly to the riverfront. Only one commercial/industrial building was built in the twentieth century on the banks of the Main Stem: the Sun-Times Building in 1957. Instead, handsome residential and office buildings towered over the river. Architect Bertrand Goldberg's Marina City took eight years from concept to completion, but when the first tower was finished in 1964 and the second three years later, it boldly proclaimed that the river could be not only a scenic view from an office window, but a resident's front yard. Though it would be some years before the Main Stem riverscape was lined practically from end to end with fancy hotels, corporate towers, and residences, this innovative circular structure must have stirred the imagination and influenced the dramatic skyline we see today along the river.

The Suburbs

When Burnham wrote his 1909 *Plan of Chicago*, he was living in the suburbs in Evanston, and suburban importance to city life did not escape the Plan's attention. He wrote that between Chicago and the suburbs there existed "vital and almost organic relations. . . . Unfortunately, however, conditions near any rapidly growing city are apt to be both squalid and ugly."[12] The occasional suburb with a university and located on the lake shore (like Evanston, though he named no names), might escape this fate. He firmly stated that "the nearby towns and villages . . . may confidently look forward to the day when the tide of Chicago's growth will envelop them, and ultimately incorporate them in the city." He assumed the creation of a metropolitan commission to plan for their orderly and attractive arrangement of parks, streets, and public buildings before they became part of the city, but until the commission came into being, "the improvement associations of each town should confer with their neighbors and agree to . . . the width and arrangement of roadways, sidewalks, planting-spaces and drainage. . . ."[13] But the suburbs jealously guarded their separate authorities and personalities, and, as we shall see in the next chapter, could not come together even on drainage.

Burnham co-authored the *Plan of Evanston* in 1917 with Dwight Perkins and others. This plan neither anticipated annexation to Chicago nor addressed, except once in passing, sanitary conditions or drainage in Evanston. He never envisioned that the North Shore Channel would become a greenway amenity akin to the forest preserves.

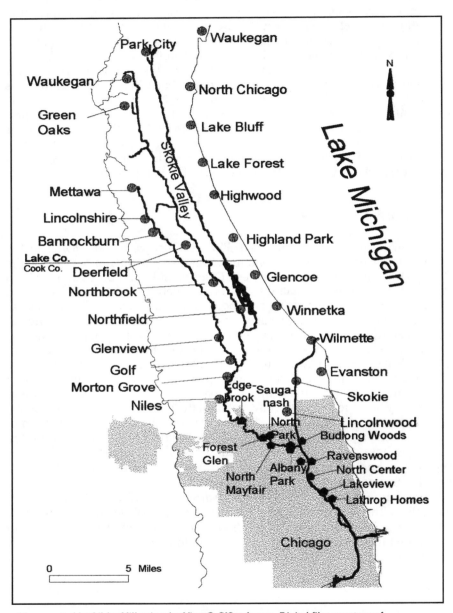

Map created by Libby Hill using ArcView® GIS software. Digital files courtesy of Northeastern Illinois Planning Commission and Illinois Department of Natural Resources.

"Northwest Branch" communities and some downstream Chicago neighborhoods.

The "Northwest Branch"

So determined are those who have been wronged by this outpouring of sewage upon them, that the Northwest association is urged to clean up sanitary conditions in the entire valley, and further injunction suits will accordingly be brought, not only against the villages themselves, but against individuals as well. . . . This organization has taken the position that there is but one sanitary problem and that every locality is concerned in its right solution.

—Philip R. Barnes, August 2, 1913

Once the North Shore Channel was built and the river below Lawrence Avenue straightened, some community members along the North Branch above (or west of) the confluence with the channel felt the need for a new name to distinguish their reach of river. They dubbed it the "Northwest Branch," referring to the Skokie Valley in particular, but encompassing all of the forks or tributaries of the North Branch. The name did not stick and was perhaps used only by the short-lived Northwest Sanitary Drainage Association, Philip R. Barnes, legal counsel.

The Burnham Plan had extolled the charm of this reach. Barnes, a resident of a North Branch community, concurred:

> Now, this stream, with its tributaries uniting at Golf, winds its way by a circuitous route in a southerly and southeasterly direction, among noble forest trees, for a distance of ten miles, finally entering the Evanston channel above Lawrence Avenue. Its banks are well defined and high and are mostly wooded to the very water's edge. The whole valley is designed by nature as a most beautiful and healthful residence district and natural park. . . .

Yet, Barnes noted, "it is rapidly increasing in population and is destined to become a great suburban district."[1] It was one thing to appreciate the valley's natural beauty and quite another to deal with the inevitable abuse to which the North Branch was subjected as the suburban district grew.

Before the new North Shore Channel could help solve the sanitary problems in the growing north suburban communities, its very existence frustrated the suburban residents because of the immediate expectations it engendered. All of the north suburban communities saw the North Shore channel as the answer to their sanitary ills. But even before the channel was built, the December, 1905, *Winnetka Messenger* aired a suspicion that:

> The trustees of the Sanitary District of Chicago brought forward a proposition at the last Legislature to include us in the Sanitary District of Chicago. We consented—the people being led to believe there would be relief for us. The policy of the board since proves—as some of us appreciated before—that we are now paying taxes for a "gold brick. . . . If we wish to connect with their

DOWNTOWN GLEN VIEW
CIRCA 1900 A.D.

Map by Donald N. Fisk, artist, published in the Glenview Area Historical Society Newsletter, *Spring, 1989. Courtesy of Glenview Area Historical Society.*

This map of Glenview in 1900 illustrates its location directly in the West Fork flood plain.

waterway *at our own expense we may do so.*"

Growth of the Suburbs

In Lake and northern Cook Counties before 1860, only small settlements of pioneer farmers existed in the inland North Branch watershed, while the growing railroad suburbs of the North Shore along Lake Michigan attracted Chicago commuters. The North Shore communities were centered on the high land associated with Green Bay Road, straddling the two watersheds of Lake Michigan and the Skokie.

Cook County's inland farming centers along the river grew into Northbrook (previously Shermerville), Northfield, Skokie (previously Niles Center), Morton Grove, Niles (previously Dutchman's Point), and Lincolnwood (previously Tessville). The lakeside towns were Evanston, Wilmette, Kenilworth, Winnetka, and Glencoe. By 1903, the time of accession into the Sanitary District of Chicago, all but two of the embryonic inland villages had incorporated into official municipalities. Lincolnwood was incorporated in 1911. Northfield was a latecomer, not being formed until 1926.

In Lake County, Highland Park, Highwood, Lake Forest, Lake Bluff, North Chicago, and Waukegan had incorporated by 1906, and inland Deerfield was incorporated in 1903. The coming of the railroads, immigration after the Chicago Fire of October, 1871, and then the automobile all contributed to local suburban growth spurts. Later westward expansion of Highland Park and Winnetka and the full development of Deerfield awaited draining the wet land. Waukegan and North Chicago were exceptions to the railroad commuting suburbs along the lakefront; both were industrialized. Sandwiched in between the suburbs along the lakefront in Lake County were two federal military bases, the Great Lakes Naval Training Center and Fort Sheridan.

Each community, each river reach along the inland waterway had its particular character. A few illustrations from Cook County follow.

Glenview

Early Glenview was practically synonymous with the river, having been settled in the low floodplain of the West Fork. One day's wagon ride from Chicago on what is now Waukegan Road, it was a logical stopping place for travelers and thus a natural location for hostelries and services for neighborhood farmers who traded their goods there or took them to market in Chicago. "The river flowed through the Grove Street bridge [near the downtown] in a curving direction along a bluff on the west and along River Road on through the Waukegan Road bridge. Under normal conditions, the river was about 60 feet wide and three to four feet deep. It provided a swimming hole for the kids. There were some fish, mostly bullheads, which were caught and eaten. It presented a scenic and pretty picture. In the winter, it was the only available place to ice-skate and play hockey."[2]

The river offered recreation, but it caused headaches for the developing town. It overflowed in spring rains and thaws. Floodwaters reached east of the intersection of Waukegan and Glenview Roads. The land to the southwest was drained by a slough leading to the river and became known as Frogtown. Another large slough drained the northeast section through a creek that crossed Waukegan Road and emptied into the river north of Grove Street. In cold weather, both river and sloughs froze, and ice would block the water under the bridges. In 1926, the village board voted to reroute the river in a straight line between the bridges and make it deep and wide enough to be controlled. Simultaneously, the village wanted to extend Glenview Road to meet Waukegan Road. This plan was problematic since the road would have run straight through the Blue Heron, a local roadhouse. The problem was resolved by cutting the building in two and moving half of it to the north.[3]

One seasonal gift of the river was ice. "Each year, during mid-winter, when the ice in the river became 12 inches thick or more, it was cut into blocks and stored in the ice house in layers, each layer being covered with sawdust. The ice was used primarily for cooling the beer served from the kegs in the saloon and also for mixed drinks. Whatever pollution there may have been in the river never seemed of any consequence."[4]

Rev. Martin C. Schmidt, once resident pastor of Our Lady of Perpetual Help in Glenview, tells a story of the earliest river "improvements" coincident with the installation of the sewer system in 1918-1919. In a taped interview, he related how he purchased delinquent property near Glenview Road for a very low price and one of the parishioners paid the back taxes on it. Not only the price, but the property, was low. It was

> down in a valley, ten feet deep from the road. Every time it rained, this was one big lake. . . . Now this river went like this (sound of pencil drawing across paper). Now what good is that land? It wasn't any good, but I had foresight. There was a time when improvements would be coming. I was almost the boss—I ran the town of Glenview. So, when improvements came, I said, "Boys, I want this river to go straight. I want all the filling to go in here. . . . [Well], while they were improving the town, putting in streets and sewers, they dumped everything here. Didn't cost me a cent! . . . They thought I was joshing them, you know. This river—see, that's the Chicago River . . . that belongs to the State. Their eyes straightened—monkey with the River? If they hear about it after all these years, I'll be in the calaboose for that. I broke up that river. See, it just cut up the land. You couldn't use it. That would always be a lake. That whole thing filled in. That was fifteen feet. . . . [I]t was about a year before I had all of it. Served two purposes. They could get rid of their garbage, and you had good land."[5]

Morton Grove

Glenview, on the West Fork, is low. Morton Grove, on the full North Branch, is high. In 1872, when the Chicago, Milwaukee and St. Paul Railroad laid track in the little settlement of 100 people that was to become the village of Morton Grove, the river was moved to accommodate bridges for both the railroad and Dempster Street. South of Dempster Street in Morton Grove at the site of John Miller's old sawmill, which the tracks covered, rerouting the river left a little island that became known as "Hobo Island." Men who worked in the nearby greenhouses hauling manure out of the benches camped there in shacks sheltered by the trees and the surrounding high banks. Sledding the steep bank down to the river at this spot was a popular winter sport in the village. Morton Grove historian Fred Huscher remembers that youngsters somehow managed to avoid the trees as they flew down to the frozen river on runs with names like "Belly Flop" and "Nutcracker."[6]

Further attesting to Morton Grove's height was Bingham and Fernald's advertisement for Morton Grove's first subdivision. "Morton Grove is only $12\frac{3}{4}$ miles from Chicago, lying 20 feet higher than the Chicago River, which is only $\frac{1}{4}$ mile distant therefrom [to the west]. Ornamented by beautiful timber of natures [*sic*] planting . . . [b]eing well drained and easily reached it is a healthy & desirable location."[7]

Today's Morton Grove spans both sides of the river and adjacent Forest Preserve District holdings. The village stretches west to the high ground of Washington Street, its boundary with Niles. From that location, barely discernible channels drain east on a gentle slope into the river's extensive natural bottomlands and floodplain. The bottomlands are easily seen in St. Paul Woods between Oakton and Dempster Streets.

George C. Klehm, a prominent village citizen, owned some land along the river south of Dempster. He built a crude dam, raised the water level to create a slightly wider opening in the river, and supplied pleasure boats. According to a *Villager* reporter, this was "the most beautiful spot near Chicago. . . . A convention of the Plattdeutsch (German middle class) Guild was held Aug. 6-8 in 1897." The reporter who covered the picnic waxed poetic as he pictured "the joy of drifting downstream between banks so heavily wooded that sunbeams only flickered through."[8] Today this spot in the vicinity of St. Paul Woods is part of the Forest Preserve District of Cook County.

Chicago Neighborhoods

The reach of the North Branch from the city limits at Devon Avenue to the North Shore Channel near Foster Avenue runs a crooked course. Its zigzag route is refreshing in stark contrast to the gentle arcs or straight lines of the neighboring reaches tamed to meet civilization's needs. This is not to say, however, that this crooked stream has been left untouched by the people and institutional landowners along its banks. Numerous creative styles of retaining walls, from flagstones to old grave stones in Bohemian National Cemetery to sturdy seawalls, speak to the continuing battle between the river and its human neighbors.

At Pulaski Road and Foster Avenue, on the north bank, are two side-by-side cemeteries, both built on converted farmland at the turn of the nineteenth to the twentieth century. Both were built in the North Branch floodplain. In this vicinity, crumbling stone seawalls restrain the flow of river water onto the land, but before seawalls, the river had to be held at bay. The nearby Municipal Coke Oven supplied city power for gas fixtures. The dry ash, or "clinkers," as the by-products of the works were called, were picked up by the wagonload and

Courtesy of Fred N. Huscher.

Boaters upstream of Klehm's dam on the North Branch of the Chicago River in Klehm's Grove, in what is now St. Paul Woods in the Forest Preserve District of Cook County, circa 1915.

Courtesy of Fred N. Huscher.

Khlem's dam on the North Branch, circa 1915.

hauled to nearby St. Luke Cemetery. There they were dumped into a low spot until the ground was at least level with that of the burial plots. Thus, the clinkers formed a dike, keeping the river from flooding the cemetery fields and graves.[9]

Neighboring Bohemian National Cemetery likewise had a flooding problem. At this location, the river meanders in a wide loop and, if left to its normal drainage, would flood the grounds. In the 1930s the cemetery installed a retaining wall to hold back the river, but in the early 1990s the wall failed, and the river spilled over into the cemetery. The Army Corps of Engineers repaired the wall. The cemetery continues to pile mounds of dirt and debris on the river bank to protect itself against floods.

Farther downstream is North Park University, formerly North Park College. This institution provides an excellent vantage point from which to observe problems and attempted solutions related to years of riverbank construction in the floodplain and even in the floodway.

Sanitary Problems

Although the industrialized, farming, and residential suburbs of Lake and Cook Counties had different sanitary requirements, Lake Michigan and the Skokie Valley united the North Branch communities of both counties geographically, if not politically or psychologically. It was tempting for the lakeshore communities to look to the Skokie Valley for relief of sanitary problems, as noted by Winnetka's December, 1905, *Messenger*.

> The drainage of the "Skokie" valley is becoming a serious problem, not only for our village but for all the North Shore suburbs. . . . To cut an outlet through the ridge to the lake is, in the first place, an expensive proposition, and, in the second, contrary to our present policy of eliminating sewage from the lake. . . . As this slope is built up sewage drainage becomes a necessity, and through-out its length sewer systems are being installed emptying into the Skokie. In our village [Winnetka] we are working on a system (which I had hoped to see in operation long before this) to give relief to as much of this slope as the present level of the water in the Skokie will permit. This sewage will be passed through what is known as a "septic tank" for purification before flowing into the Skokie.

The geographic proximity of the lakefront and the inland communities provided ample opportunity for cooperation. Influential backers proposed a sanitary district that would have united at least the lakefront communities in Cook and Lake Counties into a single sanitary district, but they could never overcome the legislative restriction that sanitary districts be limited to one county.

Upstream pollution in Lake and Cook Counties along the North Branch was a cause of concern to downstream communities, whether they were on the lake, the river, or both. The lakefront communities formed a Lake Michigan Association. The inland interests were represented by the new Northwest Sanitary Drainage Association, which also included the Lake Michigan communities.

Sanitary and drainage issues at this time were front page news on papers from such disparate towns as Waukegan and Evanston, and it is easy to follow the pace of the arguments. In the October 26, 1912 *Evanston Index*, Philip R. Barnes, counsel for the organization, recalled that problems of water quality in the North Branch of the river were first brought to his attention by citizens of Forest Glen, a small community on the North Branch in Chicago. Since Barnes made his home in Forest Glen, this is not surprising. The next to complain, he said, were three farmers in the Skokie Valley, who "objected to sewage being poured down upon their lands by the village of Winnetka." Here, then, was the nucleus for an organization that might ultimately obtain results. Barnes's professional law career included the position of general counsel to the Cook County Truck Gardeners and Farmers Association, and it was natural for them to turn to him for relief.

An article crystallizing the issue appeared in the October 19, 1912, *Evanston Index*. The article addressed the most serious needs of North Shore communities. Without exception, officials interviewed from the various towns stated sanitation and drainage as most urgent. One official suggested that, as one of three alternatives, the sewage of his and other North Shore suburbs could "be pumped westward, to some point into the Skokie." In the following week's October 26 *Index*, Barnes responded sharply,

> To such a proposition for sewage disposal our organization, the North-west Sanitary Drainage association, is unalterably opposed. The Skokie and the stream below, known as the northwest branch of the Chicago River, shall no longer be a dumping ground for sewage. This stream is fast becoming a succession of cess pools. . . . It is now up to those villages along the North Shore to find a right solution of the question. A larger view of the case at once led us to this conclusion: That, after all, there was one sanitary problem involving two questions, first, the saving of Lake Michigan from pollution by sewage; second, such sewage disposal on the part of all these villages as should not harm the stream in question to the injury of residents and property owners below. . . . The idea uppermost in the minds of many of these officials seems merely to be in what cheapest manner and method they may get rid of their own sewage, regardless of the discomfort it causes people living below them. . . . It lies within the Sanitary District of Chicago to afford ultimate sanitary relief. . . . It seems to have been assumed that the sole purpose of the Sanitary district . . . was to save the water of Lake Michigan from pollution. But our contention is that this same board should not alone seek to save the lake water, but should, under the law, relieve unsanitary conditions wherever found within the limits of its jurisdiction.

An *Index* survey reported in the November 2, 1912, issue documented finding unsanitary outfalls up through the 25 miles of the river to Waukegan and "vile odors" issuing from open drains through the entire stretch.

In December 1911, the SDC board had passed a resolution to build an intercepting sewer to collect and convey the sewage to the North Shore Channel as soon as each suburb presented a plan to build a local collection system and identify connection points.[10] The question as stated in the 1905 *Messenger* remained: who would foot the bill for these connections? The SDC's 1911 resolution had not addressed communities along the North Branch. To

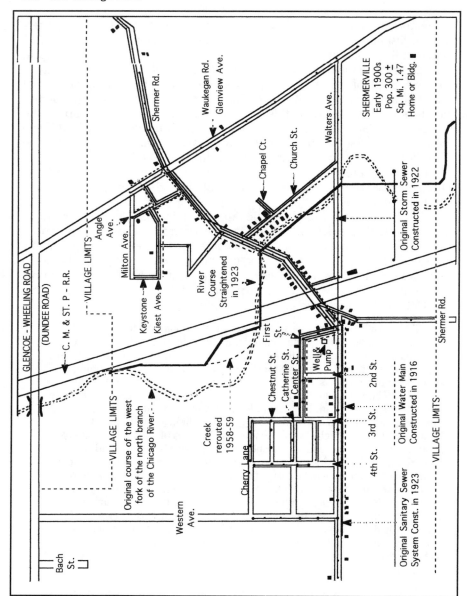

Map redrawn from original by Don Hintz, 1999. Courtesy of Don Hintz and the Northbrook Historical Society.

The original West Fork route as it ran through Northbrook before 1923 is shown by double-dotted lines. The fork as straightened in conjunction with the original sewage system is shown by the solid dark line. The fork was reconfigured again in 1958-1959 in conjunction with contruction of the Cherry Lane bridge and underpass.

keep raw sewage out of the North Branch, in 1914 the Chicago Sanitary District built a small treatment plant just below Dempster Street at the river in Morton Grove.

The preceding chapter on the North Shore Channel relates Evanston's history of connecting up with the Channel. Niles Center's negotiations with the Sanitary District resembled that of Evanston's. At first, the SDC recommended building a septic tank with an outlet into the North Branch, but the citizens "did not think favorably of the plan and requested that an outlet sewer be built connecting with the canal." George H. Klehm, relative of the creator of the boating pond on the North Branch in Morton Grove, is credited with "untiring efforts" required to shepherd the plan through. He scheduled meetings with both sides and participated actively in arranging easements, surveys, and estimates. In 1917, the District built a two-mile-long outlet sewer from Skokie Boulevard east along Oakton Street to send the untreated sewage from Niles Center to the North Shore Channel.[11]

Later, by 1923 and 1925, small sewage treatment plants came on line to serve Glenview and Northbrook respectively by removing their raw sewage from the North Branch. Northbrook rerouted the West Fork in conjunction with that project.

By 1930, a system of intercepting sewers was in place to collect sewage and stormwater from lakeside and inland municipalities and convey it to the recently completed North Side Sewage Treatment Works. After this, no raw sewage was discharged into the North Shore Channel. Whether any of the SDC projects were in direct or indirect response to the persistence of the Northwest Sanitary Association is not known. Pollution of the North Branch by agencies other than municipalities continued unabated.

Lake County:
Sanitary Solutions through the North Shore Sanitary District

Having been left out of the SDC, before the turn of the century, Lake County was left without an entity responsible for its sanitation, and local communities were fouling their drinking water by dumping sewage in the lake. In 1909, after almost a decade of study, The North Shore Sanitary Association was formed. Its work resulted in enabling legislation for the North Shore Sanitary District (NSSD) in 1911. Unlike the 1903 annexation to the SDC in Cook County, this act did not authorize construction of a new channel, but authorized construction of a sewage treatment plant by contiguous communities within a single county bordering on Lake Michigan and drawing water from it. In Illinois this could only apply to Lake County. Also unlike the 1903 Cook County annexation, this act of legislation was followed by a public petition and a vote. The North Shore Sanitation District was voted down in 1911, but the proposition passed three years later on April 8, 1914. The district formed quickly that same year. Although some voters expected that passage would mean building an intercepting sewer that would transport Lake County's sewage into the North Shore Channel, the district instead built its own small primary treatment sewage plants mostly on the lakefront during the 1920s and added new works and improvements in the 1930s.[12]

The small Clavey Road treatment plant went on line in 1952 along the East Skokie Drainage Ditch and discharged treated effluent into the Skokie River. From the beginning, that plant was beset by problems, particularly odor problems. In 1974, the Clavey Road plant was upgraded, modernized, and expanded; and the sewage of all the small facilities that had been discharging into Lake Michigan was redirected through an intercepting sewer to the plant. The effluent from this plant discharges into the Skokie River through a 48-inch-diameter pipe that skirts the Chicago Botanic Garden. (In 1999, the Clavey Road plant began a state-of-the-art upgrade that would automate its operations and improve its odor-control technology.)[13]

Drainage Districts

Lake County faced not only sewage but also drainage difficulties. Lake County is aptly named. It was, and still is, pockmarked with wetlands. The water in what is now the three forks of the North Branch of the Chicago River originally ponded in a series of ill-defined marshes, or sloughs, nothing that anyone would think of calling a river, although the West Fork flowed in a more defined channel than the other two. These sloughs did not create the Lake County communities in the sense that settlers used them as major arteries to the destination of new villages, but the sloughs did influence settlement patterns. John J. Halsey, in his *History of Lake County, Illinois*, observed that the sloughs made east-west road construction difficult from the Des Plaines Valley to Lake Michigan and dictated that "the settlements along the margins of each watercourse must have for each crest a north and south road to Chicago."[14]

Ever since homesteaders began arriving in the 1830s, before the land was surveyed by the federal government and officially available for purchase, drainage had been an everyday task in Lake County, performed on a piecemeal basis. Anyone whose property was covered with water that limited the growing season or the amount of farmland under cultivation would undertake the backbreaking manual labor of draining the water off the land through drain tile.

In the 1870s, many state statutes were written to govern drainage. The publisher of Hurd's Revised Statutes in 1880 said that the Illinois General Assembly made so many changes in drainage laws in 1879 that another revision was needed. The 1880 volume combined all of the laws in the revisions of 1874, 1875, 1877, and 1879.

Drainage districts on the forks of the Chicago River began incorporating in Lake County in the first decade of the twentieth century, under the old Farm Drainage Act of 1885. While sanitary districts are restricted to single counties, drainage districts have more leeway and may cross county lines. Those that do are referred to as "union" drainage districts.

In the cloudy crystal ball category, a member of an early settler's family, Warren Wilmot, predicted that "within 25 years all of the north shore cities and villages, as far north as Waukegan, will use the Skokie (the east fork) as a means of drainage, and motor boats will be used as a means of transporting the products of the farms and gardens to the City of Chicago, while for pleasure it will be popular indeed." Author Marie Ward Reichelt, after quoting Wilmot, notes that, "Seventeen years afterwards, nearly all of the farms in the vicinity have been converted into residence sub-divisions and golf courses, and wide concrete roads are the highways, and motor trucks have taken away business from the railroads."[15]

Drainage districts were established on the forks of the North Branch of Lake County, but not all continue in existence today. Of those that do, two are named Union Drainage District No. One. One is responsible for the West Fork from Route 22 (Half Day Road) in Lake County south to Dundee Road in Cook County, and the other is responsible for the Middle Fork (originally known as the West Skokie Slough) from Deerfield Road in Lake County also to Dundee Road. The East Skokie Drainage District is responsible for the East Skokie, or Skokie River, beginning in Park City, just west of Waukegan, but its responsibility stops at the county line. Landowners within the districts are not taxed but are assessed for the improvements to their property.

The districts used the original routes of the sloughs as guidelines for their deepened channels. Easements along the forks are inconsistent, varying from 60 to 100 feet wide. The ditches were dug project by project and then improved later, often suffering benign neglect in between projects. They were excavated out of raw clay that was often dumped directly over the adjacent topsoil, creating steep, uneven, and unsightly banks. It was difficult for any planting to

Photo by Robert M. Kaplan.

The Skokie River in Lake Bluff looking south. The steep banks have been faced with stone walls. The stone wall on the western bank is crumbling and the steep slope is eroding. A tree grows in the middle of the ditch. This photo was taken in 1994. In 1999, at the same spot, vegetation had begun to obscure the eastern wall; the tree had toppled into the stream along with others from the west bank, creating a logjam.

take hold on the banks because of the slope and the clay. Over time the ditches silted up due to erosion and debris. Trees began to grow in the channel bottoms. Floodwaters surged over the banks. Although the ditches were built to carry drainage and floodwaters downstream, partially-treated septic tank effluent also ended up in the waterway. The ditches became unsanitary and inadequate.[16]

The Middle Fork is generally representative of all three ditch designs. It was to be 20 feet wide on top, six feet on the bottom, with an average depth of six feet. The side slopes were to be uniform.

The first ditch on the Middle Fork was excavated in 1910. When the *Waukegan News-Sun* dipped into its archives on November 8, 1940, to pull out stories of importance printed on that same day in earlier years, it reprinted this about the Middle Fork: "On November 8, 1910, the [West] Skokie Canal from Rondout to the Cook County Line was finished. Originally fathered by J. Ogden Armour [of meat-packing fame], the canal drains 3,000 acres of useless swamp lands and makes it available for anything from ordinary farming to celery-raising." Drainage also enabled Armour to build one of the midwest's most lavish estates, called Mellody Farm, complete with his own sewage-treatment plant, in the vicinity of the ditch.[17] Union Drainage District No. One for the Middle Fork was probably not formed until after Armour dug his ditch. During the Depression, the Drainage District on the Middle Fork managed to obtain a grant from the Public Works Administration to reconstruct and improve the ditch. The grant proposal explained that no work had been done on the ditch since the inception of the district. With the funds, the Middle Fork was improved from Rondout to Deerfield.

Union Drainage District No. One on the West Fork was organized in 1908. "In 1910 the meandering stream which then constituted what is now known as the drainage ditch was reconstructed, graded and straightened," suggesting that someone had previously dug a ditch along the same route. "Much of the property on either side of the then existing stream was low marshland. . . ." Over the years, the district annexed other territory until it was responsible for the entire West Fork watershed from Half Day Road through Deerfield until just above Dundee Road in Cook County and even some drains from other watersheds that empty into the ditch. It dredged the ditch again in 1926; in 1931, it removed brush; and then, until 1947, it was in a "dormant" stage until residents insisted on the district's fulfilling its obligations.[18]

Where are the original outlines of the Lake County sloughs today? They are today's floodplains. If you live within their boundaries, you are likely to need flood insurance and sump pumps, unless dramatic flood control measures have been taken upstream. The separate projects that transformed the sloughs into ditches might lack the epic drama of the extraordinary construction of the Sanitary and Ship Canal or even of the North Shore Channel. The expansion of the Chicago Metropolitan area, however, just as surely depended upon creating these small, artificial forks of the North Branch as they did upon creating the major artificial channels of the Chicago River system.

Summary: A Watershed in Pieces

Although late in the nineteenth century, several parties had strongly recommended a cooperative approach to sanitation problems in the north suburban communities, they could never overcome the tendency of municipalities to control their own jurisdictions or the Illinois legislature's mandate on single-county sanitary districts. When drainage districts crossed lines, they did not cross them very far. This is the background for today's political river geography. Official responsibility for stormwater management, drainage, sewage, and clean water in the Chicago River shifts from one authority to another, or to no one, as in the case of Cook County and stormwater, as if the water in the streams were disconnected. The turn of the nineteenth to the twentieth century was too early for a watershed ideology. It remains to be seen if the different jurisdictions in the twenty-first century can unite to make watershed planning a reality.

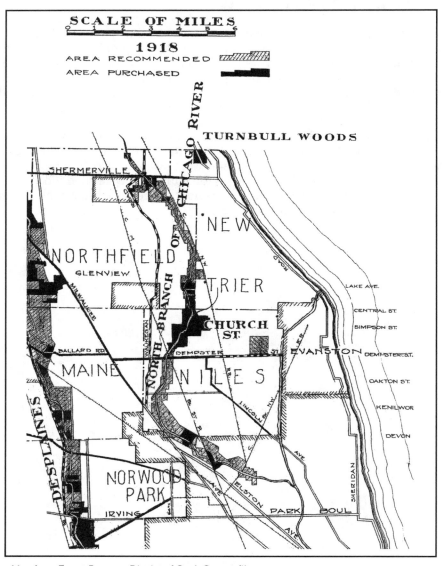

Map from Forest Preserve District of Cook County files.

This puzzling 1918 Forest Preserve District Map showing proposed
and recommended purchases along the North Branch gives no hint
of the FPDCC's historic interest in acquiring the Skokie. It concentrates
on the North Branch and the Middle Fork. The district intended to
purchase almost the entire riverway north of the confluence of the
North Shore Channel and the North Branch.

The Forest Preserve District of Cook County and the North Branch

Truly this is the People's Paradise.
Here great and small shout out contentedly.
Here I am human; here human I can be.

—Goethe's Faust

At the turn of the century, neither the Main Stem nor the South Branch of the Chicago River afforded any escape from the drama of daily life in a burgeoning city. Even though the North Branch above Lawrence Avenue was degrading in water quality because of rapid population growth, its scenery beckoned Dwight Perkins, who was roaming the entire Chicago area at the turn of the century to select land that might be included in a system of reserves. This stretch of the North Branch had not been straightened or moved, except for a small portion in Morton Grove. It retained much of the forest cover along its banks, and the expanse of the Skokie Marsh had defied attempts to drain it. The Chicago Small Parks Board and the self-proclaimed "Committee on the Universe" spawned a group called "Friends of Our Native Landscape." Predicting that the city would grow enormously, their vision was clear, their idea logical: make a series of parks out of the natural geography of the landscape, a series of green ribbons that would provide respite from a sprawling city.[1]

Influenced by this idea, the Cook County Board established the Outer Belt Park Commission in 1903 to propose a system of parks and boulevards that would encircle the city and include the outlying areas. In 1904, the Commission proposed the acquisition of land contiguous to the North Branch of the Chicago River (earlier referred to as the Northwest Branch), north from Lawrence Avenue to the Lake-Cook county line in the Skokie Valley; west to the Des Plaines River; south along the Des Plaines to a point below Riverside; then west, south, and east to the Calumet River, including Lake Calumet and its shores. They also proposed the creation of many new boulevards and small parks.[2] From these beginnings grew the Forest Preserve District of Cook County (FPDCC).

The FPDCC was approved by popular vote on November 6, 1914, and organized on February 11, 1915. In a 1990 interview, Larry Perkins elaborated on his father's passion to create these preserves:

> The concept of reserving some green intervals before the city could sweep over them was probably [born] at that lunch-eating group [the Committee on the Universe]. . . . Dad took the concept of a forest preserve and used The Prairie Club, Friends of the Native Landscape, woman's clubs, anybody that

Courtesy of Chicago Aerial Survey Co.

These aerial photographs taken in 1931 illustrate the difference in tree cover above and below Lake Avenue. There was precious little "forest"on the farmlands between Lake and Winnetka Road. The ditched Skokie, narrow and weedy, was virtually devoid of trees. The district succeeded in buying the remaining wooded areas along the Middle Fork and went on to acquire the degraded Skokie ditch and some of the Skokie Marsh. The white arrows indicate the confluence of the Middle Fork and Skokie between Winnetka and Lake and the confluence of the West Fork and the North Branch just south of Simpson Street, now Golf Road. The east-west portion of Happ Road is now Illinois Road.

would listen to his speeches. This was his golf, his tennis, his bridge, none of which he played, for 22 years. He talked with whoever was interested and would listen and he took it to the legislature. The act was passed in 1905 but turned down by the governor. A couple of years later, an amended act failed in the legislature. An act of 1909, passed by the legislature, was declared invalid by the Supreme Court.

The third time, after the Forest Preserve District Act of 1913 got through the legislature, Dad himself brought a lawsuit against the forest preserve to say it was illegal, and to his great joy he lost resoundingly. And, it having been declared legal, they started out to acquire land. One of his architect partners referred to his passion in a rather surly tone of voice as "picking flowers by the wayside." Interesting stuff, but it wasn't able to pay the grocery bill.[3]

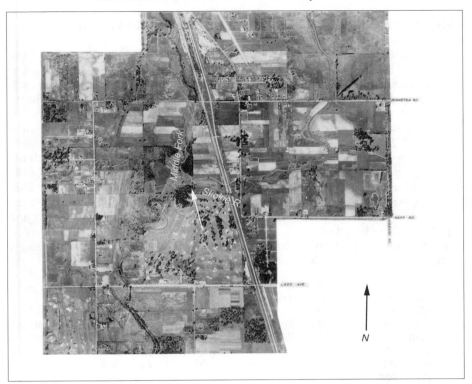

The visionaries of the forest preserves mostly headed for what the public land surveyors called "timber." The green intervals described by Larry Perkins were the cool wooded borders of the streams, the ravines in the Palos hills. They also wanted the almost treeless Skokie Marsh. Whether the woods were old or second growth was unimportant to the planners. If they had to buy farmland patches to connect their woodlands, they did. (How ironic that this happened in, of all places, the "Prairie State.") Some patches of the now rare and treasured prairie remain in the Chicago area primarily because dry and wet prairie are dynamically interwoven with the savanna and woodland in the Forest Preserve lands.

The 1904 report of the Outer Belt Park Commission had recommended purchasing land along the North Branch beginning at Lawrence Avenue, where the river joined the North Shore Channel, up to the Lake-Cook border. By 1916, however, when the FPDCC Plan Committee presented an acquisition map from Crawford Avenue (now Pulaski Road) to the county line, the land along the Chicago River east of what is now LaBagh Woods had already been purchased by other interests. (A small portion of LaBagh Woods was sold to the Chicago Park District in 1932 for the enlargement of Gompers Park.) It was the Middle and East Forks that the visionaries were after. The West Fork is represented by just one small purchase, that portion south of Golf Road where the West Fork joins the combined Skokie/Middle Fork to form the full North Branch.

The District and Water Quality in the North Branch

From its inception, the Forest Preserve District was anxious about the health of its waterways. On April 2, 1917, two years after the district was incorporated, its Plan Commission articulated a policy to "purchase wherever practicable, land on both sides of streams located along the borders of forest preserves, so that the FPD commissioners may have such control of streams and sewage disposal as would belong to the owners of land along such streams." Section 2 of this report favored "the purchase of forest lands bordering upon the Skokie as well as certain portions of said Skokie which are marshes, provided the same can be bought at prices which are reasonable in the judgment of the Forest Preserve Real Estate Committee; and provided further, that the report of the Attorneys shows that such action can be taken legally."[4] This plan put the FPD into conflict with those who would ditch and drain the Skokie Valley.

By January, 1918, shortly after it was formed, the FPD became increasingly concerned about the deteriorating condition of the river. Peter Reinberg wrote:

> I wish to call your attention to the necessity of preventing the streams
> and lakes on the preserves from contamination by neighborhood sewage.
> Cities and Villages near some of the preserves and the rapidly increasing
> population around others threaten serious injury to the most attractive natural
> features of our forests. . . . With proper protection these lakes and streams may
> be stocked with fish and used for boating and bathing purposes. To keep the
> water in them pure and fit for use, sewage and drainage pollution must be
> prevented.[5]

In 1919, property owners in the Skokie Valley along the North Branch proposed a bill in the state legislature for the creation of a special drainage district to drain "all wet or flooded lands in the Skokie Valley." This bill met fierce opposition from the four-year-old FPD. The bill failed, explained Frank Windes, the engineer for the proposed drainage district, because "it was felt that the tax would be too great and that the plans of the Forest Preserve and Sanitary District would be interfered with."[6]

By 1920, the FPD had purchased 260 acres in the valley and wished to acquire 1,832 more. Landowners were divided in their support. While many were in favor, not everyone appreciated the idea of a preserve in the midst of development. Some were so opposed that they filed a petition in County Court to form a farm drainage district covering 3,200 acres, nearly twice as much as the acreage eyed by the FPD but including all the land the FPD wanted to acquire. The district interpreted this petition as nothing less than an attempt to "change the character of the natural drainage and soil of the Skokie territory as to make it unfit for forest preserve purposes." The petitioners lost.[7] By 1933 the Forest Preserve prevailed, and the proposed plats along the North Branch were acquired to form an almost continuous green zone along the stream.

In 1925, communities along the North Branch and the North Shore began to complain about both mosquito and sewage problems. In 1931, demand increased for clean streams, and the FPD unanimously passed a resolution calling on Chicago's Sanitary District to clean up the water, focusing particularly on problems in the river at what was then known as the Caldwell or Sauganash Forest Preserve. Children wished to wade in the "supposedly clear and sparkling water of the North Branch." The FPD said the river was "polluted and laden with sewage from several towns and villages along its course, and is virtually a menace to the lives and the health of those who attempt to enjoy their recreation along its banks."[8]

It should come as no surprise then, that in 1932, the Forest Preserve District created a Clean Streams Advisory Committee. The committee's preliminary recommendations included the formulation of the principle that

> all streams . . . shall be treated, insofar as sound engineering and economics permit, so as to restore and assure an adequate seasonal flow and depth of clean water, free from pollution, and thereby conserve for the people their health and safety, their recreation spaces, water transportation, aquatic life, property values and agricultural uses. The entire program of your committee may be divided under two main heads as follows: 1. Prevention of future stream pollution and 2. Abatement of present pollution.[9]

This committee was adamant that all future construction of combined sewer systems be banned, and only separate storm and sewage systems be built.[10]

The committee also requested that the State of Illinois Sanitary Water Board study pollution in waterways throughout the county, including the North Branch above the Chicago city limits. The study was to be a combined effort of the Sanitary Water Board, the State Department of Public Health Division of Sanitary Engineering, the Forest Preserve District, the Chicago Sanitary District, and the Chicago Regional Planning Association. Research took place from November, 1931, to March, 1933. In April, 1933, the group issued an "Inventory of the Pollution of the North Branch of Chicago River and Tributaries and Recommendations for the Abatement and Prevention of Pollution."

The report noted that every community bordering on the North Branch had at least one case of outflow into the stream, but just a few qualified for the lion's share of the blame. The public sewage-treatment plants of Morton Grove, Deerfield, and Highland Park topped the list of offenders. Untreated sewage came intermittently from Glenview, Northbrook, and Highwood. Some sewers in Niles, Morton Grove, Glenview, and Lake Forest discharged raw sewage into the North Branch, resulting in pollution and unsightly conditions downstream. The North Shore Sanitary District at Lake Forest was singled out for the lack of an intercepting sewer along the Skokie River, causing untreated sewage to be released from estates, residences, and three golf course clubhouses. But the FPD's role was limited; it could arouse public opinion and advocate a study, but it could not implement any recommendations.

The advent of the automobile led to increased pressure on the land and water of the forest preserves. People roamed unchecked everywhere in the preserves, challenging the very mission of the district to preserve, protect, and restore its resources. The solution was to direct visitors to designated recreational spaces, such as trails, picnic areas, and dance floors, most of them paved.

Thus, along with increased access of people in automobiles came roads and parking lots—impermeable surfaces that prevented the slow infiltration of rain and snow into the ground, causing quicker runoff into the river. During the Depression, scores of Works Progress Administration (WPA) and Civilian Conservation Corps (CCC) men worked to create automobile control structures; safe parking spaces; barriers; bridges; hiking, biking, and horseback riding trails; and shelters. Nowhere did the work of the CCC become more renowned and romanticized than in the creation of the Skokie Lagoons.

Increased residential, commercial, and recreational development in the watershed after World War II created greater erosion and pollution in the stream, particularly from the pesticides that were the peacetime spinoffs of wartime's chemical advances. In 1953, Charles "Cap" Sauers, general superintendent of the Forest Preserve District, authorized the formation of a new Clean Streams Committee. Its members formed a volunteer force that monitored the rivers, looking for "instances of industrial pollution such as oil or chemical discharges, dumping of materials on stream banks where high water can carry it away, buildup of logjams that can aggravate flooding situations, unlawful encroachment and filling of floodplains, and debris such as oil drums, shopping carts, and picnic tables thoughtlessly thrown into our rivers." Members reported their findings at bi-monthly meetings (immediately if the situation was acute) and the appropriate authorities were to investigate and take action.[11] Ralph Frese, active in this organization since its beginning and owner of the Chicagoland Canoe Base, points proudly to this group as the oldest volunteer stewardship organization in Cook County.[12]

As Lake and Cook Counties have expanded onto virtually all the "wild" land left in private ownership, the preserves are almost the only haven for wildlife, both plant and animal, in the watershed, not to mention the human spirit seeking renewal in the natural world. The waters of the Chicago River system are a vital part of this haven.

The Ascendance of Federal Authority
Making the River Safe for Shipping and Addressing the Issue of Lake Michigan Diversion

The Chicago River, one of the indispensable arteries of commerce upon which is based the eminence among American cities obtained by Chicago is regarded by nine-tenths of the population not interested directly in commerce as a nuisance to be abated.

—Captain William L. Marshall
U.S. Army Corps of Engineers, Chicago District, 1893

By 1910, the Chicago River system had two artificial channels, the Sanitary and Ship Canal and the North Shore Channel, both withdrawing Lake Michigan water to dilute and drain away the by-products of increasing settlement and industry. But the creation of the new waterways did not come without problems. Upon completion of the Sanitary and Ship Canal, the Sanitary District of Chicago had to face issues involving not only diversion of Lake Michigan water but also of safe navigation.

The Main Stem and the South Branch were cluttered with bridges and wharves. Even if the clutter could be removed, the Army Corps of Engineers expressed concerns that the increased velocity of the current from diversion might create a safety hazard to navigation. Worse yet, the chief engineer of the War Department warned that the other Great Lakes states and Canada might become alarmed that Chicago's diversion of Lake Michigan water would lower the Great Lakes.[1]

Improving the River's Profile: the Federal Role

The two purposes of the new channel—sanitation and shipping, as described in its name—had encouraged enough state legislators to vote for passage of the Sanitary District Enabling Act, yet appeared to be in conflict. The federal government perceived the requirement for an adequate amount of Lake Michigan water for sanitation as potentially inconsistent with safe navigation. Safe navigation required a wide, deep river with no impediments and little current. The SDC spent the early years of the twentieth century addressing these issues.

In 1889, the year the Chicago Sanitary District was authorized, 11 million tons of cargo moved through the Chicago Harbor. That was enough so that in 1892, the federal government's River and Harbor Act required Capt. William L.

Marshall, the War Department's engineer in charge of harbor works, to report his views on improvements needed in the Chicago River now that construction had begun on the Sanitary and Ship Canal.

In his 1893 annual report, Marshall recounted the inadequacies of the river. Larson, in *Those Army Engineers,* summarizes the river's condition at that time:

> "The Chicago River," Captain Marshall wrote in 1893, "is the most important navigable stream of its length in the world." Of United States harbors Chicago was second only to New York in terms of tonnage "but," he said, "in capacity, depth, and width of navigation it is but a third class port." At a time when improvements were underway at many Great Lakes ports to achieve 20- 21-foot depth, the Chicago Harbor had but a 16-foot depth at the entrance to the Chicago River. The Chicago River, where most of the harbor traffic congre-gated, could not be deepened beyond 15 or 16 feet because of two tunnels under the river with no more than 16-18 feet of water over their crowns. In addition, the river was obstructed by an average of four bridges to the mile and its course was lined by wooden docks, heavy buildings, elevators, etc., many resting on piles and sheet piles but a few feet below the bottom of the channel and built up close to the water's edge so as to prohibit a channel next to them exceeding 16 to 18 feet without danger of their collapsing. At places the river had been contracted to less than half its original width by piles or riprap of stone placed in the stream to buttress inefficient bulkheads or docks. Bends in the river, with curves rigidly fixed by structures built along the edge of the channel, would not permit the passage of modern vessels. Because of these obstructions, tugs, frequently two per vessel, had to be used for movement of all vessels above the juncture of the north and south branches of the river. The cost of moving the larger vessels to the elevators above 22nd Street and back to the lake, Captain Marshall learned, was equal to one-half the cost of transporting the cargo from Chicago to Buffalo. In addition to all this, the Chicago River was an open sewer.[2]

Prior to 1893, the federal government had restricted its activities to improving the harbor. Only in 1894 did Congress begin to authorize funds for improvements to navigable stretches of the river. In 1896 the government began a three-year project to dredge the river to a 16-foot minimum depth.

Marshall, promoted to Major by 1898, concluded, however, that dredging the river once would not be enough. According to his estimates, the city of Chicago was dumping in excess of 1,000 cubic yards of waste into the river *daily.* He predicted that within four years the channel would be back where it had started and would require continued re-dredging. The city had two choices, he reasoned: either stop dumping in the river or pay for the cost of dredging it.[3] In 1899, Marshall left Chicago after 11 perspicacious, outspoken, and influential years on the job. Although an Illinois state publication accused him of breathing "an adverse spirit," his legacy was a blueprint for the river's future.[4]

By the time the Sanitary and Ship Canal was completed, a 16-18-foot depth was no longer acceptable for shipping. The War Department now required twenty-six feet. The first challenge was to remove the pedestrian tunnels under the river at La Salle and Washington Streets and a rail tunnel belonging to the Chicago Union Traction Company.

It literally took an act of Congress to make the tunnels compatible with the new depth requirements in the river. On April 27, 1904, Congress declared the three tunnels under the Chicago River to be unreasonable obstructions to free navigation. The act authorized the Secretary of War to give notice to the tunnel owners to alter them so as to have a river depth of 26 feet. The city's plan was to build new lower roofs over the tunnels and then remove the older, higher ones. Between 1906 and 1908, the Washington Street and Van Buren Street tunnels were lowered successfully, but flooding rendered the LaSalle Street tunnel useless.[5]

Meanwhile, the War Department continued to move on all fronts on Marshall's recommendations. By 1903 it had removed and replaced old docks, eliminated bends in the river that had been impediments to traffic, and authorized funds for turning basins. These basins, built between 1904 and 1907 (the same years the SDC was eliminating the North Branch meander below Foster Avenue), were to allow boats to turn around at the the junction of the South and West Forks on the South Branch and the northern end of Goose Island at North Avenue.[6] The Sanitary District was responsible for the North Branch upstream from Belmont Avenue beyond the limit of lake-going vessels. It dredged the river to a depth of nine feet. The Sanitary District was also improving the South Branch to Damen Avenue, widening it, deepening it to between 21 and 26 feet, building docks, and replacing bridges.[7]

Navigation vs. Sanitation

The War Department permits for river improvements were based on the condition that the velocity of the river's current be less than one and one-half miles per hour. The SDC was walking a tightrope. Its challenge was to increase the flow from the lake enough to dilute the sewage without exceeding the velocity of the current considered by the federal government to be safe for navigation.

Immediately after the canal opened in 1900, the War Department expressed concern on behalf of the navigation industry about strong currents in the river. The Sanitary District and the Secretary of War were miles apart on the two issues of who was in charge and what was the real purpose of the canal. The District rejected the War Department's right to interfere with a state project.

What followed was a seesaw of War Department regulations for allowable diversion. First, the allowable total was modified downward. Then the total was modified so that diversion could be higher during the evening hours of 4 P.M. through midnight when shipping traffic was slow. Soon after, allowable diversion was based on a daily average, and still later, in 1903, different levels were allotted according to season: open season for navigation meant a low season for diversion.[8]

The Cal-Sag Channel

The diversion issue came to a head over the SDC's proposed construction of a third diversion route for Lake Michigan water, the Calumet-Sag Channel. The Calumet River emptied into Lake Michigan. Its reversal through the proposed channel would keep polluted water from flowing into the lake at Chicago's southern boundary. Although in 1903 the Calumet area's population was small and dispersed, the location's potential to develop into Chicago's major port meant that both industry and population would expand and concentrate. The SDC wanted to be prepared.

In 1907, when the SDC applied for a permit to build the "Cal-Sag" to link the southeastern portion of the city with the Sanitary and Ship Canal and to divert Lake Michigan water through it, the Secretary of War denied the request. The defiant SDC pointed out that it was a creature of the state, regulated by state law. What gave the federal government authority to regulate diversion? The SDC intended to proceed on the channel without a permit. At times, during that year and in subsequent years, the SDC even openly exceeded the Secretary of War's permitted limit of 4,167 cfs.

The Secretary of War fought back with a new and potent argument. On behalf of the federal government, he alleged that the additional proposed diversion through the Cal-Sag would lower the level of the Great Lakes, obstructing navigation of the lakes' rapidly expanding shipping traffic. The federal Rivers and Harbors Act of 1899 prevented obstructions to shipping. The SDC argued that it was complying with state law and claimed that the congressional authority that had been granted for diverting Lake Michigan water for the I&M Canal was sufficient authority for building the Cal-Sag. The issue went to court.

On June 30, 1910, the Secretary of War finally issued a permit for the channel, but he limited diversion to the amount already permitted through the Chicago River. Less water would have to be diverted through the Chicago River and the North Shore Channel in order to divert water through the Cal-Sag.

The SDC began work on the Cal-Sag immediately in 1911. It took until 1922 to complete the 16-mile, 60-foot-wide, and 20-foot-deep channel, and at a cost of $14,175,000 to the SDC, because its excavation was mostly through limestone bedrock. The Cal-Sag flows west from a point on the Little Calumet River near south-suburban Blue Island to Lemont at a place on the Main Channel known as Sag Junction, 11 miles upstream of Lockport. The first construction on the Cal-Sag was not intended to reverse the flow of the Calumet River entirely. The Calumet and Chicago Rivers were not originally in the same watershed. The Calumet drained the area south of approximately 87th Street into Lake Michigan, and the Chicago River drained the area to the north. Construction of the Cal-Sag was the first step toward interconnecting the two watersheds.

Once the Cal-Sag was built, the Sanitary District naturally applied for additional diversion.

In 1925, federal authority trumped states' rights. The Supreme Court ruled that the Secretary of War, not the state of Illinois, had the authority to regulate the diversion of water from Lake Michigan. The SDC had lost its best card. It is ironic that in 1900, the infant Sanitary District, by the simple act of opening a control dam, had been able to beat Missouri's filing of a request for an injunction to prevent the opening of the Main Channel. Now, however, older and wiser, it was learning what a lawsuit really meant.

The Water Level Battlefront Expands

When the Secretary of War added the potential lowering of Great Lakes levels to his arguments against the Cal-Sag, he was presaging a new battlefront. Lake Michigan is upstream from every Great Lake except for Lake Superior. It is upstream from the states of Wisconsin, Michigan, Ohio, Pennsylvania, and New York, and the Canadian provinces of Ontario and Quebec. Any water drained out of the lake system at Chicago was perceived to affect them all.

As the country grew and industry evolved in the early twentieth century, the context for diversion issues began to shift to include not only navigational safety but also water rights. Three developments—larger capacity ships, power generation in the basin, and the expanding role of the federal government—changed the nature of the debate. Between 1890 and 1910, larger vessels began hauling iron ore and coal to newly-built steel mills in Indiana, Pennsylvania, and Ohio. These new vessels required deep-water harbors. And, extremely important in the equation, in 1896 the first hydroelectric plant on the Great Lakes opened at Niagara. Between 1900 and 1915, additional power plants nearby in both the U.S. and Canada gave new significance to the amount of water rumbling over Niagara Falls.[9] Any sort of decrease would affect the plants' potential capacity.

Was the concern of the other lake states and Canada valid? An 1895 federal commission had stated that a 10,000 cfs diversion from Lake Michigan would lower the lake level about six inches. But Lake Michigan water levels vary radically, sometimes from day to day, more often from year to year, and definitely over longer cycles, and it would be difficult to assign Chicago the responsibility for radical change. Lake levels had been very high, for example, in 1673, during the "Little Ice Age" when Jolliet and Marquette explored the region. As the lake levels lowered in the decades after 1673, the pier at Fort Michilimackinac, Father Marquette's early mission at St. Ignace, where Lakes Huron and Michigan meet, had to be extended continuously in order to reach the lake. More recently, a dry period lasting from 1895-1940, caused record low lake levels during the 1930s. Approximately 40 years later in 1979-1995 an extremely wet period set in and lasted for 15 years. Chicago was scrambling to save her lakefront from high lake levels. Lake Michigan's water level is in "dynamic interplay" with many agents, including rainfall and snowfall, evaporation rates, temperature, and the levels of rivers and streams that empty into it.[10]

Nevertheless, when lake levels were nearing an all-time low in 1925, there was much finger-pointing at Chicago. The *New York Times* reported authoritatively that, "It is beyond dispute that the Chicago abstraction has contributed greatly to the lowering."[11] In 1922, the same year the Cal-Sag opened, Wisconsin brought suit against the SDC to stop diversion *entirely* for the purposes of sewage treatment. In 1925, Wisconsin amended its 1922 lawsuit

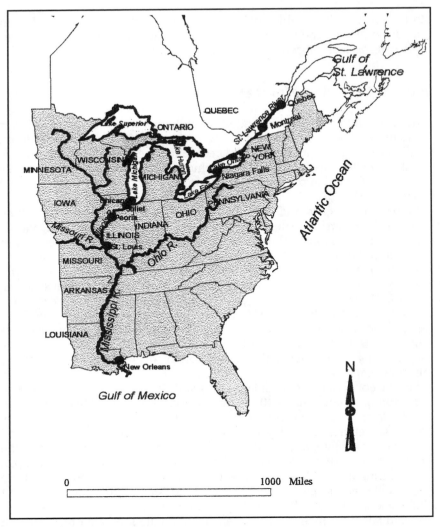

Map created by Libby Hill using ArcView® GIS software.

Geographic relationship of Chicago to the other Great Lakes states and Canada.

to enjoin the SDC from diverting more than the amount required for navigation. Minnesota, Ohio, and Pennsylvania filed as additional plaintiffs, and in 1926, Michigan and New York joined the suit. All claimed that diversion was damaging to navigation, agriculture, horticulture, and climate, and was in violation of their water rights. This suit challenged the SDC's diversion in excess of the amount required for navigation.

Big guns were aimed at the SDC. All the suits were combined into one, the "Lake States versus the SDC," and in 1930, the U.S. Supreme Court ruled in favor of both parties. In favor of the lake states, the decision, referred to as the 1930

Decree, instructed the SDC to reduce "direct diversion" of Lake Michigan water in stages. "Direct diversion" was the euphemism for water used for navigation and sewage dilution purposes and did not include drinking water. By December 31, 1938, the SDC would be allowed only 1,500 cfs.[12] In favor of the SDC, the decision continued to allow diversion. While allowing time to build treatment facilities, the decree required the SDC to complete the construction of the sewage-treatment facilities it had already begun. Also, in accordance with the SDC's own proposal, the court required the Sanitary District to build controlling works in Chicago Harbor, consisting of a navigation lock and impermeable walls to prevent the reversal (or re-reversal) of the Chicago River.

In awarding the diversion to the SDC, the 1930 Decree required that the SDC account for the annual amount of diversion for all purposes in reports to the Army Corps of Engineers. Lockport was designated as the point of measurement. Drinking water drawn from Lake Michigan, "domestic pumpage" in the court's language, by the City of Chicago and other suburbs, was not at issue in the litigation. The court simply required that it be measured and accounted for. The federal government was only authorized to regulate the amount of diversion for navigation.[13]

The Sanitary District and Sewage Treatment

Well before the suits brought by the other Great Lakes states, the SDC had begun working on new methods of sewage treatment to supplement "dilution as a solution to pollution." In 1908, in a speech to the Lake Michigan Water Commission, the head chemist of the Sanitary District advocated artificial treatment of sewage as the best method of both protecting the public health and preventing the ruination of waterways.[14] After considerable experimentation, in 1919 the Sanitary District began a 25-year program to build large activated sludge treatment plants. The heavily polluted North Shore Channel was a major priority, and the North Side Sewage Treatment Works, located on the west bank at Howard Street, became operational in 1928. The Sanitary District was also the target of many pleas for sanitation from communities upstream from Lawrence Avenue on the river's North Branch.

The "Controlling Works" at the Lake

The controlling works mandated by the 1930 Decree were to bar Lake Michigan water from entering the Chicago River except under very tight diversion restrictions. They were also supposed to prevent the river from backing up into the lake in times of storms, preventing polluted Chicago River water from reaching the Lake Michigan drinking water intakes. When the Sanitary and Ship Canal was built, there seemed to be no need for a control structure at the harbor. In the original design, lake water flowed freely into the river, drawn by gravity into the lower level in the canal. Waterflows in the canal were controlled at Lockport.

The controlling works would have to allow for the passage of navigation. In

Photo by Libby Hill, June 20, 1996.

"Locking through" into Lake Michigan on a summer evening.

1925, SDC engineers began to study types of structures and control gates that would be most effective in restraining Chicago River water and controlling water traffic. Work on actual plans and specifications began in January, 1934. The new controlling works were dedicated in September, 1938, although they were not put into operation until January 1, 1939.

The final design, still in place as of the beginning of the year 2000, consists of a 600-feet-by-80-feet lock located just east of the former U.S. Coast Guard Station. Two heavy stone and concrete walls support triangular gates that create a tight seal when moved into place on rollers. Each gate weighs in at 30,000 pounds, but only a 25-horsepower electric motor is needed to open or close them, because they are so well-balanced.

Also built in 1938 was the Chicago Inner Harbor, an enclosed basin formed by connecting walls. The south wall of the lock connects with the north-south federal Inner Breakwater, which then connects to the east-west South Basin Wall. This wall then connects to the lakefront at Randolph Street. The north wall of the lock connects with the North Basin Wall, which then connects via the federal North Pier to the made land in front of Navy Pier. The *Chicago Daily News* described this basin as an "anteroom to the river."[15] Changes begun in mid-1999 are described later in the chapter.

Because both the north-south Inner Breakwater and the North Pier were porous, built by the federal government for the purpose of breaking the impact of waves, the SDC had to make them water-tight. To accomplish the job, the SDC installed a row of sheet piling and a berm of broken rock on the river side of the Inner Breakwater. For the North Pier, the SDC built sheet pile cells filled with broken rock on the river side of the pier. Now the enclosed basin would be completely separated from the lake. The SDC built one additional feature to control the flow of water. In both the North and South Basin Walls, a set of four sluice gates is installed under the wall, out of sight but recognizable by the long and narrow low building with glass block windows. These gates can be opened to allow lake water into the river to augment the river flow. The sluice gates in the South Basin Wall are used during the summer when there is boat traffic. This minimizes the effect on river currents that might otherwise push the boats around. The gates in the North Basin Wall are used during the winter.

When the lock is opened for shipping, if the lake level is one foot higher than that of the river, 400,000 gallons of lake water pour into the river from the lake. A larger or smaller difference between the lake and river levels changes the amount of water released through the open lock. Whatever the quantity, it is charged against the diversion allowance. The purposes of the controlling works do not include direct metering of the volume of water passing through them, but by knowing the difference in lake and river levels and the number of gate openings, the volume can be estimated. The name, however, may mislead people into thinking that there should be monitoring equipment that measures or actually controls the amount of water coming through for diversion. The only purpose of controlling equipment at the lock is opening and closing sluice gates and opening and closing the gates for boats to lock through.

Chicago's Department of Public Works noted immediate problems as a result of the new lock. The department's report for 1938 reported that "the effect of reduced diversion is obvious. Floating ice in the main Chicago River is at a standstill and a section was observed between Clark and LaSalle Streets where it was practically frozen over. It remains to be seen what the future holds in the way of offensiveness from the reduced flow."[16]

In 1939, the Department of Public Works reported that the effects on navigation were negligible, except that unsafe conditions prevailed east of the lock during southeasterly and southwesterly weather and might require the

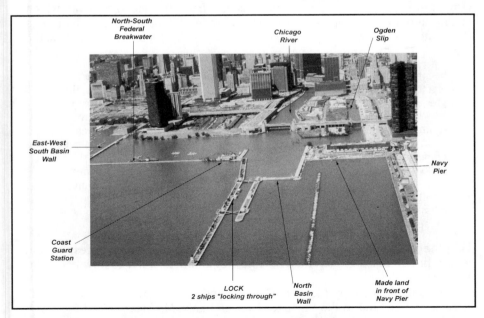

Courtesy of the Metropolitan Water Reclamation District of Greater Chicago.

The "anteroom" to the Chicago River.

construction of additional piers in the lake. Regarding sanitation, however, the situation was much worse. Reports of offensive odors from the river increased, and "the condition of the river was comparable to that of an open sewer, which in fact the river became." Since the U. S. Supreme Court could not be moved on the matter of the amount of diversion for sanitary purposes, Chicago hoped that the need for more water for safe navigation of large barges through the "Lakes-to-the-Gulf Waterway" would change its mind.[17] The Lakes-to-the-Gulf Waterway, which had been a dream since 1887, had become a reality in 1927, with the completion of locks along the Illinois River between Joliet and Alton. Hence the Sanitary District could shift its argument.

Beginning in the 1950s, increased residential development on the northern reaches of the Chicago River watershed led to more floodwater coursing down the river, and it became more common to open the locks to release river floodwater into the lake. The first time the lock was opened for that purpose was in the flood of October, 1954. When it was determined that the Willow Springs Spillway in the Sanitary and Ship Canal's Main Channel contributed to the problem by steering Des Plaines River water into the Chicago River system, the spillway was closed, but that closure did not solve the problem. Release of floodwater into the lake occurred again in July, 1957, and September, 1961, and with increased frequency thereafter.

The navigation lock gates had to be in service year round. Back in the 1960s, even in the dead of winter, boats had to visit the City of Chicago water intake cribs weekly. But in January, 1963, two events coincided to cause extraordinary trouble: the lake and river levels were the same, and the temperature plummeted. The continuous flow from the lake to the river, which usually kept the gates open, ceased. The gates froze tight and the ice had to be dynamited, and the *Chicago Tribune* of January 23, 1963, describes how the locks

> became immobilized by the crush of ice, two of the locks' four powerful electric motors burned out in an attempt to force the gates open against the press of a foot or more of ice. A team of 15 workers from the sanitary district, which operates and maintains the locks, arrived to open a battle of men against nature. As the temperature dropped to the subzero zone, the men picked away at the ice without success. The city sent a tug equipped with a crane and a giant bucket. The bucket was dropped onto the ice within the locks, smashing small chunks off. But after every two dips, the bucket jaws froze, and the bucket had to be swung ashore and saturated with gasoline, which was set afire, the bucket loosened up and once again dipped into the mass of foot-thick ice. On Wednesday a city specialist in explosives was sent to the locks.[18]

Had the weather warmed and a large winter storm occurred, excessive rain would have caused the river to rise, allowing polluted water to flow back into the lake.

Solving the local problems of Chicago and relieving the unsanitary conditions it had created in the Chicago River and Lake Michigan raised the diversion issue and led to the construction of the controlling works at Chicago's harbor. It seems improbable that the original planners of the Sanitary District ever dreamed that reversing the little river would have such widespread, national implications.

Courtesy of Chicago Historical Society.

Straightening the South Branch, aerial photo looking north from about 18th Street showing old and new channels. The new channel is still blocked at the south.

Realization of Late Nineteenth-Century Dreams

Straightening the South Branch Between
Polk and 18th Streets, and the Creation
of the Lakes-to-the-Gulf Waterway

*There will be street extensions, super-highways through to the south side,
resulting in tremendous increases in property values like the waving of a
fairy wand in improving and developing a vast section of the city.*

—*Straightening the Chicago River*, 1930

*This legislation, [Great-Lakes-to-the-Gulf Waterway] passed by Congress,
will result in opening up the markets of the world, at seven dollars per ton, to
the products of the factory and the workshop of Chicago, making of Chicago
an inland seaport and bringing to us an era of such greatness, prosperity and
wealth as the mind of man cannot now conceive.*

—Richard W. Wolfe, Commissioner of Public Works
"Our Chicago" lecture broadcast over WSPC, April 2, 1929

While the Forest Preserve District was fulfilling its visions on the North
Branch and the SDC was occupied with diversion issues, Chicago was
vigorously pursuing two other long-anticipated, related projects: straightening
an "undesirable" meander on the South Branch, and pursuing public dollars
for improvements on the Illinois River for a Great-Lakes-to-the-Gulf Waterway,
also commonly known as the Deep Waterway.

The meander was perceived as a barrier to smooth navigation on the
Chicago River and therefore as a detriment to the fulfillment of the Deep
Waterway. It was also a barrier to the extension of Chicago's streets onto the
south side. Removing the meander was a small engineering project compared
with building either the I&M or the Sanitary and Ship Canal in their times, but it
was meant to provide tremendous benefits to the heart of the city, especially in
its rivalry with Calumet as the premier port of entry. The story of straightening
the South Branch provides an example of the more sophisticated legal
approaches required during the twentieth century when it came to moving the
river. It is also a microcosm of how apparently unrelated interests in a maturing
city intertwined on one project.

AIR VIEW OF RIVER STRAIGHTENING AREA *Indicating Possibilities of Street Openings After the River Is Straightened*

The City Is Now Preparing a Definite Street Plan for This Area.

From Chicago, IL: City Council Committee on Railway Terminals and Citizens Committee on River Straightening, The Straightening of the Chicago River, *1926. Courtesy of Chicago Aerial Survey Co.*

Anticipated street extensions as of 1926.

Background

"A GREAT NORTH AND SOUTH THOROUGHFARE" proclaims the bold chapter heading in historian J. Seymour Currey's *Chicago: Its History and Its Builders*, referring to LaSalle Street.[1] With the arrival of the automobile, upgrading the Chicago street system was crucial to an orderly city. Connecting the north and south portions of the city was one of the chief goals of turn-of-the-century planners. The river was in the way.

The original South Branch of the river meandered to the east at Polk Street, and then meandered back to the southwest starting at around today's 15th Street and ending near 18th Street. Several interests considered the Polk Street bend a nuisance; eliminating it promised near-miracles. At the very least, the proposed project was to allow Franklin, Wells, LaSalle, and Dearborn Streets to be extended south and 14th Street to be extended east from Canal Street to State Street, so that traffic could proceed with "undiminished speed." At the time, only Wabash Avenue and State Street connected the south side to the city's business district. Michigan Avenue was restricted to passenger cars, and Clark Street was too narrow for trucks. As many as nine railroads squeezed their tracks into the narrow space between Clark and the river, and some railroad properties were even bisected by the river. The railroad yards were the obstacle to street extensions. The plan was to move the river westward to straighten it.

The Citizens Committee on River Straightening spoke forthrightly on the divisions and rivalries created by the river:

> The Chicago River, still the accepted boundary between the north, west and south sides, has figured in the greatest sectional struggles Chicago has had, political and otherwise. Jealousies which grew in the early days of the

city still exist in no small measure. In early days each side refused even help to build bridges across the river lest a rival section might benefit. . . . Thus we have the present-day picture, with the south side bottled up, with five square miles between Eighteenth Street, State Street, Fifty-fifth Street and Halsted Street "frozen" territory from the real estate valuation standpoint; with 1,600,000 people on the south side facing a barrier as inconvenient and almost as formidable as a Chinese wall between them and their 1,700,000 neighbors of the west side, and with vehicular traffic from the southwest side detouring over Michigan Avenue and the South Shore drives to reach the downtown district.[2]

Passenger cars didn't find the going easy on the existing street system. Commissioner of Public Works Richard Wolfe, in testimony before the Illinois Commerce Commission in 1930, described a particularly frustrating afternoon:

About a month ago or so I was invited to speak at a public school at Forty-fifth and Emerald Avenue. Leaving the City Hall to get there I should make it in about fifteen minutes, if I could go direct. Because of the congested district, because of this condition we are talking about, I had to ride over through the congested loop district to the outer drive, then go south six or eight miles to Fifty-fifth street, and then go back to Forty-fifth and Emerald, my destination. It took me one hour, practically, to get to that point, which would be reached in fifteen or twenty minutes with direct highways. . . . Straightening of this river, and the building of the thoroughfares we have in mind, will solve this problem. Then will follow railroad air rights, which will mean buildings over these forests of railroad tracks that glisten and blind the eye, as well as streets and bridges between the west side and the south side.[3]

Interested Parties

Four prominent interests were involved in the plan to reroute the river: the railroads, the city, the South Park Commission, and the War Department, which acted on behalf of shipping interests. First, there were the railroads, who lobbied for a Union Station to replace their scattered passenger terminals; they didn't necessarily advocate moving the river, they just wanted more space for more efficient operation.

Next was the city. Based on the financial benefits experienced after the completion of the Michigan Avenue bridge, the city leaders anticipated a dramatic rise in land values south of the river after major arteries connected the south side to the business district and enhanced tax revenues began to accrue. An added incentive was the financial benefit of air rights. James Simpson, president of Marshall Field & Co. and chairman of the Plan Commission, anticipated that "with the utilization of air rights and duplication of a district comparable with that Park Avenue district in New York, the benefits are so huge it would be appalling to think anybody would hesitate for a minute to lend every assistance they could to it."[4]

Then there was the South Park Commission, which wanted the lakefront land freed of the Illinois Central tracks so they could create a grand and glorious park.

Finally, there were the shipping interests, who wanted safer passage. The straighter the river, the safer the journey.

Bureaucratic and Legal Tangles

Most of the property adjacent to the original South Branch Channel was owned by railroads. The Chicago Union Station Company had applied to the city for an ordinance to build a new Union Station and other facilities between Washington Street and Roosevelt Road on the west bank of the river for the Pennsylvania; Burlington; and Chicago, Milwaukee and St. Paul Railroads. In early 1914 the city passed the ordinance, which contained a provision for removing the river's meander. In this manner, river straightening became connected to the railroads, and the City Council Committee on Railway Terminals became the sponsor for the River Straightening Project.

In 1921, several legal questions surfaced: Who would hold title to the bed of the old channel? What legal steps were necessary for the city to initiate the straightening? Was state or federal legislation necessary? What would the Sanitary District's responsibility be for navigational safety and river upkeep on the rerouted channel? It would take the city 14 years of maneuvering and arm-twisting to straighten out ownership and legal matters before it could straighten out the river.

State legislation was enacted, and the Chicago Title and Trust Company was engaged to render an opinion regarding titles to the bed and property abutting the old river. Only one question was resolved promptly. An act of Congress, passed in 1921, allowed "the City Council to pass Ordinances to change or relocate the Channel, course, or bed of any natural or artificial water course within the corporate limits of the City."[5]

Despite a revised report dated March 20, 1926, clearly stating the concerns of the Baltimore & Ohio Railroad that the width of Franklin Street as proposed would make the land "east of the street of such insufficient depth as to destroy its usefulness" to the railroad,[6] the city council passed an ordinance on July 8, 1926, giving the go signal for the project, optimistically assuming that all differences could be worked out in due course. The ordinance established real estate values for the exchange of properties among the nine railroads involved. Progress ground to a halt in April, 1927, however, because the railroads would only accept the provisions conditionally. Union Station had been completed two years earlier in 1925, and perhaps the city's issues were no longer so important to them. Mayor William Hale Thompson persisted and pushed the railroads hard. He gave Wolfe the herculean task of bargaining with the railroads to obtain agreements and financing.[7] It seemed it was easier to move a river bed than to navigate the necessary legal channels.

The 1926 ordinance had declared that the new channel would be an official part of the South Branch of the Chicago River.[8] It would be at least 850 feet farther west of Clark Street than the original channel, depending upon where you measured from. The Citizens Committee set up a fund for construction costs, based on the value of the reclaimed lands plus the increase in value of the lands transferred from the west side to the east side of the river.[9]

All that was needed now was for the railroads to convey title for the new channel to the city. The final compromise provided for each of the railroads and the city to deed holdings to the Foreman Trust and Savings Bank of Chicago as trustee. After straightening was completed, the bank was to deed the parcels to the railroads and the city according to prior agreements. By March, 1928, construction was set to begin.

Shovel Day and Construction

September 20, 1928, was Shovel Day, and as always many prominent city boosters were on hand for the ceremonies. Demands of navigation and the need to maintain a continuous flow in the river for sanitary purposes meant that a new channel had to be excavated before the old channel could be filled in. Excavated material was tossed in the lake or given to the South Park Commissioners to be used for filling in the lakefront.

The July 8, 1926, ordinance authorizing straightening spelled out detailed specifications about the infill of the old channel. Plans dictated that the channel be "filled and leveled to an elevation of seven feet above Chicago city datum. . . . Such filling shall be placed or deposited in such old channel in such manner as to avoid all unnecessary voids or interstices, the intent being that the manner of depositing such filling shall be such as to produce the least practicable amount of settlement or subsidence of the same."[10] Nine hundred forty thousand cubic yards of sand would be scooped from the bed of Lake Michigan.[11] Nothing that could be humanly controlled was left to chance.

The Great Lakes Dredge and Dock Company began work on the north end, 400 feet south of Polk Street. Mother Nature, unpredictable as always, stopped the work twice, once by bitter cold weather that moved in on January 17, 1929, and again by extremely high water levels during that spring and summer.[12]

The Deep Waterway:
Boosterism and Celebrating, Chicago Style

The first official act creating the Great-Lakes-to-the-Gulf Waterway was in 1882 when Illinois ceded the I&M Canal to the federal government with the expectation that the canal would become part of a great route from the Great Lakes to the Illinois and Mississippi Rivers. The federal government did not accept the gift. In 1887, the citizens of Chicago presented the waterway plan in booklet form. The plan sputtered along with the federal government improving the Illinois River here and there as the years progressed.[13]

In Mayor Thompson's second-term inaugural address in 1919, he "noted with much satisfaction" that the Illinois Legislature passed a bill authorizing the issuance of $20 million worth of bonds for waterway construction to dig a canal from Lockport to Utica on the Illinois River in order to accommodate barges on their way to New Orleans.[14] Finally, in 1925 the Illinois Legislature created a Lakes-to-the-Gulf Commission with former Mayor Thompson as chairman.

It took only 18 months, until January, 1927, for Congress to pass legislation creating the Deep Waterway and for President Calvin Coolidge to sign it. Thompson, now back as mayor, planned a huge victory cruise. Undeterred by raging floodwaters on the Mississippi, 500 Chicago boosters, headed by the mayor, boarded two Illinois Central trains for St. Louis on the evening of April 18, 1927. At St. Louis, they embarked on two steamers and set out on their voyage to New Orleans. The Mayor reserved a berth on each boat.

Wolfe included an account of the cruise in a lecture/radio broadcast he delivered on April 2, 1929:

> When Cairo was reached there was consternation there. On the way down the river, families were out on the housetops and in trees. Members of the cruise gave money and clothes to the suffering and frightened people. Cattle, horses, pigs, sheep were seen struggling in the wild waters, houses were afloat; men, women and children in mule carts, carrying beds, bedding, domestic animals, were fleeing in droves along the highways, behind the bursting levees. A pall of dark fear hung over New Orleans, its officials and citizens.
>
> The Victory Cruise was converted into a Crusade of Relief; out of the scenes of disaster came the campaign for Flood Control. Mayor Thompson of Chicago joined with Mayor O'Keefe of New Orleans, and the Flood Control Congress was held in Chicago. . . . President Coolidge himself, was won [over]. Flood Control legislation soon followed. . . .

In this talk embracing the fulfillment of the Deep Waterway and the river straightening that was nearly completed, he came close to outranking all former excesses of Chicago boosterism. You can almost hear him intoning:

> . . . . And in all the history of Chicago, with its record of marvelous achievements, I am prepared to state that never at any time in its history has it had to its credit projects of greater magnitude and importance, accomplished and under way, than it has at the present hour. The straightening of the Chicago River for fifty years has been the subject of controversies, discussions, resolutions and plans. The dreams are now at realization. Go down to 12th street and the River and see for yourselves. There are workmen, the giant dipper dredge, opening up the new channel, and in less than a year from today the Chicago River will be in its new channel. . . . The straightening of the Chicago River will lead to the solution of the railway terminal problem, and the erection, in time, of sky-scrapers over the network of steel rails between Clark Street and the River.

And regarding the Deep Waterway,

> Then was realized the dream of two hundred and fifty odd years, beginning with the report of the French pioneer, Father Marquette . . . of recommending a Navigable Waterway between the Great Lakes and the Gulf.[15]

Jolliet received no credit.

One month after the work of straightening was completed, a "Banquet Commemorating the Historic Event of Straightening The Chicago River" was held in the Grand Ballroom of the Palmer House on December 29, 1929. Above the title on the souvenir program cover was one of Chicago's several uplifting mottos, *"KNOW CHICAGO BY HER ACHIEVEMENTS."* Inside, along with photographs of the principal political and engineering players and of the project itself, was a short essay about the challenges of carrying out the project, both assembling the land and digging the channel, and its promise for the future of Chicago. The straightening was completed almost a month after the stock market crash on Black Tuesday, October 29, 1929. Nowhere in the celebration program is there any mention of completion of the project *despite* the crash or the spiral toward the Great Depression during November and December. Perhaps this occasion for optimism was not to be marred by a pessimistic note. Perhaps it was alluded to by the speakers but omitted from the program notes. In this time of national gloom, the celebrants feasted on "Canapé of Sea food [*sic*] à la Marsellaise, Cream of Pistachio soup, Roast Vermont Turkey Palmer House, Endive Salade, topped off with a dessert of Gatoux [*sic*] River Banks with Saboyon sauce, petits fours, mignardises, and coffee." Apparently nothing hindered the appetite of a Chicago booster.

Summing It Up

Geographically, ever since the Illinois and Michigan Canal breached the sub-continental divide, Chicago had been connected by water to the Missouri/Mississippi River system. With the completion of the Deep Waterway, Chicago, the quintessential city of transshipment, became an integral part of that system. Chicago's 1927 victory-turned-mercy crusade symbolized the recognition of the increased scope of this interdependence. Floods on the Mississippi were now of such consequence to Chicago's commerce, it was as if the Mississippi were Chicago's front yard.

While the South Branch straightening project may seem to be insignificant tinkering to today's audience, it is impossible to overstate the expectations of many of Chicago's leading citizens. The magnitude of their optimism explains the city's persistence through the tedium of ordinances, permits, legal travails, and land swaps. Even a few unresolved details, such as the fact that there was no agreement with the railroads on the street extension routes, did not deter the city authorities. River straightening, safe navigation, the commercial promise of the Deep Waterway, concern about Mississippi River flooding, parkland for Chicago's citizens, a handsome Union Station, and a city united, not divided by the river, must be regarded as parts of a combined vision for the city, separate only in the unique approaches each project required to achieve its goal.

In the end, the park commissioners got their parkland, filled with the spoils of excavation. The shippers got their safer channel. The railroads got their Union Station, bordered by Adams, Canal, and Clinton Streets, and Jackson Boulevard, as recommended by Burnham. But Franklin, Wells, LaSalle, and Dearborn Streets were never extended across the river, and the central business district never expanded to the south. More than 100 acres of abandoned property lay idle as late as 1998, although in June, 1999, the land was sold to a developer.

The final irony of the South Branch straightening project is that between the time the straightening was first proposed in the late nineteenth century until its completion, the bulk of Chicago's shipping traffic shifted to Calumet Harbor. Although the new, straight South Branch was hailed in speeches as an easily navigable channel integral to the Great-Lakes-to-the-Gulf Waterway through which many boosters projected tons of cargo would pass, it was too late for the Chicago River. From a navigation standpoint, Chicago would benefit enormously from the Deep Waterway, as the boosters predicted, but it would be primarily through the Calumet Harbor and the Cal-Sag Channel.

Transforming the Skokie Marsh

The Skokie was so vast! Sometimes with pony and phaeton our family would drive clear across it. Cat-tails and coarse grasses grew there. Prairie chickens, ducks, mud hens, snipe, killdeer, meadow larks, bobolinks, butcher birds, bitterns, and hawks, are the birds which made a lasting impression. The fenced-in "bottomless holes" were as gruesome as ghost stories. There was a big ditch at Willow Street where tiny mud turtles and queer water life could be netted for the home aquarium. "The Island" [Crow Island], rearing its heavy woods out of the grass of the Skokie, was a place to find rare song birds, and woodcock, and the nests of crows.

—Edwin F. (Ned) Walker
"Memories of Winnetka in 1880," at age 7

West of the Highland Park Moraine, beginning above what is now Lake-Cook Road and extending south to Wilmette, is a remnant back bay of Glacial Lake Chicago. An interconnected valley of sloughs beginning at today's Park City flowed south to the bay. The bay's outlet narrowed to a winding stream, when not in flood, that curved southwest, met up with the Middle Fork, and flowed around the Wilmette spit.

Over time, the bay filled in with vegetation and became a crazy quilt of plants and water. Centuries of drowned and decaying vegetation created what Roland Eisenbeis of the Cook County Forest Preserve District described as "mostly peat and muck from one to four feet deep, underlaid by glacial clays including an impenetrable rubbery layer."[1]

The Potawatomi called it the "Chewab Skokie," meaning "big wet prairie." It was an old hunting ground and probably part of an important portage route between Lake Michigan and the upper Des Plaines River in west Glenview. To the white settlers it became known as the Skokie Marsh. Many had little practical use for it in its natural state, although reminiscences of some early residents tell how the Skokie could captivate its neighbors, young and old.

Frank Windes, who became Winnetka's village engineer in 1898, claimed to have been told by some that he was the first white child born on the edge of the Skokie. He rhapsodized in 1933 about skating there when he was a child. He says that in extended periods of cold weather, when the ice was strong, he and his friends could sail ice boats on the marsh, probably in the manner described by Harold I. Orwig, whose grandparents moved to Winnetka in 1886. Orwig remembers the boys "used to go 'skate-sailing.' " They rigged up a sail from a canvas nailed to two crossed sticks, like a kite, and held it behind them. The wind blew them across the marsh at tremendously high speeds, and when they wanted to stop they turned the sail sideways."[2] From the Skokie, skaters had the potential of traveling a long stretch along the East Fork. Windes recalls skating from Winnetka down to Wells Street in Chicago, and Rev. Quincy L.

(Top) *Earl E. Sherff, "Vegetation of the Skokie Marsh,"* Bulletin of the Illinois State Laboratory of Natural History, *Urbana, Illinois, Volume IX, 1910-1913, Article XI, August 1913, Figure 2.* (Bottom) *Photo by Libby Hill.*

Looking north at the East Slough, or the Skokie, in July, 1911 (*top*), and in November, 1999 (*bottom*), just north of the Lake-Cook county line. In the 1911 photo, the lone tree would have been just south of today's Clavey Road, indicating that the marsh went beyond Lake-Cook Road. In 1911, the water moved unconfined through channels in the marsh grasses, although it had a directional flow to the southeast. The ground was too low and wet to support trees. On November 21, 1831, George W. Harrison, deputy surveyor for the General Land Office, described this area, after having walked north for one mile, as follows: "Land level and worthless marsh." After it was channelized, the water was confined between two dry banks upon which trees could grow.

Dowd recalls skating and "sled sailing" up to Waukegan.[3]

Windes also tells fish and hunting stories. He remembers:

> In the hunting season it was not an unusual sight to see thousands of water fowl in the Skokie marsh, feeding or resting. There were great flocks of wild geese, ducks, wild swan [trumpeters]. I think Mr. Fred Richardson of Winnetka shot the last wild swan, along the edges of the Skokie. . . . Coon, mink, muskrats, and weasels were found, and we had great fun hunting with our old muzzle-loading shot guns. . . .
>
> Mr. Jack Schafer of 846 Cherry St., and I, as small boys, would build two dams a short distance apart, in the Skokie stream, with an opening in one end of a dam. We would wade in the stream and beat the water with sticks, scaring the fish between our two dams. After we had some 20 to 30 good sized bass, pickerels, cat fish and perch enclosed, we would close the dam, and then shovel out the fish, and everyone in town had a fine mess of fresh fish.[4]

But Windes also remarks that, "for many years, when the seasons would permit, the only use derived from the Skokie, except for hunting and fishing, was the cutting of the 'slough hay,' for bedding, cattle, or packing ice. It was too wet to farm or use as pasture."[5]

Early Change in the Marsh

By the 1850s, change was already encroaching on the marsh. On the edges, rich, loamy soils attracted a growing number of farmers. On the high Ridge Road, running north and south below Willow Road and partially paralleling Green Bay Road, were the German truck farmers. On the west were Hollanders who raised choice "Glencoe horse-radish." As population in the vicinity increased, the growing North Shore villages eyed the Skokie for expansion. They perceived the maverick levels of the marsh as a threat to both farming and settlement. During wet weather, the marsh was a mire likely to swallow up a cow or a farmer chasing her. The peat often caught fire, and clouds of suffocating smoke and mosquitoes plagued the vicinity. In addition, its narrow outlet was prone to flooding nearby roads and homes. Windes recalls:

> In 1890-1893 there was a real estate boom, and a number of "wild cat" subdivisions were laid out, streets were platted, and wooden sidewalks constructed. We had had a long dry spell; then the floods began; in a few days we boys had all kinds of sidewalk rafts which covered the Skokie and finally floated down stream toward Chicago. The walks that did not float away that spring were burned up by the Skokie fires in the fall.[6]

Flood, fire, and mosquitoes doomed the Chewab Skokie. When in the late 1800s the villages of Wilmette and Winnetka wished to expand to the west, they built roads across the swamp at Willow Road, Winnetka Avenue, and Lake Avenue. The roads acted as dams, trapping the normal seasonal flood flow into sprawling floodwaters that damaged nearby farms and homes. Eventually, attempts at drainage nearly depleted the water table. It became so low that the physical character of the marsh changed from swamp grasses and wild rice to weeds. Denuded of its moist, naturally grassy cover, the dry peat bed with its annual accumulation of weed growth was extremely susceptible to fire. Dust and smoke devalued property, both environmentally and materially.[7]

Early Attempts at Drainage

The first serious attempt to drain the Skokie had been the Hurd Commission's Kenilworth-Skokie ditch in the late 1860s. The ditch began at Willow Road, just east of Hibbard Road, and zigzagged through the village of Kenilworth, crossing land now occupied by Indian Hill Golf Club, then Ridge Road, and finally emptying into the lake in the northern part of the village.[8] Portions of this ditch still exist; one section is easily visible at Sheridan Road from a bridge just north of Kenilworth Avenue. Funds ran dry and this ditch never attained full capacity; proposals to complete it failed for lack of money.

The December, 1905, article in Winnetka's *Messenger* observed the irony in the situation. "The people on the eastern slope of this valley look to it as an outlet for their sewage. . . . Every heavy storm causes the Skokie to overflow into the ditch at the south end of Winnetka, resulting in the flooding of both Kenilworth and Wilmette." Citizens, the writer said, considered forming a drainage district, but discarded the idea as being too complicated. They put pressure on the Sanitary District to deal with the problem, and apparently the SDC responded that the population buildup west of "the ridge" was insufficient for their attention. The author of the article states that the very reason for the slow buildup was the "unsolved sewage question."[9]

The Forest Preserve:
The Struggle to Acquire the Skokie Marsh

The Skokie had always been at the top of the Forest Preserve dreamers' list. Its vastness, mystery, beauty, and richness of wildlife made it unique. But such wildness was in too sharp contrast with the needs of civilization. Sensitive to the flood issues of the area, the FPD reasoned that if it could acquire the marsh, it would be able to design a flood control project. But what shape should it take? The FPD considered widening and deepening the North Branch, but worried that it would back up into the Skokie. The next suggestion was to create impoundments to store the flood water and as a byproduct create a recreational water landscape. By 1922, the lagoon plan made its first official appearance on the books.[10] Windes maintained, however, that he had suggested the idea of lagoons to Daniel Burnham much earlier, in 1908 or 1909:

> The main idea was to improve the Skokie Valley and make it usable at
> all times as the "Play Ground" for Chicago and the North Shore Villages.
> Lagoons, streams, drainage works, filling, roads, and landscaping were
> its main features. I urged the [Chicago] Plan Commission to make it a part
> of the "Chicago Plan", but Mr. Dan Burnham said I was "many, 25 at least,
> years ahead of the game"; "wait, some day this will be taken up"; "not now,
> young man". He was right, the 25 years have gone by—.[11]

This is the earliest mention this author has seen proposing a design that would become the Skokie Lagoons. Burnham's response seems surprising from someone who urged men to make no small plans. Perhaps Burnham himself was not ready to see the taming of the beautiful wild marsh he so admired.

In 1923, planning came to a halt. William D. Washburn, a former property owner who had sold his land to the FPD, sued the Forest Preserve for the return of his own land plus that of other former owners of the Skokie. His challenge rested on the grounds that the district was a "forest" preserve, and the Skokie Marsh did not qualify as a forest. The case continued until 1927. Washburn's idea was supported, even though he achieved neither remuneration nor the return of his land. The FPD was enjoined from acquiring any land except in strict conformity to the FPD act. This act had been amended in 1921 to allow the district to purchase land connecting preserves, but the Illinois Supreme Court essentially voided that amendment, noting that a broad interpretation would allow the FPD to purchase anything it wanted.[12]

In May, 1928, the district's advisory committee recommended acquiring only 458 additional acres in the Skokie Marsh, connecting those purchases that were already in district hands. Since land values were escalating, the committee urged the board to buy, and buy now.[13] By 1933, the district had purchased approximately 1,100 acres between Lake Avenue and County Line Road and fleshed out the plan to develop a system of lagoons.

The Civilian Conservation Corps (CCC)

When Franklin D. Roosevelt became President in 1933, he appointed Winnetka resident Harold L. Ickes as his Secretary of the Interior. Caroline Harnsberger, in her *Biography of Winnetka*, claims that Ickes's influence qualified the Skokie as an early project of the CCC.[14] Work on the Skokie Lagoons project began in May, 1933, with 1,000 men.[15]

Camp Glenview, or Camp Skokie Valley as it was also called, housed the recruits along the east bank of the North Branch of the Chicago River, at Harms Road between Glenview Road and Lake Avenue, directly east of the village of Glenview. Enrollees were divided into companies of 200 men each. The U.S. Army housed, fed, and clothed them and provided medical attention, safety demonstrations, and religious and recreational services. The National Park Service was responsible for supervising the work day.

Flood Control

The project site between Willow and Dundee Roads spanned about two and one-half miles from north to south, and approximately one-half to one mile from east to west. A system of seven lagoons was excavated and connected by broad waterways. The dredged soil was mounded into low, undulating dikes to enclose the flood plain. The FPD's 1937 annual report assured taxpayers that "Irregularities of the flood plain are being removed in order that receding waters will drain rapidly toward the central lagoons and leave no stagnant mosquito breeding pools."[16] Water covers 190 of the 1,100 acres, 133.5 acres in lagoons, and 56.5 acres in channels. The district described its design as a practical one with pleasing aesthetic results:

> The water in the lagoons was to be maintained at a depth of 5 feet or more by a series of low dams and the flood plain created by the low dikes was to be used as a huge impounding reservoir in time of flood. The storm waters in the area immediately adjacent were to be carried in diversion ditches outside the flood dikes and emptied into the stream below the lagoon system. When completed the lagoons and waterways can be maintained at a fairly constant level and the flood plain will still have much of the beauty and aspect of the original Skokie swamp. The dikes will be planted to natural forest growth so that the whole area will be enclosed by a forest belt. The project involves the moving of one and one-quarter million yards of earth. . . .[17]

The detention capacity of the dams and channels was expected to take

Photo by Robert M. Kaplan.

The confluence of the Skokie and Middle Forks after both were widened and dredged during the Skokie Lagoons project. On November 12, 1839, George W. Harrison, deputy surveyor for the General Land Office, walked north for a mile in the immediate vicinity, and when he reached what is now Winnetka Road, described the last quarter mile as a "very bad marsh," while to the south it was "level and good with oak timber generally." The marsh continued north for another eighth of a mile. The confluence of the two forks is now one-half mile south of Winnetka Road, as a result of channelizing it over the years. When the FPDCC first completed the lagoons in the late 1930s, the high prominence between the two forks was virtually bald, with one lone standing tree. This photograph was taken from the west bank of the Middle Fork at the confluence in 1997. The bicycle bridge is accessible by starting the bike path at Winnetka Road, on either side of Happ Road, or at Lake Avenue east of the river.

From the files of the Forest Preserve District of Cook County.

This photograph, taken on July 7, 1934, early in the project, shows the intensive manual labor by the unskilled workers who loaded dirt from the excavated channels and lagoon basins into dump trucks. Workers hauled the spoil to the East Dike to build it up.

care of 50-year flood stage conditions. When completed, the lagoons, channels, and flood plains would have a storage capacity of approximately 65 million gallons of flood water. The dikes on both sides of the Skokie River below Willow Road were built above the all-time flood crest in order to prevent any spillover from the Middle Fork, which ran very close to the Skokie River.

The original marsh was perceived as too huge for the ordinary human eye to appreciate its seasonal beauty, so the FPD designed and built two cross dikes as roadways from which the public could appreciate the new landscape.[18]

Progress

The Forest Preserve District maintained that this type of project was particularly suited to the use of an army of unskilled workers. They mowed weeds "well over head high, drained water pockets to eliminate the breeding of mosquitoes and quenched peat fires some of which had been burning for several years."[19]

In 1934, the National Park Service purchased two gas-powered shovels, five diesel caterpillar tractors, and one elevating grader unit with crawler-wagon to assist the enrollees with dirt handling. Three lagoons were complete with connecting channels, a fourth lagoon was on its way, two dikes were built and landscaped, and two lagoons were stocked with fish and water plants. "As fast as the major earth moving is completed, finishing work in the way of fine grading, planting and construction of trails and parking spaces is carried forward."[20]

Completion

In 1939, Tower Road and a section of Forestway Drive had been paved by the Cook County Highway Department, opening the southern half of the project to the general public for fishing, boating, and canoeing. Bridle paths topped three miles of dikes. Parking was available for 250 cars just south of Tower at the west end of Lagoon No. 3.[21] In 1940, Camp Skokie Valley was still operating at full force, with a minimum of 1,000 men. All seven lagoons and connecting channels from Willow to 500 feet beyond Dundee on the north had been completed.

Finally, in 1942, the Forest Preserve District could report:

> . . . . It is safe to say . . . that left to our own resources, we could have accomplished but a fraction of this work in the same time. . . . With the easing of unemployment, the National Defense program, and the advent of war, there was little need of such work relief, so the FPD saw the last of the CCC enrollees in May of this year. Older men participating in public works under the banner of the Works Progress Administration (WPA) continued land-

Courtesy of Chicago Aerial Survey Co.

Aerial photograph looking north at the Skokie Lagoons project. By May 17, 1935, the date of this photo, lagoon numbers one and two had been completed and work on lagoon number three was underway. In the right foreground, the straightened and widened Skokie River exits the lagoons at Willow Road. The east and west ditches that skirt the lagoons are visible, particularly the east ditch.

Courtesy of Chicago Aerial Survey Co.

This June 4, 1939 aerial photo, also looking north,
shows the lagoon project nearing completion.

scaping, planting and sodding throughout the year.[22]

The CCC men from Camp Skokie worked on other Forest Preserve projects throughout the district, and their work has stirred the imagination of those in later generations, perhaps because this CCC camp was known as the largest in the country.

Reflections

The transformation of the Skokie Marsh to the Skokie Lagoons was one of the last major deliberate alterations of the landscape in the Chicago River watershed, except for the Chicago Botanic Garden, which was built in the 1960s on the one remaining section of marsh north of the lagoons. One part of the marsh not transformed by the FPD was filled in by the town of Winnetka. According to Harnsberger, when Winnetka was looking for land onto which to expand, it put the dirt excavated for depressing the railroad tracks through the village to creative use. Between 1938 and 1943, the earth was hauled "by trucks day and night down Tower Road to the Skokie swampland. From this landfill on the north side of Tower Road there arose 'Pine Tree Village,' comprised of

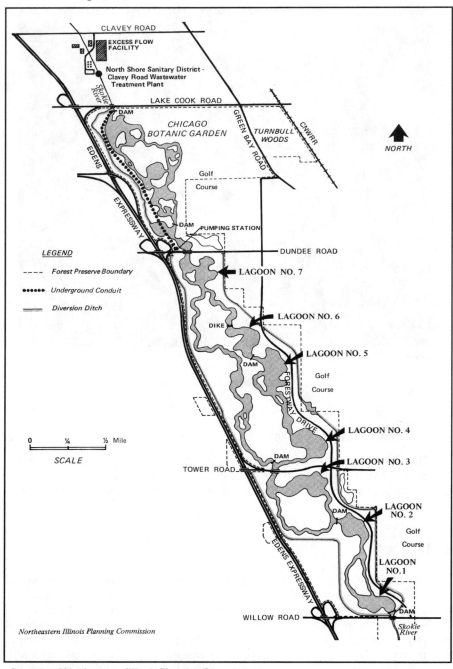

CLAVEY ROAD

EXCESS FLOW
FACILITY

North Shore Sanitary District -
Clavey Road Wastewater
Treatment Plant

Skokie River

LAKE COOK ROAD

DAM

CHICAGO
BOTANIC GARDEN

TURNBULL
WOODS

GREEN BAY ROAD

CNWRR

NORTH

EDENS EXPRESSWAY

Golf
Course

DAM   PUMPING STATION

DUNDEE ROAD

LEGEND

- - - -   Forest Preserve Boundary

•••••   Underground Conduit

———   Diversion Ditch

LAGOON NO. 7

LAGOON NO. 6

DIKE

LAGOON NO. 5

DAM

Golf
Course

FORESTWAY DRIVE

LAGOON NO. 4

0   ¼   ½ Mile

SCALE

LAGOON NO. 3

DAM

TOWER ROAD

**LAGOON
NO. 2**

Golf
Course

DAM

**LAGOON
NO.1**

EDENS EXPRESSWAY

WILLOW ROAD

DAM

Skokie
River

Northeastern Illinois Planning Commission

Courtesy of Northeastern Illinois Planning Commission.

1990s map of the entire transformed Skokie Marsh, including
the Chicago Botanic Garden project undertaken in the 1960s.

30-40 houses." The Forestview section on a no-outlet block south of Tower Road was built on the same fill during the 1950s.[23]

The re-making of the marsh illustrates the ambivalence with which we humans often approach our natural surroundings. We romanticize them; we love them. Yet, we want them changed for our health, comfort, convenience, and profit. Windes articulates the tug-of-war among our feelings: "As a boy, *I did not want it* drained or *improved.* I wanted to swim in the 'swimming holes', hunt ducks and other game, fish and play, and just enjoy it always as a mystical kind of place so different from the village or the city." As the boy became a man, however, an engineer, he accepted the premise that "if the Skokie could be drained it would 'amount' to something."[24] He had tried vigorously to drain it, but lack of money defeated every one of his plans.

Six months after the CCC boys moved into the marsh with their tools and energy, Windes shared his feelings:

> . . . . I want to warn all the "old timers": to take a last fond look at the "Old Skokie" as you knew it 50 years ago. It is fast becoming a thing of the past, a distant memory of quiet places, tall waving marsh grasses, carpets of spring and fall flowers, the wild life, the pure white snowblanket, the sheets of ice, the terrible fires, the floods of water, the soft grey mists and the colors that no artist could reproduce. From now it will be a beautiful playground—autos, hikers, aeroplanes, boats, golf grounds, drives, paths, lawns, shrubbery, trees, and colors which the artist and the photographer can reproduce. The "old timer" must let go, and the present generation improve and carry on.[25]

And in 1935, he wrote:

> There has been for centuries something menacing and yet fascinating about "Che-Wab Skokie." It was a lure to be avoided. Engineers have studied the bewitching menace and drafted plans for its abatement. Always something diverted or postponed their accomplishment. Drainage of the swamp was inevitable in this day of sanitation and engineering.[26]

Windes loved the marsh. In 1933, he had written, " 'The Skokie' has always meant a great deal to me. . . . Many years ago, Queen Mary of England, who always wanted England to keep Calais . . . said 'When I die you will find Calais written on my heart.' So when I die you will find 'Skokie' written on my heart, for I loved it too."

After nearly 70 years of trying to tame the marsh, humans finally succeeded. Frank Windes had been involved in every drainage plan proposed for the Skokie since 1894. But Windes was not the engineer in charge of this project; he was in the shadows, watching.

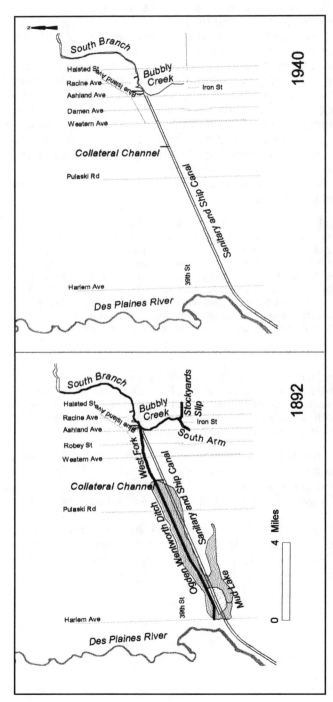

Maps created by Libby Hill using ArcView® GIS software. Digital files courtesy of Northeastern Illinois Planning Commission, the Illinois Department of Natural Resources, and the USEPA.

Comparison of the existence of watercourses in 1892 and 1940 in the vicinity of Mud Lake and the West Fork. Mud Lake disappeared during construction of the Sanitary and Ship Canal when spoil was used to fill it. The historic I&M Canal, not pictured, was south of the Sanitary and Ship Canal and began at Bubbly Creek (the South Fork). Portions remain in many locations to the southwest, beginning in Summit, west of Harlem Avenue.

Filling the Arms of Bubbly Creek and the West Fork

Money is Saved as City Fills in Historic Stream

—*Chicago Daily News*
September 14, 1938

In the early 1920s, Chicago was intent on getting rid of what it considered nuisance streams in the Chicago River system; that is, polluted tributaries of the Chicago River, streams requiring bridge maintenance, and/or streams blocking development or road extensions. Along the South Branch, the East and West Arms of the South Fork, or Bubbly Creek, and the entire West Fork all fell into this category. The only opposition to filling came from businessmen who felt the streams would be useful when the long-cherished dream of the Great-Lakes-to-the-Gulf Waterway became reality.

The "Arms" of the South Fork

The city and the SDC collaborated on filling the South Fork's East Arm, otherwise known as the Stock Yards Slip. This slip was created for use by the Union Stock Yards and therefore required no approval beyond the municipal level for eliminating it. Waste was being discharged into the slip from the stockyards and from sewers at the end of Halsted Street. Between 1921 and 1926, the SDC built and then extended a conduit along 39th Street, allowing sewage to be discharged directly into the South Fork (Bubbly Creek) at Racine Avenue and allowing the city to extend 39th Street. Stockyards drainage was provided by a ditch parallel to and south of 39th Street. Ed Lace remembers the stockyards' fire of 1934, when firemen complained that there was not enough pressure for all the hoses in use and that pumps should take water from "the ditch." He assumes they were talking about the East Arm. Exactly when it disappeared completely is unclear.

The West Arm was a different story. As part of the original Chicago River, the portion up to Ashland Avenue had been designated as a navigable stream. The non-navigable portion beyond Ashland could be filled without federal consent. In 1916, when the SDC completed the Stockyards Intercepting Sewer, it provided a new outlet for city sewers along Damen and Ashland Avenues. The stream beyond Ashland, now obsolete as a sewage dump, was filled.

Legislative maneuvering was required, however, to close the navigable section of the arm east of Ashland. The case for filling in the natural stream had to be argued in a Congressional hearing. There were opponents. They argued that the stream would play an important part "in the unloading of hogs and cattle to be shipped to the Union Stock Yards from the Illinois and Mississippi Valleys, via the new Deep Waterway route."[1] Disregarding this viewpoint, in 1923 Congress declared the portion of the West Arm between Ashland and the north line of 39th Street non-navigable, opening the way to filling.[2] It was filled east to the bridge at Iron Street, though parts of the bridge remained until the 1990s. Thus, blunt-ended Bubbly Creek is the last remaining vestige of the basin of marshes and sloughs that were once tributary to the South Branch of the Chicago River. When the west-suburban Stickney Water Reclamation Plant, the largest in the system, was completed in 1942, Bubbly Creek was no longer an official sewer and only receives sewage now during unintended overflows.

Mud Lake

The western portion of Mud Lake had been drained in the late 1860s by William Ogden and John Wentworth, and a neighbor, one Mr. Nickerson, in order to make their land suitable for farming. Both the I&M Canal and the Sanitary and Ship Canal cut diagonally through the South Arm of Mud Lake, isolating the southern end into a small patch of marsh. This portion of Mud Lake was still visible to Robert Knight and Lucius Zeuch when they made their study of the portage in 1928.[3]

The West Fork

Whatever happened to the West Fork?

Although the West Fork of the South Branch was originally a small, inconsequential-looking stream with uncertain beginnings, we know of the pivotal place it holds in Chicago history. The West Fork of the South Branch of the Chicago River was the road west, the route of the Chicago portage over the sub-continental divide, Chicago's reason for being.

The West Fork survived each major project to be built along the portage route, first the I&M Canal and then the Sanitary and Ship Canal. The fork remained and simply deteriorated into a running sore on the land, its pivotal historic legacy forgotten.

Having no use for it, in 1921 the city began the legal maneuvering necessary to obliterate it. At a Congressional hearing, there was little dissension over filling in the ditch west of the Collateral Channel at Albany Avenue. To the surprise of many, however, International Harvester Company, which owned land east of the Collateral Channel, registered strong opposition to filling in the portion of the West Fork to Robey Street, a portion not even up for discussion. The company claimed that since the West Fork and the Collateral Channel formed a loop with the Sanitary and Ship Canal the fork would become an extremely valuable segment in the Lakes-to-the-Gulf Waterway. Along with the Barrett Company, which also had riparian rights on the West Fork, it proposed that the loop be saved and improved as a barge terminal. In the interests of the city (and in return for some favors that included free city sewer connections and drainage to the Sanitary and Ship Canal), both companies expressed willingness to see the channel filled. In January, 1923, Congress declared the west portion of the stream non-navigable, the first legal step toward the disappearance of the West Fork. It left the portion east of the Collateral Channel intact for the time being.

The "Argument for the Proposed Filling of the West Fork of the South Branch of the Chicago River," written in 1923, describes both sections of the stream in the most uncomplimentary terms:

> The West Fork . . . which at one time carried some commerce, has for the last twenty years or more fallen out of use and is in a state of decay. Because it is not now navigable, because it is a barrier to the proper development of the area through which it passes, because it has been and will be a source of expense for bridges, because it is a nuisance, and because it is not worthy of improvement, the City of Chicago is desirous of having it filled up. . . The flow in the West Fork east of the Collateral Channel is from east to west. This flow is little if any more than the sewage discharged into it by four trunk and several small municipal sewers. The river bed is filled up with sewage sediment, always decomposing and passing gas and sludge. As a result the water is black, with an offensive odor. . . .[4]

The city filled in the western portion of the West Fork, though no details are recorded in the Department of Public Works annual reports. But the remainder of the channel stayed in place until the mid-1930s. In 1935, when Congress declared the eastern portion of the stream non-navigable, the city lost no time in filling it.

The September 14, 1938, *Chicago Daily News* refers to the filling of the fork as "coming to light" as part of a $75,000 appropriation to remove the Western Avenue swing bridge at 26th Street and to pave the stretch. New bridges would have cost $300,000 each, versus the $75,000 to remove them. "Inquiry disclosed that since August, 1935, when Congress passed a bill declaring the branch non-navigable, the city has filled in the stream from Pulaski east 2 miles to Western, and is continuing to fill in west from Pulaski to where the source of the river is lost in railway yards at 47th Street and Harlem Avenue." Fill, consisting of "clay from sewer and water tunnel excavations and broken street surface material from WPA projects," was "dumped in the old stream at the rate of 150 tons a day."[5] Except for the bridge appropriation and removal, none of this information was reported in the annual reports of Chicago's Department of Public Works.

On November 7, 1938, the *Chicago Daily News* waxed nostalgic:

> . . . . Although it has been deepened and can be negotiated by a motor boat down to its cutoff junction with the drainage canal [the Collateral Channel] near Kedzie Avenue, it retains its old curves and windings between high banks and perhaps looks not greatly different from its habit of 300 years ago. As one walks along the bank west of Kedzie Avenue this character becomes more and more apparent. The stream has been dredged to receive the drainage of the "Ogden ditch" farther west, but it was between these banks that leather-clad Frenchmen and silent Indians for two centuries poled their boats in the spring of the year. It was along these willow bordered banks that Jacques Marquette . . . was carried to a point where the melting snow

of March 1675 had filled Mud Lake to overflowing and sent the water swirling down to Lake Michigan. . . .[6]

The newspaper recognized that it had stumbled onto an historic moment.

Remnants of the old West Fork and perhaps of Mud Lake itself may remain in some small cattail marshes, but some would be on private land and others would be difficult to discern without diligent observation. A Friends of the Chicago River tour map of the area shows nine places where the fork and Mud Lake were still detectable in 1993.

Many momentous, almost unbelievable projects, carried out against great odds, make up the Chicago River system story. The routine filling of the historic West Fork was merely a quiet footnote.

The Metropolitan Water Reclamation District
Modern Approaches to Clean Streams

The Chicago Sewage Disposal System, generally acknowledged because of its great size to be one of the wonders of modern engineering, depends, in its operation, on the cooperation of the very small—hordes of microscopic bacteria.

—J. Kip Finch
"Seven modern wonders named," *Civil Engineering*, November, 1955

During the early part of the twentieth century, even as it was completing work on the Cal-Sag Channel, the Sanitary District of Chicago was turning away from building artificial rivers and turning toward artificially harnessing the natural ally of the germ. This change was a result of the new popular acceptance of Pasteur, Koch, and Lister's germ theory.

It is extremely important to appreciate that helpful bacteria in appropriate conditions and quantities are essential to life on our planet. Without these bacteria our bodies would not operate properly, organic matter would not decompose after death, nutrients would not be recycled, and life would simply stop. Scientists at the SDC and elsewhere were beginning to appreciate that in the normal cycle of natural events, beneficial microorganisms clean up decaying organisms in river systems. It seemed plausible that this natural process could be harnessed in an artificial environment. While dilution continued as a district strategy, new techniques based on germ theory were also refined and applied. Chicago, which had made of its river an open sewer, now attempted to undo the harm of more than half a century and reclaim the river through the agency of the Sanitary District. As the SDC changed in scope, it also changed its name. In 1955 it became the Metropolitan Sanitary District of Greater Chicago (MSDGC), and in 1989 it became The Metropolitan Water Reclamation District of Greater Chicago (MWRDGC, or simply, the MWRD).

Sewage Collection:
From Home, Business, and Industry to Treatment Plant

As of this writing, more than $4\frac{1}{2}$ million people live in the service area of the MWRDGC. Industrial waste adds the equivalent of the refuse from another $4\frac{1}{2}$ million people. This tide of refuse would have overwhelmed the artificial channels and the branches of the river if the MWRDGC had not experimented with and adopted sewage-disposal strategies other than dilution. Channels and dilution were never intended to handle the waste from a population of this size. In the 1890s when the channel system was designed, it seemed inconceivable that Chicago would grow this large.

Dealing with this huge challenge required new approaches. Waste would be delivered to centralized locations for treatment instead of being dumped into the river and diluted. The SDC would build three treatment facilities, all of them in the 1920s, and all in handsome Art Deco architecture. In cooperation with communities within its jurisdiction, it would build a system of conduits and pumping stations to steer the stormwater runoff and sewage discharge from combined sewers away from the lake and rivers and into these treatment plants. This system would begin to come on line in the late 1920s and would function effectively until the 1950s, when urban growth and development outstripped its capacity. Four other treatment plants were built much later and do not relate to the Chicago River per se.

The Activated Sludge Process

Waste delivered through the system to the treatment plant is subjected to the rather unappealing but accurate name of the "activated sludge process." The activated sludge process was in wide use by 1914. It harnesses nature's smallest organisms to break down other microorganisms in a continuous process until nothing is left but the smallest amount of organic residue, or sludge, which then has to be properly disposed of. The process mimics that of nature but is sped up enormously over the time it would take in a natural environment. All of the MWRDGC's facilities use this same approach. We will take an armchair tour of the North Side Water Reclamation Plant on the North Shore Channel in Skokie to see how it works.

The first, or primary treatment process, mimics the process of a river carrying "junk" such as stones, bottles, twigs, etc. In a natural river, the heavy inorganic materials, such as shopping carts, to use a local example, would drop out first. Coarser materials, such as the bottles, would drop out further along, and finer ones would stay in the river for the longest distance, eventually settling out onto the river bed. Biodegradable organic matter would decompose through the action of naturally occurring microorganisms.

When raw waste emerges from the intercepting sewers deep beneath Howard Street and McCormick Boulevard, it is full of typical junk in a dirty river, from rags to logs. The sewage passes through coarse screens to remove large pieces, such as timbers, that could damage pumps and other equipment. It is then lifted to the surface by huge pumps in the Pump and Blower Building, a quiet and dignified affair on the outside but near-deafening with the multitude of blowers chugging away inside. The sewage next passes through another pre-treatment process consisting of a grit tank and fine screens. The solid objects that have settled on the bottom of the grit tank or have been sifted out by the screens are removed to dumpsters and go, like household garbage, to a landfill. (On the day I visited, a ten-inch-long frog had miraculously survived the indignity of passing through all the tanks and screens. I hoped he would be released, as are survivor fish.) The remains are visibly prettier, but not

Photo by Libby Hill.

The Art Deco North Branch Pumping Station on the east bank of the North Branch at Lawrence Avenue. The station went into service in 1930 and pumps raw sewage northward to the North Side Water Reclamation Plant at Howard Street. All sewage from the area bounded by Lake Michigan, Fullerton Avenue, Clark Street, and Howard Street drains through the Lawrence sewer to this station. During large storms, extra pumps are put into service to pump excess sewage and stormwater to the river through the arches.

much cleaner organically than when they entered the plant.

After the material has passed through pre-treatment in the grit tank and fine screens, it passes to the preliminary settling tank for primary treatment. The sludge settles out on the bottom of the tank, is combined with other sludge, and the "activated sludge process" takes over. In this oversimplified description of a very complex process, the wastewater is continually mixed in football-field-sized tanks with microorganisms and a supply of dissolved oxygen. The dissolved oxygen is constantly bubbled into the tanks through large pipes that lead from garage-sized compressors in the Pump and Blower Building. Here, also, we have artificial treatment mimicking nature. This bubbling air mimics the natural aeration of rapids in a river, and it provides the microorganisms with the oxygen they need in order to live and devour the organic materials in the wastewater. In the process, these microorganisms not only produce their own waste but also reproduce another generation of microorganisms that continue the work. The organic material is subjected to this microorganism cycle for $4\frac{1}{2}$ hours, after which it enters final settling tanks to allow any remaining organic material to settle out. What settles out is called activated sludge.

Part of the settled activated sludge is cycled back to the start of the process

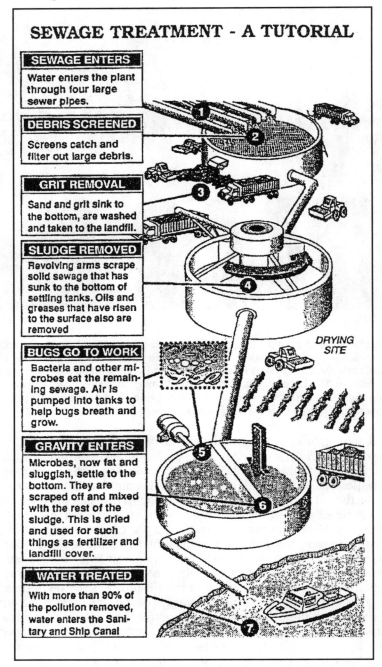

SEWAGE TREATMENT - A TUTORIAL

SEWAGE ENTERS
Water enters the plant through four large sewer pipes.

DEBRIS SCREENED
Screens catch and filter out large debris.

GRIT REMOVAL
Sand and grit sink to the bottom, are washed and taken to the landfill.

SLUDGE REMOVED
Revolving arms scrape solid sewage that has sunk to the bottom of settling tanks. Oils and greases that have risen to the surface also are removed

BUGS GO TO WORK
Bacteria and other microbes eat the remaining sewage. Air is pumped into tanks to help bugs breath and grow.

GRAVITY ENTERS
Microbes, now fat and sluggish, settle to the bottom. They are scraped off and mixed with the rest of the sludge. This is dried and used for such things as fertilizer and landfill cover.

WATER TREATED
With more than 90% of the pollution removed, water enters the Sanitary and Ship Canal

DRYING SITE

Sewage Treatment—A Tutorial; Jack Jordan. Reprinted with special permission from the Chicago Sun-Times, Inc. © 1999.

A greatly simplified diagram of the sewage treatment process for a generic treatment plant emptying into the Sanitary and Ship Canal.

to provide a source of microorganisms to continue the process described above. Clear effluent from final settling tanks is released into the North Shore Channel. "It has taken a tremendous amount of study and research to determine the most favorable conditions for bacterial growth—even down to the size of the bubbles used in aerating the sewage."[1] It would take a natural stream several weeks to achieve the cleansing feat that artificial treatment accomplishes in a matter of hours.

Any remaining sludge from the primary and secondary process is piped 18 miles to the state-of-the-art Stickney Water Reclamation Plant, where it is processed. Eventually, after three years of aging, it is disposed of on land in an environmentally acceptable manner.

The best way to appreciate the process is to take a tour of the treatment plant. Knowledgeable personnel will take you through all the steps—some of which are a little odiferous, explain the complex computer system, and show you the final product that is released into the North Shore Channel. Compared to its original condition, the effluent is astonishingly clear and organically much cleaner, with better than 90 percent of the pollutants removed.

In the early 1900s the Sanitary District not only continued to experiment with improvements in the treatment process, but it also began an aggressive investigation into the types of industrial sewage it had to treat and methods to reduce the amount. It investigated and took precautions in handling sewage from the stockyards, tanneries, corn refining, and paint manufacturing, among

Photo by Libby Hill.

North Side Water Reclamation Plant outfall to the North Shore Channel, located on the west bank north of Howard Street in Skokie. It currently treats and discharges an average of 300 million gallons of sewage per day.

others. Industrial wastes pose particular problems because they might upset the treatment process by killing the microorganisms, contaminate the sludge, cause explosions, adversely impact worker health, or pass through the process entirely to pollute the river. Even wastes from homes and businesses can be suspect, considering the variety of chemicals in use today. To protect the process from potential ill effects, the SDC initiated a program to control industrial waste.

In 1955, the American Society of Civil Engineers recognized "Chicago's Sewage Disposal System, a Herculean task in sanitation" as one of seven "marvels of civil engineering in the United States."[2] It was not the channel that finally reversed the flow of the Chicago River that impressed them, as is often thought, because the Society recognized the channel for what it was: an emergency approach to an immediate problem. It was the application of the innovative and complex process of employing tiny microorganisms for treatment of a monumental amount of waste.

Ironically, it was about this time that the effects of urban growth and development caused sewer overloads during storms to occur not once, but twice—during the fall of 1954 and again in the summer of 1957. The Sanitary District had no choice but to release the mixture of untreated sewage and storm runoff into Lake Michigan at Wilmette and Chicago. There simply was not enough capacity in the local sewers, the intercepting sewers, or at the treatment plant. The microorganisms never had a chance. Beaches were contaminated and closed until the fecal coliform counts dropped to acceptable levels.

Tunnel and Reservoir Project (TARP), The "Deep Tunnel"

In the late 1960s, federally mandated water-quality standards made it evident that the frequent overflows from combined sewers had to cease. In the Chicago area, the problem was big—375 square miles big—with over 400 locations where overflows occurred in the city and the suburbs. The objectives of the program were to prevent river backflows into Lake Michigan, to meet water quality standards in the river, and to provide an outlet for sewers in order to reduce basement flooding.

Suggestions for addressing these goals ranged from digging up all the streets to install separate sanitary sewer and stormwater systems, to placing a treatment device at each overflow point, to building another river, underground, that would temporarily hold the overflows.

The idea of building an underground river, or a tunnel, to be more precise, was not as bizarre as it might seem. The city had been building rock tunnels to convey drinking water from the lake intake cribs for over 100 years, and the city and what was then called the MSDGC were starting to excavate rock tunnels for large relief sewers. Due to advances in construction technology, the cost of tunneling was coming down. And of course, Chicago was blessed with a thick stratum of Niagaran dolomite down below. Chicago had solved its sanitation problems before by digging through this rock. Why not solve the combined-sewer problem by boring through the dolomite? This project had and still has

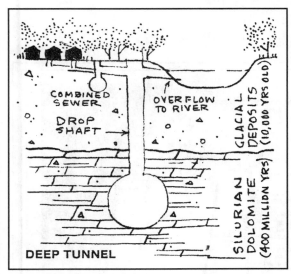

COMBINED SEWER

DROP SHAFT →

OVERFLOW TO RIVER

GLACIAL DEPOSITS (10,000 YRS OLD)

SILURIAN DOLOMITE (400 MILLION YRS)

DEEP TUNNEL

Courtesy of David Jones. Originally published in the Friends of the Chicago River's "Chicago River Trail Walking Tour of the Near North Branch Section."

its vocal opponents, who not only object to the cost but are also concerned about possible contamination of underground water in the dolomite, or the reverse, the depletion of the groundwater supply by the tunnels.

In 1972, the state and local coordinating committee decided on the Chicago Underflow Plan (CUP), the Tunnel and Reservoir Plan (TARP), or as it is popularly known, the "Deep Tunnel," as the most beneficial plan at the least cost. The tunnel portion was implemented by the MWRDGC using U.S. EPA construction grant money. The reservoir portion of CUP is being implemented through the Army Corps of Engineers. To vastly oversimplify again, vertical shafts will be drilled through the earth and rock. In times of heavy rain, overflows from existing sewers would drop 200 feet or more to a horizontal tunnel that will convey the overflows to a reservoir for temporary storage while the treatment plants worked at full tilt. As soon as capacity is available at the treatment plant, the stored overflows will be pumped there for treatment and then discharged into the river. The tunnels themselves become unintentional storage only if the reservoirs fill and back up into them.

The estimated cost, although less than for other alternatives, was a staggering $4 billion for the entire Chicago area. Funding was to come from federal, state, and local sources. This monumental project made the cost and construction of the Sanitary and Ship Canal look like a drop in a bucket.

Construction began in 1975 on tunnels between Wilmette and south-suburban McCook, following the route of the North Shore Channel, the North and South Branches of the Chicago River, and the Sanitary and Ship Canal. By 1985, the completed tunnels, shafts, and pumping station began operation. An additional segment under the North Branch between Morton Grove and the dam, or waterfall, began service in 1998. The projected completion date for the reservoir and some additional tunnels is, perhaps, 2010. Eliminating overflows from the Chicago River and its branches will eventually involve 58 miles of tunnels up to 35 feet in diameter between Wilmette and McCook. At Wilmette, the tunnel is about 200 feet below ground. At the Harlem Avenue bridge over the Main Channel, the tunnel is about 300 feet below ground, due to the tunnel's slope.

A 10.5-billion-gallon reservoir will be built near McCook between the Main Channel and I-55 from the Indiana Harbor Belt Railroad tracks to almost Route 45. This is the site of the old MWRDGC lagoons, which are being removed from

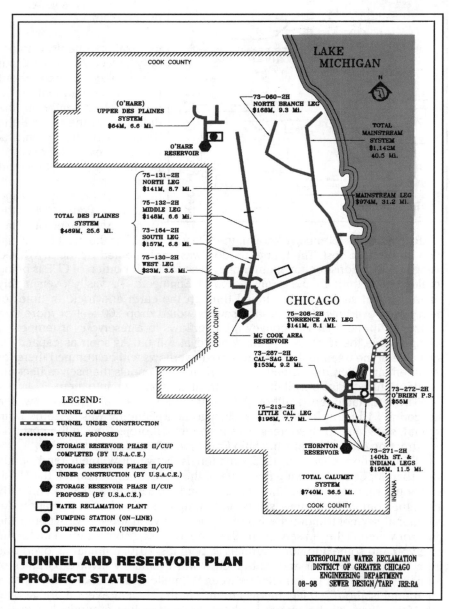

LAKE
MICHIGAN

N

COOK COUNTY

73-060-2H
NORTH BRANCH LEG
$168M, 9.3 Mi.

(O'HARE)
UPPER DES PLAINES
SYSTEM
$64M, 6.6 Mi.

TOTAL
MAINSTREAM
SYSTEM
$1,142M
40.5 Mi.

O'HARE
RESERVOIR

75-131-2H
NORTH LEG
$141M, 8.7 Mi.

MAINSTREAM LEG
$974M, 31.2 Mi.

75-132-2H
MIDDLE LEG
$148M, 6.6 Mi.

TOTAL DES PLAINES
SYSTEM
$469M, 25.6 Mi.

73-164-2H
SOUTH LEG
$157M, 6.8 Mi.

75-130-2H
WEST LEG
$23M, 3.5 Mi.

COOK COUNTY

CHICAGO

75-208-2H
TORRENCE AVE. LEG
$141M, 8.1 Mi.

MC COOK AREA
RESERVOIR

73-287-2H
CAL-SAG LEG
$153M, 9.2 Mi.

73-272-2H
O'BRIEN P.S.
$55M

75-213-2H
LITTLE CAL. LEG
$196M, 7.7 Mi.

THORNTON
RESERVOIR

73-271-2H &
140th ST. &
INDIANA LEGS
$195M, 11.5 Mi.

TOTAL CALUMET
SYSTEM
$740M, 36.5 Mi.

INDIANA

COOK COUNTY

LEGEND:

▬▬▬ TUNNEL COMPLETED
▨▨▨ TUNNEL UNDER CONSTRUCTION
•••••• TUNNEL PROPOSED

⬡ STORAGE RESERVOIR PHASE II/CUP
COMPLETED (BY U.S.A.C.E.)

⬢ STORAGE RESERVOIR PHASE II/CUP
UNDER CONSTRUCTION (BY U.S.A.C.E.)

⬣ STORAGE RESERVOIR PHASE II/CUP
PROPOSED (BY U.S.A.C.E.)

▭ WATER RECLAMATION PLANT

● PUMPING STATION (ON-LINE)

○ PUMPING STATION (UNFUNDED)

TUNNEL AND RESERVOIR PLAN
PROJECT STATUS

METROPOLITAN WATER RECLAMATION
DISTRICT OF GREATER CHICAGO
ENGINEERING DEPARTMENT
08-98   SEWER DESIGN/TARP JRR:RA

Courtesy of the Metropolitan Water Reclamation District of Greater Chicago.

service. Another reservoir will be built in the northern section of Thornton Quarry.

The project appears to be working. Even with the tunnel part of the project only partially completed, the occurrence of backflows to the lake, which used to happen about twice per year on average, has been cut back. Only when the reservoirs are on line will backflows be virtually eliminated. Other evidence that TARP is "on-line" is the columns of vapor you see (and sometimes smell) at various points along the river. These plumes occur from the warm moist air rising out of vents from the drop shafts to the deep tunnel. Because the tunnels are not completely drained, residual solids decompose and the musty odor rises with the vapor plumes.

Now that the tunnels are in operation, the final step is to construct the "R" part of TARP, the large reservoirs that will increase storage capacity to nearly 20 billion gallons. In the flood of February 20-21, 1997, four inches of rain cascaded off frozen ground into the waterways, the tunnels filled up, and the MWRDGC had to open the locks so the river could flow what is now backward into Lake Michigan. *The Chicago Tribune* editorialized,

> It's deep tunnels and reservoirs! . . . Nothing like a few thousand flooded basements to remind people in Cook County why they've been paying higher taxes over the last 20 years to build something called the Deep Tunnel and Reservoir Project. . . . And nothing like the dumping of 4 billion gallons of sewage-tainted storm water into Lake Michigan to remind everyone why [the 4-billion-dollar] TARP must be completed, in its entirety, the sooner the better.[3]

Would it also be fair to say that there is nothing like such a flood to remind Chicago that it was built on a marsh?

Requirements for Disinfection, and its Consequences

The approach used by the Sanitary (Water Reclamation) District throughout the twentieth century was based upon the knowledge that natural rivers contain helpful bacteria that decompose the organic detritus in the waterway. Despite this natural process, a practice arose in the 1960s of using various techniques to kill off the bacteria in the treated effluent discharged from sewage treatment plants into streams. (Unfortunately, the idea that all bacteria are harmful was becoming a household mantra among the public.) The most common technique used to disinfect effluent involves dosing it with enough sodium hypochlorite, or household bleach, to destroy the micro-organisms. When Illinois adopted these standards in 1972, the MSDGC began the practice at all of its water reclamation plants. It proved very costly because of the large quantity of the chemical needed to disinfect the large volumes of effluent.

Although there was some controversy when federal standards requiring disinfection were adopted, it wasn't until after the practice of using chlorination was widespread that scientists and public health experts questioned its necessity and its latent effects. The federal government became concerned

Photo by Robert M. Kaplan.

An avid angler, a member of Mayor Daley's fishing committee, catching blue-gill without bait at the dam at the confluence of the North Branch and the North Shore Channel.

about safe drinking water. Research showed three disagreeable side-effects to using chlorine to treat effluent. First, the discharge of chlorine resulted in the creation of chlorinated hydrocarbon compounds, which contributed carcinogens to lakes and rivers used as sources of drinking water for cities. Second, excessive amounts of energy were required to produce the chlorine or chlorine compounds. And third, the chlorine was toxic to aquatic life in rivers and lakes. In 1976 the federal government repealed its requirement.

Illinois was slower to change. Finally, the MSDGC received permission to conduct extensive tests of the effectiveness of disinfection at the Calumet Water Reclamation Plant from August, 1983, to March, 1984. Having demonstrated that disinfection was not effective, the district received a variance allowing it to discontinue chlorination at the Calumet, Lemont, North Side, and Stickney plants. Since 1984, the fact that effluent is no longer chlorinated has contributed both to the restoration of aquatic life and to the annual savings of millions of dollars for the district's taxpayers and ratepayers.

Midges and Fish: Success Story of Nature's Balancing Act

The elimination of chlorine additives to the Chicago River occurred at the same time the Deep Tunnel went on line, and the combination has resulted in a major rejuvenation of water quality, indicating the resiliency of nature. A dependable supply of oxygen in the water is a vital component in this success.

While standing on the bow of Pollution Control I (PCI), docked at the Wilmette Pumping Station on a gray December afternoon in 1997, passengers learned that a small amount of Lake Michigan water was being diverted from the lake through the Wilmette sluice gate. In freezing weather, a bubbler system mounted along the sides and bottom of the gate causes water to circulate. This system keeps the gate free of ice accumulations and prevents it from freezing shut. An inoperable gate could lead to disaster if a rainstorm occurred during the winter. But allowing this slight diversion from the lake during winter also maintains an acceptable amount of dissolved oxygen in the North Shore Channel.

Since dissolved oxygen is a vital component of water quality, this diversion helps to maintain a thriving community of fish. At least 25 species, including white crappie, some large and small mouth bass, green sunfish, bullheads, and many blue-nosed minnows, among others, are now found regularly by the MWRDGC through its fish-population monitoring program. During cold winter months, some fish may migrate downstream below Howard Street where the discharge from the North Side Water Reclamation Plant warms the waters of the North Shore Channel.

In the 1970s and up until the mid-1980s, the MWRDGC had been receiving complaints from residents and businesses along the North Shore Channel about midge flies—nuisance, mosquito-like, but non-biting, insects. Midge flies hatch in the bottom sediments of the channel and exist there during their larval stage. As adults, they leave the water and swarm in huge numbers around trees and bushes. Although the neighbors were bothered by these insects, the midges at least demonstrated that for some reason conditions in the channel had improved enough to allow the breeding of aquatic insects, albeit those very tolerant of pollution. Previously, aquatic life in the channel had been minimal to non-existent because of the inhospitable environment. Nevertheless, the MWRDGC did douse the North Shore Channel with a larvicide and used occasional airborne spraying to control the pesky flies.

By 1984, when TARP came on line and the chlorination stopped, conditions improved dramatically to the point where fish began to appear in the river. By the 1990s, the nuisance flies were no longer a problem because enough fish were eating enough of the bottom-dwelling midge fly larvae to keep the population in check. Working with nature once again proved its value. To maintain a high amount of dissolved oxygen for the fish, the MWRDGC has built aeration structures that look like corrugated retaining walls on the channel at Devon Avenue and on the North Branch at Webster Avenue. Bubbles coming from underwater along these walls add oxygen to the water.

Controlling the Flow of Water in the Chicago River System

After the completion of the Main Channel extension in 1907, the control of the flow of water from the Chicago River system into the Des Plaines River occurred at the Lockport Powerhouse, downstream from the Lockport Controlling Works, and the Lockport Controlling Works, including the Bear Trap Dam, was essentially put on standby. The Bear Trap Dam that the

Photo by Libby Hill.

The Devon Avenue Instream Aeration Station. Compressors in the building supply air to diffusers under the water on each side of the channel to allow oxygen in the air bubbles to dissolve in the water. The aeration is not in operation in this photograph as it is winter, and the extra oxygen is not needed.

commissioners and trustees had furtively opened on January 17, 1900, was no longer needed after 1907 and was later removed.

In addition to controlling the flow of water from the Chicago River system at Lockport, the SDC had to control water flow in all of its channels and controlling works to keep the entire system prepared to handle storms. Originally, the control center for the canal system was located at 31st Street and Western Avenue. This facility served as an operations center for the SDC and was staffed at all times. From 1907 through the 1920s, this center was primarily in control of the distribution of electrical energy brought from the Lockport Powerhouse to Chicago on transmission lines along the Main Channel. As the SDC began to operate pumping stations and treatment plants in the late 1920s, the center also took on the task of coordinating electrical switching operations with Commonwealth Edison at all SDC facilities.

It was always this center that issued orders to control the flow of water throughout the canal system. SDC engineers would make decisions and convey them to the system dispatcher on duty at the center. The system dispatcher conveyed orders by telephone to local operators at the Wilmette Pumping Station, Chicago River Controlling Works, Blue Island Controlling Works, and the Lockport Powerhouse, directing the local operator to change operating conditions. (The Blue Island Controlling Works at the eastern end of the Cal-Sag Channel was replaced in 1965 by the O'Brien Lock and Dam on the

Calumet River, completely reversing the flow of the Calumet River.) In turn, the local operator would relay information on local conditions of canal water levels, gate settings, pump discharge rates, rainfall amounts, etc. back to the system dispatcher at the control center

In 1965, the headquarters of what was then called the Metropolitan Sanitary District of Greater Chicago (MSDGC) at 100 E. Erie Street, off of Chicago's "Magnificent Mile," became the new home for what was now called the "Waterway Control Center." By this time, electrical energy generated at the Powerhouse was sent to the Edison distribution system at Lockport, and the MSDGC was no longer in the business of bringing electricity back to Chicago for distribution. The Waterway Control Center was upgraded with canal-water-level data and rainfall amounts transmitted over telephone lines from remote sensors at strategic locations. Through a direct link with a private weather forecasting service, the system dispatcher was armed with the latest information and, in collaboration with the supervising engineers, could transmit orders to the local operators to prepare the canal system for approaching storms. Further state-of-the-art upgrades to the Waterway Control Center include computerized recording and display of critical weather and operating information, including the TARP system.

With the TARP tunnels in place, there is added capacity to handle big storms. Given the realities of weather forecasting, however, every storm is handled as if it could be the big one. Typically, upon notice of imminent rainfall, the gates at the intakes at Wilmette, Chicago Harbor, and the O'Brien Lock and Dam are closed, and the discharge through the generators at Lockport is increased. This lowers the canal system water level slowly below the prescribed level for navigation and provides capacity for the channels to accept stormwater runoff and increased flow from the treatment plants. If the storm does not materialize, conditions are returned to normal. Depending on the intensity and duration of rainfall, additional flow at Lockport may be required.

If the storm turns out to be a whopper and the TARP tunnels fill up, water flow from Lockport is increased to the maximum by using the trusty 100-year-old sluice gates at the Lockport Controlling Works. Navigation interests are notified to take precautions due to fast currents in the canal. If water levels in the canal system at Wilmette or the Chicago Inner Harbor reach critical highs, preparations are made for bypassing to the lake. The harbormaster at Wilmette is notified for the safety of boats and boaters. Personnel at the water supply intakes for Chicago and North Shore communities are notified of a potential by-pass of polluted water to the lake. During the summer, the various park districts are notified due to the potential for pollution at bathing beaches.

Fortunately, with the TARP tunnels in operation, the frequency of by-passing to the lake is decreasing. When the TARP reservoirs are in operation, by-passing will be a thing of the past, just like it was prior to the 1950s, except for that rare event that swamps everything.

Diversion Revisited

The conflict over diversion continues to this day. In 1959, the U.S. Supreme Court reopened the 1930 Decree. Issues on the table included the loss in hydroelectric power revenues at Niagara and St. Lawrence power plants, public health and pollution in the Great Lakes and the Illinois River basin, and the navigability of channels and harbors on the Great Lakes—topics not easily resolved. In the 1967 Decree, the court ruled for the state of Illinois, essentially retaining the status quo. It limited Illinois's amount of diversion to 3,200 cfs and included domestic pumpage in that total. Domestic pumpage had been averaging 1,700 cfs annually. Illinois could now apportion the total allowable diversion among its many political units: municipalities, sanitary districts, and so forth. The amount could be divided between domestic use and direct diversion into the canal system to maintain it in reasonably satisfactory sanitary condition.

The 1967 Decree also specified the method for measurement and the allowable grounds for Illinois to apply for an increase. The state Division of Water Resources became the responsible accounting agent for diversion and for reporting the amount to the U.S. Army Corps of Engineers. The state set up a mechanism to allocate the 3,200 cfs to users of lake diversion through the issuance of allocation orders. Today, the MWRDGC operates under these regulations and diverts water from the lake into the river under its allocation order.

In 1980, small changes related to the administration of the decree led to large consequences. The role and responsibility of the Corps of Engineers in lake diversion accounting was increased and, as a result, an alternate means and location of measurement was implemented in 1984. The Corps of Engineers hired the U.S. Geological Survey (USGS) to install and maintain a new technology (acoustics) for measuring the flow of water at southwest-suburban Romeoville on the Main Channel. It is not entirely surprising that the new measurements did not agree with the old. Lockport had been under-measuring the flow, and Illinois had been inadvertently diverting too much water from Lake Michigan. The Great Lakes states pounced and threatened to reopen the decree. Cooler heads prevailed, however, and mediation resulted in a Memo of Understanding between the Great Lakes states, Illinois, and the U.S. Attorney General.

The memo called for the Army Corps of Engineers to reduce excessive leakage through the Chicago River lock and to recycle lock flows. It required that Illinois "pay back" the overdraw over a period of years, reduce excessive leakage through the old Chicago Harbor walls by building a new wall, and relocate the point of measurement to the intake controls on Lake Michigan. As a result of the last item, the acoustic flow meters in the Chicago River are now under the Columbus Drive bridge.[4]

Continuing Improvements to the Controlling Works

In 1984, ownership of the locks was transferred to the Army Corps of

Engineers. By the 1990s, the aging structure was leaking so badly as to jeopardize the allowable lake diversion amount. The corps performed a major overhaul, replacing motors, gear trains, and gate seals; lubricating hinges; and installing a system of air bubblers and mixers to control ice formation.

Ongoing lake diversion issues are changing the old controlling works built in the 1930s. A project launched in 1999, resulting from the Memo of Understanding, created a new wall across the Chicago Inner Harbor from the old Coast Guard station to near the south abutment of the Outer Drive bridge. This wall replaced the South Basin Wall, which was breached. The new wall has sluice gates, boat mooring for government agencies, and a pumping station to recycle flows from lock openings back into the lake, thereby reducing the amount of lake diversion.

The Future?

Past efforts to deal with wastewater barely kept pace with the population increase. As of 1998, the system had enough capacity to accommodate the current population. The next challenges will be to build the reservoirs and to plan for inevitable continuing growth. As of today, with more than 90 percent of pollutants removed from the waste that enters the treatment plants, the river is cleaner, and fish and anglers are returning. Working with natural processes has shown that a river can be resilient if approached with respect.

1938 air photo courtesy of the North Cook County Soil and Water Conservation District. 1988 air photo courtesy of the Natural Resources Conservation Service and United States Department of Agriculture.

The air photo on the left was taken in 1938. The photo on the right is of the same area around north-suburban Northbrook was taken in 1988. Peg your eyes to the arrow pointing to the intersection of the two railroad tracks near the bottom center of both photos. To its left is Shermer Road. Downtown Northbrook is near the center of both photos. The light and dark patches in the 1938 photo are farm fields. In the 1988 photo on the right, those fields have been developed for housing. Although these profound changes occurred on the West Fork, the same degree of development occurred on the Middle and East Forks.

Citizens and Their River
The Sixties through the Nineties

The Chicago River is the city's most neglected natural resource. It is overshadowed by Lake Michigan, disdained by environmentalists and outdoorsmen alike, neglected, fouled, and abused by industry and by all the rest of us. Nonetheless, it is the second greatest gift that nature has bestowed on this city.

—Robert Cassidy
"Our friendless river," Chicago, 1979

In May, 1979, Robert Cassidy put his canoe into the North Branch at Lake Avenue in Glenview for a trip down the Chicago River with Ralph Frese and a few others. Frese is a veteran canoeist, native of Chicago, and owner of the Chicagoland Canoe Base that supplies canoes and accessories for rental and purchase. Cassidy and Frese, threading through the leafy forest preserves, observed the variety of flora and fauna under a canopy that can deceive the paddler into thinking he is miles away from civilization. Cassidy discovered the treasure that lay long forgotten or ignored by the majority in their own backyard. He wrote an article for *Chicago* magazine and titled it, "Our friendless river." In it, he stated, "The task of reclaiming a city's river is hardly impossible. Other places are doing it. A recent survey of 107 major cities with waterways suitable for redevelopment showed that more than half were actually implementing waterfront-development plans. Why not Chicago?"[1]

The article triggered the imaginations of enough Chicago-area residents to raise the consciousness of many others. At last people began to consider the realities and the potential of the Chicago River system. They began to address the scars left by over 100 years of abuse.

Although people had been moving into the watershed steadily throughout these past 150 years, much of the development had come in spurts, responding to changing social conditions. Punctuated changes in runoff leave scars on the riverbanks. When the earliest settlers began to farm the watershed, they drained water off the land and channelized it into conduits of brick or open ditches. Erosion and deposition increased, producing severely unstable river conditions. The river was literally thrust up and down as any minor rain event caused its water levels to fluctuate wildly.

As large quantities of sediment entered the channel, amounts in excess of what the stream would normally carry, the stream bed would actually become elevated and the stream would flow on top of an increasing depth of sediment. The stream-channel bottom would rise during periods of severe deposition. During periods of less deposition the stream would erode the recently deposited sediments and deepen its channel. This process of deposition and erosion could repeat itself countless times, and the record would be visible in terraces along the stream banks.

Along many reaches of the Chicago River, especially where undeveloped land can be found, many depositional terraces are visible. In areas such as Harms Woods in the Cook County Forest Preserves, three principal terrace systems are present. Each terrace represents a previous heavy deposition period. The first dates from the early to mid 1800s, when the North Branch watershed was first being settled and locally cultivated in small-scale farms. A second, middle terrace dates from 1890 to the 1930s, a time of more extensive land clearing and agriculture. The third and lowest terrace dates from the 1950s, when large-scale housing development began. Recent erosion from continuing development has cut through all prior terraces, but it has not erased their traces.

Pollution:
Chemical and Biological Changes to River Water Quality

The "river continuum hypothesis" holds that persistent changes in one reach of the river can result in changes to all or most other reaches. As development continues upstream, the amount of impermeable surface, such as in parking lots, increases. Water drains quickly off the land and enters the

Photo by Robert M. Kaplan.

Intensive changes in land use on the North Branch resulted in visible terraces at the Forest Preserve District of Cook County's Harms Woods downstream. At Harms Woods, the author is standing on the middle terrace, and a friend is standing on the higher terrace. The lowest terrace, dating from the 1950s, is underwater in the river.

channels more rapidly. As the water skims the land surface, it picks up many of the same naturally-occurring chemicals it did under normal conditions, but in higher concentrations than those absorbed by slowly percolating water. Other manufactured chemicals, many of them available in quantity only after World War II, take a ride on the water. These include salt concentrates; heavy metals; oils, lubricants, and grease; combustible by-products like gasoline; and some soaps and detergents. Once they enter the stream, these chemicals, individually or in combination, are detrimental to the organisms that once relied on the life-support minerals of seepage water.

The chemicals change the biology of the stream. Some species are favored by the differences while others are eliminated, and these changes in populations occur rapidly for some species and over long periods for others. In many rivers, including the Chicago, disruption of the natural river processes completely alters the life, energy, and productivity of the river system. Animal and plant species that can adapt to the altered conditions in a river begin to invade. They often predominate, to the detriment of other species. Carp and goldfish, species bred for food for 5,000 years in other parts of the world, have become adapted to the deteriorated water quality associated with human societies in Europe and Asia. After being introduced into the United States in 1876, these species became the most frequently caught fish in the Chicago River.

Healing: National and Local Responsibilities

With all of the Chicago's erosion and chemical and biological challenges, it might seem hopeless to think of restoring this river to any semblance of health or even to consider turning it into a pleasant recreational amenity. Yet, this is exactly what people are doing. While the Metropolitan Water Reclamation District is improving the water quality, others are developing amenities along the riverbanks. Downtown streetscapes that overlook the river, continuous riverwalks that provide pedestrian access to the river along private developments, a park along Bubbly Creek, restored wetlands along the North Branch, and replanting native vegetation along stream banks to stop erosion: all are either happening or being planned.

We have already seen how the Forest Preserve District became concerned with the health of the North Branch in the latter part of the teens, how it commissioned a study of the North Branch in the 1930s, and how the Clean Streams Committee took shape in 1953 in order to address chemical, biological, and physical hazards in the river. But local action required federal support in the form of money and laws. The Chicago River was not the only waterway in trouble. Waterways were in trouble nationally, even though their stories might have been different, and widespread problems required federal attention. In the 1930s, epidemics of water-borne diseases had given rise to the New Deal's national policy to remedy water pollution. In 1948, Congress passed the Federal Water Pollution Control Act, leaving responsibility for clean water in the hands of the states but putting the federal government in a strong advisory and assistant role and setting up a grants structure. The legislation was renewed in 1956 with the support of a public grown increasingly wary of pollution from industry and municipalities. Because President Eisenhower was opposed to the program, the wheels turned slowly, if at all.[2]

Beginning in the 1950s, the combination of rapid population growth and urban development had created flooding and pollution problems of such proportions that dramatic efforts and even new agencies were required. At the beginning of the 1960s, water pollution began to evolve from a national concern into a national cause.

In 1962, Rachel Carson published *Silent Spring*. It was a galvanizing event. Although she was not the only person concerned about pollution in the late '50s and early '60s, no other publication on the topic of pollution inspired such a widespread and long-lasting passion. Carson was a scientist who could communicate with the general public. Her book supported those who were already concerned with environmental problems and helped pave the way for an increasingly active citizenry to lobby for improved general environmental health.

During the 1960s, federal authority over water quality increased steadily. In 1965, Congress passed the Water Quality Control Act, requiring states to set water quality standards. In 1969, Congress passed the National Environmental Policy Act (NEPA), mandating environmental impact statements. "This statute recast the government's role: formerly the conservator of wilderness, it now became the protector of earth, air, land, and water."[3] The national actions of the 1960s culminating in NEPA were the seed bed for the major national policies of the 1970s. On December 2, 1970, President Nixon's reorganization plan to assemble environmental agencies into one overarching organization culminated in the Environmental Protection Agency (EPA). In 1972, Public Law 92-500, the Federal Water Pollution Control Act, known as the Clean Water Act, marked a major philosophical change in that it essentially prohibited the polluting of waterways by any public or private facility and set forth new technology-based standards for treatment facilities and industrial discharges, along with a calendar for reaching the goal of zero polluting discharges by 1985. President Nixon's last-minute veto was overridden by a solid majority. "Thus did the Water Pollution Control Act Amendments of 1972, among the most sweeping, innovative environmental legislation ever considered, become law."[4] Further refining the federal government's role, President Carter signed the Clean Water Act of 1977, whose priority was to control toxic pollutant discharges into rivers and streams.

Despite these sweeping new federal laws, it would take combined local, state, and federal action to help the river. The action did not always have to be governmental. Individuals make a difference. Individuals in groups make an even greater difference. Groups working together with responsible agencies make the biggest difference. The vigilant volunteer crew of the Clean Streams Committee, for example, detected in 1965 that the Chicago Transit Authority Forest Glen bus terminal was dumping pollutants into floor drains that emptied into the forest preserves and then into a ditch that paralleled the railroad tracks. Commuters often would report that the ditch was on fire, because children would light the oil-soaked vegetation with a match. The ditch emptied into the Chicago River. Committee members did not take action themselves, but their working through authorities, including elected officials, led the CTA to acknowledge responsibility and begin steps to correct the situation. (Eventually the CTA stopped the offense, but it took nearly two decades.[5]) Because corrective measures take time to implement after responsibility is acknowledged, it takes great patience and persistence on the part of volunteers to continue their work, to neither throw up their hands in frustration nor to prematurely declare victory and go home. In the final analysis, river restoration depends upon a concerned, educated citizenry.

In 1967, a group of Lake Forest citizens became concerned about increasing development in their village and the loss of open land. They teamed up with the Nature Conservancy, became known as the Lake Forest Open Lands Association, and faced their first challenge: protecting the Skokie River floodplain. Bit by bit, over 20 years, the Lake Forest Open Lands Association purchased, accepted donations, or received conservation easements of land that culminated in the Skokie River Nature Preserve. The preserve covers 100 acres in an almost continuous stretch along the Skokie River, from Deerpath Road on the south, to near the northern limits of Lake Forest. Today the association owns and manages land along the Middle Fork as well as the Skokie.

In 1970, the year of the first Earth Day on April 22, a rash of articles about cleaning up the Chicago River appeared in newspapers. A *Chicago Tribune* headline from March 19 reads: "Grounds for fishing? Mayor [Richard J.] Daley order goes out to clean up riverbanks." Bruce Ingersoll of the *Sun Times* weighed in on October 11 in the article "Chicago River N. Branch—mucked up trout stream?" Despite its title, there is a note of optimism to the article. In March, 1970, citizens were urged to "Adopt-a-Stream." Scout troops responded, proving that often-untapped children power can do an adult-sized job. A ground swell (a river swell?) of volunteers responded to the call.

To recognize the first Earth Day, students at the former Cadwell Elementary School in Deerfield searched for a suitable project, and they turned to the polluted little creek (the West Fork) adjacent to their school; their first instinct was to do something for the river. Tom Roth, who in 1999 was President of the Deerfield Historical Society, was then in sixth grade at Cadwell Elementary School in Deerfield. He and his friends grew up around the creek and played near it, but Earth Day caused them to look at it in a different light, an environmental context. They decided to clean it up. Approaching the water, Roth realized he had on brand new gym shoes and removed them to keep them clean. With bare feet, he put one foot into the water, stepped on a rusty can, and ended up in the emergency room. "This is one of the dirtiest cuts I've ever seen," Tom quotes his physician.[6]

In 1972, the U. S. House of Representatives passed Rep. Frank Annunzio's bill to amend the River and Harbor Act of 1970 and authorize the Army Corps of Engineers to make clearing the North Branch a federal project. The amendment authorized the Corps to spend no more than $150,000 annually, in perpetuity, for cleanup of debris in the North Branch. The local sponsor is the Metropolitan Water Reclamation District, which provides 25 percent of the budget. As of 1999, no one had requested money for the past several years.[7]

Then there were the pessimists: The *Chicago Tribune*, once more:

Chicago River—it has a dirty future: Report blames population growth.
. . . Despite plans to spend more than $400 million to clean up the North
Branch of the Chicago River, many parts of that waterway will be dirtier in the
year 2000 because of continuing population growth, according to a report by
the Northeastern Illinois Planning Commission . . . reports show that although
most [water basins in the Chicago region] are rapidly improving, none will be
as clean as planners had hoped.

The report predicted that while the North Branch below Niles would improve
"from bad to good . . . an expected 30 percent increase in population in the
North Branch area, which includes Deerfield, Highland Park, and Lincolnshire,
will negate present pollution reduction efforts. . . ."[8]

The Friends of the Chicago River

Despite the pessimists, whose ideas certainly cannot be dismissed, the
optimists were out there. Cassidy's August, 1979, article in *Chicago* stimulated
like-minded people to forge a common mission: to revitalize the river and
return it as a focal point of Chicago. Within a month or so, these people made
it official. They were "Friends of the Chicago River" (FOCR, or simply, Friends).
Within a year, Friends became an official program of the Openlands Project,

Photo courtesy of Chris Parson, Friends of the Chicago River.

Education of teachers and students about the river is a crucial component in
improving river quality. Here, volunteer high school science teachers practice
water quality testing they will do with their students as part of the Friends of the
Chicago River program called "The Chicago River Schools Network."

and in 1988, Friends spun off as an independent organization.

Friends is a leading group, but not the only one dedicated to reviving the river. Canoe enthusiasts, hikers, volunteers within the ecological restoration community, river neighbors, and members of the public-at-large began to press for changes. The Chicago River, the lowest watery feature on the landscape, except for Lake Michigan, is finding a lofty place, with renewed and burgeoning interest in its ecological health.

Numerous innovative restoration projects are taking place throughout the Chicago River watershed. Restoration, meaning restoring river processes and not trying to reverse time and return the river to its original size and shape, is one. Some projects re-create adjacent wetlands and help the river store floodwater, others are vegetating riverbanks to keep them from eroding. It would take a book or a continuously updated Web site to track and discuss them all as thoroughly as they deserve. In our limited space, we will introduce just a few.

Lake County: Prairie Wolf Slough

Beginning in 1992, Friends of the Chicago River joined with the National Park Service under the leadership of Wink Hastings to initiate a comprehensive assessment and planning effort for the 156-mile-long Chicago River waterways. The effort was dubbed the Chicago River Demonstration Project, later just "ChicagoRivers." Knowing that the public wanted to see more than planning, Friends wanted to ensure that on-the-ground projects were included to demonstrate a holistic approach to the challenges facing a highly channelized river system. The U.S. Fish and Wildlife Service and other agencies provided technical assistance and spearheaded the effort to develop a list of 12 candidate sites for restoration, among them the 42-acre site now known as Prairie Wolf Slough. Aggressive fundraising by Friends and its partners led to money from the Illinois Environmental Protection Agency (Section 319 of the Clean Water Act), the Urban Resources Partnership, the Lake County Storm-water Management Commission, and the U.S. Fish and Wildlife Service. Numerous other agencies provided in-kind assistance.

On January 12, 1994, 21 people met together at Heller Nature Center in Highland Park to select the site. Because of the wisdom and necessity of involving everyone in such decisions, the group included representatives from many agencies: the villages of Deerfield and Bannockburn; the city of Highland Park; North Cook-Lake County Soil and Water Conservation District; Deerfield High School; High School District 113; Highland Park Historical Society; Highland Park Conservation Society; U.S. Fish and Wildlife Service; Lake County Stormwater Management Commission; Lake County Forest Preserve District; Heller Nature Center; Natural Resources Conservation Service; and, of course, Friends of the Chicago River.

There was strong enthusiasm for a site on Lake County Forest Preserve District land, adjacent to the Middle Fork, north of Deerfield High School, and abutting Half Day Road. The partners selected this site because of the strong interest on the part of the local community, especially Deerfield High School just to the south and Heller Nature Center just to the north. Both wanted to utilize the proposed project for nature education and ecology classes because such wetlands were increasingly difficult to find in this part of Lake County.

The first steps of this collaborative effort were fundraising and evaluation. The next steps were to convince the development committee of the Forest Preserve District Board to approve the concept and to navigate the continuous political and fundraising maze. The leadership of individuals combined with that of the Lake County Forest Preserve District and other agencies to bring about this project.

Ground was prepared in the winter of 1995-1996. An old-fashioned groundbreaking ceremony, reminiscent of the old Shovel Days, celebrated the culmination of planning and the beginning of construction. Staff and volunteers installed 51,000 plants the following spring. The site was named Prairie Wolf Slough, after Prairie Wolf (Injun John) Clark. Prairie Wolf had straddled two cultures at an important transition time in Lake County's early history. This wetland demonstration project represented another transition from one era to another in our ecological treatment of our landscape.

The purpose of the Prairie Wolf Slough project was to demonstrate how a restored wetland adjacent to the river could filter pollutants from surface drainage coming off a nearby detention basin, provide wildlife habitat, reduce flooding, and create a site for ecological education and recreation in an area of the country where such natural features are sorely lacking. Originally a wetland, the area had been drained for farming, increasing the amount of water flowing into the river and adding to flooding problems downstream. During restoration, the drainage tile installed by farmers was broken, allowing the water flowing onto the site to remain on the site rather than discharging directly into the river. Also, a berm, or dike, was constructed at the southern end of the site to divert water out into the wetland. This water had previously flowed into a drainage ditch and then into the stream. The site now contains 28 acres of wetlands and wet prairie and 18 acres of improved forest, including oak savanna.

A control structure adjacent to the Middle Fork regulates water in the wetland, maintaining a minimum water elevation in the wetlands and discharging excess flows into the stream. Because of the depth of the Middle Fork, about eight feet below grade, water from the ditch does not rise high enough to flood the wetland except in larger flood events.[9]

Carol Spielman of the Lake County Board shares her enthusiasm and commitment to the project:

> Numerous people have become stakeholders in the project. There are volunteer stewards working to manage the plan, volunteers from schools. One volunteer group holds Sunday evening sessions at Heller Nature Center, a social evening revolving around what is happening at the slough. Volunteers are monitoring the birds coming back, the plants that are starting to show, the butterflies, the water that is actually going into the Middle Fork. One volunteer wrote a history of Prairie Wolf Slough. Interpretive signs are in the works. People who planners never anticipated would appreciate the slough were coming from the neighboring office complex; a new path was created for them. Boy scouts, girl scouts, and school groups come to the slough to do

Photo courtesy of David Ramsay, Friends of the Chicago River.

Volunteers planting at Prairie Wolf Slough.

projects. All of this activity demonstrates the enormous response from the community and the great variety of people, not only from Lake County, who participate both as volunteers and as users of the slough.

In 1997, the fifth anniversary issue of *Meadowlark*, the journal of the Illinois Ornithological Society, dubbed Prairie Wolf Slough a "birding hotspot" because of all the migrants it has attracted. Over 120 bird species, particularly water birds, have been seen at the site. Before 1996, there was no open water; the land was only abandoned farm field.[10]

The Chicago Park District: Gompers Park

At the corner of Foster Avenue and Pulaski Road is 38.7-acre Gompers Park. Originally owned by the Albany Park District, it became a part of the Chicago Park District in 1934, when the 22 separate park jurisdictions in the city consolidated into one. The North Branch divides the park. The land is particularly attractive, descending gently from the residential highlands, built on the original rich prairie, to the wooded floodplain. The land's contour is a textbook case of the ecotonal nature of wetlands as a transition zone between dry land systems and rivers.

The meandering Chicago River carved the generous valley through glacial remains, eroding and depositing sediments and creating a landscape of terraces and floodplains. Over time, the river would have altered its course, as rivers do, and it is probable that the low terrain in the park adjacent to the river

Upper photos courtesy of Jim Macdonald. Lower photos courtesy of Anthony Watrobinski.

Gompers Park Project. 1995: Machinery preparing to remove the filled-in overburden from alongside the creek (*upper left*). 1995: The overburden has been scooped out and pushed up into a berm to create a lagoon which the creek can fill (*upper right*). 1999: Three volunteers stand in front of the filled lagoon and the berm. Wetland vegetation planted by volunteers covers the berm and grows at the edges of the wetland (*lower left*). 1999: A volunteer stands next to the controlling structure in the wetland. When the water gets high enough in the river, water pressure opens the valve at the end of the pipe and allows river water into the wetland (*lower right*).

is an old oxbow, an abandoned part of the river's former route. As is typical in functioning river-wetland systems, when the river overflowed its banks, as it did twice in spring, 1999, standing water collected in the low wetlands. The wetland vegetation filtered out pollutants and sediment and the water percolated slowly through the soil. During the late summer, the wetland soil would have become drier, and the river might have diminished to "a mere swampy rivulet," as U.S. Geological Survey topographical engineer W. S. Alden described it when he surveyed the vicinity on August 3, 1896.[11] As the area was settled and the natural landscape was farmed, fragmented, and developed, the river would have carried more sediment, and the wetland function and quality would have deteriorated.

Gompers Park serves as a microcosm of how people's attitudes towards the natural world have changed over time and how decisions made by public agencies reflect those attitudes. In the 1930s, when the Chicago Park District acquired the park, the district initiated an ambitious beautification plan, generally following the natural contours of the landscape. The landscaping plan retained many original trees and added a variety of others. On the high land, the district enlarged what was probably a farmer's pond into a lagoon fed by city water. Water from the lagoon trickled over into an artificially-landscaped creek that drained into the wetland. A path leading down to the river and to the other side of the park passed over concrete-block stepping stones placed in the river bed so that visitors could cross during low water periods. To keep the river from overflowing into the park or eroding its banks, the Park District built a berm and a retaining wall. The work was performed as part of a WPA contract.

Over the years, the wetland came to be considered a liability, and the Park District tried different measures to dry it up. In the 1960s, according to an article in the April 12, 1995, *News Star*, "the city poured soil a foot deep over Gomper's wetlands to eliminate standing water that could breed disease."[12] The Park District planted a lawn over the fill. The lawn never flourished and the adjacent ballfield flooded; the project proved to be an imperfect solution.

By the 1980s, the value humans placed on wetlands was on the rebound as scientists began to understand wetlands' natural functions in flood control and biodiversity. In the early 1990s, the Park District hired professionals to remove the fill, re-contour the low land at Gompers, and re-create the wetland. Restoration lowered the grade of the wetland and built up a new berm between wetland and river. Volunteers planted a variety of native plants in the wetland and on its fringe. There had always been a resident diversity of wildlife at the wetlands, ranging from muskrats to turtles to dragonflies and birds, and neighbors report that the number of animals is on the increase.

Fluctuating water levels are natural in a wetland. They are important in creating the variety of conditions, open water, and vegetative cover that encourage a diversity of habitat for wildlife. A water-level control structure was built to manage the amount of water flowing onto the site. The water level can be lowered to facilitate maintenance for planting or sediment removal.

This project was the result of the collaborative efforts of community groups, in this case, the North Mayfair Improvement Association, local and federal government agencies, not-for-profit organizations, and the Chicago Park

District. The National Park Service also played a key role, as it had in the Prairie Wolf Slough restoration. Volunteers, including students from nearby public schools and neighbors, helped plant the wetland vegetation. The wetland is now a source of great pride to its neighbors, many of whom consider it the centerpiece of their neighborhood and step up to opportunities for volunteer stewardship.[13]

The Chicago Botanic Garden: From Planning to Restoration

The Forest Preserve District's Skokie Lagoons project addressed the Skokie up to Dundee Road, but the marsh extended farther north. The FPD had considered improvement of this northern section of their land, which had been purchased early in the FPD's history. By the 1950s, however, the land was still undeveloped and was a haven for a variety of shorebirds.

The Chicago Horticultural Society, established in the late 1890s, had gone through ups and downs, including letting its charter lapse in the late 1930s. Re-energized by World War II and the wide interest in victory gardens, it flourished again, but after the war its fortunes slumped. New leadership revived the organization, and by May, 1963, having courted politicians, mastered legal matters, drawn plans, and examined sites, the Horticultural Society was ready to go with the Chicago Botanic Garden, much to its own amazement. It had received advice that its best location would be in Chicago's suburbs to the north. There, the plants could grow in an atmosphere free from the "smoke pall" of downtown. Because limited funds prevented the purchase of land, collaboration with the Forest Preserve District would make the project feasible. The Horticultural Society requested a lease on an estimated 250-300 acres in the Skokie Lagoons, including land to provide access to an island in the lagoons.

The Forest Preserve countered with a recommendation that the society use the acreage between Dundee and Lake-Cook Roads. This land had already been violated by highway department borrow pits and a toll road interchange for construction of the Edens Expressway on the west, and on the east, farmer Robert Daggitt (sometimes spelled Doggett) had used the area as a watering trough for his herds. The FPDCC knew it would have major work ahead of it to reclaim this territory, and no roadblocks stood in the way of leasing it.

Roland Eisenbeis, of FPD's Conservation Department, also recommended the site above Dundee. But, he warned, the high concentration of nitrates released into the Skokie ditch from the upstream Clavey Road sewage treatment plant led to summer concentrations of duckweed and algae. Treating the problem with chemicals would make the lagoons unsuitable for ornamental plantings.[14]

The public was not entirely sanguine. A Winnetkan questioned the wisdom of the site above Dundee:

> The Cook County Forest Preserve District is about to make a move that
> will destroy the present feeling and character of a portion of the Skokie
> Lagoon area that is uniquely rich in wildlife resources. While the land has

undergone change since the white man first came to settle, it has been allowed to revert to wildness. . . . Here, in relative quiet, almost all of the animals indigenous to the region abide—deer, fox, muskrat, woodchuck and cottontail. So varied is the landscape that birds of the forest, field and meadow abound. Ducks are seen in the several ponds and connecting streams. It is one of only a few places in the county where marsh and mud-flats afford food and rest for shorebirds on their migrations. . . . Why, we ask, is it necessary to dredge, flood, and build to provide in neatened capsule form some of what already exists so abundantly in a natural state? . . . Wildlife has diminished markedly . . . in the Skokie Lagoons [due to recreation and development]. Development to the north will result in the same decimation of wildlife. . . .[15]

Others were highly enthusiastic about the location, particularly its water attributes. The project was approved.

Ground breaking took place on September 25, 1965. The Chicago Botanic Garden and the FPD negotiated with the village of Northbrook to tap into a water main running from Lake Michigan to the Northbrook filtration plant on an off-peak basis for irrigation in dry periods and to maintain the lagoons in the garden.

It took nearly two years, from 1966 to 1968, to move the earth and water around. As the garden matured and expanded, it became a birdwatchers' haunt during migration seasons (although the shorebirds never returned); a place to seek education, exercise, and solace; and a favorite stage for wedding photographs. While many parts of the garden are complete, the continuing quest for new projects make it, as is a river, a work always in progress.

In the 1990s, the Botanic Garden undertook an ambitious Skokie River Corridor Enhancement Project, or, in other words, a river/wetland restoration. "For three years, volunteers and staff planted native vegetation, installed willow and dogwood posts and placed brush and fiber rolls to hold the slope. In-stream areas were contoured and planted, and the habitat was enhanced with rocks, which also served to aerate the water. Finally, wetlands were created along the riparian buffer, and 12 acres of prairie were seeded and planted."[16]

This streambank and wetland project is one important example of many ecologically-oriented projects of the 1990s that have brought the attention, affection, and reconnection of people to the much-abused original Chicago River.

In the late 1990s, the Chicago Botanic Garden embarked on another restoration project to stabilize its slumping shorelines. In order to make this garden beautiful to the human eye, short-rooted grass covered steep slopes all the way to the water line. Erosion was inevitable, and engineers have employed various forms of shoreline treatment.

The Skokie Lagoons Revisited

Due to population growth and pollution, water quality and aquatic life in the Skokie Lagoons began degrading almost as soon as the lagoons were created. During summers, the water surface had all but disappeared under brownish green 'algal blooms' because of the excessive amount of nutrients concentrated in the water. Sedimentation and shallow depth limited healthy populations of desirable fish, affecting recreational fishing. The beautiful appearance of the lagoons in the misty twilight disguised their illness.

By the end of the '60s, the lagoon water contained arsenic, lead, copper, zinc, and nickel in dangerous proportions, and underneath the water, polluted muck was easily stirred up by canoe paddles. The dissolved oxygen count was low-to-non-existent and fish were dying. There was concern that even the bottom-dwelling carp, which can tolerate large amounts of pollution, could become extinct in the lagoons. In addition, development along the lagoons had reduced the wetland areas that previously absorbed excessive precipitation. In heavy rain, the Skokie Drainage Ditch often backed up into the lagoons carrying sewage-loaded effluent from the upstream North Shore Sanitary District's Clavey Road treatment plant, whose conduit discharged into the ditch.

By the end of the 1990s, in cooperation with the Northeastern Illinois Planning Commission (NIPC) and other agencies, the Skokie Lagoons had undergone major rehabilitation and a face-lift. During the decade, an ambitious project to clean up the Skokie Lagoons required that nutrients entering the lagoons, particularly phosphorus, be reduced. This meant keeping the effluent from the Clavey Road wastewater treatment plant out of the lagoon water. By 1969, flooding from the polluted Skokie River had led the Botanic Garden to install a 6,000-foot-long, 48-inch-diameter pipe to divert the water around the lagoons area. Pumps were to lift the water into an existing ditch to bypass the lagoons below Willow Road. Very early on, its gas-powered pumps failed. The conduit was abandoned but left in place.

For the 1990s project, the conduit was repaired and directly connected to a new underground conduit leading directly from the Clavey Road plant. The effluent no longer drained immediately into the river. The pumps at the south end of the gardens were upgraded. Today, the effluent flows through both conduits and emerges into a ditch, otherwise known as the diversion channel, paralleling the Edens Expressway. This channel reunites with the Skokie River at Willow Road at the southern end of the lagoons below the dam.

Simultaneously, the FPD, along with other partners, including NIPC and the federal EPA, using Clean Lakes Program money, conducted a program to eliminate carp and reintroduce native fish into the improved habitat. The project focused on the Skokie Lagoons and areas upstream nearly to Lake Forest. The eradication program was very successful. It will be interesting to see whether the lagoons will remain carp-free, connected as they are to the rest of the river system. Because of the fundamental changes in the hydrology and water chemistry of the stream, and because of the regional abundance of this undesirable species, they usually reappear. Attempts to reverse biological changes in the river are often effective for only a short period of time.

The North Branch Restoration Project

Not every restoration project along the Chicago River is devoted to work on the river itself. Along the North Branch, in 1977, the North Branch Restoration Project began work on Cook County Forest Preserve District land in the adjacent watershed. Volunteers began to restore health to remnant plant communities that had thrived here after the climate warmed and temperate vegetation replaced the post-glacial, spruce-fir vegetation around 10,000 years ago. The North Branch Restoration Project is just one of numerous ecological restoration projects throughout the Chicago area, many of them modeled after the NBRP.

An example of their approach to habitat management that particularly benefits the Chicago River has been the continued eradication of buckthorn, a shallow-rooted shrubby tree native to Eurasia and brought to the United States around the 1840s. Buckthorn leafs out earlier in the spring than native species and retains its leaves longer than natives in the fall. By outcompeting other plants for light and water, it creates what might be termed a buckthorn desert. The buckthorn shades out the native understory of herbaceous plants and seedlings, and the barren ground then erodes into the neighboring stream, carrying with it the seed bank—seeds of plants adapted to the climate and fire regime that evolved over those ten thousand years. North Branch volunteers replace the buckthorn with native plants, many of them deep-rooted, to hold the soil and allow deep penetration of rainfall. Thus, soil is kept out of the river, and precipitation is held in the ground and released slowly into the stream, restoring one of the age-old watershed-river collaborations.

The use of fire as a management tool has been a major ecological restoration strategy. The current landscape evolved under a fire regime: lightning often ignited prairie fires, but tribes also set fires for hunting, agriculture, and protection purposes. Its re-introduction permitted natural processes to do part of the work of restoration. Another management technique was the culling of native trees that had grown thickly during 150 years of fire suppression in areas normally prone to periodic fire. An additional tool has been the use of short-lived, non-residual herbicides to control a few species of aggressive exotic plants.

In 1996, these three management practices came under intense criticism from some citizens. Cook County Board President John Stroger declared a moratorium on all restoration activities on September 24 of that year, leading to bitter controversy. At the same time, Stroger constituted a 21-member Community Advisory Council (CAC) with representatives from all districts in the county. Its function was to review and provide public input on the Forest Preserve District's Land Management Program. The CAC discussed management activities, heard the scientific basis for restoration, visited many restoration projects, and reviewed the management plans for all Forest Preserve restoration sites. On February 5, 1997, the County Board began to lift the moratorium in stages on selected activities for selected groups of sites. The conflict continued, however, and during the next three years a majority of the CAC consistently voted in support of all aspects of the FPD's program. As of January, 2000, the moratorium remained in place only on North Branch

Restoration Project sites along the North Branch in the Edgebrook area where the controversy first erupted. In April, 2000, resumption of some work on five of those sites was approved by the County Board. Because these Forest Preserve sites border the river, the potential positive effects of restoration that can stabilize streambanks was lost during the moratorium. (The fate of birds illustrates the complexities of the ecological restoration issue. Removing buckthorn and then replanting to stabilize a riverbank may be good for the river, but it removes habitat for birds that nest in buckthorn branches and feast on its winter berries.)

Seawalls: Their Place in Restoration

As we have learned, the Chicago River experienced periodic overbank flooding, during which the floodwaters built up natural levees of sediments along its riverbanks. Beginning in the earliest days of shipping in Chicago, natural levees were no longer acceptable; they were too changeable. People needed to stabilize the riverbanks and build durable moorings for boats close in to the docks, especially as the river was deepened. They did so by building vertical edges, or seawalls, to separate the river from the land, eliminating one more natural process of a river and its watershed.

The first seawalls built along the river's edge from 1900 through the 1940s were built of timber. Timber piles 45 to 50 feet long were driven at four-foot centers deep into the river's clay bottom. Timber sill, 6 inches x 12 inches, was hung horizontally on these piles. Next, prefabricated timber "Wakefield" sheeting, consisting of three 30-foot planks fastened together to make tongue-in-groove sheets, were driven one by one vertically alongside each other. Finally, a steel tie rod was attached to each pile and extended some 40 feet back into the bank and fastened to an anchor log buried in the earth well behind the wall. The completed timber construction was backfilled, sometimes with dredged material from the channel deepening, sometimes with granular fill.

By the 1930s, steel pan sheeting was available, and engineers turned to sheet-piling. When the timber bulkheads above the water line rotted when they were exposed to the air due to varying river levels and new seawall was required, steel "zee type" sheet piling was driven in front of the old timber structure. Thus, whatever the material, the river is confined to a channel defined by human-made walls.[17]

Today, with navigation mostly limited to pleasure craft, river advocates are asking if there are better ways to stabilize a riverbank, techniques that will create habitat for aquatic creatures such as fish fry and the small insects they feed upon, and the amphibians and dry-landers who like and need water for at least part of their life cycle. How much of an artificial edge between river and land is necessary? Are there more naturalistic treatments that are effective? Sheet piling may be functional for deep rivers with significant fluctuation levels, although some people are even questioning this assumption. Where the river is shallow, however, restoration projects are experimenting with alternative methods of shoreline protection.[18]

The Invisible Flood of 1992

Rivers, like humans and animals, have territories. If you trespass upon a river's territory, that is, its watershed, as the Chicago region has done by channelizing, rerouting, and building in its wetlands, it is best to remember that you are an intruder and that the river may try to reclaim its own. Chicago's Loop learned this lesson the hard way in mid-April, 1992, when the river seemed to find an escape route to what had been its old marshlands. The river flowed down an opening along timber pile that had been installed for bridge protection. It went on a binge, spilling into an old freight tunnel system that had been installed 42 feet beneath the city's surface 100 years earlier for delivering materials among the downtown buildings. To the casual observer above ground, the river looked exactly the same as it had the day before. It looked like business as usual. But companies in towers with basements connected to the old tunnels knew differently. It took millions of dollars and what seemed like as many days to isolate the damaged portion under the river by plugging the tunnel and then dewatering the flooded systems.[19] The unruly river was confined again firmly into the channel where people store it, thinking themselves safe from its natural tendencies. It is best to respect a river, even one as sluggish as the Chicago.

Who's in Charge Here?

An archivist assisting in this project asked "Who is in charge of this river? Who owns it?" The bemused answer we gave was, "it depends." The water in the stream belongs to the state. The state has jurisdiction over all of the animals in the stream as it does over all land animals. Beyond that, a plethora of agencies, from national to local, have decision-making powers over some aspect of the river. A landowner with riparian rights may own to the centerline of the river bottom, thus being responsible for the banks. The U.S. Army Corps of Engineers has permitting authority over wetlands and over navigable sections of the river, to ensure that no work impedes the federal navigation channel, which is strictly defined on maps. On the Chicago River, the Corps' Chicago District oversees the Main Branch, anything called the North Branch up to the confluence of the West Fork and the Skokie River/Middle Fork, the North Shore Channel, the South Branch, and the South Fork (Bubbly Creek). The Corps also has responsibility for the lock at Lake Michigan. Although it seems geographically odd, the Corps' Rock Island District has historically overseen both the O'Brien Lock and Dam on the Calumet and the Sanitary and Ship Canal.

The U.S. EPA, the Illinois EPA, and the Illinois Pollution Control Board have authority over water quality. The Illinois Department of Natural Resources (IDNR) Office of Water Resources is responsible for carrying out federal and state policies on allocation of water diverted from Lake Michigan and over the capacity of floodways to carry stormwater. Individual communities have a large measure of control through their zoning powers and use of land adjacent to the river. Any public or private agency wanting to alter the waterway must go through a wearying process of approvals. Even drainage districts are required to hold hearings and obtain permits from the Army Corps of Engineers for projects to keep the drainage ways clear, and the districts' work requires court approval before they may spend their collected assessments. A partial list of agencies with license or permit requirements for one particular project for the West Skokie Drainage District in the 1990s included the U.S. Army Corps of Engineers; the Illinois EPA; the Illinois Department of Natural Resources; the U.S. Fish and Wildlife Service; the Lake County Stormwater Management Commission; the Lake County Forest Preserve District; the Canadian Pacific Railway; the Elgin, Joliet, and Eastern Railway; METRA; the villages of Deerfield and Green Oaks; and the cities of Highland Park and Lake Forest.[20]

Acting like a Watershed

This book is the biography of a river, a river that is a microcosm of urban rivers everywhere. It is important to remember that there is an entire watershed involved here, not just a slim ribbon of water. In the beginning of the book, we emphasized that a river is only a collection of drops of water that fall upon a watershed and eventually make their way by gravity to a waterway. Thus, there is no running from the reality that, even if the land along the stream or in the floodplain is protected, river water quality will suffer if most land surfaces throughout the watershed are developed or if runoff is rapid and loaded with impurities. Scientists study non-point-source pollution, contaminants that load up the river but that do not originate from one obvious source.

Land use in our urban watershed is an ever-changing kaleidoscope. The quality of the river for its aquatic organisms reflects the historic and current land use in the watershed, which, in turn, reflects the social, political, economic, and aesthetic policies of its residents. Today, engineers, architects, planners, builders, and developers are just beginning to create environmentally-sensitive residential landscapes that combine clustered housing and open land. More projects with environmentally sound visions will be needed to come closer to a healthy river.

The polluters and drainers of the early years were most likely unaware of the specific ecological fate of the faster runoff and the contaminants they were contributing to the river. But now we know the consequences with certainty. The question is how to combat these consequences in the face of continuing development in the watershed.

A *Chicago Tribune* article on December 28, 1969, "Chicago River North Branch Cleaning Begun," features an interview with Dr. Walter Dalitsch, head of the West Skokie Drainage Ditch Commission. Quoting the article:

> The flow of water in the system has greatly increased in recent years.
> [Quoting Dr. Dalitsch:] "Much of the pasture land which used to absorb
> the rainfall has been replaced by paving. This means much more water runs
> into our system and makes the clearing of obstructions very important." . . .
> The channel south of Lake County is under the jurisdiction of the Metropoli-
> tan Sanitary District of Greater Chicago. "We are planning in the near future to
> discuss with them the possibility of their clearing their portion of the Chicago

River's north fork. . . . As it is now, the obstacles in Cook County cause the waters to back up during heavy rains and flood some land in Lake County."[21]

Dr. Dalitsch had one part wrong. The channel was not and is not under MWRD jurisdiction. But he had it right that the channel was being asked to carry additional run-off from Lake County. If the water in the channel were plugged by debris and backing up into Lake County, however, should Cook County be responsible for Lake County's flooding? It was development in the floodplain along the West Fork in Lake County that was exacerbating the consequences of flooding to humans. Could Dr. Dalitsch have looked toward controlling development in the West Fork sub-watershed rather than pointing the finger downstream? His thinking was a normal response of his times to a condition that still exists: there was, and still is, no overriding authority over the entire Chicago River watershed. The sheer size and shape of the watershed, containing as it does two counties and many municipalities who do not consider themselves linked in any way, presents a daunting challenge to planners.

We have already seen how throughout the century the MWRD, cloaked in various names, addressed the problem of sewage by improving technologies for treatment in Cook County and how, slowly, the mission of the MWRD is changing to include flood management through TARP. But flood control is not, as of 2000, the agency's statutory mission. Lake County, in 1992, created the Lake County Stormwater Management Commission (LCSMC), whose mission is to "coordinate comprehensive stormwater management efforts throughout the county. Founded on the equal partnership between municipalities and the County of Lake, LCSMC provides technical assistance, local knowledge and problem-solving skills to service local and county government agencies, groups and residents to reduce flood damage and to improve surface water quality." LCSMC has enacted a watershed protection ordinance. Unfortunately, there is no legal partner in Cook County with the same designated authority to enact a similar ordinance.

In the past, thinking about stormwater amounted to taking remedial actions along the river. To handle excess stormwater in both Lake and Cook Counties, the sanitary and drainage districts, in cooperation with the Army Corps of Engineers, built surface reservoirs as side adjuncts to rivers, to retain the water for two or three days. The deepest of these are referred to by some people as "giant toilet bowls" because this is what they look like. Pumps flush floodwater into adjacent streams when it appears that the downstream waterway can accommodate additional flow. One very visible reservoir, built by the MWRD, is behind Northbrook Court shopping mall (Lake-Cook Road, west of Route 41). It is a deep bowl that fills in times of heavy rain but usually holds only a small pool at the bottom. Occasional ducks swimming in the pool or loafing on the sides appear tiny in comparison with the enormity of the crater.

In the mid-1970s, Northeastern Illinois Planning Commission was busily assessing issues of regional water quality. NIPC is a state-created body with advisory, not regulatory powers, that encourages regional solutions to complex issues in the six-county region encompassing Cook, Lake, Kane, Du Page,

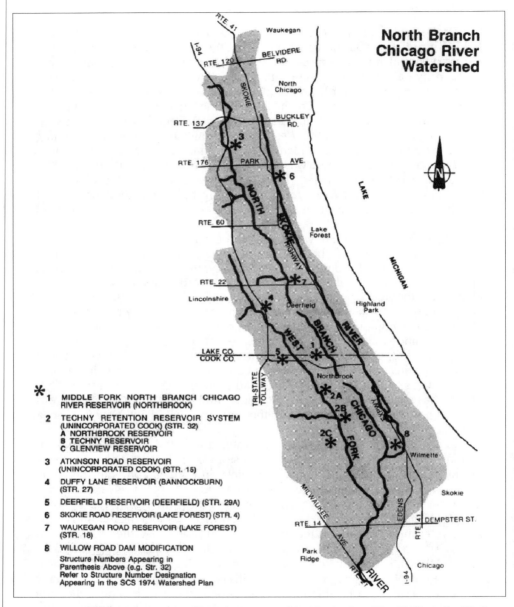

From "Our Community and Flooding," 1991, 21. Courtesy of the Metropolitan Water Reclamation District of Greater Chicago.

Distribution of flood control reservoirs in the North Branch watershed.

McHenry, and Will Counties. NIPC's involvement in an Areawide Water Quality Management Plan began in 1976, and, in 1979, NIPC formally adopted the plan. Part II, Chapter 11 of the plan is devoted to the North Branch Chicago River Basin and provides a watershed overview of water quality issues and actions, as well as computer-generated water quality forecasts based on NIPC growth forecasts for the region at that time. (This work is often referred to as "the 208 Plan," named after a section of the Clean Water Act.)

Subsequently, NIPC continued its work. It drafted model ordinances of Stormwater Drainage and Detention, Soil Erosion and Sediment Control, Stream and Wetland Protection, and Floodplain Management, the latter in conjunction with the Illinois Department of Natural Resources. These model ordinances have been widely adopted by communities throughout the region. They are indicative of NIPC's continued promotion of preventive measures that address both the quantity and quality of stormwater. NIPC's strategy includes recommendations for constructing detention ponds to prevent increases in runoff rates from individual development sites throughout the watershed, rather than constructing new remedial flood control basins. These recommendations are called "Best Management Practices" (BMPs), practices that mimic wetland functions by holding the water on-site, filtering it through wetland vegetation, and slowly releasing it into the river. NIPC has also been instrumental in planning for the restorations of the lagoons of the original Skokie Marsh—the Chicago Botanic Garden and the Skokie Lagoons, plus a one-mile stretch of the Skokie River running through the Botanic Garden.

Friends of the Chicago River has been working along similar lines. In the early 1990s, Friends received support from the National Park Service's Rivers, Trails and Conservation Assistance Program for watershed planning. The project had three major components. The first was an assessment of the natural resources of the river, performed by the U.S. Fish and Wildlife Service with assistance from the Army Corps of Engineers. At numerous sampling points, they studied the river: the fish, macro-invertebrates, wildlife habitat, and the condition of the banks. This was not a watershed assessment, because a watershed is much larger than the stream that drains it, but it provides a start toward understanding the present condition of the waterway and toward appropriate actions.

The second component was an assessment of public opinion and use of the waterway, conducted by the U.S. Forest Service and Army Corps of Engineers. The third component was the development and funding of several restoration/demonstration projects coordinated by Friends. These projects generated considerable interest in the river and its associated ecosystems. Prairie Wolf Slough and Gompers Park are two examples.

During the late 1990s, the Illinois EPA approached Friends of the Chicago River and asked the organization to create an Urban Watershed Management Handbook based on its experiences at Prairie Wolf Slough as well as its watershed planning on the North Branch. The hope is that this handbook will create a framework that can be supported by all communities in the watershed.

Often today we address the problems of the river reach by reach. We try to alleviate conditions in one reach by restoring a more sinuous shape to the stream, adding meanders and riffles and streamside vegetation to mimic

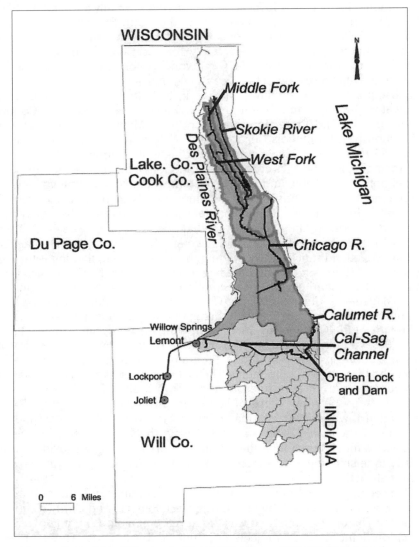

Map created by Libby Hill using ArcView® GIS software. Digital files courtesy of Northeastern Illinois Planning Commission, Illinois Department of Natural Resources, USEPA, and Illinois EPA Bureau of Water.

The present watershed and sub-watersheds of the Chicago River System, including the addition of the lighter gray Calumet River watershed. Because the West Fork of the Chicago River and the Des Plaines watershed boundaries were always a mystery and have been so disturbed, historic and current watershed boundaries are difficult to determine.

nature's processes. The hope is that if we are doing a good job, natural ecological processes will rebound and success will breed similar projects. As a microcosm of issues of urban rivers, the Chicago and its watershed are confronted by the reality of a built-up environment that is continuing to build much faster than is typically planned for. Successes in working reach by reach, project by project, can lead to a more sophisticated citizenry that will pressure its community governments to work together. But first it must understand and accept the indisputable ramifications of being connected by this stream.

"The Water Will Go Somewhere"

To complicate matters even further, we must be careful to think beyond the Chicago River watershed because we have linked the Chicago River system with the Calumet and Des Plaines Rivers and two artificial channels, all of which flow downstream through the Illinois River into the Mississippi River and, ultimately, the Gulf of Mexico. From the time of the earliest research for this book, Lake County engineer Ted Anderson advised the author never to forget the maxim "the water will go somewhere." Runoff from the land goes not only into the river but also into people's basements, even those living far from the river, before making its way to the Gulf. By our human ingenuity in providing for our human needs, we have created unintended consequences. We have worsened streambank erosion, erased or debased wildlife habitat, and affected every natural function of a river and its watershed. On a positive note, improvements in wastewater treatment have greatly enhanced water quality in the last couple of decades, although we are still not achieving "fishable/swimmable" conditions. It will take imagination, more research, more conservation, more money, and a commitment to work with nature's processes to make a healthier river system.

A Century of Progress

During the twentieth century many of the dreams articulated by the Committee on the Universe and the Burnham Plan of 1909 came to fruition. Other plans went way beyond the scope of those dreams. While the possibility of the return of the river into our lives may be attributed to projects of the Metropolitan Water Reclamation District, the amenities we have today could not have occurred without citizen effort, not only through Friends of the Chicago River but also through their cooperating partners and other individuals and groups.

Chicago's wonderful downtown riverwalk harkens back to the early visionaries. The walk on the Main Stem begins at Lake Shore Drive and continues west along Wacker Drive. On the South Branch, the riverwalk known as Riverside Plaza begins on the west bank at Randolph Street and continues south to Union Station between Adams Street and Jackson Boulevard. These riverwalks afford wonderful views of life on the river and feature many restaurants and shops.

Riverwalks are not limited to downtown Chicago. In addition to trails in the forest preserves are walks in suburban commercial or open park settings. As examples, Northbrook is planning to extend its downtown park riverwalk in conjunction with riverbank restoration, and there is a riverwalk at the North Shore Corporate Park in Glenview. Both sites are mapped in the appendix.

The Chicago River has been incorporated into more ambitious plans that span Northeastern Illinois. The Northeastern Illinois Regional Greenways and Trails Plan, known informally as the Greenways Plan, was first proposed in the late 1980s by Openlands Project. It was formalized in cooperation with NIPC in 1992. Its 1997 revision includes almost 2,000 miles of proposed and existing connected linear open space that will all be accessible to the public. The Chicago River and its banks are an integral part of this trail system.

Targeting area waterways, a 484-mile Northeastern Illinois Regional Water Trail Plan for canoeing and kayaking was proposed in 1998 and adopted by NIPC in December, 1999. The waterways trail is a cooperative venture among NIPC, Openlands Project, and the Illinois Paddling Council, with funding provided by the Illinois Department of Natural Resources. Each of the ten major waterways in the plan, the Chicago River among them, will have its own planning committee and will have access and portage sites approximately three to five miles apart on public land. The 174 proposed sites for the region will involve the cooperation of over 50 agencies.

The Chicago River is also part of Chicago Wilderness, a regional effort spanning a wide territory and functioning under the umbrella of the Chicago Regional Biodiversity Council. Chicago Wilderness is a consortium of 92 public and private agencies dedicated to preserving and restoring the 200,000 acres of protected natural areas that dot the southern crescent of Lake Michigan from Southeast Wisconsin to the Indiana Dunes. Each of these three initiatives recognizes the value of open space in general to the psychological health and well-being of the region's residents.

The I&M Canal Today

Finally, whatever happened to the Illinois and Michigan Canal? Jolliet's vision of a one and one-half mile canal was the impetus for the city of Chicago, yet the last we heard of it in this book, it had disintegrated and closed in 1933 after an inglorious chapter. Its importance, however, had not faded from the minds of those who understood its historic value. Citizen determination preserved it from tragedy.

Prospects for saving the Illinois and Michigan Canal looked bleak in the 1960s when the State of Illinois assessed the value of the abandoned canal lands and prepared to sell off parcels in order to generate state revenue. The timing was right, therefore, when the Openlands Project was formed in 1963 to conserve public open space in northeastern Illinois. By 1974 citizen action and the Openlands Project resulted in the designation of the I&M Canal State Trail, a 60-mile long park that followed the canal and towpath from Joliet to LaSalle/ Peru.

In the meantime, small but determined groups of concerned citizens organized town meetings, circulated petitions, and confronted their legislators. The grassroots effort drew support all the way to the Governor's office. Drawn in by growing public and private response, Senator Charles Percy and Congressman Tom Corcoran requested the National Park Service to draft a conceptual plan ". . . to protect and enhance the abundant cultural and natural resources of the I&M Canal while at the same time providing for economic development." More than 100 local citizens and officials helped write the National Park Service document. The bill that emerged from Congress was supported by the entire Illinois delegation and signed into law by President Ronald Reagan on August 24, 1984.

The historical significance of the Illinois and Michigan Canal in the nation's history was finally recognized. The canal became the backbone of the I&M Canal National Heritage Corridor, the nation's first national heritage corridor, and a prime example of what organized and determined citizen effort can accomplish to revive and preserve a portion of our too-often neglected and forgotten natural landscape.

Photos by Richard E. Carter.

Two contemporary aerial views of the Chicago River. (*Top*) The Chicago Harbor with Navy Pier on the right. See the labeled photo on page 189 to locate specific elements of the Chicago River's "anteroom." (*Bottom*) Wolf Point, where the Chicago River's Main Stem and North Branch meet near the Merchandise Mart in downtown Chicago.

Reflections

A river, as stated in the beginning of this book, is a work in progress. Progress is an appropriate word, but not the only one. There is looking forward and there is looking back. The river is a continuum over space and time, connecting city with suburbs, generation with generation, and humans with nature and each other.

In his 1922 book, *A Thousand and One Afternoons in Chicago*, Ben Hecht wrote a fitting ode to the river in his essay "Night Diary":

> .... We stand on the bridge that connects State Street and look at the river. There are night shapes. But first we see the dark water of the river and silver, gold and ruby reflections of the bridge lights. These hang like carnival ribbons in the water. . . . We walk away with memories. When we are traveling some day, riding over strange places, these will be things we shall remember. . . . The scene from the bridge will bring a sad confusion into our heads. . . . We shall sit staring at famous monuments, battlefields, antiquities, and whisper to ourselves: " . . . wish I was back . . . wish I was back. . . ."[1]

By 1922, when Hecht wrote this piece, the riverscape in downtown Chicago was on the brink of change. Hecht was lured to the river because, now that it was reversed, river watching had become a pleasurable activity. Though far removed from seeing the river in its original state, he was stirred by his experience. He could foretell wishing himself back to his particular time and place, but that was his limit.

His essay is instructive. We cannot wish ourselves back to the river of Marquette and Jolliet, and most of us probably would not wish ourselves back to Hecht's time, before the beautification of the riverscape. As humans, we will always tinker with the river within the context of our times and technological abilities. We have an artificial Chicago River system that extends from Park City in Lake County to Lockport in Will County. Its history as nature's creation goes back thousands of years; as a European re-creation, only 200 years. Today we try to re-create it once more. We beautify its banks to make paths along it and make it publicly accessible. We do our best to restore its processes, experimenting with remaking the river and the wetlands. While acting with optimism regarding nature's resilience, we must remember the river's power to defy our best plans. If we continue our habit of building in the floodplain, as we are doing, we must expect to pay the piper for our actions. If we believe that the Chicago River, so close to the sub-continental divide, made Chicago, we most assuredly must see that greater Chicago reworked the river not just once, or twice, but that the Chicago River's story is not over. We continue to remodel the river today, whether intentionally or unintentionally, and will continue doing so into tomorrow.

Nostalgia, tinged with reality, seems to be an elemental quality of the human condition. Like Frank Windes and the Skokie, Edwin Gale (who is quoted throughout the book) had a lifetime of memories of the Chicago River. And like Windes, he responded with ambivalence to the changes he saw during the span of his years. In 1902, at the age of 70, Gale celebrated the reversal of the downtown river, but expressed his ambivalence in the final stanzas of this poem:

> I never more at nightfall
> Shall see the birch canoe
> Propelled by paddles, softly
> Come slowly into view;
> A pine knot burning brightly,
> The savage 'neath its gleam,
> With spear, move like a phantom
> Upon its burnished stream.
>
> We hail thee, little river,
> Child of the scented plain,
> Thy sad, polluted waters
> Will soon be clear again.
> Those mighty glacial furrows,
> Thrown open by the Lord,
> Through which have passed such torrents,
> Once more shall be restored.
>
> The floods of these fresh oceans
> Through their old channels pour,
> The savage and the Trader,
> Though banished evermore,
> The portage they made use of
> Blazed well for us the way;
> Canoes with their pelt cargoes
> Led the commerce of today.[2]

Notes

Introduction

1. Extract from a report of Major Stephen H. Long, 4 March 1817, cited in testimony by Clarence W. Alvord, *United States of America v. Economy Light and Power Company*, District Court of the United States for the Northern District of Illinois, Eastern Division, in Chancery. No. 29776 (1910), 111.

2. R. Graham and Joseph Philips, 4 April 1819, cited in testimony by Clarence W. Alvord, *U.S. v. Economy Light and Power Co.*, 114.

3. Long, cited in *U.S. v. Economy Light and Power Co.*, 111.

4. J. Seymour Currey, *The Story of Old Fort Dearborn* (Chicago: A.C. McClurg & Co., 1912), 20-21. According to Bill Hinchliffe, Chicago Archicenter docent, in personal communication with author, 1 January 1999, some of Chicago's southeast siders tell an even different version of the story: that the fort was proposed for the Calumet River, but an Indian girlfriend of one of the soldiers who lived north, near the future Chicago, led the decision to build on the Chicago River.

5. Edwin O. Gale, *Reminiscences of Early Chicago and Vicinity* (Chicago: Fleming H. Revell Co., 1902), 304.

Location, Location, Location

1. Gurdon Saltonstall Hubbard, *The Autobiography of Gurdon Saltonstall Hubbard* (New York: The Citadel Press, 1969), 42-3.

2. Archer Butler Hulbert, *Portage Paths: The Keys of the Continent*, Historic Highways of America, vol. 7 (Cleveland, OH: Arthur H. Clark Company, 1903), 166.

3. R. Graham and Joseph Philips, cited in *U.S. v. Economy Light and Power Co.*, 116.

4. Robert Knight and Lucius H. Zeuch, 1928, *The Location of the Chicago Portage Route of the Seventeenth Century* (Chicago: Chicago Historical Society, n.d.), 19.

5. Wm. H. Keating, "Narrative of an expedition to the source of St. Peters River in 1823, under Major Stephen H. Long," in Henry Higgins Hurlbut, *Chicago Antiquities* (Chicago: Henry Higgins Hurlbut, 1881), 204-5.

6. R. Graham and Joseph Philips, cited in *U.S. v. Economy Light and Power Co.*, 115.

7. Knight and Zeuch, 29.

The Ice Age and the Legacies of the Wisconsin Glacier

1. Ardith K. Hansel and David M. Mickelson, "A Reevaluation of the Timing and Causes of High Lake Phases in the Lake Michigan Basin," *Quaternary Research* 29 (1988): 113-128. Scientists with the Illinois Geological Survey are re-evaluating the ancestral lakes of the present Lake Michigan. In the process, they have determined through radiocarbon dating that post-glacial Lake Nipissing, not a level of Glacial Lake Chicago previously called the Toleston, formed the Graceland spit. The chart showing tribal cultures and lake levels in the chapter "Tribal Lands" illustrates the revisions to our commonly accepted chronology.

2. Frank Leverett, *Pleistocene Features and Deposits of the Chicago Area*, Bulletin No. 2 (Geological and Natural History Survey, Chicago Academy of Sciences, May

1897), 43.

3. J. Harlen Bretz, "Geology of the Chicago Region Part I-General," *Illinois Geological Survey Bulletin* 65 (1939): 37.

The Chicago River

1. Commission on Chicago Historical and Architectural Landmarks, *Site of the Wolf Point Settlement*, 1975, 9.
2. Alfred T. Andreas, *History of Chicago from the Earliest Period to the Present Time*, vol. 1 (Chicago: Alfred T. Andreas, 1884-1886), 589.
3. Gale.
4. George P. Jenson, *Historic Chicago Sites* (Chicago: Creative Enterprises, 1953), 6.
5. George W. Harrison, *Field Notes of the General Land Office Survey for Illinois*, Book 389 (7-9 July 1840), 10-13, 32-3.
6. Alan W. Noehre, Davis S. Ellis, and Dean E. Long, *Floods in Libertyville Quadrangle, Illinois*, Hydrological Investigations Atlas, HA-88 (Washington, D.C.: Department of the Interior, United States Geological Survey, n.d.).
7. Ted Anderson, personal communication with author, 14 July 1999; soundings taken by the author and crew, 13 July 1999.
8. *Wheeling Quadrangle Hydrological Atlas and Wheeling, Ill. Quadrangle* (Washington, D.C.: U.S. Geological Survey, 1953, 1963).
9. John J. Halsey, *A History of Lake County, Illinois* (Philadelphia: Roy S. Bates, 1912), 296.
10. Bretz, 1939, 110.
11. Bretz, 1953, 32.

The Natural Chicago River: Animal, Vegetable, and Mineral

1. Jesse Lowe Smith, "Flora of Lake County," in John J. Halsey, *A History of Lake County, Illinois* (Philadelphia: Roy S. Bates, 1912), 330-6.
2. Smith, in Halsey, 333.
3. George C. Klehm, handwritten copy of a letter sent in answer to an inquiry by Ransome Kennicott, Chief Forester of the Forest Preserve District of Cook County, requesting information regarding tracts purchased by the Forest Preserve in the townships of Niles, Northfield, and New Trier, circa 1919.
4. J.G.F. in Hurlbut, 89.
5. "A Game Preserve," 23 March 1902, newspaper clipping, in Conrad Sulzer Regional Library archives, Chicago Public Library.
6. Ibid.

Tribal Lands

1. James A. Brown, personal communication with author, 8 April 1997.
2. Albert Scharf, unpublished manuscript. [Scharf JAB/JCT "(1) page-39-E I"] [First Folder], at Chicago Historical Society, 19.

Passages and Treaties: On the Path to a Canal

1. Report by Comte de Frontenac, Governor-General of New France to Colbert, French Minister, based upon Jolliet's verbal narrative to him, in Pierre Margry,

Deconvertes et Establissements Des Francais, Dans L'Quest et Dans Le Sud, De L'Amerique Septentrionals (1641-1754) Memoires et Documents Originaux Recueillis et Publies, vol. 1, cited in *U.S. v. Economy Light and Power Co.*, 26.

2. Francis Parkman, *France and England in North America*, vol. 1, written between 1865 and 1892 (The Library of America, 1983), 741.

3. Seiur de La Salle, leaves from an undated letter, quoted in Pierre Margry, *Deconvertes et Establissements Des Francais, Dans L'Quest et Dans Le Sud, De L'Amerique Septentrionals (1641-1754) Memoires et Documents Originaux Recueillis et Publies*, vol. 2, cited in *U.S. v. Economy Light and Power Co.*, 34-7. No date can be attributed because this is a letter to someone, on loose leaves, assumed to be written after 11 August 1681.

4. Clarence W. Alvord, *U.S. v. Economy Light and Power Co.*, 41.

5. Eleanor Atkinson, *The Story of Chicago and National Development* (Chicago: Little Chronicle Company, 1909), 50.

The Illinois and Michigan Canal

1. *Illinois, a Descriptive and Historical Guide*, compiled and written by the Federal Writers Project of the Works Projects Administration for the State of Illinois, American Guide Series (Chicago: A.C. McClurg & Co., 1939), 194.

2. Edgar Lee Masters, *The Tale of Chicago* (New York: G.P. Putnam & Sons, 1933), 69.

3. John Larson, *Those Army Engineers* (Chicago District, U.S. Army Corps of Engineers, 1979), 6.

4. John Clayton, *The Illinois Fact Book and Historical Almanac, 1673-1968* (Carbondale, Illinois: Southern Illinois University Press, 1970), 15.

5. Andreas, 1884-1886, vol. 1, 167.

6. Charles B. Johnson, *Growth of Cook County*, vol. 1 (Chicago: Board of Commissioners of Cook County, IL, 1960), 82.

7. Hubbard, from the introduction by Caroline M. McIlvaine, xix-xx.

8. Andreas, 1884-1886, vol. 1, 167-8.

9. Ibid., 168.

10. Hubbard, xx.

11. Andreas, 1884-1886, vol. 1, 170.

12. Ibid.

13. George Berndt, I&M Canal Corridor Interpretive Specialist, personal communication with author, 8 July 1998.

Redesigning the Harbor: Fighting Nature and Politics, 1833-1875

1. Knight and Zeuch, 22-3.

2. John F. Swenson, "Jean Baptiste Point De Sable, The founder of Modern Chicago" in Ulrich Danckers and Jane Meredith, *Early Chicago* (River Forest, IL: Early Chicago, Inc., 2000), 388-94.

3. Allan W. Eckert, *Gateway to Empire* (New York: Bantam Books, 1983), 61.

4. Andreas, vol. 1, 233.

5. Larson, 3.

6. Andreas, vol. 1, 233.

7. "The Illinois Central Depot Suit," *Chicago Daily Tribune*, 30 September 1858, 1.

8. Hubbard, 40.

9. Larson, 19.

10. Andreas, vol. 1, 234.

11. Larson, 30.

12. Larson, 24-34.
13. Larson, 30-1.
14. Larson, 37.
15. Gale, 290.
16. Larson, 62-4.
17. Paul Gilbert and Charles Lee Bryson, *Chicago and Its Makers* (Chicago: Felix Mendelsohn, 1929), 91-2.
18. Larson, 73.
19. Gale, 291.
20. Larson, 83.
21. Larson, 83.
22. Larson, 84-5.
23. Larson, 97.
24. Andreas, vol. 2, 70.
25. Larson, 106-7.
26. Andreas, vol. 1, 235.
Sand accumulation by year, as given by Andreas in vol. 1., 238:

1821-33	380 feet	[32 feet per year average]
1833-37	320 feet	[80 feet per year average]
1837-39	400 feet	[200 feet per year average]
1839-45	350 feet	[58 feet per year average]
1845-57	340 feet	[28 feet per year average]

27. Andreas, vol. 1, 589.
28. J. Seymour Currey, *Chicago, Its History and Its Builders*, vol. 3 (Chicago: S.J. Clarke Publishing Co., 1912), 178.
29. Carl Smith, *Urban Disorder and the Shape of Belief* (Chicago: University of Chicago Press, 1995), 59.
30. Harold M. Meyer and Richard C. Wade, *Chicago, Growth of a Metropolis* (Chicago: University of Chicago Press, 1969), 305.
31. Larson, 111.

Early Settlement on the North Branch

1. Eckert, 52, 143.
2. "Lake View," *Chicago Daily News*, 8 July 1929, in Conrad Sulzer Regional Library archives, Chicago Public Library.
3. Alfred T. Andreas, *History of Cook County, Illinois: from the Earliest Period to the Present Time* (Chicago: A.T. Andreas, 1884), 744.
4. Louis Werhane, personal communication with author, Northbrook, IL, 8 August 1997.
5. Andreas, *History of Cook County*, 744.
6. Philip E. Vierling, "Early Water Powered Mills of the Des Plaines River and its Tributaries" (pamphlet, 1955), 106-7.
7. Andreas, vol. 1, 566.
8. Newton Bateman and Paul Selby, eds., *Historical Encyclopedia of Illinois*, and Charles A. Partridge, ed., *History of Lake County* (Chicago: Munsell Publishing Company, 1902), 623.
9. Marvyn Wittele, *Pioneer to Commuter: the Story of Highland Park* (Highland Park, IL: The Rotary Club of Highland Park, IL, 1958), 25-7.
10. C. E. Carroll, "Our Heritage" in *Historical Essays of Libertyville* (n.p.: n.d.), 7.
11. "From Settlement to Village," *The Villager*, 19 June 1958, 16-7.

12. Gordon Fyfe, *A Short History of the Village of Golf* (printed for the village, 1970), 44-5.

13. Charles S. Winstone, *Historic Goose Island* (Chicago: Chicago Historical Society, 10 October 1938), 10.

14. "A Walking Tour, Near North Branch Section From the Waterfall (Foster Avenue) to Goose Island (Chicago Avenue)" (Chicago: Friends of the Chicago River, 1993).

Early Commerce and the River

1. Andreas, vol. 1, 554.

2. Ibid., 191.

3. *Illinois: a Descriptive and Historical Guide*, 196.

4. James Curtiss, "Inaugural Address of Mayor James Curtiss, March 9, 1847," Inaugural Addresses of the Mayors of Chicago, www.chipublib.org/004Chicago/Mayors/speeches.

5. Andreas, vol. 1, 239.

6. Otto Peltzer, *Peltzer Atlas of Chicago* (Chicago: Peltzer, Fox and Hoffman, 1872), 61.

7. Andreas, vol. 1, 191-2.

8. Winstone, 10.

9. Andreas, vol. 1, 202.

10. Andreas, vol. 2, 63.

11. Meyer and Wade, 47.

12. Andreas, vol. 2, 64.

The Chicago River: From Clean Stream to Open Sewer

1. James C. O'Connell, "Technology and Pollution: Chicago's Water Policy, 1833-1930" (Ph.D. dissertation, University of Chicago, 1980), 74.

2. Andreas, vol. 1, 191.

3. Vinton W. Bacon, "The Lake We Drink" (The Metropolitan Sanitary District of Greater Chicago, reprinted from *Chicago Tribune Magazine* with supplementary illustrations, 1966), 1.

4. Andreas, vol. 1, 190.

5. Andreas, vol. 1, 190-1.

6. Daphne Christensen, ed., *Chicago Public Works: a History* (Chicago, IL: Department of Public Works, 1973), 80.

7. Joel A. Tarr, "Sewerage and the Development of the Networked City in the United States, 1850-1930," in Joel A. Tarr and Gabriel Dupuy, eds., *Technology and the Rise of the Networked City in Europe and America* (Philadelphia: Temple University Press, 1988), 164.

8. O'Connell, 26.

9. Andreas, vol. 1, 191-2.

10. *Illinois: a Descriptive and Historical Guide*, 198.

11. Ibid.

12. Chicago, IL, *Municipal Report*, 1860-1865, 41-2.

13. Louise Carroll Wade, *Chicago's Pride, The Stockyards, Packingtown, and Environs in the Nineteenth Century* (Urbana, IL: University of Illinois Press, 1987), 37.

14. O'Connell, 76.

15. Wade, 157.

16. W. Jos. Grand, *Illustrated History of the Union Stockyards* (Chicago: W. Jos. Grand, 1901), 9-10.

17. John Anderson, "The Stockyards Open," in Stevenson Swanson, ed., *Chicago Days: 150 Defining Moments in the Life of a Great City* (Wheaton, IL: Cantigny First Division Foundation, 1997), 29.

18. Upton Sinclair, *The Jungle* (New York: Harper & Bros, 1905, 1946), ix.

19. Justin Kaplan, ed., *Bartlett's Familiar Quotations*, 16th ed. (Boston: Little Brown and Co., 1992), 634.

20. O'Connell, 78-9.

21. John Husar, "Disabled fisherman's plight hooks mayor," *Chicago Tribune,* 19 March 1997, sec. 4, 8.

The I&M Canal: From Shipping Channel to Sewer

1. Chicago, IL, *Department of Health Annual Report,* 1911-1918, 1484.

2. *Joliet True Democrat*, 7 June 1862, quoted in Mary Yeater Rathbun "Illinois and Michigan Canal" (Illinois Department of Conservation, 3M-4-81, 1980, draft), 43.

3. Rathbun, 43-4.

4. Andreas, vol. 2, 554.

5. Andreas, vol 2, 554; Wade, 69.

6. Andreas, vol. 2, 123.

7. Larson, 186.

8. Andreas, vol. 3, 136-7.

9. Chicago Sanitary District, "In the matter of the application of the Sanitary District of Chicago for a permit to divert not to exceed 10,000 cubic feet of water per second for Sanitary Purposes from Lake Michigan," 1913.

10. Andreas, vol. 3, 139.

11. Andreas, vol. 3, 141.

According to Andreas, the cost of deepening the canal from the beginning up to April 1, 1871, exclusive of interest, was $2,298,437 (vol. 2, 554). The original 1843 estimate of the difference in cost between the deep cut over the shallow cut had been only $1,600,000 (Chicago Sanitary District, "In the matter of the application of the Sanitary District of Chicago for a permit to divert not to exceed 10,000 cubic feet of water per second for Sanitary Purposes from Lake Michigan," 1913).

12. Winstone, 19.

Toward the Sanitary and Ship Canal: From 1880 to Shovel Day

1. J. B. McClure, ed., *Stories and Sketches of Chicago* (Chicago: Rhodes and McClure, 1880), 169-72.

2. Joel A. Tarr, "Risk Perception in Waste Disposal: A Historical Review," in Julian B. Andelman and Dwight W. Underhill, eds., *Health Effects from Hazardous Waste Sites* (Chelsea, Michigan: Lewis Publishers, Inc., 1987), 84.

3. O'Connell, 101.

4. Lyman E. Cooley, *The Lakes and Gulf Waterway as related to the Chicago Sanitary Problem* (Chicago: Press of John W. Weston, 1890), vi.

5. Andreas, vol. 3, 135.

6. Currey, *Chicago, Its History and Its Builders*, vol. 1, 323.

7. Andreas, vol. 3, 135.

8. Knight and Zeuch, 36-7.

9. Ibid., 37.

10. Andreas, vol. 3, 135-6.

11. O'Connell, 90-1.

12. Currey, *Chicago, Its History and Its Builders*, vol. 3, 106-7.

13. "Slow Sanitary Measures," *Evening News*, 1 August 1885, 2.

14. "The Indications," *Evening News*, 1 August 1885, 1.

15. "The Weather," *Chicago Tribune*, 2 August 1885, 9.

16. "And a Flood Came," *Daily Tribune*, 3 August 1885, 1.

17. *Chicago Tribune*, 4 August 1885, 1 and 5; *Daily News*, 3 August 1885, 1.

18. "A Pleasant Day," *Chicago Tribune*, 4 August 1885, 1.

19. "Many Basements Flooded," *Chicago Daily News*, 3 August 1885, 1.

20. "Fortunate Chicago," *The Daily News*, 17 August 1885, 2.

21. Louis B. Cain, "The Creation of Chicago's Sanitary District and Construction of the Sanitary and Ship Canal," *Chicago History*, spring 1979, 100.

22. Illinois, House, *Journal*, 26 May 1887, 1047.

23. O'Connell, 94-5.

24. Illinois, *Laws of the State of Illinois passed by the Thirty-Sixth General Assembly* (9 January 1889 - 28 May 1889), 126.

25. Illinois, *Laws*, 1889, 132.

26. Ibid., 134.

27. Ibid., 135.

28. Cain, 103.

29. Sanitary District of Chicago, *Proceedings*, 14 September 1892, 746.

30. Currey, vol. 3, 118.

31. "Recalls How Chicago River Often Caught Fire" *H&A*, 28 August 1949, in Newspaper Clipping File, Chicago Historical Society.

Building the Channel that Saved Chicago

1. Judith V. Sayad, "The Night they Turned the River 'Round," *Chicago Times Magazine*, July/August 1989, 92-5.

2. Carl Condit, *Chicago, 1910-1929: Building, Planning, and Urban Technology* (Chicago: University of Chicago Press, 1973), 28.

3. Currey, vol. 3, 120.

4. "Turn the River into Big Canal," *Chicago Daily Tribune*, 3 January 1900, Part 2, 9.

5. Sanitary District of Chicago, *Proceedings*, 17 January 1900, 6240.

6. Cain, 110.

7. Stanley A. Changnon and Joyce M. Changnon, "History of the Chicago Diversion and Future Implications," *Journal of Great Lakes Research* 22, no. 1 (1996): 104.

8. Sanitary District of Chicago, *Proceedings*, 17 January 1900, 6240.

9. "Evanstonian Credited with Being 'Father' of Chicago Sanitary District Scheme," 9 October 1914, in newspaper clipping file, Evanston Historical Society archives.

10. Arthur R. Reynolds, *Report of Streams Examination, Chemic and Bacteriologic* (Chicago: Trustees of the Sanitary District of Chicago, 1902), 8.

11. O'Connell, 131-3.

12. Harlow B. Mills, et al., "Man's Effects on the Fish and Wildlife of the Illinois River," *Illinois Natural History Survey Biological Notes* No. 57 (Urbana, IL, 1966): 3.

13. David McCullough, *The Path Between the Seas: the Creation of the Panama Canal, 1870-1914* (New York: Simon and Schuster, 1977), 25.

The North Shore Channel and Straightening the North Branch

1. Harvey B. Hurd and Robert D. Sheppard, eds., *History of Evanston*, vol. 2 (Chicago: Munsell Publishing Co., 1906), 474.

2. Ibid., 170 .

3. *Hessler v. The Drainage Commissioners, Illinois 53 Reports*, 105 (1870).

4. Evanston Board of Trustees, Minutes, March 1868, 167.

5. "The Big Ditch," *Evanston Index*, 15 June 1872, 1.

6. "The Big Ditch," *Evanston Index*, 10 June 1874, 1.

7. "West Evanston," *Evanston Index*, 10 January 1874, 2.

8. "Work on Big Ditch," *Evanston Index*, 29 October 1904, 6.

9. "Judge Hurd on Drainage," *Evanston Index*, 21 October 1899, 1.

10. "Report of Canal Experts," 25 March 1901, in Drainage Folder, Evanston Historical Society.

11. "Diphtheria Threatens Us," *Evanston Index*, 22 November 1902, 4.

12. "The Sanitary District Bonds," *Evanston Index*, 13 June 1903, 1.

13. "Discuss Sanitary Question," *Evanston Index*, 18 July 1903, 1.

14. "Peter Haual Recalls Early Ravenswood," typed from a local newspaper, 1931, in Conrad Sulzer Regional Library archives, Chicago Public Library.

15. "Interviews of Old Settlers," mimeograph, n.d., in Conrad Sulzer Regional Library archives, Chicago Public Library.

16. Sanitary District of Chicago, *Proceedings*, 16 March 1904, 9817.

17. Chief Engineer's Annual Report for 1904, Chicago Sanitary District, 14 June 1905, 10594; Circuit Court of Cook County, General No. 298,136, *Sanitary District of Chicago v. Chicago Title & Trust Company*, on Bill and Cross-Bill, Term No. 8913, Thursday, 13 April 1911, 2:30 o'clock p.m., 16, in Clerk of the Circuit Court of Cook County archives, Chicago, Illinois.

18. Richard C. Bjorklund, *Ravenswood Manor, Indian Prairie to Urban Pride* (Ravenswood Manor Improvement Association, published with revisions, 1981), 5.

19. The Sanitary District of Chicago vs. The Chicago Title and Trust Company, 278 Ill 529; 161 N. E. 161; 1917 Ill. LEXIS 1094, available in the LEXIS® service).

20. "Evanston Girl Starts Big Drainage Canal," *Evanston Press*, 28 September 1907, 1.

21. Sanitary District of Chicago, *Proceedings*, 1908, 1201-8.

22. "Evanston Girl Starts Big Drainage Canal."

23. Currey, vol.3, 130.

24. Currey, vol. 3, 129-30.

25. "Evanston Girl Starts Big Drainage Canal."

26. Bill Wente, Executive Director of Wilmette Harbor Association, personal communication with author, 2 October 1997.

27. W*ilmette's Nautical Heritage* (Wilmette, IL: Sheridan Shore Yacht Club, 1982), 12.

28. "Sanitary Board Promises Relief," *Evanston Index*, 7 September 1912, 1.

29. "Last Objection to Diversion is Removed," *Evanston Index*, 10 March 1916, 1.

30. Chicago, IL, Department of Public Works, *Annual Report*, 1938, 51.

31. Chicago, IL, Department of Public Works, *Annual Report*, 1934, 238; 1935, 280.

32. Chicago, IL, Department of Public Works, *Annual Report*, 1939, 322.

33. Chicago, IL, Department of Public Works, *Annual Report*, 1940, 245.

34. Chicago, IL, Department of Public Works, *Annual Report*, 1942, 296.

35. Richard Lanyon, Head, Department of Research and Development, Metropolitan Water Reclamation District, personal communication with author, January-December 1998.

36. Wente, personal communication with author.

37. Sanitary District of Chicago, *Maintenance and Operations Department Report*, 1975, 12.

38. *Wilmette's Nautical Heritage*, 73.

39. Bill Koenig, personal communication with author.

Reconnecting the City and the River after the Turn of the Century

1. Daniel H. Burnham, thoughts from a speech delivered to the London City Planning Conference, paraphrased by Willis Polk, Mr. Burnham's San Francisco partner, after Burnham's death in 1912. Henry M. Saylor, " 'Make no Little Plans': Daniel Burnham Thought It but Did He Say It?," *Journal of the American Institute of Architects* (1957): 27, 3.

2. Larson, 118-22.

3. Ibid., 192-3.

4. Ibid., 115-6.

5. Transcript of videotaped interview with Larry Perkins, 28 December 1990.

6. Daniel H. Burnham and Edward H. Bennett, *Plan of Chicago*, 1909 (Reprinted by New York: Da Capo Press, 1970), 97.

7. Ibid., 97.

8. Ibid., 54-5.

9. Ibid., 97.

10. Alice Sinkevitch, ed., *AIA Guide to Chicago* (Harcourt Brace & Co., 1993), 101.

11. Ann Durkin Keating, "Chicago and its river," draft, 12 July 1997, 19.

12. Burnham, 34.

13. Ibid., 39.

The "Northwest Branch"

1. "Skokie Drainage Now Demanded," *Evanston Index*, 26 October 1912, 1.

2. Glenview Area Historical Society, *Glenview at 75: 1899-1974* (Melrose Park, IL: Union Press, 1974).

3. Ibid.

4. Ibid.

5. Typed transcript of interview with Reverend Martin C. Schmidt by Denise Rossmann Christopoulos, recorded for the Morton Grove Historical Society, 21 April 1978.

6. Fred N. Huscher, personal communication with author, 1998.

7. *Morton Grove, Illinois, 100 Years; a Tradition of Service, 1895-1995* (commemorative book), 29.

8. *The Villager*, 19 June 1958, 16-7.

9. Joel Bookman, personal communication with author.

10. Sanitary District of Chicago, *Proceedings*, 1911, 1448.

11. Baudette El Palma, ed., *Niles Township, Niles Center, Morton Grove, Tessville* (Chicago: Holland Press, 1916).

12. "Judges Must Outline Five Wards in Drain District Within 20 Days," *Waukegan Daily Sun*, 9 April 1914; "The North Shore Sanitary District, Its History & Present Services," (North Shore Sanitary District, 1965).

13. Brian Jensen, North Shore Sanitary District, personal communication with author, August 1999.

14. John J. Halsey, *A History of Lake County*, Illinois (Philadelphia:Roy S. Bates, 1912), 296-7.

15. Marie Ward Reichelt, *The History of Deerfield, Illinois* (Glenview, IL: Glenview Press, 1928), Introductory Page.

16. Ted Anderson, President, James Anderson and Co., personal communication with author.

17. Bill Hinchliffe, personal communication with author, 1 January 1999. Mellody Farm has become a model restoration project during the 1990s, under the auspices of the Lake County Open Lands Association in cooperation with a developer, the Youth

Conservation Corps from Deerfield High School, and various funding agencies. Overburden is being removed from the east bank of the "ditch" to return the stream to its original level and wet prairie community. This approach will allow the river and floodplain to return to their natural processes. As land use changes in Lake County, the ditch is no longer necessary to drain the land for farming. (Casey Bukro, "Unlikely partners bridge open space and home building," *Chicago Tribune*, 27 June, 1997, Sec. 2, 1).

18. "Memorandum - Resume of Work Done by Union Drainage District No. 1, October 14, 1957."

The Forest Preserve District of Cook County and the North Branch

1. Perkins.
2. Currey, vol. 3, 164.
3. Perkins.
4. Board of Forest Preserve Commissioners for the Forest Preserve District of Cook County, Illinois, *Proceedings*, 2 April 1917, 236.
5. Forest Preserve District of Cook County, *Proceedings*, 7 January 1918, 9.
6. Windes.
7. Forest Preserve District of Cook County, *Proceedings*, 3 January 1922, 11-2.
8. Forest Preserve District of Cook County, *Proceedings*, 9 June 1931, 228.
9. Forest Preserve District of Cook County, *Proceedings*, 3 February 1932, 20.
10. Ibid.
11. "History of the Cook County Clean Streams Committee," (pamphlet, n.d.).
12. Ralph Frese, personal communication with author, 4 September 1998.

The Ascendance of Federal Authority: Making the River Safe for Shipping and Addressing the Issue of Lake Michigan Diversion

1. Larson, 202.
2. Ibid., 196-7.
3. Ibid., 201.
4. Ibid., 193.
5. Larson, 205; Chicago, IL, Department of Public Works, *Annual Report*, 1908, 232.
6. Larson, 203-4.
7. Ibid., 205.
8. Ibid., 202.
9. Changnon and Changnon, 106.
10. James A. Brown and Patricia J. O'Brien, *At the Edge of Prehistory: Huber Phase Archeology in the Chicago Area* (Kampsville, IL: Center for American Archeology, 1990), 142.
11. Changnon and Changnon, 106.
12. O'Connell, 142-3.
13. *State of Wisconsin, et al. v. State of Illinois and Sanitary District of Chicago*, October Term, 1929, Decree of April 21, 1930, Supreme Court of the United States, Washington, D.C.
14. O'Connell, 138.
15. "Control Lock Shuts Out River, Boats, Too, Causing Trouble," *Chicago Daily News*, 9 September 1938, 5. Final construction costs added up to $2,478,292.88 for the Controlling Works, including $1,960,984.70 for the lock and guide walls.
16. Chicago, IL, Department of Public Works, *Annual Report*, 1938, 353.
17. Chicago, IL, Department of Public Works, *Annual Report*, 1939, 323.

18. "Dynamite, Barge Finally Open Chicago River Locks," *Chicago Tribune*, 23 January 1963, in Chicago—River File, Chicago Historical Society.

Realization of Two Late Nineteenth-Century Dreams: Straightening the South Branch between Polk and 18th Streets, and Creation of the Lakes-to-the-Gulf Waterway

1. Currey, 377.
2. William Hale Thompson, Mayor; Richard W. Wolfe, Commissioner of Public Works; Loren D. Gayton, City Engineer, *Straightening the Chicago River*, (Chicago: Press of J.T. Igoe Co., 1930), 7-9.
3. Ibid., 26.
4. Ibid., 33.
Before Michigan Boulevard was opened by the Michigan Avenue Bridge, property between Randolph Street and the river was valued at about $22 per square foot. After the improvement, property south of the river was valued at $100 per square foot, north of the river at $80 per square foot. The Chicago Plan Commission estimated that for every dollar in assessments on property owners, the city received $12 in increased property value, and observed the effect all the way up to Evanston. [In Chicago, IL, Citizens' Committee on River Straightening; Chicago, IL, City Council, Committee on Railway Terminals, *The Straightening of the Chicago River*, (Chicago: Press of J. T. Igoe Co., December 1926), 13-5.]
5. Chicago, IL., Department of Public Works, *Annual Report*, 1921, 137.
6. *Straightening the Chicago River*, 1926, 13-5.
7. *Straightening the Chicago River*, 1930, 10.
8. *Straightening the Chicago River*, 1926, 172.
9. Ibid., 35.
10. Ibid., 171.
11. Commissioner's Report, in Chicago, IL, Department of Public Works, *Annual Report*, 1926, 15.
12. "Banquet Commemorating the Historic Event of Straightening the Chicago River," souvenir program, 29 December 1929.
13. Larson, 190-201.
14. William Hale Thompson, "Inaugural Address of Mayor William Hale Thompson, April 28, 1919," Inaugural Addresses of the Mayors of Chicago, www.chipublib.org/004Chicago/Mayors/Speeches.
15. Richard Wolfe, "Our Chicago," in *Straightening the Chicago River*, 1930, 167-70.

Transforming the Skokie Marsh

1. Roland Eisenbeis, "The Skokie Lagoons," *Nature Bulletin*, No. 646-A (10 September 1977).
2. Caroline Thomas Harnsberger, *Winnetka: the Biography of a Village* (Evanston, IL: Shori Press, 1971), 118.
3. Quincy L. Dowd, "1885-1901: Early Impressions of Winnetka," January 1921, in Winnetka Historical Society archives.
4. Windes, Frank, "Skokie Drainage," transcript of lecture before the Masonic Club, 21 November 1933.
5. Ibid.
6. Ibid.
7. "The Skokie Development" (Engineering Department, Forest Preserve District of Cook County, n.d.), 2.

8. Harnsberger, 118-9.

9. "A Serious Problem," *The Messenger*, December 1905, 6-7.

10. Forest Preserve District of Cook County, *Proceedings*, 3 January 1922, 11-2.

11. Windes.

12. *Washburn v. Forest Preserve District of Cook County*, 313, Illinois Reports, 130 (1925); *Washburn v. Forest Preserve District of Cook County*, 327, Illinois Reports, 479 (1927).

13. Forest Preserve District of Cook County, *Proceedings*, 31 May 1928, 146-7.

14. Harnsberger, 120.

15. Eisenbeis, Roland, *Nature Bulletin*, No. 646-A.

16. Forest Preserve District of Cook County, *Annual Report*, 1937, 17-8.

17. Forest Preserve District of Cook County, *Proceedings*, 21 December 1933, 192-3.

18. Ibid.

19. Forest Preserve District of Cook County, *Annual Report*, 1939, 225.

20. Forest Preserve District of Cook County, annual message of Clayton F. Smith, president, Board of Commissioners, *Annual Report*, 1935, 121.

21. Forest Preserve District of Cook County, *Proceedings*, 1939, 225-8.

22. Forest Preserve District of Cook County, *Proceedings*, 1942, 170-1.

23. Harnsberger, 48.

24. Windes.

25. Ibid.

26. "Che-Wab-Skokie, Great Marsh of Indians, Yields to Energy of CCC Corps," *The Chicago Daily News*, 20 April 1935, 5.

Filling the Arms of Bubbly Creek and the West Fork

1. Chicago, IL, Department of Public Works, *Annual Report*, 1922, 148.

2. Chicago, IL, Department of Public Works, *Annual Report*, 1923, 155.

3. Knight and Zeuch, 36-7.

4. Argument for a Bill to Declare a Part of the West Fork of the South Branch of the Chicago River Non-Navigable, Submitted to Congress by the City of Chicago, City Council, Committee on Efficiency, Economy and Rehabilitation, January 1923, 7.

5. *Chicago Daily News*, 14 September 1938, in Newspaper Clipping File, Chicago Historical Society.

6. *Chicago Daily News*, 7 November 1938, in Chicago—River File, Chicago Historical Society.

The Metropolitan Water Reclamation District: New Approaches to Water Quality in the River

1. Finch, 35.

2. Ibid., 34.

3. "It's deep tunnels and reservoirs," *Chicago Tribune*, 25 February 1997, Sec. 1, 18.

4. "The Great Lakes Mediation Memorandum of Understanding," 29 July 1996. It is signed by the Attorney General of each Lake State involved in the litigation and by the U.S. Solicitor General.

Citizens and Their River: The Sixties through the Nineties

1. Robert Cassidy, "Our friendless river," *Chicago*, August, 1979, 134.

2. Joseph M. Petulla, *American Environmental History*, 2nd ed. (Toronto: Merrill Publishing Co.,1988), 410-1.

3. U. S. EPA History Office, "The Guardian: Origins of the EPA," www.epa.gov/history/publications/origins.

4. Petulla, 415.

5. Ralph Frese and David Jones, personal communication with author.

6. Tom Roth, personal communication with author.

7. Ralph Frese, personal communication with author, 3 September 1999.

8. *Chicago Tribune*, 24 November 1977.

9. David Ramsay, Friends of the Chicago River, personal communication with author.

10. Sheryl De Vore, "Great Little-known Birding Hotspots in Illinois: IOS members share secret birding areas near their homes," *Meadowlark* 6, no. 1 (1997): 14-6.

11. W. C. Alden, Department of the Interior, United States Geological Survey, Geologic Records, Accession No. 1328, *Chicago and Calumet Quadrangles*, Index. No. WCA–1, Locality K-16, Illinois, 1896, 79.

12. Jane Friedman, "Wetlands to reappear at Gompers Park," *News Star*, 12 April 1995.

13. Chicago Rivers Demonstration Project, "What's Working on Chicago Rivers: a handbook for Improving Urban Rivers" (Milwaukee, WI: National Park Service, 1998), 14-7.

14. Roland F. Eisenbeis, Memorandum to Charles G. Sauers, 20 September 1963, in Forest Preserve District of Cook County Botanic Garden files.

15. Mrs. John M. Frankel of Winnetka, IL, newspaper article, in Forest Preserve District of Cook County Botanic Garden files, no source or date.

16. Joan O. O'Shaughnessy, "Take a Skokie River Ramble," *Garden Talk*, October 1997, 6.

17. Richard J. Sutphen, Marine Consultant, personal communication with author, September 1997.

18. "Life after Sheet Piling," *The River Reporter* 11, no. 4 (fall 1998): 1-2.

19. Richard J. Sutphen, personal communication with author.

20. Ted Anderson, personal communication with author, March 1999.

21. "Chicago River North Branch Cleaning Begun," *Chicago Tribune*, 28 December, 1969, in Newspaper Clipping File, Chicago Historical Society.

Reflections

1. Hecht, Ben, *A Thousand and One Afternoons in Chicago* (New York: Covice Frider, 1922), 227.

2. Gale, 306-307.

Map Notes

Digital files for the author's maps were used with permission from the following sources:

Chicago River

Digital files of the Chicago River were obtained from the Illinois Department of Natural Resources (IDNR). They were modified from the Illinois Geographic Information System Statewide CD-ROM Volume I, Streams, May, 1996, from the Data Set Streams and Shorelines by County, derived from the U.S. Geological Survey 1:100,000 Digital Line Graph file, hydrography layer, 1980-1986. Counties\Lake\streams has been modified by extending the East and Middle Forks of the North Branch of the Chicago River to the north, to agree with field checking.

Streets

Streets were obtained from the Northeastern Illinois Planning Commission (NIPC) 1:24,000-Scale 1990 Major Roads Centerline File, Version 1.1, 4/15/1999, from the Digital Map of the Region CD-ROM.

Land Use

Land use maps showing parks, forest preserves, and golf courses were based on NIPC's 1:24,000-Scale 1990 Land Use Inventory.

Watershed Boundaries

Watershed boundaries shown on this map were provided by the Illinois Environmental Protection Agency (IEPA), delineated at a scale of 1:24:000. For information contact IEPA, Division of Water Pollution Control, at 217/782-3362. The watershed file was modified by truncating record ILG102 at Lemont, eliminating the part of the polygon that reaches south to Joliet.

Calumet River and Cal-Sag Channel

The Calumet River and Cal-Sag Channel are from IEPA, from the U.S. Environmental Protection Agency (U.S. EPA) Stream Reach File, Version 3 (RF3).

Eastern United States and Canada

The map of the eastern United States and Canada was created using ArcView® GIS software and the following files provided in ArcView's® data set: canada\province.shp, canada\lakes.shp, canada\rivers.shp, canada\cities.shp, usa\cities.shp, usa\rivers.shp, and usa\states.shp.

Glossary

Numbers in parentheses at the end of a definition indicate the source from which it is adapted. Sources are listed at the end of the glossary.

alluvium. Sediment deposited by running water in a stream channel and in low parts of a stream valley. (1)

animal lick. Accumulation of minerals in a seep or pool that provides animals with necessary salts and other micro-nutrients.

baymouth bar. A low ridge of sand above water level, built across the mouth of a bay by littoral drift and wave action; a type of beach. (1)

bedrock. Solid rock underlying soil or other land layers such as clay.

berm. An embankment, usually made of earth, but sometimes of rocks.

borrow pit. A hole remaining in the land after earth or rock has been removed for use elsewhere.

chert. Nodules of silica or quartz, often in layers within sedimentary rock; a poor-quality flint. (1)

continental divide. The crest or ridge of a continental land mass that divides the flow of surface waters between two oceans. For example, the Rocky Mountain chain separates the drainage of streams between the Atlantic and Pacific Oceans.

continental drift. Hypothesis that the lithosphere, or earth's crust, is broken into about 12 thick plates riding on a molten inner layer, explaining the movement of continents.

cubic feet per second (cfs). A measurement of the instantaneous rate of flow past a single point (one cubic foot equals $7\frac{1}{2}$ gallons and when multiplied by 60 seconds per minute, gives almost 450 gallons of flow per minute).

detritus. Composition of parts of dead organisms, cast-off fragments or wastes of living organisms, and fragments of non-organic waste; junk; debris.

dissolved oxygen (DO). Amount of oxygen gas (0_2) dissolved in a given quantity of water at a given temperature and atmospheric pressure. (3)

divide. *noun.* The crest or ridge of a continental land mass that divides the flow of surface waters between bodies of water. *See* **continental divide** *and* **sub-continental divide.**

dolomite, "Athens Marble," Lemont Stone. Hard sedimentary rock, a type of limestone, having the composition calcium magnesium carbonate ($CaMgCO_3$). (1)

ecotone. A transition zone between two ecological communities, containing plants and animals from each.

effluent. Wastewater discharged into a receiving waterway.

end or terminal moraine. A landform composed of a thick ridge of glacial till, created from the debris that flows to a glacier's leading edge and is deposited in place when the glacier's edge remains stationary. (8)

fetch. The distance along open water or land over which the wind blows; specifically, the distance traversed by waves without obstruction. (7)

floodplain. Low, flat ground on one or both sides of a stream channel, subject to annual flooding and characterized by alluvial deposits. (1)

floodway. Defined channel of a river through which the water flows; different from the floodplain, which is the area over which the river expands laterally when in flood.

forest. Plant community dominated by trees growing close together, their crowns forming a layer of foliage that largely shades the ground. (1)

freshet. A flood or overflowing of a river resulting from heavy rains or melted snow (7); a term in common use during the nineteenth century.

glacial till or drift. Mixed, unlayered, and unsorted rock debris carried and deposited by glaciers.

glacier. Large natural accumulation of land ice. (1)

habitat. Place or type of environment where a plant or animal organism or a population of organisms lives. (2)

hardpan. A hard layer of earth beneath soil, composed mainly of clay and impervious to water. (7)

hydrography. The description of the waters of the earth's surface; the study and mapping of their forms and physical features and dynamics.

hydrology. Science of the earth's water and its motions through the hydrologic cycle, which is the movement, exchange, and storage of the earth's free water in gaseous, liquid, and solid states. (1)

ice sheet. Large, thick plate of glacial ice moving outward in all directions from a central region of accumulation; also called a continental glacier. (1)

league. *measurement.* Though indefinite and depending upon the place and time of usage, in English-speaking countries, usually meaning about 3 miles (4). It is thus unclear exactly what Jolliet's estimate was for the length of the canal he contemplated.

levee, natural. A belt of higher ground paralleling a meandering alluvial river, built up by deposition of fine sediment during periods of flooding. (1)

limestone. Sedimentary rock formed from shells, sands, and other material in the oceans that, in the past, covered today's limestone regions; mainly composed of calcium carbonate but with varying amounts of magnesium carbonate, silica, or other minerals, and clay. (10)

Little Ice Age. Climatic interlude of below-normal temperatures from about 1450 A.D.-1850 A.D., during which mountain glaciers enlarged and advanced to lower levels. (1)

littoral drift. Movement of sediment parallel to the shore when waves strike the shoreline at an angle. (9)

longshore current. A moving mass of water set up by the angled approach of waves and running parallel to a shoreline. (9)

Mackinaw boat. A rowboat or sailboat with a flat bottom, pointed bow, and sometimes a pointed stern, formerly used around the upper Great Lakes. (10)

marsh. A frequently or continually inundated wetland characterized by emergent [partly out of the water] non-woody vegetation, such as cattails, adapted to saturated soil conditions. (4)

mesic area. An area in which the soils are usually well drained, but still contain a lot of moisture for all or much of the year. (5)

mesophytic. Referring to plant species or plant communities that grow under mesic (moderate moisture) conditions. (5)

miasma theory. A theory, prevalent in the nineteenth century, holding that infectious diseases evolved from putrefying organic matter, creating sickening odors and resulting in epidemics of cholera, yellow fever, or typhoid, which led to calls for sanitation within cities. Also known as the filth theory of disease. (6)

microsite. A small, fairly distinct area, such as a ravine or the shade of a tree, with environmental conditions differing from the surrounding area and providing habitat favorable for plants and animals other than those living in the larger surrounding environment.

moraine. An accumulation of debris previously carried by a glacier or ice-sheet and deposited by the ice to become a landform. (1)

non-point-source pollution. Pollution, such as fertilizer, pesticides, or oils, originating from diffuse hard-to-identify sources such as runoff from the land or highways, etc., and entering a stream at unidentifiable locations.

oxbow lake. Crescent-shaped lake or swamp representing the abandoned channel left by the cutoff of a meander in a stream. (1)

Paleozoic Era. From *paleo* (old) and *zoic* (life); 590-248 million years before the present.

Pleistocene Epoch. A division of the Cenozoic (present) Era characterized by glaciations and the appearance of humans; 1.8 million-10,300 years before the present.

point-source pollution. Pollution from a known source that is discharged at an identifiable point, such as a culvert, emptying into a stream.

portage. A land pathway where a boat is carried over a divide between two waterways (rivers and/or lakes), or around falls and other obstructions in a river.

prairie. Plant community where grasses are dominant and broad-leaved flowering plants, or forbs, are sub-dominant. (1)

Public Land Survey. The Land Ordinance of May 20, 1795, instituted by the Continental Congress, providing for the survey of U.S. territory into a grid of townships. Townships are six miles on a side and are subdivided into 36 consecutively numbered sections, each of which is one square mile or 640 acres. The law specified that a surveyor was to note "at their proper distances, all mines, salt springs, salt licks, that shall come to his knowledge; and all water courses, mountains and other remarkable and permanent things over and near which lines shall pass; and also the quality of the lands."

reach. A stretch of water between two points in a river.

riparian rights. Rights that accrue to owners of land along rivers and streams for use of the water in the river (originally referred to land along rivers but today often used to designate land on a lakeshore, as well).

savanna. Woodland of widely-spaced trees.

seep. Groundwater that drips from a hillside or a bank adjacent to a stream; water that drains through the hillside until it hits an impenetrable layer such as clay and must flow laterally to find an outlet.

shale. A fine-grained rock formed by the hardening of clay; splits easily into thin layers when broken. (7)

Silurian Period. Subdivision of the Paleozoic Era, 440-395 million years before the present.

slough. Shallow water running or ponding on the land; used interchangeably with "marsh" by surveyor Harrison in describing Lake County.

spit. *geology.* Narrow, fingerlike ridge of sand attached to land but originally formed in open water.

spoil. *from excavations.* Excavated materials from digging or dredging, such as when deepening a channel; sometimes heaped up into spoil piles.

spring. Ground water upwelling from a point on the land or on the bottom of a stream or lake.

stream. Long, narrow body of flowing water occupying a channel and moving to lower levels under the force of gravity. (1)

sub-continental divide. Watershed divide between streams flowing into one part of an ocean and those flowing into another part of the same ocean. The Chicago sub-continental divide is between the watersheds of the Mississippi and St. Lawrence Rivers, both of which flow into the Atlantic Ocean.

swale. Narrow belt of low, marshy ground separating parallel beach ridges.

swamp. Wetland dominated by trees or shrubs. The wet areas of the Chicago River watershed were marsh, not swamp, because they were dominated by emergent plants, such as cattails, rather than trees or shrubs.

tussock sedge. A flowering herb, a member of the sedge family, which resembles grasses and rushes; found growing in low, humpy mounds on marshy ground in cold climates.

understory. The intermediate-sized tree and shrub layers of a woodland.

vernal pond. A small, shallow, temporary springtime pond fed by spring rains and snowmelt.

watershed. All the land area from which water, along with the sediment and dissolved substances that it carries, enters a stream through the force of gravity. (2)

weir. A structure built across a stream for catching fish, measuring rates of flow, or diverting water for purposes such as water mills, etc.

wetland. An area of land distinguished by four primary characteristics: the presence of water, hydric soil (soil formed under water), vegetation adapted to wet conditions, and varying water levels. (4)

Adapted from the following sources, where noted:

(1) Arthur N. Strahler and Alan H. Strahler, *Modern Physical Geography* (New York: John Wiley & Sons, 3rd edition, 1987).

(2) G. Tyler Miller, Jr., *Living in the Environment* (Belmont, California: Wadsworth Publishing Company, 7th edition, 1992).

(3) Christensen, *Global Science* (Dubuque, Iowa: Kendall/Hunt Publishing Co., 4th edition, 1996).

(4) William J. Mitsch and James G. Gosselink, *Wetlands* (New York: Van Nostrand Reinhold, 1986).

(5) Floyd Swink and Gerould Wilhelm, *Plants of the Chicago Region* (Indiana Academy of Science, 4th edition, 1994).

(6) Joel A. Tarr, in J.B. Andelman and D.W. Underhill, eds., *Health Effects from Hazardous Waste Sites* (Chelsea, Michigan: Lewis Publishers, 1987).

(7) *Webster's New Twentieth Century Dictionary of the English Language*, Unabridged, 2nd edition (Simon and Schuster, 1978).

(8) Ardith Hansel, "End Moraines—the end of the glacial ride," *Geobit* 2 (Illinois State Geological Survey, 1997).

(9) Charles C. Plummer and David McGeary, *Physical Geology*, 4th edition (Dubuque, Iowa: Wm. C. Brown, Publishers, 1988).

(10) *Compton's Interactive Encyclopedia* (Compton's NewMedia, Inc., 1995).

For More Information

Organizations

The following organizations are sources for maps, nature walks, organized walking tours, and boat tours. This list is not exhaustive. It includes those institutions that have been most helpful to the author or are most likely to be accessible to the general public. Whatever you do, get out onto the river; it is the best way to appreciate it. Organizations offering volunteer opportunities in ecological restoration and habitat management along the river are indicated by a (V).

Chicago Architecture Foundation
224 S. Michigan Ave.
Chicago, IL 60604
312/922-3432

Evanston Environmental Association
2024 McCormick Blvd.
Evanston, IL 60201
847/864-5181
Ladd Arboretum, Evanston Ecology Center.

Forest Preserve District of Cook County (V)
536 N. Harlem Ave.
River Forest, IL 60305
312/261-8400 (city)
708/366-9420 (suburbs)
630/257-2045 (to volunteer)
The North Branch bicycle trail begins at Caldwell and Devon Avenues in Chicago and extends approximately 20 miles to Lake County.

Friends of the Chicago River (V)
407 S. Dearborn, Suite 1580
Chicago, IL 60605
312/939-0490
www.chicagoriver.org

Illinois and Michigan Canal
National Heritage Corridor Commission
15701 S. Independence Blvd.
Lockport, IL 50441
815/740-2049
www.uic.edu/oorgs/LockZero/htm

Lake Bluff Open Lands Association (V)
P.O. Box 449
Lake Bluff, IL 60044
847/735-8137

Lake County Forest Preserves
General Offices
2000 N. Milwaukee Ave.
Libertyville, IL 60048
847/367-6640
forestpreserves@co.lake.il.us
www.co.lake.il.us/forest

Lake Forest Open Lands Association (V)
272 E. Deerpath Rd.
Lake Forest, IL 60045
847/234-3880
Skokie River Nature Reserve, including Shaw Prairie and Shaw Woods in the northern
section, with access at Laurel Avenue; and Haffner Meadows, Skinner Woods, and
Jones Meadow in the southern section, with access at Deerpath Road or Laurel Avenue.

Metropolitan Water Reclamation District
111 E. Erie St.
Chicago, IL 60611
312/751-6634 (public information and tours of facilities)

Northeastern Illinois Planning Commission
Natural Resources Department
222 S. Riverside Plaza
Chicago, IL 60606
312/454-0400
www.nipc.cog.il.us

Openlands Project
25 E. Washington St.
Suite 1650
Chicago, IL 60602
312/427-4256
www.openlands.org

Municipal Park Districts

Chicago Park District
North Region Office
Warren Park
6601 N. Western Ave.
Chicago, IL 60645
312/742-7879 (North Region Office)
312/742-PLAY (Main Office)

Deerfield Park District
836 Jewett Park Dr.
Deerfield, IL 60015
847/945-0650
Pine Street Park, Trail Tree Park, and Briarwood Nature Area.

Glenview Park District
901 Shermer Rd.
Glenview, IL 60025
847/724-5670
Tall Trees Park, Sleepy Hollow Park, and Riverside Park.

Highland Park Park District
Administrative Office
636 Ridge Rd.
Highland Park, IL 60035
847/831-3810
Centennial Park, Fink Memorial Park, and Devonshire Park.

Lake Forest Parks Department
110 E. Laurel Ave.
Lake Forest, IL 60045
847/234-2600
Deerpath Community Play Field.

Northbrook Park District
545 Academy Dr.
Northbrook, IL 60062
847/291-2960
Meadowhill Park, Meadowhill Park South, and Village Green Park & Village Green Center.

Historical Societies and Libraries

Chicago Historical Society
Clark St. at North Ave.
Chicago, IL 60614
312/642-4600

Conrad Sulzer Regional Library (Chicago Public Library)
Neighborhood History Research Collection
4455 N. Lincoln Ave.
Chicago, IL 60625
312/744-7616

Deerfield Area Historical Society
450 Kipling Pl.
Deerfield, IL 60015
847/948-0680

Glenview Area Historical Society
1121 Waukegan Rd.
Glenview, IL 60025
847/724-2235

Harold Washington Library (Chicago Public Library)
Municipal Reference Collection, 5th floor
400 S. State St.
Chicago, IL 60605
312/747-4526

Morton Grove Historical Museum
Harrer Park
6240 Dempster St.
Morton Grove, IL 60053
847/965-0203

Northbrook Historical Society
1776 Walters Ave.
Northbrook, IL 60062-2021
847/498-3404

Waukegan Historical Society
John Raymond Memorial Library
Lilac Cottage
1911 N. Sheridan Rd.
Waukegan, IL 60087
847/336-1859

Wilmette Historical Museum
609 Ridge Rd.
Wilmette, IL 60091
847/853-7666

Winnetka Historical Society
1140 Elm St.
Winnetka, IL 60093
847/501-6025

On the Water

Chicago Architecture Foundation cruises
312/922-3432

Chicago Fishing Hotline
312/744-3370

Chicagoland Canoe Base
4109 N. Narragansett Ave.
Chicago, IL 60634
773/777-1489

Friends of the Chicago River
312/939-0490

Mercury Skyline Cruise Lines
312/332-1353

Wagner Charter Co.
800/727-8926

Wendella Boat Lines
312/337-1446

Wendella River Bus
312/337-1446
Wendella's River Bus makes three stops—the Metra Station (Madison and Canal Streets), the Wrigley Building (400 N. Michigan Ave.), and "River East" (one block from Navy Pier)—and runs mid-April to October 31.

Selected Bibliography

Andreas, Alfred T. *History of Chicago from the Earliest Times to the Present Time*, 3 vols. Chicago: Alfred T. Andreas, 1884-1886.

Balesi, Charles J. *The Time of the French in the Heart of North America*. Chicago: Alliance Francaise Chicago, 1992.

Burnham, Daniel H. and Edward H. Bennett. *Plan of Chicago*. New York: Da Capo Press, 1970.

Chicago: an Industrial Guide. Chicago: Public Works Historical Society, 1991. This is a 50-page booklet on bridges and factories.

Christensen, Daphne, ed. *Chicago Public Works: a History*. Chicago: Rand McNally and Co., 1973.

Condit, Carl. *Chicago 1910-1929: Building, Planning and Urban Technology*. Chicago: University of Chicago Press, 1973.

Condit, Carl. *Chicago 1930-1970: Building, Planning and Urban Technology*. Chicago: University of Chicago Press, 1974.

Cronan, William. *Nature's Metropolis: Chicago and the Great West*. New York: W.W. Norton and Co., 1991.

Danckers, Ulrich and Jane Meredith. *Early Chicago*. River Forest, IL: Early Chicago, Inc., 2000.

Draper, Joan. *Chicago Bridges*. City of Chicago, 1984.

Eckert, Allan W. *Gateway to Empire*. New York: Bantam Books, 1983.

Greenberg, Joel. *A Natural History of the Chicago Region*. Baltimore, MD: Johns Hopkins University Press, in press.

Hansen, Harry. *The Chicago*. Rivers of America Series. New York: Farrar & Rinehart, 1942.

Knight, Robert and Lucius H. Zeuch. *The Location of the Chicago Portage Route of the Seventeenth Century*. Chicago: Chicago Historical Society, 1928.

Larson, John W. *Those Army Engineers: a history of the Chicago District U.S. Army Corps of Engineers*. U.S. Army Corps of Engineers, Chicago District, 1979.

Markman, Charles W. *Chicago Before History: the Prehistoric Archaeology of a Modern Metropolitan Area.* Springfield, IL: Illinois Historic Preservation Agency, 1991.
Available through the Center for American Archeology; P.O Box 366; Kampsville, IL 62053; 618/653-4688

Mayer, Harry M. and Richard C. Wade. *Chicago, Growth of a Metropolis.* Chicago: University of Chicago Press, 1969.

Miller, Donald L. *City of the Century.* New York: Simon and Schuster, 1997.

Quaife, Milo M. *Chicago's Highways Old and New.* Chicago: D.F. Keller & Co., 1923.

Saliga, Pauline A. *The Sky's the Limit: a Century of Chicago Skyscrapers.* New York: Rizzoli International Publications, Inc., 1999.

Sanitary District of Chicago, *Proceedings, 1892-1942.*
Available in the 5th-floor Municipal Reference Collection at Harold Washington Library; 400 S. State St.; Chicago.

Sinkevitch, Alice, ed. *AIA Guide to Chicago.* Orlando, Florida: Harcourt Brace, 1993.
This guide includes both bridges and buildings.

Solzman, David M. *The Chicago River, an Illustrated History and Guide to the River and its Waterways.* Chicago: Loyola University Press, 1998.
Solzman's book provides an excellent collection of maps and photographs and an excellent bibliography and guide to recreational, educational, and commercial river tours and resources.

Struever, Stuart. *Koster, Americans in Search of their Prehistoric Past.* New York: New American Library, 1979, 1985.

Wade, Louise Carol. *Chicago's Pride: The Stockyards, Packingtown, and Environs in the Nineteenth Century.* Urbana, IL: University of Illinois Press, 1987.

Maps

The maps that follow are intended as a general reference to points of interest mentioned in the book and to public lands along the river. They will not serve as detailed guides. If you wish to visit any of these sites, a good map of Chicago and the North Shore and a magnifying glass are essential companions. The mapped sites are those where the author has found easy parking and accessibility to walks along the river. The forks of the North Branch are often hidden by a screen of buckthorn, an aggressive exotic shrub with thorns, but earlier visitors have made informal trails that can lead you to the stream. The golf course map is for information only. If you wish to see the river as it winds through a golf course, you must be golfing (or, on several of them, you might be monitoring a bluebird trail).

Unfortunately, the river is not labeled along the major roads that pass over it, except for Golf Road where drivers learn they are crossing the West Fork and the North Branch, Chicago River. If members of the public are to support river-oriented initiatives for bank stabilization, flood control, and restoration of ecological health, they must be aware that what they now call a creek or a ditch is part of a long river system in a large watershed. As a beginning, signs could identify the Skokie River and the Middle and West Forks next to the bridges on Deerfield, Lake-Cook, and Willow Roads.

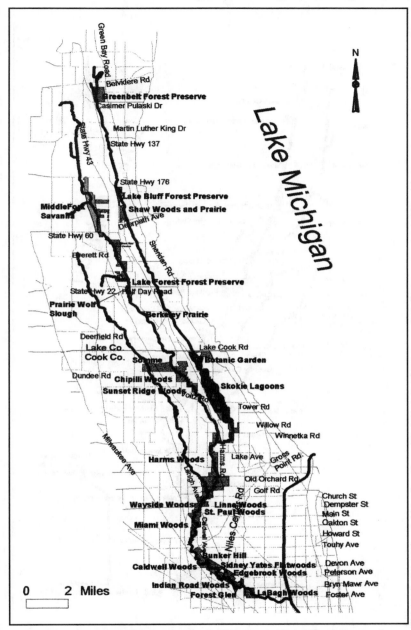

Map created by Libby Hill using ArcView® GIS software. Digital files courtesy of Northeastern Illinois Planning Commission and Illinois Department of Natural Resources.

Forest preserves along the Chicago River. Off the map to the southwest along the Des Plaines River are Chicago Portage Woods and Ottawa Trail Woods at Harlem Avenue and 47th Street, 300 acres of Cook County Forest Preserve that appear much as they did when Jolliet and Marquette crossed the portage.

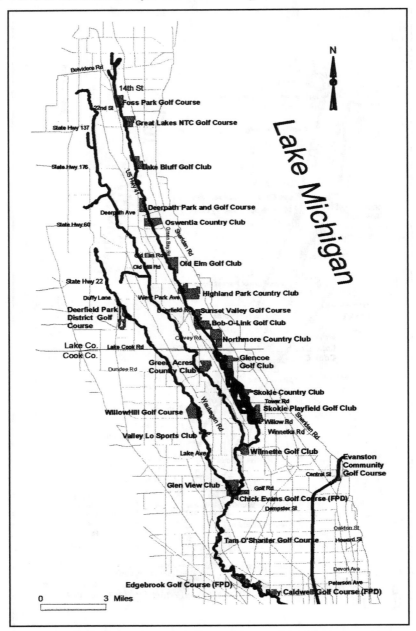

Map created by Libby Hill using ArcView® GIS software. Digital files courtesy of
Northeastern Illinois Planning Commission and Illinois Department of Natural
Resources.

Golf courses along the Chicago River.

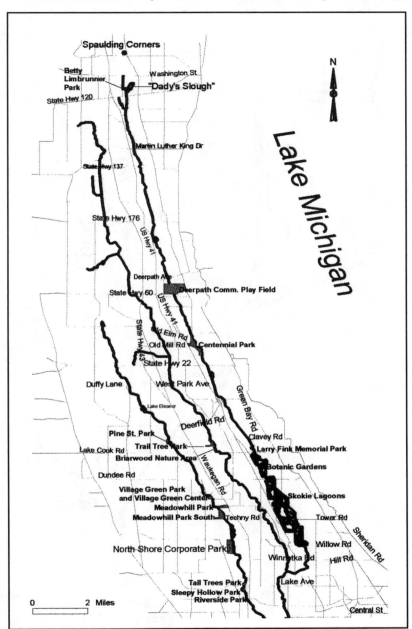

Map created by Libby Hill using ArcView® GIS software. Digital files courtesy of Northeastern Illinois Planning Commission and Illinois Department of Natural Resources.

Parks and other noteworthy features along the Chicago River:
Spaulding Corners to Lake Avenue.

Map created by Libby Hill using ArcView® GIS software. Digital files courtesy of Northeastern Illinois Planning Commission and Illinois Department of Natural Resources.

Parks and other noteworthy features along the Chicago River:
Lake Avenue to Bridgeport.

Acknowledgments

This book came about as the result of a challenge. For responsibility, or blame, I point to Peggy Bradley, Public Information Coordinator for the Metropolitan Water Reclamation District of Greater Chicago. It was she who articulated the need for a factual history addressing the questions that teachers, students, journalists, and the general public continuously request from her office about the river.

I reasoned that with my history-sociology-librarian-geography-ecology background, I would be able to write such a book. What I had in mind was to use all of the secondary resources I could find and compile them into a sort of readable reference book on the river. Because of my own natural history interests, I wanted to learn first about the "original" river before people got around to making changes and then look respectfully at the context in which the changes were made. Soon after I began my search for sources, I learned that the subject was much more complicated than I had thought. The sources conflicted; if one were right, the other had to be dead wrong or misleading at best. And it would help to have a little engineering background.

This meant calling in the experts. And so the book changed course. Instead of writing it by myself, I asked authorities to contribute. Everyone I asked accepted, and others asked if they could contribute. Some wanted to write entire sections, while others only wanted to furnish "the facts." Others wanted to copy-edit. The compromise we agreed to was that they would provide drafts and I would attempt to edit them all into one voice. Our central question would be: who did what to the Chicago River, when, how, and why, and what were the consequences?

In the process, I contributed some original research of my own, examining the Public Land Survey notes from 1821 and 1839, the two years when the river's watershed was surveyed so the federal government could sell the land to settlers. The surveys gave a picture of the landscape before large-scale European settlement: the river's route, its various widths and qualities (slough, marsh, creek, brook, river), what kind of vegetation grew in the watershed, and where. In addition, I would visit every nook and cranny where the Chicago River was publicly accessible. The Metropolitan Water Reclamation District of Greater Chicago generously offered me extended tours of the North Side Treatment Plant and a boat trip beginning on the Sanitary and Ship Canal, up the South Branch, on the Main Stem, and up the North Branch to the locks at Wilmette Harbor.

The more I learned, the more important primary sources became. I went to Chicago's old health department reports, fire department reports (did they tell of the river burning and the fire department responding, as some observers reported?), Department of Public Works reports, Congressional and legislative records, Metropolitan Water Reclamation District maps and records of early meetings, to name a few. I visited nearly every historical society and/or library in every town in the North Branch watershed and found enthusiastic assistance. I interviewed people involved with the river for recreation and as neighbors, read community histories and diaries of early settlers. I met with more enthusiastic help than I ever dreamed possible. Throughout the project, Peggy Bradley and Mary Carroll, also of the MWRDGC Public Information Office, were always available with help.

The list of people who contributed to this book is almost longer than the book itself. Without their friendship and support this book would have stopped in its tracks. Numerous people helped in small but essential ways. I have tried to name those whose contributions to the book made the difference between moving ahead or being at a standstill and who went above and beyond the call of duty.

My co-authors are: John Elliott, Ed Lace, Steve Apfelbaum, Joel Greenberg, and Richard Lanyon. John Elliott, director of River Trail Nature Center, Forest Preserve District of Cook County, wrote of the Portage, the Illinois and Michigan Canal, and the natural history of the river and watershed. Some of his passages were previously included in similar form in the Forest Preserve District of Cook County's brochure, "The Chicago Portage and Environs." Ed Lace, retired naturalist and archeologist with the Forest Preserve District of Cook County, wrote of geology, tribal peoples, the French and the Chicago portage, and Bubbly Creek and generously provided countless maps of the geology and natural and human history of the region. Joel Greenberg, naturalist and author, wrote of the Sanitary and Ship Canal and reviewed the glossary. Steve Apfelbaum, research ecologist at Applied Ecological Services, Inc. in Brodhead, Wisconsin, wrote of the ecology of the river, past and present. Richard Lanyon, director of the Research and Development Department of the MWRDGC, wrote of just about everything having to do with the district under its various names. All co-authors not only wrote sections of the book, but also made themselves available to answer countless follow-up phone and e-mail inquiries.

Numerous people were willing to answer endless questions, submit to countless interviews, comment on my written interpretations of those interviews, and offer advice and/or put in endless time on this project. The highest award in this category goes to Ted Anderson, president of James Anderson Engineering Co. in Lake Bluff, Illinois. Tied for a close second are Irwin Polls, water and sediment quality specialist for the Stickney Research and Development Laboratory of the MWRDGC, and David Jones, David Ramsay, and Chris Parson of Friends of the Chicago River.

Bill Koenig and Rob Nurre helped me inaugurate the new map room in Steve Apfelbaum and Susan Lehnhardt's house by drawing the Chicago River watershed onto ten different topographic maps. Al Westerman and David Clark helped enormously in procuring and deciphering the 1821 and 1839 deputy surveyors' notes from the General Land Office. My early fellow explorers on the ground include Bill Koenig, David Jones, Jayne Lilienfeld, Richard Carter, and my brother Bob.

For my tour of the North Side Water Reclamation Plant, I want to thank Mary Brand, Otto Quasthoff, and Steve Girsh of that facility, all of whom showed great patience in answering my incessant questions. For my MWRD boat tour aboard *Pollution Control I*, I would like to acknowledge the friendliness and professionalism of boatmen Danny Seasock and Javier Salazar of the MWRD's Industrial Waste Division. Thank you to General Superintendent Hugh McMillan of the Metropolitan Water Reclamation District, who granted the permission for these explorations.

For written sources, I went to librarians and archivists. I am certain that the three librarians who work with the Municipal Reference Collection on the 5th Floor of the Harold Washington Library Center in downtown Chicago, Ellen O'Brien, Shah Tiwana, and Lyle Benedict, are the most helpful librarians on the planet. Another standout in the library world is Glenn Humphreys, the archivist at the Chicago Public Library's Conrad Sulzer Regional Library. The reference staff of my own Evanston Public Library rewarded me by taking my exotic queries seriously and finding the answers. In addition, they have an impressive collection of books about Chicago history. The Transportation Center Library and the Government Documents Depository at Northwestern University Library were extremely helpful. David Clark, at the Illinois Regional Archives Depository at Northeastern University, introduced me to interesting maps of old Chicago. Diana Dretske of the Lake County Museum first pointed me in the direction of natural and human histories of Lake County. Jeanie Child and Phil Costello of the Office of the Circuit Court Clerk of Cook County Archives assisted me in finding the old case of the *Sanitary District of Chicago v. Chicago Title and Trust*. Matthew Cook of the Chicago

Historical Society was particularly helpful in answering questions regarding copyright issues.

I offer particular thanks to the staffs of the Winnetka Historical Society, the Wilmette Historical Society, and the Waukegan Historical Society; Beverly Dawson and staff at the Glenview Area Historical Society; and Judy Hughes of the Northbrook Historical Society. Adele Sturgis and Lona Louis of the Village of Northbrook provided necessary and interesting information and leads. Fred N. Huscher generously shared his time and invaluable knowledge of Morton Grove's history. Tom Roth of the Deerfield Historical Society was the first to share a personal story about the river. Carol Edwards, head of the U.S. Geological Survey Field Records Library in Denver, Colorado, became caught up in the project and supplied me with useful historical maps that assisted in validating my understanding of the area's geology. Arlene Stanger, office manager of Union Drainage District No. One on the West Fork in north Cook and Lake Counties, uncovered essential information in old files. Rick McCandless of the North Cook County Soil & Water Conservation District helpfully provided a variety of air photographs for me to choose among.

Others who contributed information and reprints and volunteered expertise include Robert Easton, chairman of the Department of Geography and Environmental Studies at Northeastern Illinois University; James Brown, professor of Anthropology at Northwestern University; Nancy Spencer, Department of Anthropology, Northeastern Illinois University; and Ralph Frese, unofficial dean of Chicago's waterways and owner of the Chicagoland Canoe Base. Ardith Hansel and Don Mikulic of the Illinois State Geological Survey edited the geology section and shared their recent research into lake levels in the Michigan Basin.

Many others went out of their way to help. Carol Spielman provided a lengthy interview about Prairie Wolf Slough and was supportive throughout. John and Jane Balaban edited the section on the North Branch Restoration Project, and Mike Branham of the Illinois EPA Bureau of Water helped me interpret IEPA's digital files of the Chicago River watershed. Geri Weinstein, Sofia Refetoff Zahed, and Michaelene Brown, all formerly with the Chicago Park District; and Jim Macdonald, volunteer steward of Gompers Park, helped me sort out the complicated story of that park. Joel Bookman, director of the North River Commission, and Richard Bjorklund, who lives in Ravenswood, helped me with the history of the neighborhoods along the North Branch of the river. Bill Wente, executive director of the Wilmette Harbor Association, graciously spent several hours with me discussing Wilmette Harbor. Dan Weber, Dave Kircher, Chris Merenowicz, Dick Newhard, and Jim Havlat helped by pulling old files, maps, and photos of the Forest Preserve District of Cook County. Chet Ryndak, my bird-banding mentor, searched his files for helpful materials regarding native tribes and climate. My colleagues at Northeastern Illinois Planning Commission (NIPC) gave generously of their time. They include Max Dieber, Kim Soulliere, Nina Savar, and Marc Thomas of the Research Department and Bob Kirshner and Holly Hudson of the Natural Resources Department. Carol Massar of the Army Corps of Engineers was always available to answer questions or direct me to others for information. Jack Tindall, a trustee of the Village of Mettawa, helped me untangle the complex ownership of the headwaters of the West Fork, and Dennis Bracco of W.W. Grainger, Inc. generously arranged access for me to explore their land there. Robert Ahlberg, village planner for Glenview, informed me about the village role in plans for redevelopment along the West Fork at the North Shore Corporate Park, where there is a pleasant riverwalk along a nice stretch of river. Kent Fuller obligingly drove me around the former Glenview Naval Air Station to find "Navy Ditch."

People who read and corrected sections of the manuscript include Dennis Dreher and Tom Price from NIPC and George Berndt, interpretative specialist for the I&M Canal National Heritage Corridor. Many friends carefully read every word of a draft. Ira

Pilchen copy-edited an early version. David Jones, Chris Parson, Bill Hinchliffe, Lynn Needham, Roland Eisenbeis, Phil Peters, Jim Macdonald, and Carl Duncan, mentor to my husband and me, read and commented upon the entire manuscript. Richard Sutphen, retired marine consultant formerly with the Chicago Dredge and Dock Company, not only critiqued the manuscript but patiently helped me to understand sheet piling construction and the Loop flood of 1992. Betsy Mendelsohn read the manuscript and provided copious insightful commentary as well as leads to esoteric resources. Bill Howenstine, my once and always advisor from Northeastern Illinois University, read for accuracy. My long-time, wonderful friend Marilyn Williams is the champion, having copy-edited the entire manuscript in its different forms at least three times. I am grateful to them all and I hope I haven't introduced wording into the text that undercuts their efforts.

My appreciation to Gary Little Dog Middle Rider of the Blackfeet/Lakota Sioux, who helped me understand how indigenous tribes think of themselves in today's United States.

Thanks to Karen Hewitt for believing in the book and putting it into the constructive hands of others.

Of course, my thanks to Lake Claremont Press, especially editor Bruce Clorfene and most especially to publisher Sharon Woodhouse. Lake Claremont was exactly the kind of press I had in mind for a publisher when I conceived of the book in 1994, but I never dreamed I would find such a perfect fit.

Finally, there are my two essential partners. My brother, Robert Kaplan, flew out from Boston as the project was beginning and was captivated by the river. He became the official photographer, official critic, and, being the photographer/computer buff that he is, a one-person illustrations coordinator. And my husband, Win Hill, a wonderful writer and reader, companion on many Sunday jaunts to every imaginable spot on the river, was my steady rock in the midst of this sometimes turbulent stream.

Index

Page numbers in italics refer to items in maps and photos; bold page numbers refer to items in appendices.

About the Author

Photo by Marc Thomas.

Libby Hill grew up in the suburbs of Baltimore. After high school, she attended what was then the Woman's College of the University of North Carolina in Greensboro, majoring in history and sociology. Soon after graduation, she met and married her husband, and they moved to Evanston, Illinois where they have lived ever since. They have two daughters and two grandchildren.

In 1969, Libby received her graduate degree in library science from what was then Rosary College, now Dominican University, in River Forest, Illinois. For 22 years, she was the librarian for grades 5-12 at Roycemore School in Evanston, a near north suburb of Chicago. Wanting to learn more about the natural world led her to a graduate degree in Geography and Environmental Studies from Northeastern Illinois University. She now teaches one course in that department and also works for the Northeastern Illinois Planning Commission (NIPC), where she teaches workshops about the Geographic Information System ArcView®.

Libby and her husband have always enjoyed travel. They love rivers and have sought out the headwaters of the Yukon, Mississippi, Missouri, and Suwanee, among others. She also loves searching for birds in the wild. Her ambition is to see every National Wildlife Refuge in the United States, a goal that's always out of reach because, fortunately, refuges are being created faster than she can visit them.

Lake Claremont Press Books in Print

Graveyards of Chicago:
The People, History, Art, and Lore of Cook County Cemeteries
By Matt Hucke and Ursula Bielski, 0-9642426-4-8, $15

Chicago Haunts: Ghostlore of the Windy City, Revised Edition
By Ursula Bielski, 0-9642426-7-2, $15

Hollywood on Lake Michigan: 100 Years of Chicago and the Movies
By Arnie Bernstein, with foreword by writer/director of *Soul Food*, George Tillman, Jr.,
0-9642426-2-1, $15

A Native's Guide to Chicago, 3rd Edition
By Sharon Woodhouse, with South Side coverage by Mary McNulty, 0-9642426-0-5, $12.95

A Native's Guide to Chicago's South Suburbs
By Christina Bultinck and Christy Johnston-Czarnecki, 0-9642426-1-3, $12.95

A Native's Guide to Chicago's Western Suburbs
By Laura Mazzuca Toops and John W. Toops, Jr., 0-9642426-6-4, $12.95

A Native's Guide to Chicago's Northwest Suburbs
By Martin A. Bartels, 1-893121-00-3, $12.95

A Native's Guide to Chicago's Northern Suburbs
By Jason Fargo, 0-9642426-8-0, $12.95

Forthcoming Titles

"The Movies Are": Carl Sandburg's Film Reviews and Essays, 1920-1928
Edited and with historical commentary by Arnie Bernstein (September 2000)

Ticket to Everywhere:
The Best of the Sun-Times "Detours" Midwest Travelogue Column TENTATIVE TITLE
By Dave Hoekstra, with foreword by Studs Terkel (September 2000)

Literary Chicago: A Book Lover's Tour of the Windy City
By Gregory Holden (October 2000)

More Chicago Haunts: Ghostlore of the Windy City TENTATIVE TITLE
By Ursula Bielski (October 2000)

Haunted Michigan: Recent Encounters with the Supernatural TENTATIVE TITLE
By Reverend Gerald Hunter (October 2000)

A Native's Guide to Northwest Indiana
By Mark Skertic (Spring 2001)

All Lake Claremont Press books are available directly from the publisher. You may order via
mail, e-mail, fax, or phone, and pay with a check, money order, Visa, or Mastercard.
All of our books come with a 100% money-back guarantee.

For orders of 2 books, take a 10% discount; 3-4 books, a 20% discount; 5-9 books, a 25% discount;
and 10+ books, a 40% discount. Shipping is $2 for the first book and $.50 for each additional book,
for a maximum shipping charge of $5. Illinois residents, add 8.75% sales tax.

To receive offers on future titles and LCP sales flyers, send us
your name and address or e-mail address for our mailing list.

Lake Claremont Press · 4650 North Rockwell Street · Chicago, IL 60625
773/583-7800 · 773/583-7877 (fax) · www.lakeclaremont.com · lcp@lakeclaremont.com